Reaction Formations

Berkeley Forum in the Humanities

Reaction Formations
The Subject of Ethnonationalism

Edited by Joshua Branciforte
and Ramsey McGlazer

Townsend Center for the Humanities
University of California, Berkeley

Fordham University Press
New York

Copyright 2023 © The Regents of the University of California

All rights reserved. No part of this publication may be reproduced, stored in a retrieval system, or transmitted in any form or by any means—electronic, mechanical, photocopy, recording, or any other—except for brief quotations in printed reviews, without the prior permission of the publisher.

The publishers have no responsibility for the persistence or accuracy of URLs for external or third-party Internet websites referred to in this publication and do not guarantee that any content on such websites is, or will remain, accurate or appropriate.

The publishers also produce their books in a variety of electronic formats. Some content that appears in print may not be available in electronic books.

Library of Congress Cataloging-in-Publication Data is available.

Printed in the United States of America

25 24 23   5 4 3 2 1

First edition

Contents

Introduction: On the Subject of Ethnonationalism
Joshua Branciforte and Ramsey McGlazer
1

I. Psychic Economies

**1. Fascism Without Men:
On the Gender Politics of the Radical Right**
Joshua Branciforte
23

**2. Navigating Mass Psychology:
The Political Myth of Trumpism**
Chiara Bottici
58

**3. Challenging the Outlaw Thesis:
New Configurations of Sexuality, Politics, and Aesthetics**
Ty Blakeney
88

**4. The Myth of What We Can Take In:
Global Migration and the "Receptive Capacity"
of the Nation-State**
M. Ty
118

II. Ethnostates

5. The Return to Exile: Critical Shifts in the Age of Neo-Zionism
Shaul Setter
145

6. The Alt-Right: From Libertarianism to Paleolibertarianism and Beyond
Melinda Cooper
166

7. Nationalisms By, Against, and Beyond the Indian State
Rahul Rao
190

8. Giving the Heimat a New Home: National Belonging and Ethnopluralism on the German Far Right
Julian Göpffarth
207

III. Counterrevolutions and Culture

9. Planetary Technology and Reactionary Accelerationism
Benjamin Noys
241

10. "The New Conservative Humanism": Reflections on a New Ethnonational Counterrevolution
Bruno Perreau
263

11. Authoritarian Neoliberalism and Neocolonial Subordination: Beyond the National Question (Argentina, 2015–2019)
Gisela Catanzaro
297

12. Gramsci's Grave
Ramsey McGlazer
324

About the Contributors
349

Index
353

Reaction Formations

Joshua Branciforte and Ramsey McGlazer

Introduction: On the Subject of Ethnonationalism

THE FAR RIGHT is here. By its own account, it has returned.[1] Until recently, an observer from a wealthy country in the global North could regard fascism as an ideologically vacant, politically vanquished anachronism.[2] As postwar liberalism gave way to neoliberal hegemony, there seemed to be less place than ever for a politically salient far right.[3] The cosmopolitan, globalizing outlook prevalent during the 1990s, as we find it in Francis Fukuyama, for example, was aware that right-wing nationalism persisted, but it had become virtually axiomatic that this right resided elsewhere.[4] To be sure, signs that this was wishful thinking were there all along.[5] The French far-right leader Jean-Marie Le Pen took increasing shares of the French vote throughout the 1990s; now rebranded and led by his daughter Marine, the Rassemblement national has become even more successful. In Hungary, Viktor Orbán, leader of the nationalist Fidesz party, took power in 2010. Narendra Modi became prime minister of India in 2014, running on a Hindu supremacist platform. A tipping point came in 2016, when Rodrigo Duterte won the presidency in the Philippines, Donald J. Trump was elected president of the United States, and Brexit passed in the UK. Jair Bolsonaro then won the presidency of Brazil in 2018. Right-wing governments in Russia, Israel, Turkey, and elsewhere found more overt, sometimes startling sympathies in these governments. While substantial differences exist between these actors and movements, by 2016 it was clear that versions of right-wing nationalism with notable family resemblances had become potent political forces in many countries and world regions.

With these political victories, the reinvigorated right became increasingly defined and legible at the level of culture and increasingly preoccupied with shaping right-wing subjects of the present and future. "Politics is downstream from culture," argued Andrew Breitbart, founder of a U.S. media company that became known as a mouthpiece for "the Alt-Right."[6] In the United States, the cleavage between the newly radicalized right led by Trump and the old center-right Republican Party—a dwindling remnant of which organized itself as a cohort of "never Trumpers"—was stark. The policy differences between the party of Reagan and the party of Trump were muted: once Trump was in power, these factions made common cause on tax cuts, deregulation, and court appointments, while he moved foreign policy toward protectionism and away from military adventurism. It was the new right's change of political style and cultural self-presentation that broke with the old conservative posture of decorum. This shift was calculated to disorient the left, which was used to thinking of itself as in an antagonistic relation to conservative normativity and the "post-political" aversion for political conflict typical of the neoliberal era. It now faced an adversary with a subversive style who embraced a persona at once libidinous and seductively brutal, perfectly calibrated for viral self-replication in the digital attention economy.

However, most of the right's foundational values were little changed. Even Trump's slogan, "Make America Great Again," was cribbed from an old Reagan campaign motto.[7] The difference, it was frequently noted, was that Trump "said the quiet part loud," openly owning aspects of conservatism that his predecessors had veiled in euphemism. For his supporters, who had been addressed a generation earlier as the "Silent Majority," conservative values evolved from commonly held norms to the positions self-styled as those of a virtuous minority standing in embattled opposition to liberal hegemony, whose strongholds were perceived to be higher education and the "mainstream media." Kellyanne Conway's claim that there was such a thing as "alternative facts," which became a tagline for the era, expresses how, in the far right's understanding, truth and fact were detached from the public realm of debatable normativity and privatized as transcendent matters, akin to religious beliefs, to be adjudicated by a tribal conclave.

In this situation, the nineteenth-century fantasy of national community described by Benedict Anderson—in which a public imagines itself waking up every morning reading the newspaper, situating itself imaginatively in a shared national theater of political disputation, and supposing itself connected in a general project of seeking a common truth—has collapsed.[8] In the typical media situation today, news is presorted by algorithm, and partisan outlets do not acknowledge each other as legitimate competitors engaged in a common activity. This enabled the finale of the Trump presidency, the January 6 takeover of the U.S. Capitol by right-wing groups who believed the "Big Lie" that he won the 2020 election. This takeover was reprised—even more farcically, many observers noted—by supporters of Bolsonaro in Brazil in January 2023. Seeing themselves as radical minoritarian subjects, these protestors lurched to the centers of U.S. and Brazilian legislative power by imagining a spiritual majority behind them. This spiritual majority, which, by their account, may not be of this world (but should be), will always trump the outcome of the mundane democratic process, which they feel sure is, like everything else, rigged against them.

This brief sketch of radical-right subjectivity, somewhat specific to the United States, points to one of many lines of analysis pursued in this volume. The collection grows out of a conference, "On the Subject of Ethnonationalism," held at the University of California, Berkeley in 2018.[9] We envisioned that event as an occasion for responses to the right's emergent cultural politics, and although several years have passed since the conference was held and the cultural and political situation has changed in many ways, the questions that prompted us to organize the conference remain timely. Trump has left office, as have Bolsonaro and Duterte. But the far-right movements that these figures represented and emboldened are still potent—in some cases all the more potent in that they are again aggrieved and conceive of themselves as oppressed minorities. Meanwhile, an updated list of far-right electoral victories would now need to be expanded to include the case of Italy, where the fascist-sympathizing Giorgia Meloni took power in 2022. In Israel, Benjamin Netanyahu returned to office the same year, after a brief departure, this time leading the most right-wing administration in the country's history. For their part, Orbán, Modi, Putin, and Recep Tayyip Erdoğan remain in power. Putin is perhaps the most established ultranationalist world leader today; in February 2022, he launched a full-scale invasion of Ukraine inspired by a version of the traditionalist and neo-imperial ideology discussed in this volume.

Our aim in assembling the chapters in *Reaction Formations* has been to study the contemporary far right in this global context and through the lens of culture and subjectivity. Each contribution, in its own way and within its own context, takes seriously the distinctive cultural and stylistic features of today's radical right. While many national contexts are considered—Argentina, Brazil, France, Germany, India, Israel-Palestine, the United Kingdom, and the United States—the volume is far from exhaustive. We note that it would be fruitful to read this work alongside scholarship on Erdoğan's Turkey, for instance, or on the former communist world, particularly Russia and China, or on the revival of movements with links to white nationalist parties in the Nordic countries. In these contexts, movements with quite different histories from their counterparts in the United States have encountered both sympathies and tensions.

There are competing keywords used to describe the broad sociopolitical trend that is the subject of this volume. As Joshua Clover notes, this trend is also economic. Both in the capitalist core and in the periphery, national economies have been forced to confront what Marx calls "the limit to capital" and the reality of climate catastrophe: "The increasing unification of global processes under the law of value, even as value production wanes, and the shared planetary awareness of 'climate,' even as it collapses: these put a heretofore unseen pressure on the status of *the nation*."[10] Indeed, one feature that all of the movements addressed in *Reaction Formations* share as they seek to respond to this pressure is an avowed nationalism. In some cases, the word "fascism" is appropriate, but that word can imply a continuity with twentieth-century European movements that is not always salient, especially outside of Europe and the United States.[11] None of the groups, regimes, or figures discussed in this volume positions itself as a linear continuation of the old fascist or Nazi regimes. Each of the contributions to *Reaction Formations* instead emphasizes an aspect of the newness of the radical right today: its emergent discursive strategies, frameworks for concept formation, cultural logics, and patterns of subjectification. These are tailored to the present moment even as today's right-wing regimes reinvigorate and take forward the tradition of twentieth-century fascism and its fellow travelers.

These developments are often described as nativism or right-wing populism. The keyword "nativism" emphasizes the ubiquitous antipathy for outsiders and immigrants and an ideology of national belonging, while "populism" points to the right's adoption of appeals to the masses often associated with democracy. We use the somewhat less colloquial term "ethnonationalism" as a framing and defamiliarizing device for this collective inquiry, in order to slow down the impulse to place contemporary developments too hastily within familiar categories. What is the "ethnos," the "people," envisioned by the radical right today? Where does this right continue the legacies of the fascism, and where has it evolved, modified, or simply rebranded itself to parry familiar critiques and reflexive social rejection? How, above all, does it invoke or create subjects who belong and others who must be excluded or annihilated?

Reaction Formations is divided into three thematic sections, each addressing a set of common problems and offering a range of answers to the questions we have just posed. Part I, "Psychic Economies," centers on subjectivity. The chapters in this section analyze salient fantasy structures and key strands in the right's cultural logic, following mutations as well as continuities with the predecessors of contemporary right-wing formations. In "Fascism Without Men: On the Gender Politics of the Radical Right," Joshua Branciforte focuses on the sphere of gender politics. He shows that the "commonsense view ... that fascist regimes simply want to reinstate 'traditional, patriarchal gender roles'" cannot account for the logic that the right deploys to oppress gender and sexual minorities. Discussing the work of right-wing ideologues Alexander Dugin and Julius Evola, Branciforte argues that today's radical right is committed to the destruction rather than the shoring up of the paternal function and normative masculinity. In fact, for Branciforte, "the radical right is much more thoroughgoing about subversion than its minoritarian counterparts. Minoritarian subjects, like typical neurotics, ultimately acknowledge the legitimacy and desirability of a different and better normativity." By contrast, the radical right begins with a posture of perversion and ends in paranoid delusion, so that "dealing with fascist violence is to deal with psychosis." In a reading of Luca Guadagnino's 2018 film *Suspiria*, Branciforte considers the workings of contemporary psychosis, which shed light on the "structural reason for the contemporary radical right's special animus against trans and nonbinary people."

Chiara Bottici's reflections on Trumpism follow from a different kind of engagement with psychoanalysis. Bottici asks us to attend to the limits as well as the affordances of the Freudian theory of the subject, informed as this theory is, for Bottici, by "patriarchal and racist biases." At the same time, Bottici's chapter highlights the continued salience of Freud's "mass psychology" in an age of neofascist reaction. Bottici looks to Adorno's essay "Freudian Theory and the Pattern of Fascist Propaganda," which calls attention to what Bottici names "the emptiness of the fascist agitator's speech, the absence of anything [this agitator] can actually 'give,' and the consequent prevalence of the register of threat and violence." For Bottici, this register accounts for the centrality of race in Trumpism and in fascist and neofascist discourse more generally; here "race can function as an 'empty' space that defines the group negatively." This Adornian insight has implications for our understanding of the gender politics of contemporary neofascisms as well, and Bottici proceeds to analyze the current "crusade against 'gender ideology'" and the right's abiding investments in the patriarchal family.

For both Bottici and Branciforte, the vilification of so-called "gender theory," also known as "gender identity theory" or "gender ideology," endemic to the new right does not offer a substantial, normative alternative to what it deplores. In the typical situation, people on the right find themselves triggered by the presence of others who do not conform to their notion of a stable scheme of two sexes assigned at birth. But these people often direct their complaints, with studious, myopic precision, away from persons and toward "gender theory," the discourse that makes a place for gender nonconforming people within a shared world. Those on the right will usually say—and no doubt frequently believe—that trans, nonbinary, and queer people may have the right to exist, just not in a country, city, or conceptual world shared with them. There is no violence, it is thought, in hating a theory. Likewise, the attack on antiracist activism singles out "critical race theory" as the problem. Typically, in both cases, the less of the theory one understands, the better it functions as a scapegoat. If the theory goes away, one hopes, then those who are figured in it will go away, too. In the case of opposition to "gender theory," the strategy consists in transforming whatever conception of "natural" sex or gender the complainant may or may not hold from a publicly agreed upon norm to a private matter. If the complainant has not bothered to work out any theory of cis-sexual or white supremacy and is just vexed to be asked to think about it at all, a rejection with a vague-to-nonexistent rationale may be more effective, because it will avoid alienating compatriots with competing superiority theories. The right has thus discovered that it need not demand that everyone agree with any particular theory of sex, gender, or race. Instead, one can simply demand that people stop talking about these issues altogether. "Gender" and ethnic belonging, it is held, should be non-issues, matters so obvious, indisputable, and socially frictionless that they scarcely bear discussion. (That this claim contradicts the right's obvious reliance on transphobia and racism to prolong already protracted "culture wars" does not seem to register openly in this context.) One does not need to care whether others think that binary gender is "natural" or not provided that one doesn't have to face those who challenge this schema or trigger a sense of not fitting. In this headspace, there is no need to explain why the right's subversive postures are good and the left's offending subversions are bad, because the process of deliberating and deciding on public norms has been privatized. The thinking goes: I like my subversion (of liberal cultural power in education and media) better than your subversion (of conservative power almost everywhere else), and my reasons are ultimately none of your business. In the United States, these hostilities, swaddled in euphemism and indirection, seem to have increasingly given way to openly repressive measures including "anti-grooming" bills, bans on gender-affirming care, book bans, and genocidal sentiments openly expressed, as when, for example, conservative newscasters publicly describe trans people as "demonic."[12]

Ty Blakeney's chapter centers on another set of right-wing engagements with "theory," analyzing the "Great Replacement" thesis and its main proponent, the gay French novelist Renaud Camus. In "Challenging the Outlaw Thesis: New Configurations of Sexuality, Politics, and Aesthetics," Blakeney contends that Camus's history "as both a celebrated, avant-garde gay author and an odious right-wing ideologue ... forces us to hold these seemingly irreconcilable positions together in a way that challenges the deconstructive consensus that has animated literary studies and queer theory for decades." This reading of Camus also challenges what Blakeney calls "the outlaw thesis," "the idea that homosexual subjects are somehow inherently outlaw to, and thus in some way outside of, the nation-state." Camus forces a reexamination of gay and even queer complicities with a range of racist and nationalist projects, and Blakeney's chapter prompts us to consider the queerness of figures on the contemporary far right, if not the queerness of the far right itself. Instead of emphasizing, like Branciforte, the right's slide into perversion and psychosis—and thus the normativity that we miss when it's gone—Blakeney emphasizes the "coherent social self" for whom homosexuality and racism, avant-garde aesthetics and reactionary politics, are not at all strange bedfellows.

In "The Myth of What We Can Take In: Global Migration and the 'Receptive Capacity' of the Nation-State," M. Ty returns to Freudian psychoanalysis to show how a "militarized ego" comes into being and how understandings of subject formation comes to shape geopolitics. Through a remarkable and sustained close reading of *Beyond the Pleasure Principle*, Ty argues that Freud's theory of the fraught, inextricable processes of excitation and individuation, intrusion and self-defense, can shed light on the contemporary politics of militarized borders. Ty contends that "the biocultural myth that Freud delineates survives … lethally as the unspoken kernel of contemporary formations of right-wing populism and is tapped into whenever a 'receptive limit' of an imagined community is defensively evoked." Ty revisits Freud's myth, then, in order to challenge the ethnonationalist presumption that it discloses: the "foundational presumption that survival," whether individual or collective, "is only accomplished by strategically deadening one's own affectability." It is this "deadening" that Ty's galvanizing psychoanalytic reading seeks to counter. Their reading rounds out the volume's first part by reminding us of the continuing vitality of some versions of psychoanalytic theory. Like Bottici, Ty brings this theory into conversation with theories of race and racism and suggests that reckoning with subjectivity remains indispensable to the search for antiracist and antifascist alternatives, the ongoing effort to change the subject of ethnonationalism.

PART II, "ETHNOSTATES," turns from theories of subjectivity to forms of nationalism. In each of the four chapters in this part of the book, the figure of the nation—always entwined with some understanding of who does and who does not belong—operates in significant tension with the state, or with the idea of the state. This complicates a facile understanding of the radical right as straightforwardly endorsing a strong, securitarian state that defines and polices a national people, the view that the radical right seeks an even stronger link between state and nation. The analyses in this section show that, on the contrary, the far right often profits from and foments anti-state sentiment, or alternatively that nationalist discourse can be used as a mode of resistance to the state, which right-wing governments must then counter or neutralize. A right-wing state government can thus foster a sense of national dispossession and failure to belong rather than sell a utopia of naturalized belonging. Indeed, a major reason that the radical right today is so ambivalent about the state is that it feeds off the discontent produced by the ravages of neoliberalism and positions itself as neoliberalism's antagonist, opposing the policies that state actors in both center-right and center-left parties have implemented. The financial crisis of 2008 showed the weakness of neoliberal economics, and the ensuing years saw the erosion of the optimistic cultural narratives that supported or accompanied it: globalization, multiculturalism, and a new "post-racial," "post-political" era characterized as technocratic and meritocratic, as both inevitable and beneficial for all.[13]

As these cultural narratives and the policies underwritten by them have lost credibility, in most regional contexts the right has been quicker to coalesce around a political and cultural alternative than the left. Unlike classical fascism, which defined and marketed itself as the great antagonist of revolutionary communism, the radical right today defines itself against two distinct liberal and left politico-cultural formations. One is made up of the center-left politicians who colluded with neoliberal policies and spoke neoliberalism's language; these political actors are today, implausibly yet sincerely, denounced as "socialists." The other enemy of today's right is the more radical left that has managed to consolidate limited cultural power in academia, the media, and the secondary educational system, and to translate demands for social justice, reparations, and reclaiming power for minoritarian subjects into many new cultural norms and some policy "wins."[14] In the United States, the right had long grumbled about the supposed prevalence of leftist ideas in university seminars, but as this discursive mode and set of positions expanded into a new, algorithmically regulated matrix of discourse on social media, right-wing subjects reframed these demands as a truly revolutionary attack on their way of life, a militant campaign led by a "woke mob." The fact that the left discourse to which the right objected came from within institutions that were fully acquiescent in restructuring according to neoliberal protocols, and, in the case of academia, whose primary activity is forming and certifying subjects for privileged occupations in the supposedly meritocratic knowledge economy at an ever increasing cost and diminishing return, paradoxically deepened the suspicion that center-left political actors are really occupied with prosecuting a radical "socialist" agenda. In the United States, the right quickly expanded its alternative media network from its strongholds in talk radio and Fox News to a constellation of partisan outlets and acquired a robust presence on the main social media platforms, led by Trump's masterful use of Twitter to drive news cycles and capture attention. Lavishly funded by billionaires such as the Mercer family and tech investor Peter Thiel, proliferating right-wing public discourse doggedly links frustration with neoliberalism to the left's cultural power, even though the latter usually thinks of itself as opposing the former.

In "The Return to Exile: Critical Shifts in the Age of Neo-Zionism," Shaul Setter studies the fate of one form of left opposition, showing how Israeli nationalism works today by prolonging and maximizing the experience of exile. In his chapter, Setter identifies a shift in the meaning of exile, which he argues is "not subversive nowadays but hegemonic": "What started as a critical position in Israeli academia with very few social agents has become widespread in the last two decades and penetrated mainstream politics, in quite an astonishing process of osmosis from critical discourse to social and cultural activism and from here to mass media and state politics." But this critical position's "oppositional edge has been diminished if not completely eradicated, and it seems to have been internalized by the new hegemonic ideology: whereas classical Zionism was based on the negation of exile, Neo-Zionism sponsors a revaluation of exile." What was once a hallmark of minoritarian subjectivity, the plight of the exile or refugee, has become "aligned with contemporary socioeconomic tendency to dismantle the centralized state and break the population into communities of identities; and it does both of these things while reinforcing an ethnonational ethos." The critique of Zionism must therefore take a different form today, Setter argues forcefully, given that its old tools have been co-opted and all too successfully wielded by the state that it sought to oppose.

Melinda Cooper's contribution to this volume considers another form of right-wing ambivalence toward the state. Cooper's chapter traces a strand of radically anti-state ideology on the U.S. radical right from the work of the right-wing economist Murray Rothbard to the alt-right under Trump. In "The Alt-Right: From Libertarianism to Paleolibertarianism and Beyond," Cooper describes Rothbard's understanding of libertarian politics as culminating in "nothing less than the complete dismantling of the state, the abolition of central banking, and the return to so-called honest money." In a striking intellectual history, Cooper shows how Rothbard forged alliances between libertarianism and paleoconservatism in the movement around Patrick J. Buchanan, in opposition to the then-dominant neoconservatives driving a neoliberal economic agenda. Cooper's chapter also considers the ambiguous decline of these ideas in the alt-right movement around Trump, although the latter gave paleoconservative ideas a national platform. With the emergence of a "national social or 'anti-capitalist' far right unthinkable only a few years ago," Cooper writes, Trump "arguably triggered a deep shift in the alt-right's center of equilibrium, from paleolibertarianism to a new, post-libertarian, paleo-national socialist position." On the one hand, the right has become less anti-state as it has become more sanguine about the possibility of taking control of the state; on the other hand, its racist and nativist vision of the American nation is deeply rooted in a Southern Agrarian, states' rights, anti-state legacy that has not been metabolized or left behind. Indeed, the secessionist impulses that informed Rothbard continue to animate "the national social turn" as it seeks to fashion "a white ethnostate to come."

Rahul Rao analyzes a differently structured ambivalence toward the state in India, where nationalism has, he argues, been used by the left against the state. In "Nationalisms By, Against, and Beyond the Indian State," Rao studies recent responses to the Citizenship (Amendment) Act (CAA), passed in 2019. The CAA created a pathway for Indian citizenship for Hindu, Sikh, Buddhist, Jain, Parsi, and Christian migrants from the Muslim-majority countries of Pakistan, Afghanistan, and Bangladesh, while barring Muslims from this access to citizenship. The Act's passage prompted enormous and widespread protests, and Rao considers the redeployment of national symbols in this context. How were these symbols wrested from the Hindu Right, and what were the limits of this effort at reappropriation? Borrowing a phrase from David Lloyd, Rao calls these examples of "nationalism against the state," writing that they "marshal the symbolic repertoire of nationalism to shame the state for its betrayal of the nation, with a view to repairing the disconnect between state and nation." But Rao argues that these critical responses to the CAA betrayed "a naive Habermasian faith in the possibility of consensus on the rules of communicative reason." The Indian state's response, by contrast, gave the lie to such persistent faith, pointing up the hard limits of even those nationalisms that oppose or seek to go beyond the state without at the same time going beyond "the humanist discourses of liberal constitutionalism."

In his chapter, Julian Göpffarth observes similar failures on the left in the German context. "Giving the Heimat a New Home: National Belonging and Ethnopluralism on the German Far Right" traces recent center-left efforts, including environmentalist efforts, to reclaim the concept of the "Heimat" (Homeland) from the far right. Efforts to rehabilitate the Heimat concept even in its more banal or "mainstream" forms, Göpffarth argues, ignore its racializing function and its deep ties to the "visions of white supremacy" that persisted in both East and West Germany after World War II. Uncovering the racial unconscious of the Heimat even in its apparently more benign forms, Göpffarth also examines the "ethnopluralist" imaginary of the contemporary far right in Germany. In this context, Göpffarth concludes, no true pluralism will be possible without ongoing "critical engagement with Germany's and Europe's colonial past."

Just as some form of heightened nationalism is a constant on the far right—with the nature and level of investment in the state variable across regional contexts—we also see some investment in a national subject defined along racial or ethnic lines. Every essay in this volume notes this phenomenon. However, the particular logics of racialization operative in these movements—and their continuities with and divergences from the logics of racism observable in liberal-centrist and the old fascist regimes—strike us as an ongoing and urgent topic for further research. Likewise, these movements' relationships to climate change warrant more sustained analysis, although these relationships are obliquely addressed in several of the chapters that follow, including those by Ty and Göpffarth, which center on race. From one point of view, as the right has become more radical, its racial discourse has become more forthright, echoing the racial discourse of the old fascism.[15] For instance, in the United States, one segment of the very-online discourse has emerged under the innocuous-sounding heading of "human biodiversity." A group of bloggers and (mostly amateur) scientists has taken to identifying biological evidence of the existence of supposedly genetically based differences between racial groups.[16] If racial difference is real at the invisible level of genome, they believe, then racial populations are not equal in their endowments. The driving conclusion is that racial inequities should be attributed to "innate" differences. Historical factors, even massively obvious ones like chattel slavery and its aftermath, are usually not even disputed but simply ignored. This tendency's overall thrust, therefore, is to revive the old eugenics with an updated, slick new vocabulary.

But there are two key differences between partisans of "human biodiversity" and proponents of classical eugenics: a relentless and deeply internalized commitment to euphemism (allowing them to maintain the self-perception that they are "not racist") and an understanding of "race" that is quite distinct from that of their eugenicist predecessors. Both of these features are laid out conceptually in Alexander Dugin's main work. He makes a show of rejecting classical fascism as one of the three failed political theories of modernity, drawing special attention to its flawed eugenicist theory of racism. The old fascist racism, he contends (in a surprising confluence with theorists of liberal racism),[17] is actually a deeply embedded latent feature of Western liberalism, inherent to and inextricable from liberal meritocracy. His conclusion: the problem with the old fascism is that it was not fascist enough; his "fourth political theory" proposes "a really fascist fascism," purged of the materialist and eugenicist racism that was basically liberal in origin. One can see in this striking phrase how the provocatively subversive demand for a more fascist fascism coexists with the ingenuously maintained belief that of course a "really fascist fascism" also means the disappearance of racism. All the work of old racial science can be accomplished far more discretely by a total, straight-faced commitment to deadpan euphemism. It is unsurprising to see the cloak of disavowal gradually slip, revealing open genocidal sentiments, which are then followed by openly genocidal actions, such as the forced adoption and cultural reeducation of Ukrainian children conducted by Putin's regime, inspired and advised by Dugin.

What these racist thinkers reject in the old model is any overall conception of superiority. Racial differences are still treated as natural and innate, but the natural order of things is not stabilized in and through a unified, self-present idea of what makes the superior position superior, beyond the brute, temporalized fact of its having ended up where it did. This discourse's striking similarities to the old eugenics should not blind us to its strategic pivot from an idealistically unified conception of race to a difference-based, privatized, and temporally disunified conception of race that makes it possible for a discourse as maligned and left for dead as eugenics to be revived. During the period in which eugenic thinking was culturally latent, particularly after the civil rights movement in the United States, the dominant strategy for ensuring racist outcomes was the open secret: Hold the racist cant, go heavy on dog whistles. As the right radicalized, instead of naively resuming the old cant, it doubled down on the fiction that racist discourse was over; a canny subterfuge intended to be decoded by addressees (preserving plausible deniability for everyone else) became a matter of true belief. Race-based cant was then free to return, only in a different guise, one based on the firm belief that racism as a set of propositional, idealized contents does not exist, at least not in the mind of the speaker. Once euphemism is radicalized, it is impossible to convince someone engaging in pernicious race-speech that they hold racist ideas because their speech is founded on the belief that racist ideas are over.

Dugin's Heidegger-inspired account of "race" is a specimen of a more general tendency. Increasingly, the far right shifts its vision of communal belonging from a model that polices community boundaries through public norms to one that polices tacitly. The people may be imagined as an organic emanation of the biosphere that, like a plant, does not need to know what it is, only the bare fact of its being where it is. It occupies territory in an eternal present that erases the history of conquest or appropriation, nourished by its self-generated perception of being under threat.[18] Expulsion occurs whenever something disrupts the unspoken, silent flow of belonging. Whoever has the misfortune of being deemed a social irritant in this context will experience violence, displacement, or death, whether or not there is a commonly held ideological justification accounting for why exactly that person is "different." The dominant group does not require a conception of its own unity and superiority. It can construe itself as "different" (marginalized, minoritarian, oppressed) and then reject the other as different from its difference: Once dominance is based on difference and exceptionalism—say, on a claim to exilic status, as in Setter's chapter—the other is condemned for being differently different. Some normative rationale may be given, an appeal to nature, "indigeneity," or to the divinely ordained order of things, but this rationale has the character of a post-facto rationale for a rejection that was preordained before any norm was found to justify it. Unlike in normative center-right conservatism, in this situation, any rationale will do, or several incompatible rationales, or none at all. You can be a perfectly effective protector of your ethnos with a flimsy theory of race or even no theory of race at all beyond the raw existential kernel of feeling that your place in the world, and the place of those who are like you, is threatened.

THE VOLUME'S THIRD and final section, "Counterrevolutions and Culture," attends to the consequences of these complex dynamics, which put pressure on a number of familiar political categories, both temporal and spatial. Familiar distinctions are blurred, and oppositions become difficult if not impossible to uphold: between the old and the new, the retrograde and the innovative, the backward-looking and the futuristic, the archaic and the techno-utopian, the center and the periphery, the adult and the child, the dead and the living. As they investigate various challenges to these distinctions, the contributors to this section show how those whom Bruno Perreau calls today's counterrevolutionaries thoroughly depend on and weaponize culture. Their "culture wars," Perreau shows, take different forms, which the chapters in this section seek to delineate. Contemporary right-wing movements deploy cutting-edge legal strategies in order to acquire protections from discrimination of the kind that have been granted to minorities. As Benjamin Noys argues, they combine accelerationism and reaction. Likewise, as in Gisela Catanzaro's analysis of Argentina, they bring together authoritarian neoliberal policies, on the one hand, and, on the other, neocolonial forms of subservience in peripheral countries. For Ramsey McGlazer, something called "Cultural Marxism" appears as an undead red menace that must at once be killed and be kept on afterlife support in order to sustain the political fortunes of its opponents.

The four chapters in this part of the book also share a preoccupation with what, in his chapter, Noys calls the "illiberal 'common sense' at the heart of the liberal present." In this present, even liberal institutions—or their remnants—come to shelter such an "illiberal 'common sense'" under conditions of neoliberalism, austerity, and authoritarian resurgence. Under these conditions, we cannot assume that ethnonational ideology is only "over there," only on the far right, because it also shapes the liberal institutions, practices, and political tendencies that would hold it at bay. Consider Kamala Harris's warning, delivered in Guatemala to those "thinking about making [the] dangerous trek" north to seek asylum in the United States: "Do not come. Do not come."[19] The self-styled corrective to Trump's brand of xenophobic nativism thus came to embrace nativist talking points, or rather *came home* to these talking points, since here Harris in fact echoed Obama. Our aim, though, is less to denounce Harris's hypocrisy (which is not exceptional, after all) than to ask, with Noys, how versions and valences of ethnonationalism cut across the divide that ostensibly separates the political right from the center and center-left.

In "Planetary Technology and Reactionary Accelerationism," Noys reads the work of a range of right-wing thinkers with an eye to their engagement with another set of conditions structuring contemporary politics. In his analysis of Heidegger, Ernst Jünger, and Nick Land, Noys shows that today's reactionary politics is connected to an ambivalent critique of technology. Noys asks "how racist and reactionary politics tries to traverse and engage planetary technology as the condition of its own project," tracing continuities between fascist and neoreactionary, futurist, and post-humanist fantasies. Contemporary reaction, Noys shows, draws not only on conservative nostalgia for the past but also on "accelerationism," a longing to heighten the contradictions in the present in order to bring about a breakdown that will lead to another beginning. Technology is a key "site of contestation and conflict" for these tendencies.

In his chapter, "'The New Conservative Humanism': Reflections on a New Ethnonational Counterrevolution," Perreau looks to another context and another set of rearguard actions with vanguardist aspirations. He studies an ethnonational ideology that "claims to be both a majority and a minority." Focusing on France, Perreau undertakes to show how a "new conservative humanism" informs "anti-gender" protests, right-wing ecological activism, and populist movements, among other ongoing developments. Perreau's wide-ranging analysis culminates with a call to reexamine "the very notion of minority." This call resonates with others delivered throughout *Reaction Formations*, which, again, seeks to interrogate a range of political concepts and categories, from fascism to liberalism and, in Catanzaro's chapter, from neocolonialism to nationalism itself.

Catanzaro's study, "Authoritarian Neoliberalism and Neocolonial Subordination: Beyond the National Question (Argentina, 2015–19)," analyzes the apparent eclipse of a national ideal. Catanzaro considers the ideology of Mauricio Macri, president of Argentina from 2015 to 2019. As Catanzaro emphasizes, the policies of Macri's administration combined ruthlessly punitive measures at home with postures of ingratiation and subservience with respect to Euro-American "great powers." Showing how Macri's neocolonial policies take us "beyond the national question" and even the category of nationalism as such, Catanzaro complicates sweeping accounts of global ethnonationalism and describes a radical-right government working in lockstep with key aspects of the neoliberal program. Macri's willingness to suspend or subordinate national interests in a peripheral country, whose citizens are now asked to "know their place," uncovers a "dialectic of aggression and submission," one that Catanzaro sees as characterizing the current "punitive" phase of neoliberalism.

In "Gramsci's Grave," McGlazer notes that this phase has by some accounts cast doubt on the very possibility of hegemony. For this reason, the theories of Antonio Gramsci have been pronounced "dead," declared outmoded, seen to be out-of-date and devoid of contemporary political utility, and yet he continues to live a surprising life, or to survive undead, in the Americas. For the Brazilian far right, McGlazer argues, Gramsci—possessed of uncanny and even demonic capacities for mind control—poses a still-real threat to Brazilian schoolchildren, whom the Programa Escola Sem Partido (Program for a School without Party, or a Nonpartisan School) undertakes to protect and serve.

McGlazer's reading of this movement seeks to account for the striking and apparently strange afterlife of Gramsci in Brazil, an afterlife that is at once part of the history of global anticommunism and related to the recent co-optation of Gramsci's texts by the right. Analyzing this co-optation lets us see why schooling—defined as a site of indoctrination and place of students' susceptibility to "cultural Marxist" violence—matters so much to reactionary movements in Brazil and beyond.

"Gramsci's Grave" is an afterword of sorts—a postmortem—that also returns readers to the scenes of subject formation with which the volume begins. Here this scene is not, as in Ty's reading of *Beyond the Pleasure Principle*, the setting of Freud's parable of monocellular life but rather the classroom recast as a site of formative, even fatal, seduction. For in the fantasies of Escola Sem Partido, the student is both infantilized and feminized, rendered at once helpless and available for an exploitation that is consistently sexualized. Like broken mirrors, McGlazer argues, these fantasies show us the persuasive power that the left might yet retain. Indirectly, he argues—writing against calls to move "beyond education"—they challenge us to reimagine the scene of teaching as one to which we might return.

The chapters that follow engage with a wide range of cultural objects and open onto an equally diverse range of critical and political questions. The authors do not subscribe to any orthodoxy or belong to any single school of thought. They write from various locations, both geographic and disciplinary. But what their contributions do share is a commitment to close and sustained cultural analysis, to the patient and painstaking work of tarrying with the contemporary right. They take the claims of this right—its claims to be minoritarian, exilic, secessionist, insubordinate, and indeed queer—seriously, and they proceed to draw out their structuring logics and implications. Rather than discounting these claims as self-evidently preposterous and unworthy of scholarly scrutiny, the chapters assess them carefully on the grounds that doing so is indispensable to the effort to create and sustain antifascist alternatives. Even when, as in Göpffarth's case or Rao's, authors attend to the possibilities for left appropriations of concepts claimed by the right or sanitized in liberal discourses, they insist on a recognition of these concepts' fraught histories, which they argue cannot be ignored or willed away. To ignore or seek to will away what we oppose is to be unresponsive to a present in which, as Setter writes, our old critical and "oppositional edge" has been worn down. This is not to repeat the now-tired claim that critique itself has "run out of steam."[20] On the contrary, it is to note the need for more critique, rather than less, on still-shifting political ground. It is to respond to the demand that we develop what Catanzaro calls a "critique of authoritarian social sensibilities." All of the chapters that follow are contributions to this critique, and all work to respond to challenges that remain unrelenting.

Notes

1. Daniel Friberg, *The Real Right Returns: A Handbook for the New Opposition* (London: Arktos Media, 2015).
2. On this historiography of fascism, see, for example, Roger Griffin, *Fascism: An Introduction to Comparative Fascist Studies* (Cambridge: Polity, 2018). On fascism as discursively vacant, see Zeev Sternhell, *The Birth of Fascist Ideology: From Cultural Rebellion to Political Revolution* (Princeton: Princeton University Press, 1994).
3. However, scholars of neoliberalism have shown that its architects were allied with right-wing social positions. See Melinda Cooper, *Family Values: Between Neoliberalism and the New Social Conservatism* (New York: Zone Books, 2019); and Quinn Slobodian, *Globalists: The End of Empire and the Birth of Neoliberalism* (Cambridge, MA: Harvard University Press, 2020).
4. Francis Fukuyama, *The End of History and the Last Man*, 2nd ed. (New York: Free Press, 2006).
5. See E. J. Hobsbawm, *Nations and Nationalism Since 1780: Programme, Myth, Reality*, 2nd ed. (Cambridge: Cambridge University Press, 2012), chap. 6.
6. This would-be Gramscian observation has, in the right-wing milieu, been elevated to orthodoxy and is referred to as "the Breitbart doctrine." For a document of the times, see Allum Bokhari and Milo Yiannopoulos, "An Establishment Republican's Guide to the Alt-Right," breitbart.com, March 29, 2016, https://www.breitbart.com/tech/2016/03/29/an-establishment-conservatives-guide-to-the-alt-right/.
7. Bill Clinton also used it once. See Sam Dangremond, "Who Was the First Politician to Use 'Make America Great Again' Anyway?" townandcountrymag.com, November 14, 2018, https://www.townandcountrymag.com/society/politics/a25053571/donald-trump-make-america-great-again-slogan-origin/.
8. Benedict Anderson, *Imagined Communities: Reflections on the Origin and Spread of Nationalism*, 2nd ed. (New York: Verso, 2016).
9. We thank the cosponsors of the 2018 conference: the Townsend Center for the Humanities, the Department of English, the John F. Hotchkis Chair, the Rachel Anderson Stageberg Endowed Chair, the James D. Hart Chair, and the Center for the Study of Sexual Cultures, all at the University of California, Berkeley.

10 Joshua Clover, "Parties of Order Right and Left," *Identities: Journal for Politics, Gender and Culture* 19.1–2 (2022): 28, 31, https://doi.org/10.51151/identities.v19i1-2.501.

11 Dylan Riley, "What Is Trump?" *New Left Review* 114 (2018): 5–31; Enzo Traverso, *The New Faces of Fascism: Populism and the Far Right* (London: Verso, 2019). For a counterargument, see Zeynep Gambetti, "Exploratory Notes on the Origins of New Fascisms," *Critical Times: Interventions in Global Critical Theory* 3.1 (2020): 1–32.

12 See, for instance, "Candace Owens: 'The trans agenda is demonic. Any actor, actress, individual that supports this is supporting something that is demonic,'" *Media Matters for America*, February 7, 2023, https://www.mediamatters.org/candace-owens/candace-owens-trans-agenda-demonic-any-actor-actress-individual-supports-supporting.

13 See Wendy Brown, *In the Ruins of Neoliberalism: The Rise of Antidemocratic Politics in the West* (New York: Columbia University Press, 2019); Lauren Berlant, *Cruel Optimism* (Durham: Duke University Press, 2011).

14 For a critique of the current liberal discourse of "wins," see Savannah Shange, *Progressive Dystopia: Abolition, Antiblackness, and Schooling in San Francisco* (Durham: Duke University Press, 2019). See also Ruth Wilson Gilmore, "In the Shadow of the Shadow State," in *The Revolution Will Not Be Funded: Beyond the Non-Profit Industrial Complex*, ed. INCITE! (Durham: Duke University Press, 2007), 48; and for a critique of policy, see Clover, "Parties of Order," 36–37.

15 On the Black radical tradition's recognition of a "racial fascism" that persisted after the fall of historical fascism, see Alberto Toscano, "Incipient Fascism: Black Radical Perspectives," *CLCWeb* 23.1 (2021), https://doi.org/10.7771/1481-4374.4015.

16 The ur-text is Charles Murray and Richard J. Herrnstein, *The Bell Curve: Intelligence and Class Structure in American Life* (New York: Free Press, 1996). This discourse largely ignores epigenetics.

17 See Domenico Losurdo, *Liberalism: A Counter-History*, trans. Gregory Elliott (London: Verso, 2014).

18 Lev Gumilev, *Ethnogenesis and the Biosphere* (Moscow: Progress Publishers, 1990).

19 "'Do Not Come': VP Harris Sends Anti-Migrant Message in Guatemala, Visits Mexico amid Deadly Election," *Democracy Now!* June 8, 2021, https://www.democracynow.org/2021/6/8/kamala_harris_immigration_mexico_election_killings.

20 Bruno Latour, "Why Has Critique Run Out of Steam?: From Matters of Fact to Matters of Concern," *Critical Inquiry* 30 (2004): 225–48. For a sense of this claim's influence, see, for instance, Rita Felski, *The Limits of Critique* (Chicago: University of Chicago Press, 2015); and for rejoinders, see Ellen Rooney's essays, including, "Symptomatic Reading Is a Problem of Form," in *Critique and Postcritique*, ed. Elizabeth Anker and Rita Felski (Durham: Duke University Press, 2017), 127–52.

PART I
Psychic Economies

Joshua Branciforte

1. Fascism Without Men: On the Gender Politics of the Radical Right

Revisiting the Psychic Life of Fascism

For the men we are dealing with here ... they want something other than incest, which is a relationship involving persons, names, and families. They want to wade in blood; they want an intoxicant. ... They want a contact with the opposite sex—or perhaps simply access to sexuality itself—which cannot be named. ... They want to penetrate into its life, its warmth, its blood. It seems to me that they aren't just more intemperate, dangerous, and cruel than Freud's harmless "motherfucker" Oedipus; they are of an entirely different order. And if, in spite of everything, they have a desire for incest, it is, at the very least, with the earth itself ("Mother Earth").
—Klaus Theweleit, *Male Fantasies*

FEW OBSERVATIONS ABOUT fascism impose themselves more forcefully than the preference for inflated masculinity. George Mosse describes its ubiquity in the Nazi regime.[1] For Barbara Spackman, the posture of "virility" was indispensable to Italian Fascism; women were alternately pressed into the traditional wife/mother role and given access to their own mode of militant virility.[2] Thanks to psychological analyses by the Frankfurt School and others, one can readily see—in fact, it has now become common sense—that fascist hypermasculinity compensates for a perceived emasculation or experience of abjection. As the radical right regains strength and visibility, a phenomenon that Alexander Reid Ross aptly calls, acknowledging that not all the movements on today's radical right accede to generic fascism, the "fascist creep," performances of hypermasculinity have as well.[3] To some degree, the old pattern, according to which abjection is repressed and femininity is siloed into the childbearing function, is still observable on the radical right today. However, the subject of this essay is another strand of the psychic life of fascism, which Klaus Theweleit identified in Nazism and which plays an important role in how gender politics support far-right politics today.[4] Turning to psychoanalysis, I describe how the repression that dominated the fascist experience of femininity has today become relaxed and let into consciousness and into public discourse. Increasingly, fascist hypermasculinity and fascist nonmasculinity coinhabit the same bodies and public personae without regard for the apparent incongruity. Some quantum of nonmasculinity or nonnormative masculinity becomes necessary to root the radical right's vision of the people and power, which take on a matriarchal coloration. Today's fascistic revival, hyperphallicism and all, turns out to work better without men.

Our analysis must begin with the fraught question about the relationship between fascism and perversion. Many critics, from Hannah Arendt to Judith Butler, have pointed to fascism's perverse psychic ambiance.[5] As stressed by early observers, such as Wilhelm Reich and Ortega y Gasset, fascism is "rebellious" and subversive.[6] Walter Benjamin describes its admiration for masculinity and war as a "depraved mysticism."[7] Georges Bataille saw in fascism the same radical search for "heterogeneity" (passing through "debasement") that animated his own project.[8] It is antinormative and turns that subversive thrust toward reinstating authority. Until the 1990s, it was common to disparage fascism by linking it with perverse sexuality. Noting how it idealized the homosocial "band of men," Theodor Adorno links fascism to male homosexuality construed as perversion with gleefully phobic venom.[9] To be sure, there is no shortage of evidence of fascism's appeal over the years to gay men, lesbians, and women in general.[10] The issue is further complicated by the secondary phenomenon of kinky fetishistic appreciation of fascist iconography, costumes, and pornography by otherwise liberal, unfascist subjects.[11] A few critics working in the tradition of Bataille, such as Leo Bersani and Jack Halberstam, have leaned into the fascism/perversion link, countenancing a perverse core to fascism and a fascist kernel in queer subjects.[12] However, most critics since the 1990s, notably Andrew Hewitt and Eve Kosofsky Sedgwick, have sought to undo this linkage, pointing out its potentially phobic implications.[13] For Dagmar Herzog, this move, particularly when it entails interpreting Nazi violence as individual sadistic psychopathology, is reductive and ahistorical.[14] As perversion became increasingly rehabilitated as an ethical category, within both queer theory and cultural studies more generally, the perversion/fascism link became increasingly suspect.[15] With sadistic violence as the template of perversion in mind—and Slavoj Žižek's *éloge* of perversion in his ear—the Lacanian critic Antonios Vadolas wrote a book refuting in detail the postwar discourse on fascism as perverse, refusing to attribute any psychopathological structure to fascism.[16]

Keeping these warnings in mind, I will now give a brief account of the perverse structure that avoids taking sadism as the template for perversion—which Freud does not—as well as the danger of reducing fascist violence to individual pathologies.[17] Psychoanalysis distinguishes three psychopathological structures: neurosis, perversion, and psychosis. Subjects are thought to favor one structure over the other, but all three happen frequently in everyday life and everyone has some experience of all three. My aim is not to reify a profile of "the pervert" or "the psychotic" and map it onto fascist subjectivity but rather to ask whether and how fascism (as ideology and/or political practice) activates or presupposes one of these drive patterns. Querying the psychic life of fascism does not entail describing it reductively it as a mere matter of individual psychology. Each structure is distinguished by a psychic mechanism: repression for neurosis, disavowal for perversion, and foreclosure for psychosis. The mechanisms are ways of dealing with the demand made by others that some gratification be renounced, a demand first experienced in infancy when a child realizes that it must share its first love object (typically the mother) with someone else (typically the father). As a child becomes aware of a dynamic of adult desire that it cannot understand or participate in, it encounters what Jacques Lacan calls the "paternal function." The posture one takes toward it determines how one relates to lawfulness and language.[18] It centers on the phallus, the signifier of adult desire; everyone, regardless of gender assignment, starts out life lacking it. The neurotic accepts the lawfulness of the father function and uses repression to forget about desires that do not conform to this law. Perversion offers a compromise solution: it accepts lawfulness as valid in principle but rejects any real father who pretends to fill it.

Unlike the neurotic, who recognizes the "phallus" that the mother desires as belonging to someone else, the pervert pretends to be that special object conjoined with the mother. The pervert knows in theory that the mother desires something it lacks, but they nevertheless act as though they have no lack and the real paternal subject does not exist. Perverse desire thus always comes back to the figure of the phallic mother. And the perverse subject, longing for boundless intimacy, sees itself as/in her phallic appendage. Disavowal is the mechanism of this make-believe: the fiction that repression is unnecessary, the repression of repression.[19] Neurotics often find perverts seductive and fascinating because they act as though lack and law and normalcy do not apply to them. But in this ingenious solution where "instinct is allowed to retain its satisfaction and proper respect is [also] shown to reality," Freud explains, "everything [still] has to be paid for in one way or another, and this success is achieved at the price of a rift in the ego which never heals but which increases as time goes on."[20] If the happy side of perversion gets to have it both ways, on its hidden side the pervert acknowledges the absolute validity of lawfulness. Lacan jokes that this norm-adoring side of perversion is *pèreversion*, the inclination toward the father and his lawfulness, which is concealed behind the pervert's transgressive posture of rejecting all law-bearers.[21]

In psychosis, one goes a step further, refusing to acknowledge the paternal function at all. One still faces desires and demands from others but they are foreclosed and cannot be recognized and assimilated as such. Instead of the pervert's split consciousness, there is a split at the level of the body: disarticulated voices, delusions, and somatic disturbances. Everyday low-key manifestations of the psychic structure are paranoia, jealousy, and even, Lacan claims, the search for knowledge itself, as well as much religious experience.[22] Nothing is more common than for perverse and psychotic patterns to be embedded in subjects who otherwise accept the lawfulness of their world. To capture the distinction between perverse and psychotic patterns in their raw state and those patterns when they have been reabsorbed into neurosis, Paul Verhaeghe differentiates the perverse (or psychotic) *structure* itself from what he calls perverse *traits*.[23] Of course, this process of reabsorption is a matter of degree and intensity; traits and structure regularly collapse into each other and there is no stable hedge separating them from each other. We may nevertheless distinguish between them analytically. Perverse traits are particularly prevalent because, Freud argues, we all begin life in a "polymorphously perverse" state where disavowal predominates, gradually to be superseded by repression when the child comes to accept the paternal function via the Oedipus complex.[24] Remnants of these early disavowals float ubiquitously in adult sexuality. They surface in much autoeroticism, in some configurations of same-sex desire, and in most kinks. Yet they are perverse *traits* because one goes about gratifying them in law-abiding ways, for instance by seeking consent. In structural perversion, the subject refuses to accept the lawfulness of the other's No. Instead of accepting the law from the other, the pervert reassembles their own lawfulness in the veiled form of the fetish, the adult substitute for the phallic mother; in it the longed-for law appears veiled behind a petrified thing. Typically, Masud R. Khan emphasizes, the structural fetish is overwhelmingly monological and adherence to its "law" typically drowns out pleasure.[25] This is quite unlike the multiple, highly socialized, consensual pleasures described by kinksters and queer theorists. Whenever "perversion" is held up as an ethical position, in queer theory and elsewhere, what is being defended are perverse traits.

The ethical pervert minimizes the norm-adoring aspect of perversion, the *pèreversion*, for the good reason that most queers and ethical "perverts" are not structural perverts. Figures who do embody structural perversion, such as Harvey Weinstein or Nabokov's Humbert Humbert, are seldom taken as models of ethical perversion or queerness. Of course, as Halberstam and Bersani remind us, the would-be good and healthy "perversity" of queer and kinky subjects cannot cordon itself off from the more robust structural form encountered in real perverts. However, my emphasis is less on the possible collapse of neuroticized queer perverse traits into structural perversity, present though it is. Instead, I draw our attention to how the perverse structure is inherently and ineluctably a motor for reconstituting broken phallic authority. A rigorous model of the perverse structure must acknowledge that it always entails the return of the figure of the master, but of a master hiding behind a mask. The consolidation of the paternal function by fascist revolt is not a surprising diversion of a subversive thrust we should expect to be authority-undoing but actually inherent to perversion—not a bug but a feature. Queer and kinky subjects, who may like to style themselves as subversive or perverse, actually fully embrace their own style of normativity, the law of consent and the primacy of erotic taste. The normativity inherent to queerness, in my view, should be celebrated rather than neurotically repressed in favor of a narrative of subversion that no longer fits the political facts in a world of resurgent fascism. Today, it is they and not us who play the part of the pervert—and we should say so.

Distinguishing between perverse traits and the perverse structure will help us open back up the question of the psychic life of fascism while avoiding the concerns of Vadolas and Herzog. In his survey of the historiography of fascism, Roger Griffin describes how the first generation of scholarship avoided treating fascism as an ideological framework with a consistency on par with that of liberalism or communism, defining it in terms of (usually destructive) external features.[26] In the 1990s, Zeev Sternhell, Mosse, and others taught us to read it as a coherent-enough ideology.[27] I make the same pivot from attributing fascism to the malign influence of pathological perverts to the claim that fascist ideology steers adherents to activate the drive along the structural paths of perversion and that the authority whose restoration it pursues has the structure of a fetish. The link between fascism and perversion, which so many critics notice, occurs at the level of ideological elaboration, not atomized individual psychology. However, when fascism is implemented in practices of brutality, dehumanization, and genocide—when we witness *practices* exceeding their own (or any) ideological justification— we should speak of fascism as activating the psychotic structure and as upheld by delusion. Dealing with fascistic ideology is to deal with perversion; dealing with fascist violence is to deal with psychosis. I make this distinction against a certain kind of common sense that attributes authentic subversion to queer and other minoritarian subjectivities and regards fascist subversion of the law as posturing, or not truly subversive, or otherwise inauthentic. On the contrary, the radical right is much more thoroughgoing about subversion than its minoritarian counterparts. Minoritarian subjects, like typical neurotics, ultimately acknowledge the legitimacy and desirability of a different and better normativity.

George Mosse argues that in classical fascism the radically rebellious thrust was eventually, often with a great deal of ambivalence, submitted to bourgeois "respectability."[28] This pattern is *not* perverse lawfulness; it is a momentary activation of the perverse structure followed by a timid return to repression and neurotic normalcy. Herzog complicates Mosse's thesis by documenting the continuing importance throughout the Nazi era of a (eugenicist) pro-sex discourse that defied respectability: "what a broad array of Nazi writings on sex suggests is that no prior regime in history had ever so systematically set itself the task of stimulating and validating especially young people's sexual desire—all the while denying precisely that this was what it was doing," employing "a variety of disavowing mechanisms."[29] In a Foucauldian manner, Herzog describes the "sexually exciting" aspects of Nazism not as something to be repressed but as a core part of its disciplinary practices, which are guided by the perverse mechanism of disavowal. I follow Herzog in seeking to replace less sophisticated versions of the fascism-as-perversion thesis with a model based on disavowal rather than on the presence of sadistic violence. However, the composite picture emerging from both accounts is of a classical fascist regime that activated rebellious and subversive affects, some of which were directly turned to enable a eugenicist agenda, while in another they were submitted to repression in a lurch toward normalcy. Today, the Mossean trajectory toward liberal respectability seems to decline in importance, while the Herzogian trajectory of disavowed perverse incentives is more prominent than ever.

The most important postwar ideologues of the radical right are aware of classical fascism's residual attachments to liberal respectability and they are concerned to undo this link. In his influential book about its future after the war, Julius Evola articulates what became the fountainhead for the radical-right program of today. Its key features are syncretic cosmopolitanism, a spiritual racism that is anti-eugenic and anti-materialist, and a notion of the desired traditional origin as plural and rhizomatic. His "world of tradition" stands outside of history and therefore belongs equally to prehistorical times and to the immanence of the present moment, if only there are "men" enough to find it.[30] For him, actually existing fascism failed because it was too compromised by modern liberal ideas, particularly the preoccupation with progress and its crass materialist racism. Evola was an avowed anti-Semite, racist, and misogynist, but his models of race and male superiority, inspired by the Hindu caste system and Roman patriarchy, were quite unlike the eugenicist Nazi/liberal one. For instance, he held that most Germans were more spiritually "Jewish" than actual Jews.[31] He also rejects fascist nationalism. "The sacred character and inviolability of 'nation' and 'people'" pushed by the Nazis, he writes, "are merely the transposition of features attributed to the Great Mother in ancient plebeian gynocracies and in societies that ignored the virile and political principle of the *imperium*. Thus, it has rightfully been suggested by Bachofen ... that 'men' uphold the idea of the State, while feminine natures, which are spiritually matriarchal, side instead with 'fatherland', 'nation', and 'people.'"[32] Apparently, the real problem with fascists is that they are too soft and feminine and their Volk-concept is at bottom a matriarchal concept that rejects the transcendent masculine principle! This complicates our commonsense view, recently voiced by Jason Stanley in *How Fascism Works*, that fascist regimes simply want to reinstate "traditional, patriarchal gender roles."[33] (Evola's concept of tradition, I would add, is a fetish, the veiled phallus worshiped by the pervert; it therefore does not elude the matriarchal streak he deplores in classical fascism.) Following the traditionalist René Guénon, Evola rejects everything modern, particularly all political ideas stemming from the French Revolution, as bad "subversions."[34] However, he argues that the radical right must be *more* revolutionary and more radical than anything in the modern revolutionary tradition. Against the malignant "subversions" of modernity, Evola demands the absolute subversion of modernity itself.

Alexander Dugin, the most important ideologue on the radical right today, situates himself in Evola's tradition, reinvigorating the (to me) terrifying vision of countering the "subversions" of liberal modernity with a more extreme, more absolute subversion, a "really fascist fascism."[35] He rejects classical fascism for its commitment to a notion of progress conceived technologically and its eugenic model of racism, which he argues belonged to the liberal tradition (a view of racism also held on the left).[36] His "fourth political theory" is based on a self-deconstructing notion of identity as dwelling in territory without recognition, which he develops from a questionable reading of Heidegger. Dugin attempts to purify fascism of its residual commitment to respectability and bourgeois normativity, heightening the perverse trajectory that Herzog traces in Nazism. In the classical situation, this trajectory was usually supplanted by a lurch toward respectability: the compromised paternal function would be repressed by elevating a viable father figure, one whose virility was the virility of the nation. As Freud pointed out before the war, in patriarchy the place of the original father is always empty and the (for Freud, ultimately murderous) feelings of actual men under patriarchy for the ultimate father figure are repressed, a process that classical fascism succumbs to as well.[37] Particularly attuned to the perverse current, Theweleit calls the Nazi regime a "filiarchy": "nothing but sons as far as the eye can see—Hitler too is one of their number."[38] In the postwar radical-right ideology of Evola and Dugin—the fountainheads of today's radical-right ideology—the key shift is that the empty place of the father is *openly owned* instead of repressed. In the name of a sublimely archaic patriarchal lifeworld, they propose to subvert and undo every last scrap of the ruined paternal function available in modernity, up to and including the old fascist ones. The classical fascist was a polymorphously perverse child sometimes playing at being an authoritarian father. Whatever quantum of repression upheld this situation is increasingly dispensed with. Rebellion against modernity becomes its own justification. What makes the radical-right radical is that it no longer assumes the existence or validity of any particular unitary, self-present, M-coded point of origin to be returned to.

Fascist Disavowals and the Matriarchal Radical Right

Devotees of the abject, she as well as he, do not cease looking, within what flows from the other's "innermost being", for the desirable and terrifying, nourishing and murderous, fascinating and abject inside of the maternal body.

—Julia Kristeva, *Powers of Horror*

THE HEIGHTENED IMPORTANCE of the perverse structure today comes out nicely in the meme shown in Figure 1, which Donald Trump tweeted without comment in November 2019. It is based on the poster of *Rocky III* (1982).[39] *New York Times* columnist Jamelle Bouie gives an apt analysis: "Whoever created this meme image of Trump just wanted to show him as a powerful man. And Trump obviously wants to present himself as such. But when you consider the racial politics of the film itself, it's hard to imagine a more apt piece of symbolism. Adams [sic—Adam Serwer] writes that 'The Rocky films are a product of a sense of white pride and humiliation, and the desire to overcome it by restoring the proper order of things.' You can say exactly the same for Trump himself."[40] Bouie's analysis can be supplemented by specifying *how* the image transmutes white humiliation into white pride and proper order: a disavowal and not a repression. The genre of memes is built on disavowal: you know that the cut-and-paste is not meant to be real but, taking it "as if," you enjoy the wit of the juxtaposition. The fantasy of Trump as boxer is not a fantastic preview of his actual torso; it has all the realism of toned body printed on an XXL T-shirt. The muscular body is supposed to be the ethereal manifestation of his fighting spirit.

The meme's creator made a number of tweaks that reinforce the artifice, heightening the perverse ambiance. The natural sky background in the original, rhyming with and naturalizing the patriotic

Figure 1. Anonymous. *Meme: Trump as Rocky* (2019). Source: Twitter.

blue of the flag, is replaced with a darkened indoor rally. The small undefined features of the audience around his fantastic sovereign body recall the minuscule subjects populating the phantom body of the sovereign in the famous frontispiece to Hobbes's *Leviathan*. In choosing a promo shot rather than a film still, the meme maker removes Trump's body from any possible scene of action with a real opponent; the entire social relationship compassed in the image is between the sweaty sovereign and a crowd of viewers—including Trump too, gazing at himself. Smoothing out the contrast between a septuagenarian blond head and a buffed young Italian body, the meme's color brightness is heightened, subtly whitening Stallone's bronzed Mediterranean skin. As Richard Dyer points out of the white hero in this vein of popular culture, "the tanned built body affirms [heroic] whiteness as … both unmistakably yet not particularistically white. The muscle hero is an everyman: his tan bespeaks his right to intervene anywhere."[41] But the meme downplays the vital freshness of the tanned white male, even though this famously orange figure is not indifferent to the bronzed heroic whiteness look.

Whereas the original image tended to ideologically naturalize Rocky's white ethnic body as a rock of American masculinity, the meme denaturalizes that body. It dethrones Stallone as a real father figure, snickering at the Cold War regime of ideological naturalization these films supported in order to recast that body as the mere shadow of a transcendent paternal authority (Lacan's *pèreversion*) whose more perfect instrument is the Trumpian figurehead. Smirking at the original, the meme's details converge on the suture-point at the neck, where the eye is drawn to look for the collage's seams. There is an eeriness to the fact that this projection of virility depends so directly not only on a rather extreme castration that lops off everything below the neck but also on mobilizing the fantasy most associated with revolutionary violence, namely decapitation. Yet Trump blithely shares himself as/in this perverse regicidal fanboy fantasy. Of course, the neurotic liberal gaze is baked into the image. Trump, along with his followers, is staring belligerently at us, ready with boxing gloves, red-and-blue tinsel, and a giant gold coin shielding his midriff. Perverse subjects can seldom resist exposing their feigned immunity to the lack entailed in acknowledging real norms to fascinated and/or horrified neurotics. As Joan Copjec reminds us, perverse subjects typically lure in and vent aggression upon their neurotic counterparts, a part willingly played by liberal hysterics.[42] A neurotic looking at this meme sees an illusory projection of masculine potency. Because it is so hyperbolic and the illusionism is so paper-thin, they will try to unmask the illusion and point to the material reality, in this case perhaps by sharing the meme alongside an unflattering shot of his corpulent body. But the meme maker does not engage in ideological naturalization, a process based on repression. They see his authority as justified not by its naturalness or realism but by its transcendence.

Consider now a fleshed-out specimen of this type of response, a statue of Trump created by the American Activist Collective and placed in Union Square in August 2016 (Fig. 2). It hardly needed to be called *The Emperor Has No Balls* for the castrating intention to be clear.[43] However, the title inadvertently lets slip its fatal concession. Not only does it give him a penis, but it recognizes in spite of itself that his imposing phallic presence does not track with how big that penis is. In fact, he may seem more phallic the less penis there is, which is just what we would expect in perverse disavowal, where the phallus is always attached to the maternal body. Like other instances of revenge porn, this coarsely executed insult is a projection of how the makers feel at having lost the election and being stuck with some-

Figure 2. American Activist Collective, *The Emperor Has No Balls* (2016), Union Square, New York City.

one who, with or without visible "balls," is nevertheless "emperor." Its gesture of unmasking Trump's abject and feminized "real" body can only unmask the collective's own impotence. Furthermore, it interpellates the viewer into a Trumpian scoffing at liberal inclusion and political correctness. To take the joke, you must tacitly assent that it is somehow damning, risible, and disqualifying to be fat, intersex, not well-endowed, or (practically) a woman.

One of its few aesthetic choices that merit discussion is making his obviously dyed orange hair rhyme with an abundant mound of glowing orange pubic hair. Transposed to an area of the body we would not expect such strong coloration in a man of his age, it confers on him a burning youthful glow. Presenting his supposedly lackluster genitals, it pays unintentional homage to a libidinal vigor that seems to do well enough with what it has, erectly imposing itself on the public square. The statue dramatizes the neurotic liberal playing at being a pervert confronted with the real thing, namely someone who disavows their lack. It reveals the failure of liberal critiques, evident in much less nakedly crass content, to counter fascism by exposing a material lack that it is not actually trying to repress. This abject sovereign body installed, to both merriment and groans, on a square at the center of the union ultimately suggests something more unsettling: his vitality, relevance, and success *is* his castration, abjection, and failure, and not his repression of those things. His strength *is* his nonmasculinity: his gross corporeality, his crone-like obesity, his veneered accoutrements. The neurotic liberal critique ultimately uncovers a figure that is both very potent and "castrated." Monstrous like a multimamia, its power to activate archaic affects is indicatively feminine. Behind such a fatphobic representation is a fear of feminine power and a fear that the fascist leader has activated this power and that he (or they) enjoy(s) in a way that is not routed through the position of having the phallus. Although they may masquerade as one, the prototypical fascist subject today does not need a dick because, like the phallic mother they secretly adore, they are one.

Slavoj Žižek has long been sensitive to the obscene underside that supports public authorities, describing the figure of the perverse "anal father," analysis that undoubtedly applies to Trump.[44] However, the "anal father" is not necessarily a man, and this analysis should be supplemented by inquiry into how the perverse structure mobilizes the feminine (more crudely: the weaponized cunt). Julia Kristeva, in a book on abjection that centers on the fascist novelist Céline, writes that "at the doors of the feminine, at the doors of abjection ... we are also, with Céline, given the most daring X-ray of the 'drive foundation of fascism.'"[45] In an insightful and prescient article, Andrew Hewitt develops this insight, arguing that the fascist construction of a "Volk" (the national people) depends on what he calls the "fascist feminine." Rebelling against actually existing patriarchy, fascism, he argues, justifies itself as "a quasi-utopian return to matriarchal totalitarianism ... rendered concrete through the figure of the biological mother. Matriarchy becomes a model for 'natural' society." This matriarchal "family," he continues (echoing Evola's assessment), "is to be identified with the Volk, that is, with a social and political collective that is organic and natural rather than the product of political deliberation. The mother, not the father, is the lynchpin of the mythology of the Volk."[46] The foundational theorist of matriarchy is Johann Jakob Bachofen, who described "mother right" as an intermediate developmental stage between the patriarchal model of the classical world and the earliest primitive "haeterism," characterized by nomadic free sexuality.[47] According to Bachofen, matriarchy binds promiscuous sexuality, providing a foundation for the restrictive patriarchal order that it develops into. Once patriarchy proper is installed, mother right remains as its underside, the source of kinship feelings and national adherence (111). In his reception history of the matriarchal idea, which captured the imagination of writers across the political spectrum (while remaining scientifically questionable), Peter Davies argues that matriarchal theories "represent the return of a genuinely repressed, powerful maternal origin, but because ... narratives of masculinity themselves require it and create a gap to be filled ... myths of matriarchy are [ultimately] created by mythologies of masculinity."[48] Matriarchal ideas tend to appear, I would add, when phallic projects take a perverse twist. The signifier of patriarchy, the phallus, is then construed as the invention and property of women.

There are signs of the "fascist feminine" all over radical-right revivals today. The alt-right agitator Ann Coulter, following in the footsteps of the older New Right activist Phyllis Schlafly, has built a persona around combining a phallic thrill with an intensely feminized physical presence. Schlafly herself is the subject of the mini-series *Mrs. America* (2020), in which she is played by Cate Blanchett. The apparent paradox of the militant conservative woman has become a fascinating subject in the age of Trump. Likewise, in *Bombshell* (2019), Nicole Kidman, Charlize Theron, and Margot Robbie play television anchors exposed to sexual harassment at the conservative Fox News. In a 2015 Bloomberg profile on the radical-right strategist Steve Bannon, who made a number of propaganda films, including *Fire from the Heartland: The Awakening of the Conservative Woman* (2010), a journalist observed that in his home, "about the only sign that I hadn't teleported back to the 1860s was a picture on the mantle of a smiling woman on a throne with a machine gun in her lap (it was Bannon's daughter Maureen, a West Point grad and lieutenant in the 101st Airborne Division; the throne belonged to Saddam Hussein—or once did)." The icon of order is a phallic woman sitting on a despot's throne; no father figures are in sight.[49] In France, Marine Le Pen took over the far-right Front national from her father, Jean-Marie. Breaking with his aesthetic and personnel residues of classical fascism, she rebranded her party as mainstream and led it to greater successes than ever before. The British series *Years & Years* (2018) makes its leading radical-right politician a woman, clearly inspired by Marine Le Pen. Viv Rook, played by Emma Thompson, bursts onto the scene with the credo of "not giving a fuck," whose television-inappropriate obscenity (and thus perversity) is underlined. Her movement becomes the "four-star" party and this not giving a fuck eventually leads to concentration camps in Britain. What is fascinating about these feminine figures (and attractive to the top actors playing them) is not a story about being co-opted by patriarchy or selling out. In *Years & Years*, that narrative arc is given to the normative good-enough white dad who loses his job and finds himself administering the British camps. Instead, these women seem to be—or seem to fully embody—patriarchy, and they can therefore be imagined as rightfully phallic. To show that fascist affects are routed through phallic non-men (that is, women and perverts) is not to blame them for fascism. But it is to note that nonmasculine figures have become indispensable figurations and media surrogates for a patriarchy that cannot bear to look at its actual cis-masculinity in the mirror. Once it takes leave of the imperative to respectability, enjoyment under the sign of fascism is a mode of feminine enjoyment, even when it presents as ultraphallic. We glimpse the borrowed nature of this phallus in a fleeting moment toward the end of *Years & Years*, in a rare scene when Rook actually interacts with the main characters as opposed to being seen on TV. She mutters that if she left her role "they" would kill her. We now turn to a film that tries to imagine what "they" might look like. (Hint: "they" is not a masculine position.)

Fascism Without Men in Suspiria

Hitler's way will also be a descent to the Mothers.
—Herman Wirth, *Die Ura-Linda-Chronik*[50]

WE CANNOT REVISIT the question of the psychic life of fascism without also discussing psychosis and its delusions. As I argued above, fascist ideologies tend to activate the perverse structure, but when fascist practices turn hallucinatory and brutal, exceeding all ideological armature, they typically activate the psychotic structure. We will now follow the trajectory of the "fascist feminine" as it devolves from perversion into psychosis in Luca Guadagnino's remake of Dario Argento's *Suspiria* (2018). This film follows Susie Bannion, a young American dancer who moves to Berlin to join the Markos dance company, which is secretly run by witches. The coven is in the midst of a succession crisis dividing those faithful to the old ways of the company's matriarch, Mother Markos, and those ready to pass the leadership to Mme. Blanc, the company's charismatic choreographer. Susie arrives just as Patricia, the lead dancer, has disappeared. We eventually learn that Patricia is being held in the secret cellar with Markos, whose body is falling apart. Patricia was supposed to be the vessel for her revitalization, but the ritual failed and her mind disintegrated. The ambitious Susie takes Patricia's place as lead dancer and candidate for the ritual. Meanwhile, Patricia's psychoanalyst, Dr. Josef Klemperer, a melancholic Holocaust survivor, is convinced there was foul play in Patricia's disappearance and plays detective. When the time for the ritual comes, the witches lure him to the building with a hallucination of his wife, making him their witness. The conflict between Blanc and Markos comes to a head when Blanc tries to stop the ritual and Markos kills her, defending her claim to be anointed as the third of the three primal mothers, Mother Suspiriorum. Then comes the twist: Susie declares that *she* is the infernal mother and summons a dark, ungendered skeletal creature who destroys Markos and her followers. In the final scene, Susie, now undisputed leader of the coven, visits Klemperer, tells him how his wife, Anke, died in the camps, and then wipes his memory. The film's final shot pans out from his cottage, where an attractive shirtless young man passes, then a mother and her young daughter, then to a woman carrying Erich Neumann's book *The Great Mother*, finally to a long shot of Josef and Anke's initials in a heart engraved in the wall on the corner, dividing them on separate planes (Fig. 3).

The metaphor of a linkage across divided planes of reality captures rather well how the signifiers of fascism crammed into *Suspiria* connect with its main storyline, which has nothing to do with fascism per se. Its narrative plays out against the backdrop of the "German Autumn" crisis of 1977. In the first scene, the frightened Patricia travels to see Klemperer through shouting protesters sympathetic with the Baader-Meinhof terrorists, who just kidnapped Hanns Schleyer, a former SS officer who became a prominent industrialist in postwar Germany. Later, we hear on TV and radio about the failed hijacking of the *Landshut* flight and the apparent suicide of three prominent RAF members. When the doctor leaves his home, the camera dwells on student posters expressing solidarity with the Palestinians whose militants' release was one of the hijackers' demands. Directly in front of the dance building is the Berlin Wall, covered in graffiti by

Figure 3. Film still, *Suspiria*, dir. Luca Guadagnino (2018). Photograph of the corner in Dr. Klemperer's office in the opening scene, with a voice-over evoking the transference theme.

leftists, angry at Nazis criminals secretly living on. In a further link, Klemperer's search for the missing Patricia merges with his dream of refinding his beloved wife, Anke, who died in the camps. The main plot floats in this politicized ambiance without narrative synthesis. We learn almost immediately that the witches have "been underground since the war," but we have no idea if they were in league with Nazi occultists, members of the anti-Nazi underground, or uninvolved.

We do know that the main piece they are rehearsing is titled *Volk*. "I don't know how aware you are of what times we lived through forty years ago, out of which this piece was made," Blanc tells Susie when she suggests a more "emphatic" alternation to the choreography. "We learned at great cost through those years the value of the balance of things." While she seems to imply that the company were bystanders during the Reich, there is one "great cost" of those years in evidence, namely the mysterious physical deterioration and subterranean existence of Markos. We cannot tell if the film wants us to see the coven as an analogy for fascists secretly holding on to positions of power in postwar German society or if we should liken them to a secret revolutionary antifascist group—or if it even distinguishes between these positions.

Critics either did not know what to make of these "disconnected" references[51] or were overtly hostile to the absence of historical and moral anchoring. Richard Brody's vicious *New Yorker* review condemns these "static, but attention-getting, details of vast historical import" as vain "toys that can be defended as educational while offering little substance. ... The movie has nothing to say about women's history, feminist politics, civil violence, the Holocaust, the Cold War, or German culture."[52] But *Suspiria* declines to "say something" about the historical trajectory of fascism in order to study the psychic life of fascism as an emergent phenomenon. Like other contemporary directors, such as Jordan Peele and Ari Aster, Guadagnino turns to the horror genre to study the psychology of political violence. What he reveals is more disturbing than a sadistic man with an inflated (or nonexistent) ego and a weapon. Pointing out that the first scene in which the witches act out violently toward a dancer who crosses them blurs the moral meaning to linger instead on a beautiful shot of a trail of blood disappearing into a mirror door (Fig. 4), Brody screams, reacting as though the film were advocating Holocaust denialism: "his camera sees nothing." But it is this lack—a lack of normalized meaning, a self-supporting ideological ground, a lack of men (and the crypto-fetishistic presence of a female shoe), a lack spanning the perverse and psychotic structures—that the film presents as the affective core of fascism. It is particularly concerned with what it means for fascist violence to return in a new shape that is not simply the survival or imitation of the older model: a general psychopathology of fascism distinct from the specific German historical trauma. It is no doubt with an eye to Trump's America that the film makes Susie the American a fresh new vehicle to replace the decrepit German leadership whose main activity is rehearsing and performing Volk. Appropriately then, Blanc intends to replace their staple dance with a new piece about "rebirths" called *Open Again*. This new dance, Blanc says, will be based on Susie's "instincts": the American-lead remake of a German classic from the 1940s, with an updated sensibility.

The film is almost as steeped in psychoanalysis as it is in fascism. It is particularly interested in delusion, specifically the mediated transfer of delusion from one person to another. Klemperer explains over lunch: "You can give someone your delusion, Sara. That's religion. That was the Reich. The Reich had these things. Insignia. Esoteric ritual. These 'Mothers' they could be code names for founding members with metaphoric histories, I don't know. But I do know that you are living with dangerous people." The key phenomenon is not spontaneous delusion but the transference process that spreads it. The transference theme is rooted in its psychoanalytic meaning. In the first

Figure 4. *Suspiria*.

scene, in which a disordered Patricia has a session with Klemperer, she glances through the books in his office, resting her hand on Jung's *The Psychology of the Transference*. Appropriately enough, in this text Jung maps the Freudian model of transference onto psychic transfer processes described in occultism. Recalling Blanc's obscure reference to "the balance of things," Jung seeks an "equilibrium" between the ego and the chthonic imaginary forces of the unconscious.[53] The film does not neglect the more familiar Freudian sense of transference as a parent-child relationship projected onto the therapist. In flashbacks, it juxtaposes Susie's real ailing mother in America with her two competing mothers in Berlin, the nurturing mother Blanc teaching class and the devouring mother Markos in the basement. Having identified the witches with a Jungian transference playing out in the imaginary and a Freudian transference grounded in the symbolic, the film goes on to imagine a supernatural transference in the real—a staple of the horror genre. This occurs when, in its most virtuosic scene, Susie dances an audition for the lead part in *Volk* and Blanc bridges her movements into a mirror room in which Olga, a dancer attempting to defect, is violently beaten. This scene is the heart of the film's understanding of neofascist violence—it was screened separately as a teaser—and it shows the *Volk*-leader causing violence secretly, at a distance, without consciously realizing it herself. The film's intense interest in following psychic phenomena to the level of the Lacanian real is teasingly signaled when it tells us early on that Klemperer decides to pass on attending a lecture by Dr. Lacan, who is in Berlin at the time of the events, a reference that sets up Lacan as an absent presence over the narrative.

Susie's *Volk* solo, the matron Tanner warns ominously, could "put the others at risk" if, say, someone gets "kicked in the ribs." This is just the beginning of what happens to Olga. Before the dance starts, we hear Blanc's instructions to Susie piped into Olga's room, causing Olga to look away from herself in the mirror and out, as if someone is coming toward her (Fig. 5a). This is one of several devices the film uses to make Olga's experience bleed into Susie's room, reaping a boost in tension by giving us in the audition room a partial awareness that something more is going on (Figs. 5b and 5e). Once underway, the horror-effect of the beating is constructed using sound as much as image. In Susie's room, a simple minimalist piano phrase is repeated (and later varied), so that the editing's cross-cut to the mirror room takes up (especially initially) roughly the length of the phrase, creating the effect that the cracking bones, thuds, and screams in the mirror room are continuations of the same phrase. Timed with the first inhale of Susie's dance, the camera toggles from a ceiling view of her gazing upward to a close-up of her looking ahead and back up again (Figs. 5c and 5d), mirroring her gaze and extending it out of the space of her room. It both points to Olga and mimics the mirror room she is trapped in. Corresponding to those sounds, Olga's body takes on grotesque brown bruising—twisted to the max, she eventually spews saliva and urine—but not blood. The violence is subtly racialized: her clothing is shades of brown and as her body is bruised her skin takes on matching physical shades of brown, and eventually zombie-like shades of black (Fig. 6a). As Olga is wrung into an extreme contortion, a parasitic growth seems to appear in her midsection (Fig. 5f). Susie's violence is additive rather than subtractive, the traumatic fertility of a forced feminine impregnation. At the end, Susie collapses and the camera catches a tear in her waistband (Fig. 5g), a tiny visual echo of Olga's muffled suffering.

The scene's success lies in splitting the viewer's identification between two scenes and two subjects. Pre-identified with Susie dancing her solo, the viewer is induced into the split consciousness of the perverse structure. We know that Susie is beating Olga, and yet we see no one in the mirror room. The scene formally simulates the structure of disavowal. Ultimately—and her eventual apotheosis as Mother only confirms this—Susie's corporeal enjoyment in dancing is perverse too. The details linking the split spaces suggest that on some level Susie, like us, knows that her movements are unwittingly being put to an obscure and potentially violent use. The pervert takes enjoyment in being the instrument of the other's desire; there is scarcely a clearer illustration of that dynamic than a prospective soloist auditioning to be the instrument of the witches' creative vision. In Olga's room, her being beaten has all the horror of the psychotic's delusional voices, a mode of violence that forecloses all recognition. Therefore, the scene models a mode of violence stemming from the dynamic between a perverse and a psychotic subject. In the more typical situation, a demagogue or cult leader is a pervert (or occasionally a psychotic) and they attract neurotic followers mesmerized by their seeming absence of lack. Here, Susie is the perverse leader and her aestheticized choreographic suggestions of violence, wrapped in disavowal, then trigger psychotic irruptions of seemingly spontaneous anonymous violence. This scene of violence, centered on a latter-day *Volk* performance, illustrates the psychic dynamic of aleatory terrorism.

The film supplements this split scene with a third scene in which the witches gather around Olga's broken body, pierce her flesh with hooks, and drag her through the mirror door (the shot Brody pointed out) and down to Markos. In order to help us understand it, we will take a short detour through Freud's key essay on perversion, "A Child Is Being Beaten."[54] Freud analyzes eroticized beating fantasies into three psychological levels, which are reflected quite well in the three filmic moments of Olga's beating. He begins with the conscious level, where beating spectatorship fantasies are imaginary formations that seem sadistic in appearance. The conscious fantasy, he argues, is a distortion of an unconscious fantasy with two features kept down by repression: the agent of the beating is the father and the one being beaten is the rival for his love, usually a sibling. Because of "a convergence of the sense of guilt and sexual love," the subject represses their place in the symbolic and the father figure who symbolizes it (182). But there is a deeper fantasy beneath this one, Freud says, which is never actually remembered, wherein *"I am being beaten by my father"* (185; his emphasis). Although it is merely an analytic construct, this fundamental masochistic fantasy explains the root of sexual excitement in perversion (191). This fantasy is a defense not only against the violent demand of the father's norms but against the violence that installed these norms in the first place: with how the subject was beaten into the symbolic, with its enjoyment of that capture (which gave it name and identity), and with the paternal violence that first installed this relation. In short, the fundamental beating fantasy, from which sexual excitement derives, happens at the level of the real. The film achieves its horror-effect by bridging the "conscious" imaginary

BLANC: Remember, you start on one with the music,

And...

Figures 5a–g. *Suspiria*.

plane of Susie dancing with the terrifying level of the real where Olga "is being beaten." What is left out is the repressed contents from the symbolic level, Freud's first phase of the unconscious fantasy: the father who beats and is beloved. As argued above, the invisible hand beating Olga in a mirror room is a near-perfect illustration of how disavowal works.

Figures 6a, b. *Suspiria*.

The third scene, in which the matrons gather around Olga's living-but-broken body and pierce her flesh repeatedly with curved hooks, provides the missing intermediate link, the first phase of unconscious fantasy in which it is enframed in the symbolic (Figs. 6a and 6b). The scene is narratively dispensable. It is there, I believe, to underscore that the symbolic is not necessarily masculine. Suddenly, these hyperphallic, yonically curved hooks grotesquely pierce and gangrape Olga's flesh. Giving us a suite of close-ups of the witches' vengeful and accusatory glares, the camera tells us: *here* is the masculine, penetrative, blood-letting mode of violence. Until this scene, the lack of visible beating agency placed the viewer uncomfortably in the triangulated position of the gaze that masters the transfer of violence. Promptly, the behooked witches snatch back the phallus from the viewer, beating Olga all over again to absolve us of our tacit complicity as witnesses who, no less than Susie, are "behind" the violence. The third scene makes visible the symbolic level mediating the *Volk*-imaginary and the *Volk*-real to insist that the paternal function, the one who beats, does not (this time at least) belong to a man.

One reason the film explores fascist violence without men, I suggest, is because it is interested in violence emanating from the private sphere, traditionally associated with nonmasculine actors and premasculine stages of development. Its narrative tends to remain within private spaces, particularly the monumental domesticity of the building. Yet it is preoccupied with how happenings cordoned off by privacy ramify, resonate, reactivate, and intrude upon the happenings outside, which it is torn off from and does not recognize, at least not consciously. Violence without symbolized recognition is private violence that manifests out in the open, but without the detour through publicity and its normative mediation. After the final performance of *Volk*, Blanc visits Susie, who addresses her telepathically: "It's all a mess, isn't it. The one out there. [Spoken out loud:] The one in here. The one that's coming. Why is everyone so ready to think the worst is over?" Susie's media-shift from private telepathy to public speech happens against the grain of her propositional content. The mess "in here" (in the domestic space of the coven) is spoken aloud, while the mess "out there" (survival of fascists and antifascist terrorism) is indicated using secret communication. The film thus asks us to see its ostensibly private witch drama not as a counterpublic separated from the political world but as an analogue to it that ciphers its psychic life. Unmistakably, "the worst" points to Nazism. Coming into her own as the infernal Mother of Sighs, Susie cryptically announces not its historical perdurance or its belated imitation but its "rebirth" in a new shape, her shape.

Although it explores nonmasculine, nonpublic, nonrecognition-based sources of fascistic violence, the film goes to some length to avoid essentializing these affects as somehow primordially feminine, presenting all gendered positions as artificial constructs. We will now consider how it deploys and subverts the standard gendered storylines of the occult horror film as analyzed by Carol Clover. The classical occult film, Clover argues, is built around a "dual focus" that pits a possession narrative, which is feminized and racialized, against a masculine "White Science" consisting of doctors, detectives, or priests trying to master it.[55] "The business of the occult film at every level," she argues, "is to confront the reigning masculine with problematic feminine and to arrive at some compromise or syncretic position" (99). The genre's central ambition is for the indicatively teenage male viewer to accept a feminine world, sometimes ludicrously exaggerated as possession and contagion phenomena, a "sex-gender swamp of male and female bodies collapsing into one another" in which castration largely doesn't matter but feminine insides do (107, 109). The ethical-therapeutic outcome of these films, for Clover, is a masochistic chastening of impulses toward masculine mastery. It is masochistic because the assumed viewer's position migrates from the White Science position to the occult(ed) feminine position: in slasher movies, the viewer identifies with the "last girl" who turns the violently leering male gaze back on its sender. This analysis is aligned with other critical works from the 1990s, notably those of Kaja Silverman and Leo Bersani, that look to masochism (and thus to the perverse structure) as an ethical model for a "hygenics" of violence.[56]

Suspiria's investigation into fascist affects without men, I argue, casts a profoundly skeptical light on masochism or perversion in general as a viable solution to the problem of violence by relentlessly tipping perverse structures into psychosis. The film lays out the expected "dual narrative," providing a company/coven storyline alongside that of Klemperer, the psychoanalyst-cum-detective, who (in spite of his witchy library) gives the rationalist analysis we expect from White Science. Having faithfully constructed the dual plot, the film makes a great meta-narrative feint by casting Tilda Swinton, under mounds of makeup, as the eighty-year-old Klemperer. According to the *New York Times*, Swinton's costume even included a bulky prosthetic penis and testicles.[57] The credits list him as played by "Lutz Ebersdorf" and those involved kept the conceit going as long as possible. Swinton created an IMDb page for Lutz filled with delicious details: he was a Holocaust survivor, involved in Actionist experimental theater, and a practicing Kleinian analyst specializing in mother/daughter relationships. At an awards ceremony in Italy, she solemnly read a statement on his behalf, to chuckles from members of the audience in on the joke. When asked about Lutz's improbably good skin, Guadagnino told interviewers that so was the skin of his own eighty-six-year-old father.[58] When pushed to admit that Swinton played him, he protested that this was "fake news!"—yet another (albeit low-key) inscription of the film into contemporary radical-right politics.[59]

Instead of synthesizing M- and F-coded positions, as the classic horror film does according to Clover, the film pulls the foundation out by making men and their White Science a prosthetic fiction. When Klemperer sends the police to inquire about Patricia, the witches effortlessly hypnotize the policemen, pull down their pants, and full of cackles flick their diminutive cis-penises with comparatively impressive hooks. The "reigning masculine" is either the ponderous Ebersdorfian masquerade or a joke. At one point, Sara steals a witch-hook and gives it to Klemperer, who tries to dispose of it in the river; the next thing we know the witches have recovered it, loudly exclaiming "look how dirty he made it!" Apparently, men do not even want the phallus; they try to get rid of it and just end up dirtying it. In the final ritual, Blanc brings Klemperer in as a witness, his naked body splayed out on the floor, rather like a big wrinkly baby, awkwardly turned up to expose his large white prosthetic penis (Fig. 7a). Once the frenzy of phallic violence belongs totally and unambiguously to nonmasculine subjects, the White Science position itself starts to seem like mass delusion and all of patriarchy a long enchainment of possessions. Klemperer is possessed by the traumatic loss of his wife, possessed by memories of the Holocaust—just as the Baader-Meinhof were possessed by revolutionary ambitions to rectify its aftermath. (At lunch with Sara, the film gives him a slip of the tongue, referring to one of the three infernal mothers as "Mother Meinhof.") The public world becomes possession all the way down; the historical "mess out there" is and always was a mess of mass witchery. If the masculine position from which to get to the bottom of feminine mischief becomes illusory, the prospect of reaching Clover's synthesis through masochistic self-chastening disappears.

This is what Brody hysterically responds to when he detects something close to Holocaust denialism in the film.[60] When Susie visits Klemperer at the end, she tells him how his wife died and then makes him forget everything that took place in the film, liquefying the White Science position of the witness, a position necessary to anchor the Holocaust as a real historical phenomenon. His role as official witness to the ritual is explicitly connected to his status as witness to the Holocaust. Of all the guilty men in Germany, he groans during the ritual, why should he, who continually relives the first holocaust he witnessed, be punished thusly? But Klemperer does not end up witnessing anything beyond the repetition of his own helplessness before the Reich, this time as helplessness before the nonmasculine subjects of the coven. With his character, the film is willing to pay the price of

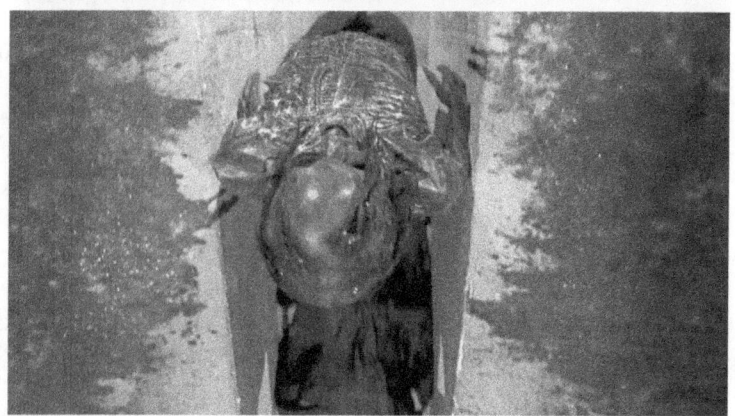

Figures 7a–c. *Suspiria*.

liquefying the witnessing of the Holocaust as a historical narrative so that he can bear witness *that it can happen again*—that the worst is *not over*—*and that it is happening again here*. Susie explains that she grants him amnesia because "we need guilt, and shame, but not yours." We do not need his guilt and shame in remembering historical wrongs that he can do nothing about and that he did not even commit in the first place. We need, I take the film to assert, the capacity to feel guilt and shame at what is happening now and at what is coming. The masochistic solution, like all perverse solutions, chastens behavior while disavowing guilt and shame. It sheds the phallus, mocks it, dirties it, diminishes it, puts it on a woman (and adores it behind a veil). But fascism can perfectly well return cloaked in disavowal, in the hands of someone nonmasculine. And the liberal masochistic pervert, just like Klemperer, will be helpless to stop it.

The film also cuts off the possibility of blaming fascist affects on a naturalized essentialist femininity by giving Swinton a third character to play. Now under truly enormous mounds of prosthesization, she plays the ghoulish mother Markos. The prosthetics used to create her abject crone body are not simply bulbous exaggerations of aging female corpulence: there is a tiny hand protruding from her elbow, and the protrusions in her loins evoke someone permanently trapped in the state of giving birth (Fig. 7b). She is naked except for dark glasses, which evoke her blindness, placing her within the castration complex. Markos inhabits, both spatially and narratively, the first level of unconscious fantasy, where, according to Freud, the agency of the father appears—here as a woman. She gives her name to the company and, symbolically "anointed" as Mother Suspiriorum, she carries the symbolic matrix, in all its monstrous deformity, in her body.

But as we saw in Freud's essay, there is a secondary unconscious fantasy behind the (maternal) symbolic and a secondary crypt below the secret crypt where the ritual takes place. "Which mother were you anointed for?" asks Susie at the ritual climax; when Markos answers, "Mother Suspiriorum," she replies, "I am she," trumping Markos's symbolic motherhood with her real motherhood. A dark monster then ascends from the subcrypt and kills all the Markosites (Fig. 7c). The demonic creature has no particularly feminine signifiers; its lean, hairy, nonbinary body reads as an inhuman death-head. As this occurs, Susie rips open her chest, revealing similarly black flesh resembling a dark beating vulva (it is instantly and inexplicably mended a moment later). The perverse secret coven is thereby confronted with a psychotic break manifesting the real. Neumann's book of Jungian analysis of the "Great Mother" archetype, which is flashed in the final scene, provides a helpful category for understanding this figure. Beneath the common feminine archetypes, he argues, one encounters a more fundamental archetypal level, which he calls the "uroboric," a nonbinary level where both gendered signifiers mingle, comparable to our experience of the natural environment, the unconscious itself, and our own bodily insides.[61] In a more Lacanian register, the monster discovered at the bottom of the feminine is (and looks like) pure phallus. If one goes searching for the primitive source of patriarchy and phallic domination, one is led to matriarchy, that is, to patriarchy without men.

The film's overarching interest, culminating in Susie's real-uroboric hairy black monster, is how perverse lifeworlds devolve into psychosis. Whenever the perversely monosexual world of the coven comes up, the film escalates it from disavowal to a more disturbing foreclosure. In the first scene, one of the first things Patricia says is "they want to eat my cunt on a plate." We barely register the lesbian frisson because it is overshadowed by the prospect of being devoured—which eventually happens when Patricia is eviscerated in the final ritual. Likewise, after her audition, Susie tells Blanc that performing *Volk* "felt like fucking," to which a startled Blanc replies, "A man?" "No," Susie answers, "an animal," leaving it unclear whether she means fucking like an animal or with an animal. Dance as perverse corporeal enjoyment blurs into the psychotic manifestation of pure animal phallus. In the final ritual, Markos is a perverse subject howling at Susie to formally disown her first mother in favor of a second motherhood that has no use for a man, and Susie one-ups her by psychotically manifesting the mother in her own body. The film anticipates this break in a shocking premonitory scene in which one of the matrons, disillusioned for reasons that are not clarified, abruptly stabs herself in the neck. Crucially, the psychotic break manifests itself not as the murderous rampage of a masculine slasher subject but as suicidal self-dissolution, a bad, transferentially induced self-shattering. After Susie has seized power, her first act is granting death to the abused Patricia and Sara, who ask to die. The film is less concerned about revivals of sadist masculinity than about delusion-animated destructive terroristic suicide. In this situation, signifiers of perversity, and even of femininity, are not repressed but worn with depraved pride. The possibility of a woman or a gay man as a fascist leader was present from the beginning. Increasingly, some mark of non-normativity becomes almost obligatory as a mark of authenticity, a perverse anchor for psychotic violence.

It is not reassuring news that the fascist phallus, like Swinton's prosthetic penis, is a cyborg supplement sutured onto femininized flesh that is shown off at every turn. The scapegoating mechanism is reconfigured. Once the fascist structure of feeling switches from fearing collapsing into womanliness into welcoming womanliness and the castration it implies, what it now fears is the collapse of sexual difference itself, or, as Patricia colorfully puts it, the threat of having one's cunt devoured. The object of fear and loathing becomes the nonbinary body, that is, any body in which sexual difference is not immediately legible, particularly trans bodies and queer bodies that withhold unambiguous cis-genderhood. Swinton's trans masquerade alludes obliquely to this new taboo. Therefore, there is a structural reason for the contemporary radical right's special animus against trans and nonbinary people. They are not exactly concerned with propping up masculinity that threatens to collapse into femininity and abjection: the psychic life of fascism thrives on that collapse. Once patriarchy outsources the phallocratic order to womanhood as the bedrock of the social, it becomes terrifying not knowing in which bathroom one may be found. To analyze the transphobic logic of contemporary fascism is not to reductively attribute it to individual psychological factors but to trace its psychic life, above all in the transferential delusions between people that sustain it. In spite of the occasional rhetoric of the "natural," bioscience is not decisive anymore in the psychic life of fascism. Once "nature" is construed in a spiritual register—either in a monotheistic-traditionalist or in a pagan-Evolian register—the radical-right subject does not care whether or how sexual difference is ideologically naturalized. The only thing that matters is that it is self-evident. One might call this the evidence of non-experience, which is to say of delusion. *Suspiria* suggests that this psychotic affective structure is the source of a fascist current that has become, as Blanc put it in the title of her projected sequel to *Volk*, *Open Again*. The perverse structure offers very limited resources to keep this performance unrealized.

Notes

1 See George L. Mosse, *The Image of Man: The Creation of Modern Masculinity* (Oxford: Oxford University Press, 1996), 155–80.
2 Barbara Spackman, *Fascist Virilities: Rhetoric, Ideology, and Social Fantasy in Italy* (Minneapolis: University of Minnesota Press, 1996), 34–48.
3 See Alexander Reid Ross, *Against the Fascist Creep* (Chico, CA: AK Press, 2017). I follow the standard practice of using "Fascism" for Italian Fascism proper

and uncapitalized "fascism" for movements with similar attributes that do not themselves embrace this label. Like Reid, I generally refer to the "radical right" for fascistic movements that may not accede to generic fascism, on which see Robert Paxton, "The Five Stages of Fascism," in *Fascism: Critical Concepts in Political Science*, ed. Roger Griffin and Matthew Feldman, vol. 1 (New York: Routledge, 2004).

4   Klaus Theweleit, *Male Fantasies*, trans. Stephen Conway, 2 vols. (Minneapolis: University of Minnesota Press, 1987). My epigraph is taken from 1:205.

5   Hannah Arendt describes pan-nationalist "tribalism" as "perverted" in *The Origins of Totalitarianism* (New York: Harcourt, 1968), 231, 234, 242. Judith Butler describes how "many people thrill to see embodied in their government leader a will to destruction that is uninhibited, invoking a kind of moral sadism as its perverse justification" in Masha Gessen, "Judith Butler Wants Us to Reshape Our Rage," *New Yorker*, February 9, 2020, https://www.newyorker.com/culture/the-new-yorker-interview/judith-butler-wants-us-to-reshape-our-rage. See also (without the psychoanalytic elaboration of the perverse structure I give here) Erik Swyngedouw, "The Perverse Lure of Autocratic Postdemocracy," *South Atlantic Quarterly* 118.2 (April 2019): 267–86.

6   Wilhelm Reich, *The Mass Psychology of Fascism*, trans. Vincent R. Carfagno (New York: Farrar, Straus & Giroux, 1970), xiv; see Ernesto Laclau, "Fascism and Ideology," in *Politics and Ideology in Marxist Theory* (London: NLB, 1977), 81–142, here 81–82.

7   Walter Benjamin, "Theories of German Fascism: On the Collection of Essays *War and Warrior*, ed. Ernst Jünger," trans. Jerold Wikoff, *New German Critique* 17.1 (Spring 1979): 119–28, here 121.

8   See Georges Bataille, "The Psychological Structure of Fascism," in *Visions of Excess*, trans. Allan Stoekl (Minneapolis: University of Minnesota Press, 1985), 137–60.

9   "He-men are thus, in their own constitution, what film-plots usually present them to be, masochists ... [a masochism which is] repressed homosexuality presenting itself as the only approved form of heterosexuality," he writes in *Minima Moralia*, trans. E.F.N. Jephcott (London: Verso, 2005), 46. On the *Männerbund*, see George Mosse, *Nationalism and Sexuality: Respectability and Abnormal Sexuality in Modern Europe* (New York: Howard Fertig, 1985), 23–48.

10 See "On Homosexuality and French Fascism," in George L. Mosse, *The Fascist Revolution: Towards a General Theory of Fascism* (New York: Howard Fertig, 1999), 175–82. On gay fascists in U.S. counterculture, from the punk and neofolk scene through Milo, see Ross, *Against the Fascist Creep*, 133–64, 281–328. On lesbian fascists in the UK, see Jack Halberstam, *The Queer Art of Failure* (Durham: Duke University Press, 2011), 151–52. For bibliographies of work on fascist women, see Dagmar Herzog, *Sex After Fascism: Memory and Morality in Twentieth-Century Germany* (Princeton: Princeton University Press, 2005), 269nn3–4; and Peter Davies, *Myth, Matriarchy, and Modernity: Johann Jakob Bachofen in German Culture, 1860–1945* (Berlin: De Gruyter, 2010), 358n25.

11 The classic statement is still Susan Sontag, "Fascinating Fascism," in *Under the Sign of Saturn* (New York: Picador, 2002), 72–105.

12 See Leo Bersani, *Is the Rectum a Grave and Other Essays* (Chicago: University of Chicago Press, 2010), 3–30; and Jack Halberstam, "'The Killer in Me Is the Killer in You': Homosexuality and Fascism," in *The Queer Art of Failure*, 147–72.
13 See Andrew Hewitt, *Political Inversions: Homosexuality, Fascism, and the Modernist Imaginary* (Stanford: Stanford University Press, 1996), 1–78; and Eve Kosofsky Sedgwick, *Tendencies* (Durham: Duke University Press, 1993), 48–51.
14 Herzog, *Sex After Fascism*, 10–63.
15 For the former, see Teresa de Lauretis, *The Practice of Love: Lesbian Sexuality and Perverse Desire* (Bloomington: Indiana University Press, 1994); for the latter, see any of Slavoj Žižek's books from the 1990s.
16 This does not stop him from titling it *Perversions of Fascism* (London: Karnac, 2009), casually flinging the psychopathologizing he deplores back on critics (like myself) who make the fascist perversity argument.
17 The individual pathology thesis is frequently associated with the collaborative volume, Theodor Adorno et al., *The Authoritarian Personality* (London: Verso, 2019). In a special issue on its pertinence today, Benjamin Y. Fong argues that thinking in terms of this "anthropological type" may not be completely exhausted. See "The Psychic Makeup of the New Anthropological Type," *South Atlantic Quarterly* 117.4 (October 2018): 757–71.
18 Jacques Lacan, "The Signification of the Phallus," in *Écrits*, trans. Bruce Fink (New York: Norton, 2006), 175–84.
19 Disavowal and foreclosure are complications of the basic procedure of repression. On disavowal as the mechanism for perversion, see Sigmund Freud, "Fetishism," in *The Standard Edition of the Complete Psychological Works of Sigmund Freud*, ed. James Strachey (London: Hogarth Press, 1966) (hereafter *Standard Edition*), 21:149–57.
20 Sigmund Freud, "Splitting of the Ego in the Process of Defense," in *Standard Edition*, 23:273–78, here 275–76.
21 Jacques Lacan, "Préface à L'éveil du printemps," *Ornicar?* 39 (1986): 7.
22 Jacques Lacan, *The Psychoses: The Seminar of Jacques Lacan, Book III*, ed. Jacques-Alain Miller, trans. Russell Griggs (New York: Norton, 1993), 39.
23 See Paul Verhaeghe, *On Being Normal and Other Disorders*, trans. Sigi Jottkandt (New York: Other Press, 2004), 397–428.
24 Sigmund Freud, "Three Essays on the Theory of Sexuality," in *Standard Edition*, 7:191.
25 M. Masud R. Khan, *Alienation in Perversions* (London: Routledge, 1987), 139–76.
26 See Roger Griffin, *Fascism: An Introduction to Comparative Fascist Studies* (Cambridge: Polity, 2018).
27 Zeev Sternhell, *The Birth of Fascist Ideology: From Cultural Rebellion to Political Revolution* (Princeton: Princeton University Press, 1994), and in broader historical perspective, *The Anti-Enlightenment Tradition*, trans. David Maisel (New Haven: Yale University Press, 2010).
28 See Mosse, *Nationalism and Sexuality*.
29 Herzog, *Sex After Fascism*, 18.

30 Julius Evola, *Men Among the Ruins: Post-War Reflections of a Radical Traditionalist*, trans. Guido Stucco and ed. Michael Moynihan (Rochester, VT: Inner Traditions, 2002).
31 See Julius Evola, *The Path of Cinnabar*, trans. Sergio Knipe (London: Arktos, 2010), 164–79.
32 Evola, *Men Among the Ruins*, 129.
33 Jason Stanley, *How Fascism Works* (New York: Random House, 2018), 4. Stanley does not hesitate to call all radical-right movements fascist. For the opposite view, which describes radical-right populism sympathetically as continuous with the center-right, see Roger Eatwell and Matthew Goodwin, *National Populism: The Revolt Against Liberal Democracy* (London: Penguin, 2018).
34 For more on Evola, see A. James Gregor, *The Search for Neofascism* (Cambridge: Cambridge University Press, 2006), 83–110.
35 Alexander Dugin, *The Fourth Political Theory*, trans. Mark Sleboda (London: Arktos, 2012). On his influence, see Ross, *Against the Fascist Creep*, 165–86.
36 See, among others, Domenico Losurdo, *Liberalism: A Counter-History*, trans. Gregory Elliott (London: Verso, 2014).
37 See *Totem and Taboo* in *Standard Edition*, 13:1–164.
38 Theweleit, *Male Fantasies*, 1:108. On fascist perversity, see 84–90. On the primacy of the phallic woman, see 73–74. On the importance of suboedipal affects, 204–15.
39 Poppy Noor, "Trump Posted a Picture of Himself as Rocky. No One Knows What to Make of It," *The Guardian*, November 27, 2019, https://www.theguardian.com/us-news/2019/nov/27/donald-trump-rocky-picture-twitter.
40 B-boy bouiebaisse [Jamelle Bouie], Twitter, November 27, 2019.
41 Richard Dyer, *White* (London: Routledge, 1997), 162–63.
42 Joan Copjec, *Imagine There's No Woman: Ethics and Sublimation* (Cambridge, MA: MIT Press, 2002), 227.
43 Kami Thomas et al., "So There's a Naked Trump Statue with a Micropenis in Union Square," *The Tab*, July 18, 2016, https://thetab.com/us/2016/08/18/trump-statue-48716.
44 On the "anal father," see Slavoj Žižek, *Enjoy Your Symptom!* (London: Verso, 2008), 124–46. On Trump's perversity, see Žižek, *Sex and the Failed Absolute* (London: Bloomsbury, 2020), 335–36.
45 Julia Kristeva, *Powers of Horror: An Essay on Abjection*, trans. Leon S. Roudiez (New York: Columbia University Press, 1982), 155. The epigraph is taken from page 54.
46 Andrew Hewitt, "A Fascist Feminine," *Qui Parle* 14.1 (Fall 2001): 29–55, here 41–42, 44.
47 J. J. Bachofen, *Myth, Religion, and Mother Right*, trans. Ralph Manheim (Princeton: Princeton University Press, 1967), 80.
48 Davies, *Myth, Matriarchy, and Modernity*, 233–34.
49 "Until Bannon showed up," he continues, "the only sounds I heard were faint noises from the basement, which might have been the young women he calls the Valkyries, after the war goddesses of Norse mythology who decided soldiers' fates in battle." Joshua Green, "This Man Is the Most Dangerous

Political Operative in America," *Bloomberg*, October 8, 2015, https://www.bloomberg.com/politics/graphics/2015-steve-bannon/.

50 Wirth was a Nazi ideologue, cited in (and translated by) Davies, *Myth, Matriarchy, and Modernity*, 357.
51 This was Christy Lemire's reaction in her review (undated), https://www.rogerebert.com/reviews/suspiria-2018.
52 Richard Brody, "Review: Luca Guadagnino's 'Suspiria' Is the Cinematic Equivalent of a Designer Che T-Shirt," *New Yorker*, October 30, 2018, https://www.newyorker.com/culture/the-front-row/review-luca-guadagninos-suspiria-is-the-cinematic-equivalent-of-a-designer-che-t-shirt.
53 Carl Jung, *The Psychology of the Transference* in *The Collected Works of C. G. Jung*, vol. 16, ed. Sir Herbert Read, Michael Fordham, Gerhard Adler, and William McGuire, trans. R.F.C. Hull (Princeton: Princeton University Press, 1975), 395.
54 Sigmund Freud, "'A Child Is Being Beaten': A Contribution to the Study of the Origin of Sexual Perversions (1919)," in *Standard Edition*, 17:177–204.
55 Carol Clover, *Men, Women, and Chainsaws: Gender in the Modern Horror Film*, 2nd ed. (Princeton: Princeton University Press, 2015), 70.
56 See Bersani, *Is the Rectum a Grave and Other Essays*; and Kaja Silverman, *Male Subjectivity at the Margins* (New York: Routledge, 1992), 185–298.
57 See Kyle Buchanan, "How 'Suspiria' Transformed Tilda Swinton into an 82-Year-Old Man," *New York Times*, October 10, 2018, https://www.nytimes.com/2018/10/10/movies/tilda-swinton-suspiria.html.
58 See Patrick Shanley, "Who Is Lutz Ebersdorf? A 'Suspiria' Mystery Deepens," *Hollywood Reporter*, August 24, 2018, https://www.hollywoodreporter.com/heat-vision/who-is-lutz-ebersdorf-a-tilda-swinton-suspiria-mystery-deepens-1137192.
59 See Buchanan, "How 'Suspiria' Transformed Tilda Swinton into an 82-Year-Old Man."
60 See Brody, "Review."
61 Erich Neumann, *The Great Mother: An Analysis of the Archetype*, trans. Ralph Manheim (Princeton: Princeton University Press, 1963), 40.

Chiara Bottici

2: Navigating Mass Psychology: The Political Myth of Trumpism

THERE IS A lot of talk today about whether contemporary forms of right-wing populism represent a new political formation or indicate that fascism has come back.[1] This discussion often fails to take into account that, in some important ways, fascism has never gone away. To be sure, history never repeats itself, and there are characteristics of the regime that created the term, and explicitly embraced fascism in the 1930s, that will not come back. But how do things look if we, as philosophers and social scientists, treat "fascism" as an ideal-type, as a heuristic tool that can be used to think about and compare different forms of power?

Consider for a moment some of the features that characterize the regime that reigned in Italy between 1922 and 1943 and gave fascism its name: hypernationalism, racism, sexism, machismo, the cult of the leader, the replacement of history and empirically formulated notions of truth with political myths, the cult of the state, extreme conceptions of enemies, perceived as existential threats to the nation, and the consequent endorsement of violence against them.[2] We can thus see how, after its formal fall in 1943, different aspects of that form of power continued to exist in different guises and shapes not simply in

Europe but also elsewhere.³ We can point to how fascist parties continued to survive in Italy as well as elsewhere, how fascist discourses remained alive, and how different postwar regimes exhibited some, or even many, of the fascist traits listed above, even when they did not formally embrace fascism in its entirety. When a regime shows a critical mass of the traits characteristic of historical fascism, we can then usefully speak of neofascism. Similarly, when focusing on a single trait of a political ideology, such as, for instance, its underlying mass psychology, we can speak of a fascist mass psychology without thereby implying that the state or the government under which that happens is fascist in its entirety.⁴

If we use the concept of fascism as a polyhedral heuristic tool, we can see how Trumpism, as an ideology, embodies a form of neofascism that presents its own peculiar features, including some respect for the formal features of representative democracy, the combination of free-market ideology and populist rhetoric, and the paradox of a critique of the state and its "corrupt" elites accompanied by the massive recourse to its institutions. But Trumpism also exhibits features, such as an extreme form of nationalism, systemic racism, macho-populism, and an implicit legitimation of violence against enemies, that are indeed typical of fascism. Therefore, I propose to consider fascism here as a tendency of modern power and its sovereign logic, a tendency that, like a Karstic river, can flow underneath formal institutions but can also always erupt in its most destructive form whenever the structural conditions allow that to happen.

In this essay, I would like to explore the psychological ties that bind fascist followers to their leaders and then move on to argue that Trumpism, as a psychological and political phenomenon, relies precisely on such a fascist libidinal bond. After briefly discussing Freudian mass psychology, I will move on to explore the insights provided by Adorno's and the feminist reinterpretation of it, in particular as it concerns the specific type of mass psychology that is the fascist one. This will enable us to throw some light on the neofascist traits of Trumpism and its underlying political mythology.

Adorno with Freud, Adorno Beyond Freud

IN ORDER TO discuss the features of the mass psychology that sustains fascist leadership, I would like to focus on a text written by Theodor Adorno in the 1950s to address U.S. American fascist agitators,

"Freudian Theory and the Pattern of Fascist Propaganda."[5] Although written in reference to the American fascist leaders of that time, this text provides key insights into fascist mass psychology and thus helps us illuminate the type of libidinal bond that links fascist leaders to their followers more generally. Certainly, the rise of Nazism was also present in Adorno's mind when he wrote this text. But the fact that this text directly addresses American fascist agitators of the 1950s, and not Hitler or Mussolini, is in my view already an indication that fascist propaganda did not stop with the dismissal of fascist regimes of the 1940s and, on the contrary, that it was well present in the United States before Trumpism.

Adorno's "Freudian Theory and the Pattern of Fascist Propaganda" is a strange text. It presents itself as a dynamic interpretation of Freud's *Group Psychology and the Analysis of the Ego*, which, in its turn is, also, according to Adorno, a "dynamic interpretation" of Gustave Le Bon's description of the mass mind.[6] It is, therefore, technically speaking, a dynamic interpretation of a dynamic interpretation. Despite Adorno's pledge to adhere to Freudian theory, he departed from Freud on crucial points, and, precisely by doing so, he provided particularly powerful insights into the nature of fascist propaganda, including the type we have recently witnessed in Trumpism. Hence the image of fascism as a Karstic river I proposed: a tendency of modern political power that can erupt here and there, in specific political movements or even in single agitators, resembling little rivulets that do not change the general landscape but that can also occasionally erupt like a virulent torrent that reshapes what it finds in its way.

Despite Adorno's dynamism, Freudian theory remains the starting point of his approach, so his text cannot be understood without reference to Freud's.[7] Let's therefore briefly recall the structure of Freud's *Group Psychology*, as well as its main insights. In the first few chapters, full of long quotations from Le Bon and other theorists of mass psychology, Freud takes into consideration both stable and unstable masses, emphasizing the existence of all kinds of such groups.[8] Much emphasis is placed on the exaltation and intensification generated by imitation and by the affective contagion that members of a mass exert on each other. In chapter 3, Freud insists that the most noteworthy and important phenomenon in a collective formation is the intensification of affects created by participation in a mass. Freud subsequently defines our tendency to imitate the affective state of a person with whom we are in contact as an "incontestable fact" (chapter 4).[9] The varieties of the affects imitated, we may add, can thus also explain why Freud insists so much on the diversity of possible collective formations. In chapter 3, by means of a beautiful metaphor, he states that there are different types of masses, some temporary and open like high waves, others fixed and closed, which are more like a groundswell in the open sea, as well as all other types that situate themselves in between them.[10]

However, after reconceptualizing such affectivity in terms of his general theory of the libido, Freud suddenly shifts to the question of whether the presence of a leader is a *conditio sine qua non* for the existence of a mass.[11] And his positive answer is consequently based on the observation that followers identify with one another through the idealization of the figure of the leader, which comes then to provide the cement that keeps the crowd united. It is at this point that Freud also explicitly shifts to his two main examples, the church and the army, which, as Adorno among others noticed, are in fact two peculiarly hierarchical groups.[12] Not only do the church and the army depend on defined ranks; they are also highly institutionalized social structures, which sets them apart from other types of masses, such as spontaneous, open crowds.[13] Yet, it is through these examples along with the analysis of the process of identification via idealization that Freud arrives at the analogy between the mass and the primal horde that then becomes central to this text and to his mass psychology more generally.

Notice, however, that it is therefore late in the text, to be precise in chapter 10, that this analogy is introduced: Freud states that the head of the mass is the psychological equivalent of the father of the primal horde, the archaic phantasy that mass psychology revives in the midst of civilization.[14] Interestingly enough, though, there is here no sustained argument for why this analogy between mass and primal horde would be justified. Quite on the contrary, Freud seems to be aware of possible criticism and the lack of a robust argument in favor of such an analogy. For instance, at the beginning of chapter 10, Freud himself mentions those who have criticized his theory of the primal horde as a "just so story," and yet he continues to insist on this "just so story" by stating that it should not be discarded because it can be applied to so many different fields—as if the variety of possible applications would by itself be a justification of its validity.[15]

On the other hand, the analogy between the mass and the primal horde with its powerful male figure remains the major reply offered to the question of whether masses need a leader in order to come into being and persist over time. All the different types of masses that were mentioned at the beginning of the text seem to be reduced to just one type: the cephalic type, which is held together by identification with the leader, and which feeds on the reactivation of the archaic father figure of the primal horde. Notice the gendered element introduced by the analogy itself: the primordial horde analogy revolves around the figure of the patriarchal father, the male who is presented as both the head of the family and the head of the horde, according to the patriarchal tropes of the time.

Here Freud effects the same sort of *reductio ad penem*[16] that has been observed in many other parts of his work—from his writings on feminine sexuality to his writings on religion and culture—where everything revolves around the figure of the father and that of the mother is persistently marginalized.[17] The entire Freudian theory of the libido reflects this bias, which is also patent in his incapacity to explain female sexuality without using male sexuality as the yardstick for assessing sexuality and the development of the libido more generally.[18] Apart from Freud's biography, this certainly reflects the patriarchy of the epoch, which Freud embodies so well but which—it should be remembered—he also provides important tools to understand and to unpack.[19] This I take to be the virtue of an intellectual genius: transforming one's own sickness into a medicine for it; in the case of Freud, this means transforming the cure for his own neurosis into an entire discipline that can potentially treat it.

And yet, because it reduces all types of masses to the cephalic type, on the basis of the patriarchal story of the primal horde, Freud's approach to mass psychology is misleading in a number of ways, beginning with the fact that it can, at best, only account for certain types of masses. Besides the hierarchical cephalic masses, held together by identification with the leader, there are other types of masses, most notably those Elias Canetti termed "open crowds." Canetti, like Freud early in his text, insists on the importance of the imitation of affects, which is the cement for all types of masses. Canetti even concludes, on that basis, that "the open crowd is the true crowd, the crowd abandoning itself freely to its natural urge for growth. An open crowd has no clear feeling or idea of the size it may attain; it does not depend on a known building which it has to fill; its size is not determined; it wants to grow indefinitely and what it needs for this is more and more people."[20] Open crowds are thus the true crowds because they are not held together by a leader or a closed, hierarchical structure but rather by the pure desire to be part of the crowd, free to just follow its own immanent size and urge to grow. These are very different crowds from those identified by Freud via the examples of the church and the army. Yet, for Canetti they are the true crowds because they show why people in general come together—through the imitation of affects, which is itself contagious and which generates that special pleasure arising from overcoming the fear of touch. Only certain types of crowds are cemented together via cephalic forms of identification with the "head" of the crowd.

And this is precisely the point where Adorno's reflections come in. Certainly Adorno did not live in a less patriarchal environment. Yet, in contrast to Freud, he manages to avoid any simplistic *reductio ad penem*. The reason he does so is because, despite his reference to the story of the primal horde with its omnipotent father, he limits that diagnosis to fascist masses. Adorno openly states that the type of psychology described by Freud in his mass psychology is the psychology of the *fascist* masses and explicitly denies that it could be applied to other types of masses. As Adorno puts it:

> Furthermore, one may even ask: why is the applied group psychology discussed here peculiar to fascism rather than to most other movements that seek mass support? Even the most casual comparison of fascist propaganda with that of liberal progressive parties will show this to be so. Yet, neither Freud nor Le Bon envisaged such a distinction. They spoke of crowds "as such" similar to the conceptualizations used by formal sociology, without differentiating the political aims of the group involved. ... Only an explicit theory of society, by far transcending the range of psychology, can fully answer the questions raised here.[21]

Adorno's argument here is twofold. First, Freud's reconstruction of the formation of masses via identification with the leader does explain the peculiar psychology that sustains the fascist community of the people, although this should not be mistaken as the psychology of all masses: it only applies to the fascist ones. Second, however, fascism is not solely a psychological issue, because an entire theory of society is needed to explain it. These two claims may appear to be in tension with one another, so let us unpack them further.

Despite the fact that, as Adorno observes, both Freud and Le Bon had in mind early socialist masses when they wrote (rather than the fascist crowds that followed them), Freud does not share with Le Bon his reactionary contempt for the mass movements of the time. In the perspective of Freudian psychoanalysis, we are all to a certain extent sick. And this more neutral attitude leads him to a far deeper understanding of its mechanism of formation: the cement that keeps them together is a specific type of libidinal tie, that is, narcissistic identification. The members of the mass can identify with one another as members of the same group because they have substituted one and the same object, which is the image of the leader, as their ego ideal.[22] They are, so to speak, equal in the image of the leader. This, in turn, explains why the leader has to appear as the big narcissist and why he can actually do so while also appearing as a rather average person.

As an example of such narcissism, consider Trump's declaration on January 23, 2016, during his first presidential campaign: "I could stand in the middle of Fifth Avenue and shoot someone and I wouldn't lose any voters." As Jay Bernstein noted, it is in reference to this type of declaration that Adorno's essay is particularly insightful and can indeed help us understand the kind of libidinal bond with his fellows that Trump is thereby presupposing.[23] And I would say, also creating at the same time. Who is this big narcissist who can claim that he could be shooting people in the street and yet get elected?

In order to explain the role of narcissism, Adorno quotes Freud, once again, who stated that "the leader himself needs to love no one else."[24] But then Adorno rephrases the same sentence by saying that "the leader can be loved *only if* he himself does not love."[25] The issue of love, as Jamieson Webster has pointed out, is crucial in this essay.[26] But notice how Adorno actually goes beyond Freud by adding that little qualification: "only if." By doing so, Adorno further emphasizes a feature that is not only typical of but I would even say essential to fascist propaganda: the emptiness of the fascist agitator's speech, the absence of anything they may actually "give," and the consequent prevalence of the register of threat and violence.

This is what Adorno calls hatred and aversion for others as a "negatively integrating force," which, in fascism, according to Adorno, takes the peculiarly empty name of race.[27] Race and bourgeois individualism go hand in hand. As we read in the *Dialectic of Enlightenment*, the enigmatic text that Adorno coauthored with Max Horkheimer, trying to make sense of the failed promises of modernity: "Race today is the self-assertion of the bourgeois individual, integrated into the barbaric collective."[28] It is important to remember that, despite the rhetoric of the melting pot, race-based segregation has been a crucial feature of the United States from its very inception: as a country built through a settler-colonial project, its history is inseparable from the recourse to race-based negative integration.

As an example of the "empty character" of race and the way it has helped the self-assertion of the bourgeois individual in the history of the United States, consider for instance the differential roles assigned to Blackness and redness. Whereas the one-drop rule in the case of Black bodies assured that enslaved persons remained at work on the plantations and that their labor force could be exploited, the project of annihilation of Native Americans was carried out in the name of the myth of the "vanishing Indian" so much so that for them the opposite rule worked: only full-blooded Indians could reclaim their right to the land and their entitlements under the treaties. The law established in most cases stipulated that having even a single drop of non-Indian blood would be sufficient to deny Native American origins and thus the right to the land.[29] This is a clear example of how "empty" the notion of race is by itself and how it can fill up with the most contradictory elements even in the same context.

There is an intimate link between the U.S. settler-colonial history and systemic racism, a link that has been a source of inspiration for other racist regimes.[30] It may be worth remembering, for instance, that the genocide of Native Americans was highly praised by Hitler as a major source of inspiration for the Holocaust, that is, for the physical annihilation of a people based on their racial belonging. As he imagined his expansion toward eastern Europe, Hitler made explicit reference to the example of the elimination of Native Americans, hoping that Nazism would deal with the Slavs in the same way in which the United States dealt with Native Americans in its westward expansion.[31]

The fascist agitators of the 1950s as well as today's American neofascists can thus draw from a long history of racialization. Certainly history does not determine the future but rather presents possibilities and, in this case, a powerful symbolic reservoir of myths, images, and symbols of racialization that any newly appointed neofascist agitator can draw from. Particularly in settler-colonial histories such as the United States', Adorno's insights apply very well: race can function as an "empty" space that defines the group negatively ("we are *not* them") and can thus take form by pointing to all different kinds of targets: as we see it today in Trump's propaganda, Mexican people, Chinese people, Muslims, and those who do not match the image of the leader, including, as we will now see, sexual and gender minorities who do not conform to the heteronormative patriarchal family embodied in Trump's propaganda and his mythical "America."

Trump's Neofascist Propaganda

ALTHOUGH MUCH HAS been written about race and nationalism in the scholarship around the contemporary resurgence of authoritarianism worldwide, much less emphasis has been placed on the central role of gender in this new constellation. And yet, as Judith Butler has argued, we cannot understand the former without the latter.[32] This, we can add, is because neofascism thrives on hatred for others as a negatively integrating force, and gender minorities play a central role among such "others."

The explicit battle against so-called "gender ideology" began in the 1990s when the Roman Catholic Family Council warned against the idea of "gender" as a threat to the family and to biblical authority.[33] According to Butler's reconstruction, "the furor began some years ago when the Pope's family council, then directed by Joseph Ratzinger, warned that gender theorists were imperiling the family by questioning the notion that appropriately Christian social roles could be derived from biological sex. It was in the nature of sex for women to do domestic work and for men to undertake action in public life. The integrity of the family, understood as both Christian and natural, was said to be imperiled by this gender ideology."[34] "Gender ideology" has since become a signifier for any questioning of the family understood as rooted in a supposedly given biological sex and thus in God's own creation: questioning the idea that biologically determined sex is destiny therefore means questioning both the institution of the family and the authority of God, and can therefore literally be seen as "diabolical."[35] This enables their detractors to unify both feminists and LGBTQI+ activists in the same plot involving a conspiracy to subvert what God intended: the natural division of tasks between the two biological sexes, with woman subordinated to man just as the rib from which Eve derived is subordinated to the rest of Adam's body in the Book of Genesis.

Although the crusade against "gender ideology" takes different shapes in different contexts, ranging from the closure of gender studies institutes in recent years to the incitement of violence against all those who teach and practice gender studies, what all these episodes have in common is that they proliferate in contexts where right-wing populism and neofascism are on the rise. This does not come as a surprise, since patriarchy has been a component of fascist ideology from its very inception. The slogan of the regime that invented the term "fascism" summarizes this connection explicitly: "Dio, patria, famiglia" (God, fatherland, the family). The triad begins with the invocation of the God of Christianity, which, as Simone De Beauvoir noted, is a religion so imbued with patriarchy that it even spared its god the stain of being born through the body of a woman.[36] Thanks to the dogma of immaculate conception, which, in the history of Christianity, is later reinforced by that of the immaculate birth, Christian (male) gods appear as so omnipotent that they can be born through the female body without ever touching it. The Italian fascist triad (God, Fatherland, and the Family) thus recalls the Christian trinity of Father, Son, and Holy Spirit, in its conspicuous denial of any godly status to "the second sex."[37] This is a peculiarity not only of Christianity but of all the three great monotheistic religions of the book, none of which has much space for female goddesses.

Apart from the fact that Christianity and Islam remain the largest religions in the world,[38] so that we cannot easily dismiss their power in purporting a patriarchal view of the world, consider how this inbuilt patriarchal bias can provide a much broader ideological justification for what Butler has termed the "doubling of the two fathers (familial and state masculine leadership),"[39] which is one of the hallmarks of contemporary right-wing and neofascist propaganda. The role of patriarchy is indeed central to understanding fascist ideology, as emphasized not just by Adorno and Butler but also by other critical theorists inspired by the Frankfurt School. For Max Horkheimer, for instance, patriarchy is not just important but even central to any understanding of the psychological foundations of the authoritarian personality. As he openly states, "the patriarchal family is the creator of the authority-oriented cast of mind."[40] And we could add that it is the creator of the authority-oriented cast of mind not only because, as Horkheimer emphasized, it instills a habit of obedience to the "head" of the group but also because it shapes authority in the form of the domination of one sex (cisgendered heterosexual man) over all others.

Although Adorno does not specifically focus on sexual and gender minorities in his essay on fascist propaganda, he stresses how hatred for others as a negatively integrating force is indeed one of its distinctive features, and thus one that unifies the American fascist agitators of the 1950s that Adorno refers to at the beginning of his essay with Hitler and the other fascist agitators of the 1930s, who are also central to Adorno's thinking in this essay. With an operation similar to Adorno's, we can extend his analysis of fascist leaders of the 1950s to Donald Trump and the other fascist agitators of our time and see a very similar type of group formation via narcissistic identification with the image of the leader. Certainly Trump is not Hitler, and we did not live under Nazism during Trump's presidency, but, as Butler, among others, has emphasized, the rhetoric that Trump uses and the libidinal ties that bind his followers to him are fascist.[41]

So many features of Trump's propaganda correspond to those enumerated by Adorno: from the rigid distinction between the "beloved in-group" and the "rejected out-group" to the technique of personalization centered on the "great little man" figure; from the "sheep and goat" device to the repetition and standardization of slogans, so typical of stereotypical thinking; and so on. As Jay Bernstein has noted, in reading Adorno's text today one has the impression that it was literally written to describe Trump because many features that Adorno ascribes to the American fascist agitators of the 1950s read like a description of the American fascist agitators of our times.[42]

As an example of typically fascist propaganda, let me focus on the central slogan of Trump's campaign, "Make America Great Again."[43] Although this is a short slogan, it is in my view particularly crucial as it is able to condense[44] in a few words the gist of Trump's political mythology. Political myths are not narratives that are given once and for all but rather processes of elaboration of a narrative core that respond to a changing need for significance. As I have argued elsewhere, a political myth consists in the entire "work on myth" that takes place not only at the moment of production but also through the reception, and thus constant reelaboration, of a single narrative core.[45] Otherwise stated, this slogan works as an "icon," that is, as an image that, by means of synecdoche, reproduces and intensifies the whole affective work on myth that lies behind it.[46] Consequently, when assessing the power of a political myth one must look not only at its initial explicit statements but also at the entire process of its production-reception-reproduction.

"Make America Great Again!" Every word is important. Let us explore each one by one and unpack the "work" that lies behind them.

"America": The term points to the idea of a nation, of a spiritual entity that is different from the state apparatus and from the immanent series of bodies composing the citizenry of the United States. A lot of Trump's rhetoric points precisely to this separation: "Make *the United States* Great Again!" would have included all of those people who currently reside within the country, acknowledging the diversity of its racial and ethnic composition. Yet, by speaking of "America," the slogan clearly refers to a further entity, a mythical nation, a space that is at the same time linked to but also distinct from the state, its territory, and the sum of bodies currently inhabiting it.

If we analyze Trump's propaganda, it is not difficult to detect a few features of this supposed nation. For instance, Trump consistently speaks of the United States as if all the people within it belonged to the middle class. This effect is accomplished by presenting specifically middle-class problems as if they were universal: how to make U.S. airports look as nice as those in Singapore and Abu Dhabi is a good example.[47] Needless to say, one has to be fairly well-off even to perceive the aesthetics of airports as a problem. Yet by speaking *as if*, Trump manages to feed into the desire for social mobility, so that the middle class becomes a mythical space where everybody is supposed to be and thus, implicitly, invited to be.[48] And, most importantly, through this mythical representation the enormous class differences existing in the United States are swept under the rug.

Similarly, Trump's mythology of the American middle-class nation is reinforced by his systematic targeting of socialists, and thus of those who most insist on class inequalities. In a tweet from July 2019, for instance, Trump stated: "We will never be a Socialist or Communist Country. IF YOU ARE NOT HAPPY HERE, YOU CAN LEAVE! it is your choice, and your choice alone. This is about love for America. Certain people HATE our Country ..." (Donald J. Trump, July 15, 2019 @realDonaldTrump). The socialists cannot belong to "America" because their ideas about class inequalities question this mythical middle-class America: any questioning of such a mythology amounts to "HATE" of America itself, and thus to exclusion from it. This is the unconscious power of political myth as a lens through which a world is implicitly constructed: if you question a crucial piece of the founding myth of white middle-class America, then you are automatically categorized as an outsider, as one of America's enemies.

This is just one example of Trump's many statements against socialist and left-leaning Democrats but one that is particularly significant because it shows how the mythical construction of a homogeneous, white, middle-class America actually works. See, for instance, a parallel tweet, from several days before, in which immigrants were targeted along similar lines as being, allegedly by their own choice, not American: "If illegal immigrants are unhappy with the conditions in the quickly built or refitted detention centers, just tell them not to come. All problems solved!" (Donald J. Trump, July 3, 2019 @realDonaldTrump). Thus, by targeting immigrants, Trump also implicitly suggests they do not belong here, that they are different. As such, a divide is created between the individuals who currently reside within the United States and those who belong to a mythical and far more ancestral "America"—although that myth conveniently stops short of recognizing the actual indigenous inhabitants of this land, thereby depicting America as an essentially white entity. An example of how this can be accomplished is Trump's proposal to make classical architecture mandatory for federal buildings: by feeding the narrative that "America" derives from the Greek and Roman past, and not from its Native American heritage, Trump's rhetoric and (proposed) policies fed the settler-colonial mythology of a *terra nullius*, of an America that the white settlers had to "fill" with their European history, because nobody was present before their arrival.[49]

"Again": this is the most important word in the entire slogan. Had it been "Make America Great!" the sentence would have amounted to the usual invitation to greatness, which is not fascist per se. On the contrary, what is typical of fascism is the precise combination of nationalism with the mythologem of "greatness-decline-rebirth": this narrative plot enables adherents to single out those who are the perceived cause of the decline, target them as guilty, and thus channel and fuel hostility toward them.[50] One can then further distinguish between different degrees of fascistization of the state, according to whether this generates an incitement to violence by "do-it-yourself groups" and self-appointed individuals or by state apparatuses. But the mythologem of the scapegoat remains the same. Fascism fundamentally relies on xenophobia, racism, and sexism precisely because its founding narrative of "greatness and decline" is predicated upon such a mechanism: it incites degrees of hostility and violence toward others—in the case of Trumpism, the establishment politicians who corrupt the system, the Mexican immigrants who steal our jobs, the Chinese people who spread Covid-19, the sexual minorities who question the heteronormative traditional family, Muslim immigrants, in sum, all those others who are responsible for the decline of a mythical white, middle-class patriarchal "America."

"Make": this imperative verb is the pivot in the call for identification. Trump has repeatedly suggested that he is the only one who can fix the situation.[51] His success as a businessman and the incendiary and exaggerated tone of his rhetoric are all meant to instill a sense of exceptionality. Here lies the appeal of identifying with the charismatic leader: "only you can vote for me" is the other side of "only I can fix this." The invitation to "make" is thus an invitation to be part of this exceptional movement, of this unique effort to fix things, to restore what has been lost, what the diabolical people took away from us.

"Great": it is noteworthy that, in the original slogan, this modifier is followed by an exclamation mark. The latter reinforces the sense of vertical identification, of a greatness going upward. Throughout both presidential campaigns, a lot of emphasis was placed on this language of greatness and a corresponding language of size. The apparent frivolity of the discussion regarding the size of Trump's hands during his first presidential campaign[52] served precisely to underline the notion that everything else could be great, as great as the size of Trump's tower, which is the epitome both of his phallic rhetoric and of his corporate power.

The myth of the nation, the "greatness-decline-rebirth" narrative, the call for identification with the leader, and the rhetoric of greatness all show significant continuity with the mass psychology of the past: such is a very traditional form of identification with state leaders who exhibit exceptionality and phallic grandeur. It suggests a form of incorporation within the political body, where the face of its leader becomes the head of the body, and where the individual bodies are subsumed in a vertical movement upward. In that sense, Trump's rhetoric can also rely on a much longer history of vertical forms of identification with the "head" of state—a story that goes at least as far back as the appearance of the sovereign state, if not, as Freud suggested, to that of the church and army. In this sense, it can feed on and display the power of the imaginal appeal of the modern state.[53]

Think of the similarities between Trump's rhetoric of vertical incorporation through identification with the leader and the image of the sovereign that Thomas Hobbes chose for the frontispiece of his *Leviathan*, one of the founding texts of the modern theory of the state.[54] Not by chance did the image of the Leviathan depicted on the frontispiece of the 1651 edition prove to be one of the most successful and famous book covers of Western political philosophy.[55] The image does not simply reflect the circulation of affects within a sovereign state, as culminating into the upward movement of its composing bodies—the people literally walking into the head of the state, as if the latter were a vacuum cleaner of political affects. It is also an invitation to make the movement happen, to join into a form of (in)corporation that, in the case of Trump, combines the language of the neoliberal corporation with that of the state corporate body, as we have seen in his fortunate reality TV series *The Apprentice*.[56]

The persistence of a vertical political identification with the leader (whether the president, the head of the state, or the prime minister) shows how pervasive the imaginal appeal of a sovereign state remains. If it is true that, as Eric Hobsbawm argued, it is not nations that makes states but states that create both nations and nationalism,[57] then we cannot come to terms with Trump's nationalism without considering the role of the state in shaping a fertile terrain for it: despite Trump's occasional critiques of the federal state, state ideology is an essential component of Trumpism. To begin with, Trump is first of all the president of the United States, and thus, as such, inseparable from the ideology of the modern sovereign state that sustains him.[58] Here, it is worth remembering that "sovereign" literally means *superiorem non recognoscens*, that is, a power that does not recognize any other power on earth as superior to itself. Hobbes tried to suggest this by adding on the head of the Leviathan the following quotation from the book of Job: "*Non est potestas super terram quae comparetur ei*" (There is no power on earth that is comparable to him). We are now so used to this rhetoric that we can no longer perceive what a great novelty in the history of political forms it represented. Before that time, only God could have been said to be sovereign.

Trump's rhetoric can thus draw from a much broader history of mythological representations of the "head" of state, one that, in the case of the U.S. presidency, also retains almost royal characteristics. In contrast to other presidencies that were instituted much later, that of the United States, which was established in the eighteenth century through the separation from the British Crown, still retains many royal overtones: think for instance of the rituals surrounding the very family of the president, with the cult of the "first lady," and the ceremonies around the residence of such a (heteronormative) family, not by chance called the "White House" and taking the shape of a Greek temple. We can see here, once again, the doubling of the two fathers mentioned before: the head of the family and the head of the state.

To sum up on this point, the icon of the head of state, the call for a vertical form of identification with the leader, and the rhetoric of greatness all show significant continuity with the past. Yet Trumpism is not just a repetition of the old. Trump's political myth does not simply draw from an old mythological reservoir: it also exhibits new elements that powerfully transform it.

Note, for instance, that the motto "Make America Great Again!" is emblazoned on red baseball caps. Not only that: Trump has often been shown wearing one of these caps when dressed more casually. As we have seen in Adorno's essay, it is typical of fascism to rely on little men, who can appear as one of us, and thus facilitate the identification process. But why baseball caps and this register of sport and game? For external observers, the baseball cap appears as the typical "American" hat, something that distinguishes the citizens of this nation from others.[59] The ritual gesture of wearing a cap works both as a way to connect Trump's rhetoric to a preexisting, traditional, symbolic reservoir (in which the baseball cap is the American hat) and to (re)produce a new version of this reservoir, one that responds to American citizens' need for significance in the second decade of the twenty-first century: becoming good players in the (in)corporation game. The reference to sports and baseball caps clearly points to "America," the mythical entity that is different from the United States and that excludes all other Americas (including Central and South America), as well as the U.S. citizens who originally came from them. References to sport point to a marriage between nationalism and the language of competition that is typical of neoliberalism. Trump's motivational speeches, his sports metaphors, and the "us" versus "them" in the global economic competition all point to the language of economic antagonism and the struggle for survival within it. As Christian Fuchs observes in his study of Trump's ideology, social Darwinism is a crucial component of Trump's ideology, as it emerges from an analysis of his entire lifestyle, his digital persona, and his statements. Consider the following examples: "The world is a vicious and brutal place. We think we're civilized. In truth, it's a cruel world and people are ruthless. ... People will be mean and nasty and try to hurt you just for sport. Lions in the jungle only kill for food, but humans kill for fun. ... When somebody screws you, screw them back in spades. ... Go for the jugular so that people watching will not want to mess with you."[60]

More than the Big Daddy figure associated with past fascisms, feeding on archaic fantasies of fear and protection such as those invoked by Freud's primal horde, Trump presents himself as the ideal team coach, a bit daddy, but also a bit mommy, the parental figure who has gone through the very same hard game and therefore knows how best to lead his followers through it. There is a lot that is old in this form of fascism, but there is also a lot that is new: the identification with the protective paternal figure, who will keep the "evil" people out of the motherland, but also the maternal figure who will privilege you over others and train you to be a good team player, as in any good corporation. This, as we will now see, is a particularly powerful performance when transmitted through social media such as Twitter that directly reach Donald Trump's millions of followers with messages such as the following: "All Democrats just raised their hands for giving millions of illegal aliens unlimited healthcare. How about taking care of American citizens first? That's the end of that race" (Donald J. Trump, June 27, 2019, @realDonaldTrump). Once again, by presenting the Democrats as those bad people taking care of "aliens," Trump's rhetoric attains a double effect: on the one hand, to attack his political enemies, and, on the other hand, to present himself as the right parental figure, as the one taking care of "us," despite the contradiction that may prima facie appear between this "taking care of American citizens" and the performance of his absolute narcissism. Indeed, Trump has most often been incapable of truly taking care of others, but that is exactly where the power of myth lies: it does not wait for reality to confirm its truth but rather goes on to create its own.

The Imaginal Politics of Social Media: Phony Leaders and the Digital Performance of Facist Identification

MANY CONTRADICTORY FEATURES of Trumpism, beginning with that between his role as a president, who cares for his own people, and the absolute narcissist, who cares only for himself, which have left commentators astonished and unprepared could be summarized with Adorno's succinct formula: the paradox of the fascist leader, who appears at the same time as a superman and as an average person, "just as Hitler posed as a composite of King Kong and the suburban leader."[61] Since, for most of his followers, their ego ideal is not very distant from their ego, the fact that Trump appears as simply a little bit better than they are, just richer and more audacious, facilitates the process of identification. As Adorno explicitly puts it:

> The category of "phoniness" applies to the leaders as well as to the act of identification on the part of the masses and their supposed frenzy and hysteria. Just as people do not really believe in the depth of their hearts that Jews are the devil, they do not completely believe in their leader. They do not really identify themselves with him but enact this identification, perform their own enthusiasm, and thus participate in

their leader's performance. It is through this performance that they strike a balance between their continuously mobilized instinctual urges and the historical stage of enlightenment they have reached, and which cannot be revoked arbitrarily. It is probably the suspicion of this fictitiousness of their own "mass psychology" that makes fascist crowds so merciless and unapproachable.[62]

The distinction between "identifying with the leader" and "enacting this identification" is crucial. We can add here that it is perhaps not by chance that Trump, like other authoritarian agitators of this new generation such as Silvio Berlusconi, was also a professional performer: the point is not so much hatred for others as the performance of it, which explains the ambivalence and irony of such performances.

While reflecting on Adorno's contributions to understanding contemporary neofascism, Vladimir Safatle introduced the notion of "the fascist laugh": what is typical of contemporary forms of fascism, by this account, is that they embody a form of power that laughs at itself, thus enacting a form of "ironic" identification with the leader, a falsehood that affirms itself sarcastically.[63] As an example of such a "fascist laugh," consider a tweet that Trump wrote in March 2018: "Lowest rated Oscar in HISTORY. Problem is, we don't have Stars anymore—except your President (just kidding of course!)" (Donald J. Trump, March 6, 2018 @realDonaldTrump).

"HISTORY," written in capital letters, registers the absence of stars from the scene: "except your President," also written with a capital letter. Whereas all other U.S. presidents before Trump used social media as a way to announce the result of a policy that had been discussed for a long time or to make some other formal public declaration, Donald Trump uses social media, and Twitter in particular, as a tool to express his own opinions and state of mind, *as if* he were one of his followers, which, at the moment of writing amount to 88.8 million.[64] With his incendiary and passionate communication reaching such an astronomical number of users, he can thus literally appear as "one of us," while signaling himself out as exceptional: if you are one of his 88.8 million followers, you participate in a performance with "@realDonaldTrump" as both one of the many people you interact with daily on social media *and* the "only Star" available at this moment in history, a Star who is even able to laugh at himself.

This, according to Safatle, is something that Adorno had already understood as typical of the production of ideology in the age of television: ideology is not simply false consciousness but, through the culture industry, becomes a falsehood that knows itself to be such, and yet nevertheless affirms itself ironically.[65] Although this is certainly a feature of media images ever since the invention of television, social media adds a further dimension to this logic. To begin with, social media has exacerbated both the quantitative and the qualitative change in the nature of images that mediate contemporary politics. As I have argued at length elsewhere, virtualization has changed the phenomenology of the image, the way in which we relate to images by suspending their reality, whereas the increase in the competition for our attention has exponentially increased their spectacularization: while in the case of the big screen, or the movie theaters that Adorno considered, one could count on a spectator committed to sitting down for a certain amount of time, in the case of individual media, consumed by distracted spectators on the subway, at the park, or in the barbershop, images have to compete for attention with many more sources of distraction and thus fight for access to people's imaginations through a much tougher competition.[66] Hence, the increased recourse to the register of the spectacular and its concomitant virtualization and suspension of truth: because of this affective surcharge, images are no longer simply what mediates our way of doing politics but also what threatens to do politics in our stead.[67]

While pushing the register of the spectacle and changing attitudes toward the truth of the image, the imaginal politics triggered by social media also turn all of their users into equal actors within the performance: this deeply subverts the logic of the spectator/audience that the television Adorno was referring to still implied. It is not just that a personality like Trump, with his (largely delusional) narrative of the self-made man, fits the new social media: it is consubstantial with them, because it is inseparable from the type of performance that these new technologies enable.[68] By interacting on Twitter with their leader and his other followers, Trump's supporters do not simply feel but literally become protagonists of the performance of "rebirth-in-greatness" that Trump's invocation to "Make American Great Again!" triggered. They do not even have to imagine what their president looks like or what he would think about X and Y and Z in this moment in space and time. These images are constantly there, buzzing on their mobile phones. And some of them even become unexpected stars of the spectacle: like the fire lieutenant in Tuscaloosa, who on the evening of April 29, 2019, tweeted to his scant followers: "Granted I am in Alabama but most of the firefighters I talk to are voting @realDonald Trump"

(Ben Rawls, April 30, 12.10am @firemanbrawls), and then woke up the morning after to discover he had become a Twitter celebrity with 14,000 likes in a few hours, just because he had been retweeted by the president himself.

Social media such as Twitter, Facebook, and Instagram are a crucial component of today's resurgence of authoritarianism worldwide, and their power can hardly be overestimated: when you are navigating on various social media, with their promise of friendship and community, you are literally navigating a certain form of mass psychology. In order to emphasize how much authoritarian capitalism feeds today on such media, Christian Fuchs helpfully labels them "digital demagogues."[69] It is not just that authoritarian personalities such as Trump can skillfully manipulate his followers but that these media have by themselves such a manipulative logic because they deeply feed on and exacerbate affects circulating in the social unconscious.

Think, for instance, of how the algorithm that decides on which tweet, which Facebook post to show next on a newsfeed, works: by selecting the image and content that is most likely to keep you glued to the media itself, the one able to capture your imagination and your emotions. Hence the tendency to produce emotionally laden and polarized versions of reality that progressively alienate those who literally see it and feel it differently: by reading only the news that confirms your own opinion and that fuels the emotions that the algorithm expects from you, some of Trump's 88.8 million followers end up living in a true "society of spectacle," one that, in contrast to what Guy Debord expected, now lives on the palm of your hand. By selecting content that elicits similar emotional responses, the algorithms regulating social media feed on the performance of the friend/enemy divide and the psychological symbolic reservoir that sustains it. The point is not deeply believing that the enemies are evil but performing that hate, except that that hate then becomes the algorithm that builds the reality you live in and thus your own emotional constitution. This, in turn, shapes the content that adept users decide to post, and it does not therefore come as a surprise to learn that Trump has attacked someone or something in more than half of his tweets.[70] It is the power of hatred as a negatively identifying form.

And yet, as Adorno observes in the passage quoted above, the performance of identification, which lies at the basis of the psychology of fascist masses, and which is exponentially increased by the new social media, cannot explain fascism per se. Psychology can at best describe the mechanisms triggered by fascist propaganda, but it does not explain why they are triggered in the first place. We need an entire theory of society in order to explain why such propaganda arises in the first place and what kinds of interests sustain it. To begin with, as Nancy Fraser observed, we need to connect the new forms of authoritarianism with the current crisis in the capitalist mode of production: although crises are endemic to capitalism, what characterizes the ongoing current one is that finance and financialization play a much weightier role than they did in previous crises. A crisis at the structural level, with a more and more predatory financialized capitalism, is accompanied by one at the hegemonic level, leading to a widespread feeling of disorientation and disconnection.[71]

This is the juncture where "speculative communities" proliferate: the enormous success of contemporary social media is indeed inseparable from the emergence of financialization, that is, from the incredible polarization of wealth produced by the abstraction of capital from materiality, and the feeling of uncertainty created by lives that are structured by debt and financial uncertainty.[72] For Aris Komporozos-Athanasiou, financialization facilitates (and at the same time relies on) the widespread circulation of a speculative imagination, and social media are key "nodes" for that circulation, as an increasingly anxious society relies on them to "cope" with the uncertainty of everyday life. Thus, the forces of finance work in tandem with new social media to cultivate (from the ground up, as it were, rather than merely from the top down) such a "speculative imagination," which is often populist, nationalist, and regressive in its nature. The axis of inequality here forms precisely as a result of uneven exposures to uncertainty, which yields huge profits for finance (and political gains for the authoritarian right worldwide), while it sows further anxiety for those without resources who still need to play the game of speculation effectively (and who therefore can only participate in speculation through social media activity).

By ideologically depicting such uncertainty as the result of those evildoers who dare to question "American values and tradition," digital demagogues such as Trump can protect their own interests, those of corporate capital, while pretending to protect those of all everyday Americans. The feeling of uncertainty is there, but its sources are fundamentally displaced through the spectacular performance of scapegoating.

To sum up, the mass psychology that sustains Trumpism is a fascist mass psychology, but the latter can help us understand the *how* of neofascism but not yet the *why*. For that, like Adorno and with Adorno, we need to go beyond mass psychology and certainly beyond Freud.

Even more so: if we remain confined to the level of the psychology of the masses in our understanding of fascism, Adorno argues, we may end up reinforcing the very same ideology that sustains it. In a puzzling passage Adorno states:

> Fascism as such is not a psychological issue and ... any attempt to understand its roots and its historical role in psychological terms still remains at the level of ideologies such as the ideology of "irrational forces" promoted by fascism itself. Although the fascist agitator doubtless takes up certain tendencies within those he addresses, he does so as the delegate of powerful economic and political interests. Psychological dispositions do not actually cause fascism: rather, fascism defines a psychological area which can be successfully exploited by the forces which promote it for entirely non-psychological reasons of self-interest.[73]

Whether Adorno is right in saying that self-interest is not also a psychological issue is a tricky question that goes beyond the scope of this essay. But we can certainly agree with him, on the one hand, when he says that fascism defines a certain psychological area and that is precisely this that we see mobilized by both the American fascist agitators of the 1950s and their contemporary versions; on the other hand, remaining at the level of pure psychoanalytic explanations could be very dangerous, because it risks reproducing the ideologies that justify fascist mass psychology itself.

Adorno's formulation, in the passage just quoted, is very synthetic and leaves space for different interpretations, but it also hints at a number of further questions we may want to raise while rereading Adorno's text today: What kind of ideology do we end up reproducing when we remain exclusively at the level of psychoanalytic explanations? Is it the patriarchal ideology that, as we have seen, is reflected in Freudian theory or, perhaps much more radically, in psychoanalysis itself? Can we understand the nature of the psychology that sustains fascism today by applying the psychoanalytic tools elaborated by Freud to unpack the foundations of the European bourgeois family structure, centered as it is on the triad of mom, dad, and child, without reproducing this structure? To what extent can psychoanalysis be exported to non-Western contexts, for instance, if it is true that, as Frantz Fanon argues, some people, like the Antillean, do not have the Oedipus complex?[74]

By uncritically applying Freudian theory to such different contexts, there is indeed the risk of Eurocentrism, of implicitly reproducing the very same European bourgeois family model as *the* model whereby to measure all others. We may think that, through our own psychoanalytic investigation, we are reaching out to the "childhood of the world," but in the process we may also end up discovering that we are reaching only down to the European unconscious.[75] The danger is not just Eurocentrism, and thus a bias based on a peculiar history that may prevent us from understanding radically different contexts, such as those with a very different family structure. By making the European bourgeois family structure implicitly appear as the normal family structure, centered as it is on the mother-father-child relations, we risk presenting a historically situated social arrangement as a natural one, which is indeed the typical operation of ideology. Even worse: while trying to understand fascism, together with the racist and patriarchal ideology that sustains it, we may even end up reinforcing its very conceptual foundations.

If that is the case, then in our attempt to understand contemporary fascism, we too should proceed with Adorno, but also beyond him, thereby adding to his mass psychology not only an entire theory of society but also a rethinking of the potential patriarchal and racist biases that Freudian theory carries within itself.

Notes

I am grateful to Lucas Ballestin for his invaluable research assistance and his help with endnotes. For reading and commenting on earlier drafts of this piece, as well as for the many conversations on this topic, I wish to thank Amy Allen, Aris Komporozos-Athanasiou, Benoit Challand, Judith Butler, Simona Forti, and Jamieson Webster. An earlier version of a part of this essay appeared in *Public Seminar* in 2016, https://publicseminar.org/2016/11/the-mass-psychology-of-trumpism/, and in the journal *Recherches en psychanalyse/Research in Psychoanalysis*, no. 32 (2022).

1 See, for instance, *Global Resurgence of the Right*, ed. Gisela Pereyra Doval and Gaston Souroujon (New York: Routledge, 2021), which, through its collection of different voices, ponders the usefulness of various categories, such as "neofascism," "right-wing populism," and even "neoliberal totalitarianism," to describe the resurgence of the right on a global scale. As an example of a journalistic approach, see Gregor Aisch, Adam Pearce, and Bryant Rousseau, "How Far Is Europe Swinging to the Right?" *New York Times*, May 22, 2016, sec. World, https://www.nytimes.com/interactive/2016/05/22/world/europe/europe-right-wing-austria-hungary.html.

2   I am here implicitly drawing from Federico Finchelstein's definition of fascism, which, very usefully, provides an approach that takes into account the Latin American historical examples of fascism. Federico Finchelstein, *From Fascism to Populism in History* (Oakland: University of California Press, 2017), 7. Although Finchelstein differentiates between historical fascism and contemporary forms of right-wing populism, because the former tends to produce dictatorships while the latter is compatible with democratic legitimacy, I will argue in this essay that the mass psychology upon which they rely is identical. This, in my view, is in agreement with his statement that right-wing populism is the contemporary reformulation of fascism, which rejected some of its extreme forms such as the systematic use of violence, in order to make it compatible with democratic legitimacy. See also Federico Finchelstein, "Returning Populism to History," *Constellations* 21.4 (2014): 467–82.

3   For instance, Matteo Albanese and Pablo del Hierro reconstruct the way in which, through the Italian-Spanish connection, a global fascist network of ideas, movements, and leaders built up transnationally over the course of the twentieth century. The authors thereby provide a very useful map for understanding the ramification of fascist ideas and movements in the last century. See Matteo Albanese and Pablo del Hierro, *Transnational Fascism in the Twentieth Century: Spain, Italy and the Global Neo-Fascist Network* (London: Bloomsbury, 2016).

4   Among those who have rejected the concept of neofascism to describe Trumpism, see, for instance, Slavoj Žižek, who has asserted provocatively that the fear that Trump could turn the United States into a fascist state is a "ridiculous exaggeration" and that we should rather look at Trump's election as a great opportunity to reinvigorate the left. Slavoj Žižek, *The Courage of Hopelessness: Chronicles of a Year of Acting Dangerously* (London: Allen Lane, 2017). We can now say that Žižek's idea that having Trump as a president could help the consolidation of the left was itself a "ridiculous exaggeration." The left did not prosper under Trump as much as it did under Obama; the eruption of the Occupy Wall Street movement, the most significant nonviolent episode in the history of the U.S. left since the 1960s, did not happen under Trump but under Obama. Similarly, in European history, we saw that the left did not prosper under the fascist and authoritarian regimes of the 1940s but rather under the liberal democracies of the 1960s.

5   Theodor W. Adorno, "Freudian Theory and the Pattern of Fascist Propaganda," in *The Culture Industry*, ed. J. M. Bernstein (London: Routledge, 1991), 132–57.

6   Ibid., 134.

7   Mass psychology has a much broader history than what I can reconstruct in the brief space of this essay. For a useful reconstruction of the history of mass psychology, from the point of view of its possible application to an analysis of Trumpism, see Eli Zaretsky, "The Mass Psychology of Trumpism," *London Review of Books* (blog), September 18, 2018, https://www.lrb.co.uk/blog/2018/september/the-mass-psychology-of-trumpism.

8   Sigmund Freud, *Group Psychology and the Analysis of the Ego* (New York: W. W. Norton, 1949), 52.

9   Ibid., 26.
10 Ibid., 21.
11 Ibid., 53. This important shift happens in chapter 5, after chapter 4's introduction of his theory of the libido, thus suggesting that it is in the latter chapter that a bias toward a certain type of libido is introduced.
12 Adorno, "Freudian Theory and the Pattern of Fascist Propaganda," 149.
13 As we will see, other authors, such as Elias Canetti, also took distance from such a view and insisted on the substantial difference between two types of crowds, the "open" and the "closed" ones, and even went so far as to state that open crowds are the true crowds. Elias Canetti, *Crowds and Power* (New York: Continuum, 1973), 20.
14 "Thus the group appears to us as a revival of the primal horde. Just as primitive man virtually survives in every individual, so the primal horde may arise once more out of any random collection; in so far as men are habitually under the sway of group formation we recognize in it the survival of the primal horde." Freud, *Group Psychology and the Analysis of the Ego*, 70.
15 Ibid., 90.
16 The operation is indeed a form of *reductio ad unum*, that is, of reduction to the one, but with the important qualification that the one is the development of the libido in bio-males.
17 Feminist psychoanalysts have emphasized this aspect of Freudian theory for a very long time. See, for instance, Karen Horney, "On the Genesis of the Castration Complex in Women," *International Journal of Psychoanalysis* 5.1 (1924): 50–65; Luce Irigaray, *This Sex Which Is Not One* (Ithaca: Cornell University Press, 1985), 23; and Julia Kristeva, *Revolution in Poetic Language* (New York: Columbia University Press, 1984), 46; more recently, see Jill Gentile, *Feminine Law: Freud, Free Speech, and the Voice of Desire* (London: Karnac, 2016).
18 For instance, in his (in)famous essay on female sexuality, which he begins to address with reluctance and which he concludes is a "puzzle to be left to poets." Sigmund Freud, *New Introductory Lectures to Psychoanalysis* (New York: Norton & Norton, 1965), 167. Freud nevertheless presents an entire reconstruction of female sexuality done from the point of view of the development of the libido in bio-males, leading to his very controversial statements about women's supposed penis envy.
19 Joel Whitebook, in his very innovative intellectual biography of Freud, adduces new historical evidence as to why Freud himself could not really deal with feminine sexuality. Joel Whitebook, *Freud: An Intellectual Biography* (Cambridge: Cambridge University Press, 2017), 52. According to Whitebook, Freud's mother suffered from a chronic depression that left little beloved Sigmund in an emotional vacuum, only partially filled by his Czech nanny (43).
20 Canetti, *Crowds and Power*, 20.
21 Ibid., 149.
22 Adorno, "Freudian Theory and the Pattern of Fascist Propaganda," 138; Freud, *Group Psychology and the Analysis of the Ego*, 99–100.

23 Jay Bernstein, "Fight Club: Enlivenment, Love, and the Aesthetics of Violence in the Age of Trump," in *Metacinema: The Form and Content of Filmic Reference and Reflexivity*, ed. David LaRocca (New York: Oxford University Press, 2021).

24 Adorno, "Freudian Theory and the Pattern of Fascist Propaganda," 141. It is worth noting that, according to a *New York Times* study of Trump's usage of Twitter, published on November 2, 2019, "the person he most often singled out for praise was himself." Michael D. Shear, Maggie Haberman, Nicholas Confessore, Karen Yourish, Larry Buchanan, and Keith Collins, "How Trump Reshaped the Presidency in Over 11,000 Tweets," *New York Times*, November 2, 2019, https://www.nytimes.com/interactive/2019/11/02/us/politics/trump-twitter-presidency.html. Note also that he has repeated this feat apropos the Covid-19 pandemic: J. W. Peters, E. Plott, and M. Haberman, "260,000 Words, Full of Self-Praise, from Trump on the Virus," *New York Times*, June 11, 2020, https://www.nytimes.com/interactive/2020/04/26/us/politics/trump-coronavirus-briefings-analyzed.html.

25 Adorno, "Freudian Theory and the Pattern of Fascist Propaganda," 141.

26 Jamieson Webster, "Freudian Theory and the Pattern of Fascist Propaganda," *Public Seminar*, October 5, 2017, http://publicseminar.org/2017/10/freudian-theory-and-the-pattern-of-fascist-propaganda/.

27 Adorno, "Freudian Theory and the Pattern of Fascist Propaganda," 144.

28 Max Horkheimer and Theodor Adorno, *Dialectic of Enlightenment* (Stanford: Stanford University Press, 2002), 138.

29 Sue Grand, "The Other Within: White Shame, Native-American Genocide," *Contemporary Psychoanalysis* 54.1 (2018): 92; see also Ryan Schmidt, "American Indian Identity and Blood Quantum in the 21st Century: A Critical Review," *Journal of Anthropology* (2011): 9.

30 On whiteness and the settler-colonial property regime, see Aileen Moreton-Robinson, *The White Possessive: Property, Power, and Indigenous Sovereignty* (Minneapolis: University of Minnesota Press, 2015), xi–xxiv; for a more general take on the role of labor control in the history of colonization of the Americas, and how the capitalist division of labor systematically relied on racism, see Aníbal Quijano, "Coloniality of Power, Eurocentrism, and Latin America," *Nepantla: Views from South* 1.3 (2000): 533–80.

31 As Coates observed: "The East was the Nazi Manifest Destiny. In Hitler's view, 'in the East a similar process will repeat itself for a second time as in the conquest of America.' As Hitler imagined the future, Germany would deal with the Slavs much as the North Americans had dealt with the Indians. The Volga River in Russia, he once proclaimed, will be Germany's Mississippi." Ta-Nehisi Coates, "Hitler on the Mississippi Banks," *The Atlantic*, January 16, 2014, https://www.theatlantic.com/international/archive/2014/01/hitler-on-the-mississippi-banks/283127/. See also Grand, "The Other Within," 84–102.

32 On this last note, see Judith Butler, "What Threat? The Campaign Against 'Gender Ideology,'" *Glocalism: Journal of Culture, Politics and Innovation*, no. 3 (2019).

33 Ibid., 1. Although Butler does not explicitly mention this, I would like to suggest that this timing is not accidental: it can be seen as a reaction to the feminist and queer waves of that and previous decades, when many powerful critiques of the heteronormative and patriarchal family were advanced, including the critique put forward in Butler's pathbreaking *Gender Trouble: Feminism and the Subversion of Identity* (New York: Routledge, 1990).
34 Butler, "What Threat?" 3.
35 Ibid., 3–4.
36 De Beauvoir writes: "Christianity's repugnance for the feminine body is such that it consents to doom its God to an ignominious death but saves him the stain of birth: the Council of Ephesus in the Eastern Church and the Lateran Council in the West affirm the virgin birth of Christ. The first Church Fathers—Origen, Tertullian, and Jerome—thought that Mary had given birth in blood and filth like other women; but the opinions of Saint Ambrose and Saint Augustine prevail. The Virgin's womb remained closed." Simone de Beauvoir, *The Second Sex* (New York: Vintage, 2011), 186.
37 By "second sex" de Beauvoir means women, but we can understand this phrase in such a way that it includes all other gender minorities who are equally second to the "first sex," i.e., to the cisgendered bio-male.
38 Conrad Hackett and David McClendon, "World's Largest Religion by Population Is Still Christianity," *Pew Research*, May 31, 2020, https://www.pewresearch.org/fact-tank/2017/04/05/christians-remain-worlds-largest-religious-group-but-they-are-declining-in-europe/.
39 Butler, *Gender Ideology*, 9.
40 Max Horkheimer, "Authority and the Family," in *Critical Theory: Selected Essays* (New York: Continuum, 2002), 112.
41 Judith Butler, "Reflections on Trump," *Society for Cultural Anthropology*, https://culanth.org/fieldsights/reflections-on-trump; "Trump, Fascism, and the Construction of 'the People': An Interview with Judith Butler," *Versobooks.com*, https://www.versobooks.com/blogs/3025-trump-fascism-and-the-construction-of-the-people-an-interview-with-judith-butler.
42 Jay M. Bernstein, "Adorno's Uncanny Analysis of Trump's Authoritarian Personality," Public Seminar, https://publicseminar.org/2017/10/adornos-uncanny-analysis-of-trumps-authoritarian-personality/.
43 Trump's iconic "Make America Great Again" (MAGA) slogan was inspired by former president Reagan's "Let's Make America Great," which Trump acknowledged, but he also claimed it to be his own invention. Brooke Seipel, "Trump: 'Make America Great Again' Slogan 'Was Made Up by Me,'" *The Hill*, April 3, 2019, https://thehill.com/homenews/administration/437070-trump-make-america-great-again-slogan-was-made-up-by-me.
44 On the condensational power of political myth, see Christopher Flood, *Political Myth* (New York: Taylor & Francis, 2013), 84; and Henry Tudor, *Political Myth* (London: Macmillan, 1972), 40.
45 I take the expression "work on myth" (*Arbeit am Mythos*) from Hans Blumenberg, who emphasized this processual aspect of myth in his major work of the same title. See Hans Blumenberg, *Work on Myth* (Cambridge, MA:

MIT Press, 1985). Blumenberg, however, does not explicitly focus on political myth in this work.

46 On this definition of the icon, see C. G. Flood, *Political Myth: A Theoretical Introduction* (New York: Garland, 1996). Icons are an important vehicle to access the social unconscious within a social context; Chiara Bottici and Benoît Challand, *The Myth of the Clash of Civilizations* (London: Taylor & Francis Group, 2010), 27.

47 Sarah Ferris, "Trump Compares US Airports to 'Third-World Country,'" *The Hill*, September 26, 2016, https://thehill.com/policy/transportation/297935-trump-compares-us-airports-to-third-world-country.

48 Steven Pressman, "Donald Trump and the Middle Class," *Dollars and Sense* (January/February 2017): 8–10; Sean Tracey, "Trust, Trump, and the Turnout: A Marketers Point of View," *American Behavioral Scientist* 61.5 (2017): 526–32, doi:10.1177/0002764217701218.

49 I have explored the significance of this proposed policy in more detail in "Philosophy, Coloniality and the Politics of Remembrance," *Graduate Faculty Philosophy Journal* 41.1 (2020): 87–92.

50 Robert Paxton, *The Anatomy of Fascism* (New York: Knopf, 2004), 35–36; Roger Griffin, *Modernism and Fascism: The Sense of a Beginning Under Mussolini and Hitler* (London: Palgrave Macmillan, 2007), xv, 332.

51 Yoni Appelbaum, "Trump's Claim: 'I Alone Can Fix It,'" *The Atlantic*, July 22, 2016, https://www.theatlantic.com/politics/archive/2016/07/trump-rnc-speech-alone-fix-it/492557/.

52 Kim Soffen, "Yes, Donald Trump's Hands Are Actually Pretty Small," *Washington Post*, March 30, 2019, https://www.washingtonpost.com/news/morning-mix/wp/2016/08/05/yes-donald-trumps-hands-are-actually-pretty-small/.

53 Chiara Bottici, *Imaginal Politics: Images Beyond Imagination and the Imaginary* (New York: Columbia University Press, 2014), 93–95.

54 See Thomas Hobbes, *Leviathan* (Cambridge: Cambridge University Press, 1996).

55 On the frontispiece, see A. P. Martinich, "The Frontispiece to *Leviathan*," appendices, in *The Two Gods of Leviathan: Thomas Hobbes on Religion and Politics* (Cambridge: Cambridge University Press, 1992), 362–68, doi:10.1017/CBO9780511624810.018. On the metaphor of the state as a person in Hobbes's political philosophy, see the very influential Quentin Skinner, "Hobbes and the Purely Artificial Person of the State," *Journal of Political Philosophy* 7 (1999): 1–29.

56 For an analysis of Trump's state ideology and the role of the reality TV show *The Apprentice* in it, see Christian Fuchs, *Digital Demagogue: Authoritarian Capitalism in the Age of Trump and Twitter* (London: Pluto Press, 2018), 182.

57 Eric Hobsbawm, *Nations and Nationalism Since 1780: Programme, Myth, Reality*, 2nd ed. (Cambridge: Cambridge University Press, 1992), 10.

58 Fuchs insists on this point: see, for instance, Fuchs, *Digital Demagogue*, 118, 166, 195.

59 In the United States, one can see baseball caps on the heads of people across all different social classes, from pop stars and American presidents to gas sta-

tion workers and urban youth. See, for instance, Carol Motsinger, "We Know Why You Wear a Baseball Cap," *The Enquirer*, April 2, 2017, https://www.cincinnati.com/story/sports/2017/04/02/we-know-why-you-wear-baseball-cap/99689202/; and Maude Bass-Krueger, "Everything to Know About the History of the Baseball Cap," *Vogue Australia*, May 28, 2019, https://www.vogue.com.au/fashion/accessories/everything-to-know-about-the-history-of-the-baseball-cap/image-gallery/879d3161b0faa82c8e453fa7eb410b29.

60 Quoted in Fuchs, *Digital Demagogues*, 170. Besides social Darwinism, Fuchs also identifies three other crucial components, along with state ideology. As he writes: "Given that Trump is the US president, his general view of the world is relevant for understanding the state's ideology (ideology by the state) during his rule. Having a look at his ideological views may also reveal what role he assigns to the state in society (ideology on the state). Trumpology is Trump-style ideology. It is not the ideology of a single person, but rather a whole way of thought and life that consists of elements such as hyper-individualism, hard labour, leadership, the friend/enemy scheme and social Darwinism" (ibid., 166).

61 Adorno, "Freudian Theory and the Pattern of Fascist Propaganda," 141.

62 Ibid., 150; translation modified.

63 Hence the ironic character of the fascist leadership, the phoniness, which Vladimir Safatle emphasizes, and which indeed explains how disinhibition is possible. See Vladimir Pinheiro Safatle, "The Fascist Laugh," in *Théorie critique de la propagande*, ed. Pierre-François Noppen and Gérard Raulet (Paris: Éditions de la Maison des sciences de l'homme, 2021), 123–34.

64 Matt Mathers, "Trump 'Haemorrhaging' Twitter Followers in Wake of Election Defeat," *The Independent*, November 26, 2020, https://www.independent.co.uk/news/world/americas/us-election-2020/trump-losing-twitter-followers-election-defeat-b1762502.html.

65 Pinheiro Safatle, "The Fascist Laugh."

66 For an illuminating analysis of the transformation of the spectator in the age of individual media, see Gabriele Pedullà, *In Broad Daylight: Movies and Spectators After the Cinema* (London: Verso, 2012).

67 Bottici, *Imaginal Politics*, 106.

68 Bart Cammaerts, "The Neo-fascist Discourse and Its Normalisation Through Mediation," *Journal of Multicultural Discourses* 15.3 (2020): 241–56, doi:10.1080/17447143.2020.1743296; Christian Fuchs, *Nationalism on the Internet: Critical Theory and Ideology in the Age of Social Media and Fake News* (New York: Routledge, 2020), 279; Fuchs, *Digital Demagogue*, 197.

69 Fuchs's *Digital Demagogue* focuses on Trump, while his *Nationalism on the Internet* focuses on European cases.

70 Shear et al., "How Trump Reshaped the Presidency in Over 11,000 Tweets."

71 See Nancy Fraser's essay significantly titled "Mass Psychology of Crisis," *Public Seminar*, April 23, 2019, https://publicseminar.org/2019/04/mass-psychology-of-crisis/. Although Fraser is skeptical of the use of fascism as a scare tactic, she takes up the challenge of connecting contemporary forms of authoritarianism and financialization.

72 Aris Komporozos-Athanasiou, *Speculative Communities* (Chicago: University of Chicago Press, 2021).
73 Ibid., 151; translation modified.
74 Frantz Fanon, *Black Skin, White Masks*, trans. Richard Philcox (New York: Grove Press, 2008), 130.
75 Ibid., 166.

Ty Blakeney

3. Challenging the Outlaw Thesis: New Configurations of Sexuality, Politics, and Aesthetics

IN 2000, THE French author Renaud Camus belatedly published the 1994 edition of his *Journal, La Campagne de France*. Camus had been publishing his personal journal since 1985 and had gained notoriety and a cult following, but this edition would be different. The publication of an article in the magazine *Les Inrockuptibles* that criticized certain anti-Semitic passages in the journal led to a legal proceeding against Camus under laws forbidding anti-Semitic speech. A media debate known as the *affaire Renaud Camus* ensued during the following months, first over whether the passages in question were in fact anti-Semitic, and then over questions of freedom of speech after Camus's publisher removed the book from shelves under legal pressure and published a new version from which the offending passages had been expurgated.[1] Within a week after the crisis erupted, however, Camus was on a plane to the United States to attend a conference at Yale University entirely dedicated to his work.

The existence of such a conference demonstrates that, before the scandal, Camus had gathered a small but loyal following of "Renaldians," scholarly readers in the United States; but after the *affaire*, these scholars were forced to come to grips with Camus's reactionary comments. Some, like Lawrence Schehr, denounced Camus's statements as clearly anti-Semitic. In an earlier article on the first volume of Camus's journal, *Journal romain,* Schehr had offered a postmodern, post-structuralist reading of Camus's "bathmological" analysis of gay identity. He wrote, "for Camus, homosexuality has its own inherent trope of irony in every situation: to be homosexual or to talk about homosexuality is necessarily to be ironic."[2] And yet, for Schehr there was nothing ironic about Camus's anti-Semitic statements. He felt the need to suspend his previous mode of reading Camus's text in order to address the seriousness of the issue: "Here I am not splitting hairs; I am not thinking of performatives, or ironies, or any deconstructible remarks that might nuance or overturn a statement. ... I am thinking of hate speech, racism."[3] Charles A. Porter, the organizer of that conference at Yale, took a middle ground, emphasizing the literary and ironic quality of Camus's statements in order to justify what he saw as a "critical examination" of anti-Semitic beliefs within the text. Here is his most forceful defense of the remarks, the most infamous of which dealt with Camus's claim that Jewish presenters were overrepresented on the television channel Panorama:

> Is there a difference between the following statements?
> 1) There are too many Jews on Panorama.
> 2) "There are too many Jews on Panorama."
>
> For a student of Roland Barthes like Camus, who is an enthusiastic proponent of "bathmology," Barthes's science of levels (or "degrees") of discourse, there is a great difference. Statement 2, the quoted statement, is less a claim or opinion than a contemplated notion, set down to be examined. It is not a call to action, not a part of a dictator's harangue. It may be ugly and unpleasant, but it is not criminal.[4]

Porter bemoans that "so many of Camus's severest critics are literary critics" who nevertheless fail to grasp the complex ironies and layers of discourse operating in *La Campagne de France.* The key question for Schehr and Porter seems to be whether Camus's comments must be taken literally or literarily. For Schehr, some forms of language (Porter's "dictator's harangue") must be understood only referentially, kept outside the "hair-splitting" of literary reading, with its endless "overturning" of statements and "deconstruction" of meaning; the racism and hatred underlying Camus's statements meant that irony was somehow no longer operative. For Porter, on the other hand, it was precisely the literary status of Camus's work that meant that it could never really be interpreted as, in his words, "a political tract."

Looking back on these scholars' responses to the *affaire Camus* twenty years later, a reader in the Trump age might feel a queasy sense of recognition. Porter and Schehr's debate over the degree to which hate speech could be ironic feels prescient given the way in which irony is deployed within the internet culture of the so-called "alt-right" today. Porter's insistence that a true "Renaldian," a reader in the know, would grasp the complex network of ironies and layers of discourse that would make Camus's statement appear innocuously in invisible quotation marks feels eerily like the fans of the YouTuber PewDiePie who insist that, if we only understood the full ecology of the streamer's persona, we would see that his statements about Hitler and Holocaust denial are "just for the lulz."⁵ The time since the *affaire Camus* has seen the emergence of a viral, ethnonationalist right that has taken advantage of what Damon R. Young has aptly described as "the prevalence in contemporary digital culture of an irony of infinite reversibility, of texts that offer no critical vantage point for determining to what extent they mean what they say," to circulate a racist ideology of hatred that has increasingly led to violence. Confronted with this appropriation of irony by the right, scholars and critics committed to combatting this new movement are in much the same position as Schehr and Porter were at the turn of the century. Do we open ourselves up to the critique that we are "bad readers" in order to denounce racist speech? Do we abandon our "hair-splitting," our close attention to what Young calls the "reversibility inherent to language," in order to insist on the referentiality of language, to call racist speech racist? Or do we continue to hew the postmodern, deconstructionist line, insisting on the near-infinite reversibility of meaning even if that means accepting speech that might be "ugly or unpleasant"? Young ends his essay "Ironies of Web 2.0" where Schehr and Porter ended their debate about Camus's anti-Semitic language, laying out what we might think of as the deconstructive double-bind, the impossible choice between, in Young's words, "retreating to the modesty of simple description or giddily embracing the inexorability of a system with no outside."⁶

Renaud Camus is a key figure for understanding this deconstructive double-bind and the limits of the deconstructive method in the face of the ironic new right. Camus started as a literary avant-gardist whose early texts were formally innovative and daring in their stark representation of same-sex sexuality. His most famous early text, *Tricks*

(1978), was even prefaced by Camus's friend Roland Barthes, who feared that it might be condemned as pornography without his protection. Camus's career in France also coincided with the rise first of gay and lesbian studies and then of queer theory in the U.S. academy, and within the French iteration of those disciplines Camus became the model for a queer writer whose formal experimentation with irony and bathmological discourse analysis led to a deconstruction of heteronormativity.[7] And yet, these accounts of the implicit politics of Camus's literary and sexual practices don't seem to line up with the political positions he took explicitly later in life. The *affaire* was only the beginning of Camus's embrace of a far-right politics that affirms the threat posed to "autochthonous" French by invading outside forces, be they Jewish or Muslim. Camus did, in fact, publish political tracts, and has twice run for the presidency of France on a platform that claims that the far-right Marine Le Pen isn't doing enough to combat immigration. (Le Pen, for her part, has kept Camus at arm's length, part of a larger strategy to distance herself from extreme elements of the far right in order to broaden her appeal to the French public.) Camus's key concept, the "Great Replacement," is the idea that there is a conspiracy to replace the "traditional" French people with an entirely new people consisting mostly of Muslim immigrants from North Africa; it has become a rallying cry for white nationalists, including protestors in Charlottesville, Virginia, in 2017 ("You will not replace us!") and terrorists like Brenton Tarrant, who published his manifesto *The Great Replacement* on Twitter and 8chan in 2019 minutes before he killed fifty-one Muslims in two mosques in Christchurch, New Zealand. In spite of its association with the most violent extremes of the far right, the "Great Replacement" has become an article of faith within more "mainstream" right circles in the years since Christchurch and Charlottesville: Tucker Carlson has repeatedly used the term to characterize Joe Biden's immigration policies and their harmful impact on "legacy Americans," while the French magazine *Causeur* endorsed the theory with a provocative cover featuring images of non-white babies in their September 2021 issue.[8] While I do not wish to further amplify this harmful conspiracy theory, I believe that a careful analysis of the particular history of Camus as both a celebrated, avant-garde gay author and an odious right-wing ideologue is vital because it forces us to hold these seemingly irreconcilable positions together in a way that challenges the deconstructive consensus that has animated literary studies and queer theory for decades.

"Removed from Reality": The Police Logic of the Outlaw Thesis

WHEN THE CHRISTCHURCH terrorist Brenton Tarrant named his manifesto after Camus's concept of the "Great Replacement," John Gallagher published an article on the center-left website *LGBTQnation.com* titled "A Gay Academic Created the New Zealand Shooter's Racist Worldview."[9] The article introduces readers to Camus's career as a gay writer and the ideology of the "Great Replacement" in a cursory way, but its primary purpose is not informational, as the title might suggest. To see Gallagher's true aim, we need to look to his subtitle: "Renaud Camus believes that whites are in danger of being replaced, but doesn't see the irony of a gay man being a hero to white supremacists." The article reinforces the idea that being gay and being committed to gay rights are incompatible with being a xenophobic demagogue. Throughout the article, Gallagher refuses to accept that Camus's sexuality and supposed contributions to the gay rights movement could somehow be integrated into an understanding of his racism. He enforces a strict temporal distinction between the two periods of Camus's career, going so far as to say that Camus is a "former academic."[10] After discussing Camus's political theories, Gallagher shifts to talking about Camus's past gay activism: "Early in his career, Camus was a pioneer for gay rights. He wrote openly about his own sexual adventures in a book called *Tricks*, published in 1981, and contributed to the gay magazine *Gai Pied*."[11] Gallagher cites Camus's statements that his commitment to gay rights and his racist fantasies are intimately related: "It's because I could write a book like *Tricks* [that] I could write a book like *Le Grand Remplacement*," he said in one interview.[12] But Gallagher rejects the possibility that right-wing homosexuality could be a part of "reality." He writes, "No doubt, Camus would reject anti-LGBTQ violence, which is a core belief of white supremacists. But the fact that he doesn't see the irony of a gay man being a hero to bigots who oppose us underscores just how removed from reality he is."[13] Camus's own claims are rejected because they don't fit within a certain framework of gay identity. Because of Gallagher's implicit understandings of the way in which gay identity and political identity are structured, Camus's claim that there is in fact a link between his work promoting homosexuality and his racist theorizing is seen only as an indication of the degree to which Camus is "removed from reality." Why, in an article whose ostensible purpose is to inform readers of the existence of this gay "hero to bigots," does Gallagher end up denying the reality

Figure 8. *Le Causeur* 93 (September 2021). "Smile, you've been Great Replaced! From Limoges to Nîmes, the new French demography in maps and numbers."

and coherence of Camus's social position, relegating him to the realm of the ironic and the laughable?

Gallagher's paradoxical position here is a result of the dominant mode of understanding the relationship between sexuality, politics, and aesthetics within both left gay and queer circles, what I call the outlaw thesis. This is the idea that homosexual subjects are somehow inherently outlaw to, and thus in some way *outside of*, the nation-state. Here I build on the work of Jasbir Puar, who questions the relevance of the critical tradition within queer and LGBT studies that emphasizes "the 'outlaw' status of homosexual subjects in relation to the state" in the era after the incorporation of gay subjects into the capitalist project of the 1980s and 1990s (the "pink dollar") and into the mainstream of Democratic Party politics (with landmark Supreme Court decisions that expanded gay rights in the 2000s).[14] I argue that the outlaw thesis is in fact a kind of "police logic" in philosopher Jacques Rancière's sense, in that it enforces a certain way of understanding who is "perceivable" within a certain representational regime. I want to be careful here to note that while I think it is important to take the arguments of these right-wing gays seriously, I do so only in order to better counter their arguments. In calling the outlaw thesis a police logic, I do not wish to make any kind of moral judgment in favor of Camus or other gay xenophobes. (Rancière is clear that what he calls "the police" is not necessarily negative, writing, "The police can provide all kinds of benefits, and one police can be infinitely preferable to another. This doesn't change its nature, which is our only concern here.")[15] Gallagher's response to Camus's racism nevertheless demonstrates the existence of an implicit law that defines a certain "reality" of gay and queer politics: the sexually non-normative are necessarily on the side of those who contest state power, which is necessarily heteronormative (the outlaw thesis). In the particular liberal idiom of the outlaw thesis he deploys, Gallagher projects the binary of queer and normative onto the binary of left and right. In denying that Camus *exists*, Gallagher polices the boundaries of that reality and reproduces gay conservatism as an impossibility. According to Rancière,

> The essence of the police is to be a distribution of the perceptible [*partage du sensible*] characterized by the absence of void or supplement: in the police, society consists of groups dedicated to specific ways of doing, to positions in which these occupations are carried out, to ways of being that correspond to these occupations and these positions. In this adequation of func-

tions, of positions, and of ways of being, there is no place for any void. It's this exclusion of "that which there isn't" that is the police principle at the heart of state practices.[16]

"Gay bigots," queers who take up the defense of normative structures like racism and heterosexuality, are exactly "that which there isn't" within the framing of the outlaw thesis: figures like Camus are precisely the kind of void or supplement that is written off in the media as a joke and excluded from the realm of civil discourse.[17]

In order to understand how this police logic functions, I would like to turn briefly to an event called "WAKE UP!" held in tandem with the Republican National Convention in 2016. The event was organized by the group Gays for Trump, and key speakers included the Breitbart provocateur Milo Yiannopoulos, Pam Gellar (who organized a "Draw the Prophet" cartoon contest in the wake of the *Charlie Hebdo* shootings), and Dutch far-right leader Geert Wilders. The event drew protestors outside, and *Vox.com* journalist Carlos Maza live-tweeted his attendance. Both of these responses to "WAKE UP!" demonstrated the same kind of police logic of the outlaw thesis that we saw in Gallagher's critique of Camus. For example, one sign from the protest outside of the "WAKE UP!" event enacts exactly the kind of exclusion that Rancière describes. In a video of the protestors posted on Maza's Twitter, a young woman can be seen carrying a sign that reads, "There is nothing fabulous about racism."[18] Rather than simply denounce Yiannopoulos's racism, the sign contests whether Yiannopoulos has a right to lay claim to the aesthetic and perceptible markers of gay maleness, designated here under the umbrella of the "fabulous." The sign performs Yiannopoulos's exclusion from the out, proud, progressive gay identity that is associated with an affirmative embrace of "fabulous" qualities. In his own tweets, Maza also uses a kind of gay aesthetics to prevent Yiannopoulos and the other party attendees from legitimately laying claim to gay identity: he attacks the party attendees not for their deplorable views or their willingness to laugh at jokes that denigrate minorities but for their bad taste in clothing, their subpar dancing skills, their lack of sexual prowess, and even their unattractiveness. "The speeches have ended so now all the cool conservative gays are dancing like cool not virgins," reads a tweet which includes a video of a man dancing alone.[19] Another tweet reads, "Never mind I've decided I don't want to have sex with anybody here," and is accompanied by images of a slightly overweight man in an ill-fitting white T-shirt and baggy jeans.[20] Maza even frames his rejection of his own experience through the perceptual lens of the popular dating app Tinder, in which users swipe left on a picture of a potential mate to indicate that they are not interested in dating: "Milo just got on stage and I tried to swipe left on my OWN VISION."[21] Far from being innocent quips about the taste-level of the Gays for Trump, these tweets present reality through the lens of a certain queer aesthetics and enforce a queer "way of being" that is supposed to be held separate from a host of other ways of being embodied by Yiannopoulos and the other party attendees: racist, misogynistic, transphobic, xenophobic, politically incorrect, gun-owning, and fascistic, but also fat, ugly, poorly dressed, unable to dance, and sexually inexperienced.

From these responses, and continuing to draw on Rancière's theorization of the police, we can deduce certain characteristics of the outlaw thesis:

> 1. The outlaw thesis presents itself as, and is perceived by its adherents as, the natural way of things. Rancière writes, "It is the very principle of the police to present itself as the realization of the essence of the community, to transform the rules of governance into the natural laws of society."[22] The insistence that Camus and Yiannopoulos exist outside of the realm of the "real" produces instances at which this police state are enforced. The outlaw thesis, the idea that gays are left wing, not right, is put on the side of social reality, while the "homocons" are relegated to the realm of the unintelligible or the insane, those who "deny reality." The protester's sign presents itself almost as a mathematical equation, a kind of natural law: fabulous ≠ racist.

> 2. The outlaw thesis is a logic of the police that renders certain forms of sexuality unintelligible. Rancière writes that the political moment "makes us see that which didn't have the right to be seen, makes us hear as speech that which was only heard as noise."[23] It is precisely this kind of moment of becoming-visible that the discourse of those responding to the event tries to disavow. Yiannopoulos and the homocons are occulted from the realm of the visible as Maza "swipes left on his own vision"; Camus is "removed from reality." Their language is not taken seriously, as *speech*, but treated as a joke (one attendee of WAKE UP! called it "an SNL skit").[24] Even though the event manifestly occurred, its representation makes it an incomprehensible, nonsensical, self-contradictory anomaly.

3. The outlaw thesis unites identity, aesthetics, and politics. For Rancière, the political and the aesthetic are linked, insofar as the political is an intervention in the realm of what can be seen or heard, the *partage du sensible*, that is, the representation (in both the political and aesthetic sense of the word) of the world. This idea is foundational for Rancière's thought and can be found in almost any of his texts, but a particularly condensed formulation comes at the beginning of his article "The Politics of Literature": "Politics is first of all a way of framing, among sensory data, a specific sphere of experience. It is a partition of the sensible, of the visible and the sayable, which allows (or does not allow) some specific data to appear; which allows or does not allow some specific subjects to designate them and speak about them. It is a specific intertwining of ways of being, ways of doing, and ways of speaking."[25] The outlaw thesis relates not only to sexual identity and politics. In Rancière's terms, it is "a specific intertwining of ways of being," with sexual identity understood either as an inherent biological fact or as a social construct that nevertheless inherently places the individual in a certain relationship with society, "ways of doing," radical left politics, understood as ways of critiquing the norm and arguing for an expanded legal rights, and "ways of speaking," understood broadly as challenging aesthetic practices that disrupt normal ways of making meaning. The critiques of Yiannopoulos or Camus take place in the realm of the aesthetic; they are debates over Yiannopoulos's ability to lay claim to the category of the "fabulous," or critiques of the sartorial sensibilities of the RNC event's attendees. Or consider Gallagher's assertion that Camus is "the sort of French academic who gives intellectuals a bad name, fulminating about linguistic distinctions that defy logic and reality."[26]

In aligning those who speak out against Camus and Yiannopoulos with Rancière's police, I do not mean to be critical of their aims or to suggest any kind of sympathy on my own part for Camus, Yiannopoulos, and their abhorrent statements and actions. My goal is rather to take these responses as opportunities to understand our own epistemological limits, the root of the double-bind represented by Schehr and Porter's debate over Camus's anti-Semitic statements. The existence of these gay right-wing demagogues represents a kind of shock to the system that momentarily reveals the invisible tectonic architecture of our own distribution of the sensible, the way in which many queer thinkers have constructed a particular intertwining of ways of being, ways of doing, and ways of speaking. The degree to which Yiannopoulos and Camus are simultaneously disturbing and inassimilable within gay and queer thought in the United States reveals a fault line of gay and queer politics, one that Camus and Yiannopoulos exploit in order to fracture the gay and queer left in the hope of inoculating themselves from critiques of their thought. ("Racist? Me? But how could I be? I'm gay, darling!") In order to combat this danger, we need to decouple non-normative sexuality from left politics; we need to reject the idea that aesthetic experimentation is only the purview of the left.

Readers well trained in queer theory might bridle at my grouping of "gay and queer" here, arguing that queer theorists like Leo Bersani, J. Halberstam, Heather Love, and Jasbir Puar have acknowledged the existence of gay conservatives. While some of the particular expressions of the outlaw thesis I have cited here occur in a centrist-liberal idiom (Gallagher particularly), it is central to my argument that the concept not be limited to a critique of gay identity politics. The problem posed by figures like Yiannopoulos and Camus is not their investment in a sanitized or normative form of homosexuality that needs to be critiqued with the tools of queer deconstruction. Yiannopoulos's explicit deployment of queer aesthetics returns us in many ways to the deconstructive double-bind that I laid out in the first section of this essay. Following scholars like Laura Doan, Robyn Wiegman, and Elizabeth A. Wilson, I want to push against the binary framing of queer theory and its liberal, identitarian other to think through the unacknowledged continuities between the LGBT and queer projects.[27] While some in queer theory and queer of color critique have certainly acknowledged the existence especially of white gay men who have aligned with the right wing, the epistemological framework of queerness, with its emphasis on a binary opposition between the normative and non-normative, nonetheless participates in the broader *partage du sensible* of the outlaw thesis that I diagnose here.[28] Yiannopoulos and Camus are powerful demonstrations of the limits of a queer critique rooted in anti-normativity, and their existence demonstrates the need to find new methodologies in the face of a new nativistic, alt- (or, we even say, queer) right wing that turns the politics of anti-normativity against the normative assumptions of the left.[29] As a way out of the outlaw thesis, we need a new way of understanding how sexuality, politics, and aesthetics interact with each other within a complex social field. In the section that follows, I will return to the work of Renaud Camus and his reception within France to present a new way of understanding how any text comes to have meaning as it circulates within a given context, one that understands literature as a social phenomenon rather than as an inherently ironic play with society's norms.

"It's Too Complicated for Me": A New Approach to Sexuality and Politics in the Literary Field

CAMUS IS UNLIKE Yiannopoulos in that, first, he is a "real" artist, who, as he frequently mentions in his journal, is barely able to eke out a living by producing literary texts. (This is even more true since the author has been dropped by his publisher; his website gives a helpful breakdown of all the different ways in which you can buy his works, and the percentage of the sum that you pay that ultimately makes it back to the author within each medium.) Camus is also a real politician, even if his two candidacies for the French presidency and his candidacy for the European Parliament never had any real public support; he frequently publishes political manifestos, often through his social media accounts, which offer concrete (if completely absurd) policy proposals that would stop the "Great Replacement" and protect European culture.[30] And yet Camus's position within each of these fields is precarious, always contested by others in a conflict over the validity of his ideas. On the one hand, because he is an artist and a public intellectual, his far-right supporters argue that we need to respect his freedom of thought, that his language shouldn't be held to the same standard as that of a politician. On the other hand, Camus's detractors often denigrate his literary work, essentially casting him out of the literary field because of his political views. In this section I will attempt to read Camus outside the triangular logic of the outlaw thesis. I will focus on the way in which two different agents (the TV pundit Caroline Valentin and Camus himself) link sexuality, aesthetics, and politics. Rather than drawing on deconstructionist frameworks, I will ground my analyses within the lineage of Pierre Bourdieu's writings on art and literature, most notably in *Les règles de l'art* (The Rules of Art) and his lectures at the Collège de France, published under the title *Manet, une révolution symbolique* (Manet: A Symbolic Revolution). My sociological approach to literature, which also owes much to Bourdieu's student Gisèle Sapiro, provides a lens that is more open to the surprising ways in which these different agents link ways of being, ways of doing, and ways of speaking.[31]

As I stated earlier, Camus's status as a literary figure and the cultural capital he gains or loses from his standing (or lack thereof) in the literary field play an important role in the way his political message is received and repackaged within the French media. But there is no one way in which his literary status is coded, no one way in which "a way of speaking" (literature) and "a way of being" (gay) relate to "a way of doing" (politics). The literary is not *only*, as it is presented for example in Schehr's reading, a disruptive realm that challenges normative structures more broadly; literature is a social phenomenon whose autonomy from or embeddedness in the social and the political is, at different times and in different places, mobilized in different ways by different agents for different effects. The literary field is traversed by and overlaps with other differential fields of power in many different ways and directions, not only as a force that disrupts normativity, and to focus only on "queer art," defined in narrowly poststructuralist terms, is to render invisible the majority of literature's social uses. Sapiro writes that, in taking for granted the idea of "la littérature engagée [politically engaged literature]," intellectual historians neglect the contingent and tactically motivated ways in which engagement on the part of an author is a product of both social custom and individual choice:

> Writers (or artists, or sociologists, etc.) become politically engaged in their capacity as writers (or as artists, as sociologists, etc.), and ... they argue for a continuity between their interventions in the public sphere and their conception of their trade. ... The sociological theory of Pierre Bourdieu reveals that the ethical, aesthetic, and political choices individuals make are closely bound together, on the one hand through *habitus*, and on the other through the positions they occupy in social space and within a given field. His theory invites us to search for the relationships between the means of writers' political interventions and their conception of their profession and the practices habitual to that profession.[32]

In other words, a certain linkage between politics and literature that has come to be taken for granted is in fact the product of the way in which politically engaged authors have tried to produce continuity between their two forms of intervention; it is not some inherent quality of literature but the product of individual choice, which is constrained at once by that individual's habitus and by their position within a social field. According to Sapiro, the idea that literature is associated with the political left has a long history; this orientation was set during debates about government censorship of literary and journalistic texts during the Bourbon Restoration and the July Monarchy in France.[33] These battles throughout the nineteenth century over the freedom of the press would eventually polarize ideas around the relationship between literature and politics. The penchant within theoretically inclined literature departments within the U.S. academy that I am resisting here is slightly different from the French debate about the history of *engagement* that Sapiro rejects, but it follows a similar structure. The particular intertwining of non-normative sexuality, challenging aesthetics, and radical left politics that characterizes the outlaw thesis is of course distantly influenced by the nineteenth-century French writers whom Sapiro mentions. As a crucial inflection point in this history, we might add the Oscar Wilde trials of 1895, which cemented the link between literature, non-normative sexuality, and state reprobation, and the Vietnam War protests in the late 1960s, which made the university a central locus of political activism in the United States. Rather than being a matter of the ontological truth of literature, the outlaw thesis's linkage of non-normative sexuality, challenging aesthetics, and radical left politics is a historically contingent phenomenon, the product of the choices of individual agents (writers, but also critics, academics, and theoreticians, even administrators and students) within a changing set of norms and constraints within the social field.

Such an approach to literature offers a different methodology to Schehr's, one that allows us to see the ways in which the sexual, the literary, and the political come to be connected by specific agents within specific contexts and fields. In order to explore exactly how this functions, I would like to turn first not to a literary text itself but to a discussion of Camus on *Points de vue*, a news show produced by the center-right newspaper *Le Figaro* and published on their YouTube channel, Le Figaro Live. My goal is not to analyze the program as if it were literature but rather to understand how Camus's status as a queer literary figure is brought to bear on a discussion of his politics. The program is a U.S.-cable-news-style panel show, with representatives from different points on the political spectrum, all responding to the Christchurch shooter's use of the term "Great Replacement" as the title for his manifesto. The question is precisely oriented around the acceptability of the term within public discourse, the "reality" of the phenomenon it describes, and the conspiratorial underpinnings of the idea that perhaps led to violence in New Zealand. The first panelist who gets to speak after host Guillaume Roquette's introduction is Caroline Valentin. Roquette's introduction, which lasts over two minutes, seems to respect the prohibition against bringing Camus into public discourse: while Roquette goes in detail into Camus's ideology, he never names Camus himself. Valentin, by contrast, refuses this occultation and names him immediately. Fascinatingly, though, on this program for political talking heads, it is not Camus's status as a politician that she emphasizes. Rather, she begins immediately talking about his status within the literary field:

> This expression, the "Great Replacement," refers to Renaud Camus. Where there's a theory, there's a theoretician. I don't believe that many of the people here, and especially not that horrible guy who carried out that vile attack in New Zealand, have ever read a book by Renaud Camus. Well, I've read *In Praise of Appearances*, which is a wonderful book. I tried to read *Buena Vista* [*Park*] ... it was too complicated for me.[34]

These references to obscure works from Camus's bibliography, which as Valentin asserts few people have read, may seem completely out of place in a conversation about a man who killed fifty-one Muslims, but then this is precisely the point. Valentin presents Camus's literary credentials, which she shrewdly invents out of thin air, as a kind of alibi for his implication in the political world in which the violent attack took place; ultimately, this serves to sanitize the "Great Replacement," to make it into a literary concept that should be discussed and taken seriously within the pure and disinterested realm of ideas, as opposed to the unreasonable, unspeakable act of the terrorist whose name Valentin refuses to speak ("that horrible guy that carried out that vile attack"). Valentin has not cited Camus's most famous works; these are truly deep cuts from Camus's extensive bibliography, but in a way their obscurity makes them better suited for Valentin's purposes. More important is the way in which she refers to them, dropping them casually in her conversation as if they were titles that, because of their great literary merit and acclaim, everyone *should* know. On the one hand, she cites *Éloge du paraître* (In Praise of Appearances), a moralistic treatise from 2000 that, like many of Camus's texts from the early aughts, deals with what Camus saw as a moral and linguistic degradation of the various forms of normativity and politeness that, in texts written after 2007, would become explicitly focused on Muslim French. The work, really a very minor one even within Camus's expansive but decidedly minor oeuvre, seems carefully chosen—of interest to Valentin and those who share her alarmist views on the influence of Muslims on French society but respectable enough precisely to provide cover for the more racist underpinnings of those ideas (and, unlike almost all of Camus's other texts, *Éloge du paraître* conveniently happens to be under one hundred pages). The ostensible reason Valentin gives for citing this work, however, is not its precise position within Camus's evolution into an openly racist conspiracy theorist but its literary merit: its status as "a wonderful book." Valentin frames it purely as a literary text, to be understood only through the lens of its aesthetic value and not as a work that could have any potential political significance. It does not ultimately matter whether the work cited is a major or a minor one: simply naming a book published by the author *as if* we all should have heard of it serves as a guarantor of Camus's good standing within the literary field (especially a book with such a pompous title as *Éloge du paraître*, whose nominalization of a verb marks it as syntactically different from normal speech). Camus (and, consequently, his theory) belongs not in the realm of mass murderers and "fascists" but within the recognizable category of the serious man of letters, of the type: authors whose titles one cites and then adds, if only to prove that one has read the book, "it's a magnificent book."

Valentin's next citation does even more work. She references *Buena Vista Park*, one of Camus's early and much more formally challenging works that also deals explicitly with homosexuality. In claiming that she tried to read *"Buena Vista"* but found it too challenging, Valentin further establishes Camus as a serious writer, of the type: one who writes challenging books; one whose books are so well-known that they are referred to in abbreviated form. At the same time, she distances herself from his explicit representations of sexuality and, crucially, positions herself as the populist voice among the more learned panel of experts weighing in on the question of the Great Replacement for *Le Figaro*, which includes Julia de Funès, introduced as a philosopher, and the international relations professor Anne-Sophie Letac. Valentin effectively uses this pivot to position herself as the voice of practical reason on the panel, who, although she can't draw on scientifically founded demographic statistics like other panelists, "sees what she sees" when it comes to the idea of the "Great Replacement." Valentin's answer masterfully sets the terms of the debate to follow, using a reference to Camus to pivot away from the most extreme elements of the far right toward the substance of Camus's claims:

> But Renaud Camus is not a fascist, is not a man who advocates for violence, and to use this term in that way is actually to take it as a given that Renaud Camus is at the origin of this massacre. So, let's put that subject of debate to the side. It's absolutely absurd. ... Let's not talk about it in those terms, in terms of Christchurch. We don't have anything to do with Christchurch. Christchurch isn't in France. This guy can make all the references he wants, but it's not for that reason that we would be responsible for what happened over there.

Valentin uses Camus's literary status to position herself in relation to the rest of the panel and to effectively reject the host's framing of the question in terms of the potential dangers of the idea, as evidenced by the violence in Christchurch. She calls on the shared ideas of the panelists around the autonomy of the literary field, the freedom of thought granted to literary figures by their particular status within society, to create a consensus that effaces the violent entailments of thinking that the government is working to wipe out the "race" of "les français de souche" (literally "French by the root," or "pureblood French," a common term in French right-wing circles that refers implicitly to white French people). As Valentin says, "Let's not talk about it in those terms, in terms of Christchurch," the camera cuts from a close angle on Valentin to a shot that includes both Valentin and her fellow panelist Julia de Funès, as if to suggest that this moment is the pivot from Valentin's singular opinion to one that will form more common ground with the other panelists. While de Funès later denounces the conspiratorial logic that lurks behind the idea of the "Great Replacement" in forceful terms, here she nods in reluctant agreement and, eventually, smiles.

I now turn to a second example, this time from Camus himself in a 2017 appearance on the radio program *Répliques*, hosted by his friend Alain Finkielkraut. After he published *The Great Replacement*, Camus was effectively blacklisted from mainstream media outlets in France. Controversially, after a debate erupted about the concept in French media, Finkielkraut invited Camus onto his program, on the prestigious France Culture radio station, in order to defend his concept. Finkielkraut also invited a demographer, Hervé Le Bras, who opposed the idea of the "Great Replacement." (Le Bras has long been skeptical of the uses of demography by the far right, publishing a book in 1998 titled *Le Démon des origines: Démographie et extrême droite* [The Demon of Origins: Demography and the Far Right].) In his first intervention, Le Bras tests Camus's claims against statistics published by France's National Institute of Statistics and Economic Studies (INSEE) about the places of origin of the parents and grandparents of recent births, arguing that the demographic changes show not, as Camus claims, the replacement of one "people" by another "people" but rather a shift from a relatively closed and homogeneous society to one that is open and mixed. Camus, much like Valentin, challenges the legitimacy of Le Bras's statistics, drawing on the critique of the social sciences developed within the other fields of the humanities:

> For me, I'd have a tendency to widen the field of debate, if I can put it that way, and to contest the notion of numbers. Personally, I agree deeply with the philosopher Olivier Rey, who highlights the incapacity of the number to account for the world. For forty years, we have been inundated with numbers; I fear that the human sciences are increasingly becoming an aporia, an oxymoron. And that's for the best, perhaps. Man is constantly trying to escape from numbers. And numbers have been unable to account for what is happening.[35]

If we can see past the racist undertones and the universalizing claim about "Man," this critique of positivism echoes a certain current of deconstructionist queer theory, which has also historically been skeptical of sociology and the human sciences.[36] Sociologist Steven Seidman summarized the queer theoretical critique of classical sociology in 1993—that is, right at the beginning of queer theory's entrance onto the academic scene—noting that the founders of sociology reinforced rather than critiqued ideologies about the naturalness of the oppression of women and the repression of non-normative sexuality. "At the very time when the social sciences materialized, announcing a social understanding of the human condition," he writes, "they assumed a natural order linking sex, gender, and sexuality."[37] Viewed in this light, sociology, as a tool of social modernization, appears as part of the "heteronormative, biopolitical nation-state," an instrument used in the control of populations that categorizes, classes, and makes individuals productive, antithetical to a queer way of thinking that disrupts categorization and heteronormativity. Camus's position certainly echoes these critiques but is different in a nuanced but important way—his appeal to the nation as he criticizes the state:

> Not only has sociology not warned the French population and the European population of the enormous thing that has been going on, this gigantic phenomenon, what I call the changing out of peoples and of civilizations. But, as it's been occurring, sociology has denied it, and has been the most perfect form of its denial.[38]

Camus continues to cite what he thinks of as misleading statistics put out by the government to cover up poor conditions in schools, the level of immigration (because, as he says, immigrants statistically are magically transformed into "French people"). Camus thus decouples the nation and the state, arguing that an ethnically defined national community is being betrayed by a state bureaucracy that aids the forces of replacement in their attempts to change the makeup of the French people. Camus places sociology on the side of shadowy ("deep") state forces, serving monied, globalized (although Camus never goes quite so far as to say Jewish) interests that, in his fantasy, are working *against* the interests of the national community: "Sociology hasn't warned the French population."[39]

More surprisingly for those of us in literature departments in the United States who have tended to think of literature, in a post-structuralist vein, as constantly undoing forms of normativity and oppression, Camus similarly cites literature as an alternative form of knowledge that reveals something about the world that cannot be captured in statistics and sociological categories. He cites the example of a philosopher, invited on Finkielkraut's show to talk about marriage, who argued that the institution had changed greatly over time because, in the nineteenth century, people only married for five or six years. The proof? In the early nineteenth century, life expectancy was only thirty-five years old. Camus unpacks the example, and says:

> But it's completely false! And what proves that it's false? Literature! What tells the truth? Literature! We can easily see that the characters [in nineteenth-century novels] don't live such short lives. And if you don't want to believe the reality of characters from a novel, you only have to look at literary history itself. Chateaubriand died at eighty. Victor Hugo at eighty-three, Corneille at eighty-two, Voltaire ... Le Fontenelle ...[40]

Certainly, the realist mode in which Camus presents literature is not quite the same as the post-structuralist conception of anti-mimetic plays with language that characterize most discussions of "queer literature." Even as he draws literature into a comparison with sociology, he frames the two fields of knowledge in different ways than queer theorists in the United States. In Camus's mind, sociology, as a tool of the globalist "replacists" (*remplacistes*), is a way of thinking at a global scale that misses and even, through a kind of police logic, *denies* the lived experience of particular individuals. Literature, on the other hand, captures individual experience that is irreducible to numbers and codification and, at the same time, with the long list of great writers, also evokes the rich cultural history which this "replacist" ideology is trying to destroy. This turn to literature allows Camus to craft the foundational fable of the theory of the "Great Replacement," the trip to the French village or city that has been overrun by non-white, Muslim immigrants:

> You bring up the relevance of statistics that would tell the truth about the world. But that's exactly the problem that I'm trying to underscore, and it's one of the components of what I've called globalist replacism. One of the elements that is replaced is the replacement of the eye by statistics. The replacement of the experience of a people, of what it lives, of what it sees every day, of what it feels, of its grief even which they don't let us feel, which they can't stand, telling us, "No, the numbers don't align with what you're saying." You gave the example of someone who arrives in England and who, on seeing one redhead, concludes that all English women are redheads. But it's not like that at all. It's the simple question of a people that lives in its homeland and that lives day by day, and not only in some cities, but now absolutely everywhere, lives the certainty that there has been an ethnic substitution, that another people is present, a people that changes absolutely everything: the countryside, the street, the way in which we feed ourselves, dress ourselves, the way we live. ... [This ethnic substitution] is visible everywhere, especially in public transportation.[41]

Camus's language here has slipped into a kind of political dramaturgy, evoking a scene of the French person who, arriving in a particular area of the city, has a certain experience that leads him or her to believe that "one people has been replaced by another." This literature of the Great Replacement takes account of the rich experiences that the cold statistics cited by the state demographer Le Bras lack, the feeling of this experience of being in France and outside of it at the same time. His list of the characteristics that have changed ("the countryside, the street …") reads almost like the details of the *incipit* of a novel, a new kind of *Père Goriot* that, rather than being set in the *Maison Vauquer*, would be set in a housing project somewhere to the northeast of Paris.

Indeed, more than the term itself, this originary fable is Camus's greatest political success. It is repeated by Lauren Southern, a rightwing YouTube personality whose video "The Great Replacement" was key in popularizing Camus's idea in the anglophone world. Southern tries to give her viewers the experience of this change through a quick series of cuts, substituting old photographs of the supposed "No Go Zone" Molenbeek, Belgium (an area that was literally occupied by the army after the Bataclan attacks were planned there), with more recent ones.

First we see, in black-and-white, a street populated only by white people and tourists (including children), filled with iconic Belgian and French landmarks (Escargots! Fries!). We then see a new photo of similar composition, clearly taken in a different location, which includes a man with a beard, a strip club, and several women wearing hijab.

Southern seems to miss that, in the old picture, there is actually a sign in Arabic, next to another that seems to include the word "Pak[istan]." In its own way, the Great Replacement is thus a kind of *partage du sensible* that shapes how its adherents see the world. Camus's fable of the Frenchman in the street is repeated by Valentin on Le Figaro Live when she cries at the end of her passionate response: "To claim that people are conspiracy theorists because they see what they see when they're walking through the suburbs of Paris, or in Rubaix, etc. Because they judge that there is a replacement. I find that to be profoundly, profoundly patronizing. To say that people don't even have the right to draw consequences from what they see."[42] The myth was also propagated by and circulated around the Christchurch shooter, who was radicalized when he arrived in France and saw whole cities "overrun" with Muslim immigrants. He supposedly wrote, "I found my emotions swinging between fuming rage and suffocating despair at the indignity of the invasion of France."[43] Camus has deployed a particular aesthetic and literary form (this fable of the stupefied Frenchman) that has circulated and produced a wide range of different effects. In the United States, through Southern's video, it gave a united voice to the torch-carrying neo-Nazis who marched through the University of Virginia campus, in a demonstration that

Figs. 9a, b. Sequence of images purporting to show the "replacement" of white Europeans by Muslim immigrants. Lauren Southern, "The Great Replacement," YouTube, July 3, 2017, https://www.youtube.com/watch?v=OTDmsmN43NA. (The video has since been made private.)

would lead a man to drive his truck into a group of counterprotesters, killing one young woman. In France, it leads Valentin to propose rolling back state censorship around racialized demographics, reclassifying this kind of discourse as mainstream rather than far right, and moving to put in place "a serious politics of immigration," which, one would assume, would curtail immigration from Africa and Western Asia. In the South Pacific, Brenton Tarrant found Camus's tragedy so moving that it led him to commit a horrifying act of mass violence.

With this context, we are also better able to understand the ways in which Camus's writing about sexuality is linked to his politics. It is of course important to note that Camus's sexuality rarely comes up in his discussions of the "Great Replacement." Unlike Yiannopoulos, Camus does not foreground those characteristics of himself that are most recognizably gay. We might be tempted to think that this is a strategic choice on Camus's part to appeal to his (necessarily homophobic) right-wing audience, but this would be to fall back into the trap of strictly bifurcating Camus's oeuvre, dividing it into a "gay" early period and a "political" late period, as we saw in Gallagher's article in *LGBTQnation*. I have sought to challenge this bifurcation, arguing that Camus holds his right-wing politics, his non-normative sexuality, and his avant-garde literary practice together to produce a coherent social self. In fact, in spite of the explicitness of such texts as *Tricks* and the *Notes achriennes* (1982), Camus has meticulously deemphasized his sexuality since the very beginning of his career. In his preface to the first edition of *Tricks* (1978), Camus wrote, "This book attempts to tell sex, in this case homosexuality, as if that combat had already been won, and the problems that such a project poses already resolved: peacefully."[44] Throughout his career, Camus has insisted that homosexuality is not a privileged topic that needs to be represented more in literature out of some political imperative; he claims, and I think that we should take him seriously on this point, that he writes about it simply because it happens to be a part of his life.[45] Camus is invested in the French Republican model and critical of what he sees as the importation of an American-style, "communitarian" model of gay rights that depends on privileging sexual identity over other categories of identity (like French citizen, or writer).[46]

For these reasons, Camus has never shied away from writing openly about his sexuality in his journal, which is still being published today. Although he does not emphasize it in the way Yiannopoulos does, Camus throughout his career has written openly about sexuality and his political beliefs in a way that helps us see how his understanding of sexuality is connected to his fears of a changing French society. One entry from Camus's journal particularly connects the shadowy forces of globalism with homophobia in a way that helps us see how Camus understands his homosexuality as a central part of his political project. (Remember that Camus said in an interview: "It's because I could write a book like *Tricks* [that] I could write a book like *The Great Replacement*.") As for Yiannopoulos, for Camus one of the great sins of the immigrant Muslim population that is supposedly taking over France is its intolerance toward homosexuality. Camus's May 11 entry from 2010 begins with the author fully assuming his position as a cranky sexagenarian, bemoaning the "calamity" of telemarketers:

> *Tuesday, May 11, one in the morning (the 12th).* Telemarketing calls are a real calamity. A young woman, with a decidedly African accent, but who was undoubtedly calling from Kyrgyzstan, was happy to announce that I had been chosen to receive a gift this afternoon. She wanted to know if this news made me happy.
> "Ummm ..."
> She wanted to know, too, if my wife was over fifty. I had to *announce* that I didn't have a wife.
> "You're not in a couple?"
> "No, I am in a couple."
> "Well then you have a wife!"
> "No, I don't have a wife."
> "Fine, but your girlfriend, at least, is she over fifty?"
> I had the good sense to stop it there, but it's much earlier that one should interrupt such absurd exchanges, absurdly chronophagous [chronophages].[47]

The passage begins as a denunciation of the absurdities of late-stage, globalized capitalism, represented metonymically here by the telemarketer who pretends to offer a gift when really fishing for data about Camus's household. Camus's critique of globalization is quickly racialized, as he notes the "decidedly African accent" of the caller. (Of course, there is more than one African accent in French, but Camus doesn't feel the need to specify.) In Camus's paranoid imagination, the woman on the other end of the phone is fully integrated into a nefarious globalized network that stretches from Africa to France to Kyrgyzstan. In this context, her implicit heteronormativity becomes just another marker of her foreignness. Her inability to imagine that Camus could have a partner who is a man rather than a woman marks her, for Camus, as coming from a culture in which homosexuality is invisible and repressed, not liberated like it is in France. Importantly for our purposes, Camus doesn't make this "homonationalist" point in the straightforward language of his political treatises but through hyperbole ("undoubtedly"), irony ("happy to announce"), a manipulation of narrative voice (the use of free indirect discourse in the first paragraph heightens the sense of irony), and the kind of wordplay and neologism that represent a mastery of the French language ("chronophage"). The exchange plays out as a kind of joke between Camus and the reader from which the telemarketer is excluded because of her inability to master either the French language (the "decidedly African accent") or French culture (the acceptance of homosexuality). Camus promotes an intertwining of sexuality, politics, and aesthetics here that is very different from the one we saw in Schehr's reading of the *Journal romain*: the literary, as in his intervention on *Répliques*, stands for a particularly French tradition, a particular way of using language, a particular *way of speaking*, that is tied to a particularly French tradition of being open to homosexuality, a particular *way of being*. But this passage also allows us to glimpse the ways in which these conceptions of sexuality and aesthetics are tied to Camus's broader sense of the current state of politics. In his interview with Finkielkraut, Camus makes the preposterous claim that "Europe is much more colonized today than Africa ever was." In this excerpt from his journal, we see the twisted logic by which Camus makes such a claim: the African woman on the phone is not the heir to a legacy of colonialism that has put her in the position of making unwanted calls to strangers for a living (perhaps in a country impoverished by European domination) but the representative of an invading global capitalism that reaches into Camus's personal life, causing the "calamity" he mentions in the first sentence of this entry. Part of the richness (for lack of a better term) of Camus's theorization of "replacement" and "replacism" is that it refers not only to the fantasy of a wide-scale attempt to replace "a people" but also to the logic of post-Fordism and post-capitalism, the economy of the internet in which individuals become "replaceable" within new forms of economic production.[48]

Thinking about the position taking of Camus and Valentin together, we see the need for a more complex method of modeling the ways people take positions that are simultaneously related to sexuality, politics, and aesthetics than that provided by what I have called the outlaw thesis. The outlaw thesis was structured around binary oppositions at each of its three points. For politics, left/right and outside/inside the heteronormative nation-state; for sexuality, queer/heteronormative; and for aesthetics, avant-garde/mimetic. These binaries were mapped onto each other in a way that allowed the three points of the triad to relate to each other; all of these oppositions could be mapped onto the pair radical/normative in a way that allowed for a transitivity between them. The ways in which these agents take up these three terms, however, don't fit neatly within the binary of state agent/outlaw. Camus decouples the nation and the state and delocalizes heteronormativity.

He uses the opposition of literature and sociology to stake out a politics that is *against* the globalist, capitalist, bureaucratic state (which, in its anti-particularism, is also cast as anti-gay) but *for* the French nation (and for a particularly French, individualist form of homosexuality). Valentin exploits an autonomous vision of the literary field in order to separate Camus and his concept from its uglier echoes in the world. None of these positions is legible from within the deconstructionist double-bind that I laid out in the beginning of this essay. The recent rise of a new gay right has revealed the tectonic architecture of the outlaw thesis, as figures like Yiannopoulos and Camus have exploited its contradictions in order to provide a kind of political alibi for their ethnonationalist screeds. These challenges point to the limits of the outlaw thesis and reveal the need for a new way of thinking about the relationship between non-normative sexuality, aesthetics, and politics.

Notes

1. A helpful summary is given in Marc Schachter, "L'Affaire Camus: An Introduction and Some Provoc," *Politics and Culture* 4 (2000), https://politicsandculture.org/2001/02/26/laffaire-camus-an-introduction-and-some-provoc/. See also Ivan Jaffrin, "D'un scandale à l'autre: L'affaire Renaud Camus et la faillite de la critique intellectuelle," *Contextes* 10 (2012), https://journals.openedition.org/contextes/4975.
2. Lawrence R. Schehr, "Renaud Camus's Roman Columns," *SubStance* 21, 1.67 (1992): 115.
3. Lawrence R. Schehr, "Monicamus? or, Sighting/Citing/Siting Antisemitism," *Politics and Culture* 4 (2000), https://politicsandculture.org/2010/08/10/monicamus-or-sighting-citing-siting-antisem-2/.
4. Charles Porter, "What Did Renaud Camus Really Write?" *Politics and Culture* 4 (2000), https://politicsandculture.org/2010/08/10/what-did-renaud-camus-really-write-2/. It is important to note, as Porter does later in his article, that the original statements in Camus's text do not appear within citations.
5. Damon R. Young, "Ironies of Web 2.0," *Post45* 2 (May 2019), https://post45.org/2019/05/ironies-of-web-2-0/.
6. Young rejects this double-bind, arguing, "Facing up to the contemporary requires paradoxically affirming the critical negativity that is writing and thought. We must become even more suspicious in our hermeneutics." I wonder, though, whether it's really very different to engage in deconstructive hermeneutics "giddily" or "suspiciously," or whether we need a more thorough rethinking of the way in which certain strands of deconstructive thought have come to frame the world.
7. Schehr, "Roman Columns." See also Pierre Force and Dominique Jullien, "Renaud Camus," *Yale French Studies*, special issue (1988): 285–89; and Bruno

Vercier, Charles A. Porter, and Ralph Sarkonak, "An Interview with Renaud Camus," *Yale French Studies* 90 (1996): 7–21.

8   On Carlson, see Media Matters Staff, "Tucker Carlson Calls Biden's Immigration Policy 'the Great Replacement' and 'Eugenics,'" *Media Matters*, September 22, 2021, https://www.mediamatters.org/tucker-carlson/tucker-carlson-calls-bidens-immigration-policy-great-replacement-and-eugenics. The 2022 presidential election made clear the degree to which the Overton window has shifted on the Great Replacement in France. Camus did not run again, but Eric Zemmour, a Jewish right-wing TV editorialist who has embraced and promoted the Great Replacement, gained a significant following and placed fourth. The candidate for Nicolas Sarkozy's supposedly more centrist Les Républicains party, Valérie Pécresse, embraced the conspiracy theory in a speech given on February 13, 2022, in an unsuccessful bid to revitalize her flagging candidacy. Although members of Le Pen's Rassemblement national party (formerly the Front national) have increasingly voiced support of the Great Replacement, at the time of this writing at least Le Pen is ironically the most critical of the three major right-wing candidates.

9   John Gallagher, "A Gay Academic Created the New Zealand Shooter's Racist Worldview," *LGBTQnation*, March 16, 2019, https://www.lgbtqnation.com/2019/03/gay-academic-created-new-zealand-shooters-racist-worldview/.

10 It is important to note that Camus has never been an academic; he has always made his living through writing, not through teaching, and while he has certainly courted the interest of scholars over the course of his career, he has never himself been employed by a university. Gallagher is mapping on a U.S. model, in which the university is the main source of cultural production, onto a French social context in which the world of letters outside of the university is quite distinct.

11 The idea that Camus was "a pioneer for gay rights" is somewhat misleading. Certainly, *Tricks* was a radical book, but Camus himself felt ambiguously toward the new forms of gay identity politics that were activated in France around the debate for the abrogation of discriminatory laws and the presidential election of 1982.

12 David Sexton, "Non!" *Spectator*, November 3, 2016, https://life.spectator.co.uk/2016/11/non/.

13 Gallagher, "A Gay Academic."

14 Jasbir K. Puar, *Terrorist Assemblages: Homonationalism in Queer Times* (Durham: Duke University Press, 2007), 4. I do not use Puar's term "homonationalism" to describe the new gay right represented by figures like Renaud Camus and Milo Yiannopoulos. While these new thinkers draw on some of the same Islamophobic tropes as Puar's homonationalists, they do not advocate assimilation into existing "heterosexual nationalist formations." In this case, it is Gallagher who most closely represents the kind of incorporation of gays into the capitalist and normative project; remember he is writing for the website *LGBTQnation.com*. Camus, on the other hand, holds out the ideal of an ethnically homogeneous nation against a state that is privileging the interests of a small group of "globalist" business owners over the sanctity of the "autochthonous" French people.

15 Jacques Rancière, *La Mésentente* (Paris: Galilée, 1995), 54. This translation and all subsequent translations of French text are my own. Rancière's vision of the police differs substantially from Foucault's, which has tended to be more influential in queer theoretical circles. See, for example, D. A. Miller's influential account at the beginning of *The Novel and the Police* (Berkeley: University of California Press, 1988), in which the police is primarily an organ of the exercise of power. Rancière's conception of the police as a logic opens up ways of thinking about norms that are not necessarily aligned with state power.

16 Jacques Rancière, *Aux Bords du politique* (Paris: Gallimard, 1998), 241.

17 Wiegman and Wilson make a similar point in their critique of queer theory's investment in binary antinormativity: "Antinormative stances project stability and immobility onto normativity. In so doing, they generate much of the political tyranny they claim belongs (over there) to regimes of normativity. For in taking a stand against normativity, antinormative analyses must reduce the intricate dynamics of norms to a set of rules and coercions that everyone ought, rightly, to contest": "Introduction: Antinormativity's Queer Conventions," *differences* 26.1 (May 2015): 13.

18 Carlos Maza, "Outside the party. God bless them," July 19, 2016, 8:30 p.m., tweet.

19 Carlos Maza, "The speeches have ended so now all the cool conservative gays are dancing like cool not virgins," July 19, 2016, 9:20 p.m., tweet.

20 Carlos Maza, "Never mind I've decided I don't want to have sex with anybody here," July 19, 2016, 9:24 p.m., tweet.

21 Carlos Maza, "Milo just got on stage and I tried to swipe left on my OWN VISION," July 19, 2016, 9:00 p.m, tweet.

22 Rancière, *Politique*, 115.

23 Rancière, *Mésentente*, 53.

24 Sean Mandell, "There Was a 'Gays for Trump' Party at the RNC and It Was Absolutely Insane—Videos, Photos," towleroad.com, July 20, 2016, https://www.towleroad.com/2016/07/gays-for-trump/. See the comment by reader "Tim."

25 Jacques Rancière, *Dissensus: On Politics and Aesthetics*, ed. and trans. Steven Corcoran (London: Continuum Books, 2010), 152.

26 Gallagher, "A Gay Academic."

27 Laura Doan, *Disturbing Practices: History, Sexuality, and Women's Experience of Modern War* (Chicago: University of Chicago Press, 2013). Doan argues that queer theory, with its investment in projecting current notions of normativity onto the past, is part of the larger genealogical project. Wiegman and Wilson write, "Even as it allies itself with Foucault, queer theory has maintained an attachment to the politics of oppositionality (against, against, against) that form the infrastructure of the repressive hypothesis" ("Introduction: Antinormativity's Queer Conventions," 12).

28 The archive of texts I draw on here also serves to complicate the binary between "queer" and "liberal LGBT" around which so many queer theoretical arguments are articulated. It might be easy to identify Gallagher as a gay liberal, but what of Schehr and Maza? Each of these individuals is, in their

own way, invested in queer politics and critical of liberal center-left politics. Schehr was himself a practitioner of queer theory, even if he was sometimes critical of its limits and often tended to use "homosexual" as his main analytical category over queer, while Maza identifies himself as "queer scum" in his Twitter bio. And how do we situate the protestor, whose embrace of a feminized gay identity ("the fabulous") could itself be described as queer? These figures demonstrate the factitiousness of any strict distinction between queer and liberal as the concept "queer" circulates outside of the careful theorizations of academicians.

29 In some ways, this essay is a response to Wiegman and Wilson's call for an anti-normative study of gay sexuality that offers a more rigorous account of the ways in which normativities, sexuality, and politics interact. On the other hand, I am less convinced than Wiegman, Wilson, and their contributors that it is possible to "think queer theory without assuming a position of antinormativity from the outset" (Wiegman and Wilson, "Introduction: Antinormativity's Queer Conventions," 2).

30 In the run-up to the 2019 European parliamentary elections, Camus released a program he called "La Ligne Claire" on his Twitter and (surprisingly active) Flickr accounts, which consists of 101 concrete propositions. The strangest is perhaps Camus's proposal that Latin be taught to children across Europe so that it would become a living language again, on the model of Hebrew.

31 Some readers might find the coupling of Rancière and Bourdieu in this essay surprising, given that Rancière has been critical of Bourdieu, most notably in *The Philosopher and His Poor*. I find Rancière's conception of the police helpful as a diagnostic tool for understanding the outlaw thesis, but the aesthetic politics that he offers as a solution is less helpful because it conflates precisely what I am trying to separate out. Bourdieu's later writings on art and literature (which were published well after Rancière's 1983 critique) provide a more helpful framework for stepping outside of the assumptions of the outlaw thesis.

32 Gisèle Sapiro, *Les écrivains et la politique en France: De l'affaire Dreyfus à la Guerre d'Algérie* (Paris: Seuil, 2018), 21.

33 This is one of the reasons that I have chosen the July Monarchy as the period of the first historical case study in my book project. It allows me to trace this concept back to its origins, in my case through the exemplary figure of an "engaged" author, Victor Hugo.

34 Le Figaro Live, "Faut-il parler du 'Grand remplacement,'" YouTube, March 18, 2019, https://www.youtube.com/watch?v=eODaSMjl0pA&.

35 Renaud Camus ("Le grand déménagement du monde"), interview with Alain Finkielkraut and Hervé Le Bras, *Répliques*, June 10, 2017, *France Culture*, https://www.franceculture.fr/emissions/repliques/le-grand-demenagement-du-monde-1.

36 See Ki Namaste, "The Politics of Inside/Out: Queer Theory, Poststructuralism, and a Sociological Approach to Sexuality," *Sociological Theory* 12.2 (1994): 220–31; Guy Oakes, "Straight Thinking About Queer Theory," *International Journal of Politics, Culture, and Society* 8.3 (1995): 379–88; and Steven Seidman, "Queer-ing Sociology, Sociologizing Queer Theory: An Introduction," *Sociological Theory* 12.2 (1994): 166–77.

37 Seidman, "Queer-ing Sociology," 167.
38 Camus, "Le grand déménagement."
39 As others in this volume demonstrate, the pitting of nation against state is a common tactic of the ethnonationalist right.
40 Camus, "Le grand déménagement."
41 Camus, "Le grand déménagement."
42 Le Figaro Live, "Grand remplacement."
43 Qtd. in David D. Kirkpatrick, "Massacre Suspect Traveled the World but Lived on the Internet," *New York Times*, March 15, 2019, https://www.nytimes.com/2019/03/15/world/asia/new-zealand-shooting-brenton-tarrant.html.
44 Renaud Camus, *Tricks*, 3rd ed. (Paris: POL, 1988), 19.
45 See Vercier, Porter, and Sarkonak, "An Interview."
46 On Camus's skepticism, see his 2002 appearance on the panel show *Un Livre, un débat*. The program has been uploaded to YouTube by a fan page of another one of the contributors, Alain Soral. Sevda Utanmaz, "Alain Soral sur LCI: Débat sur l'Homosexualité 1/2," YouTube, May 31, 2016, https://www.youtube.com/watch?v=ajocAhvnRMA&.
47 Renaud Camus, *Parti pris: Journal 2010* (Paris: Fayard, 2011), 173–74.
48 Camus's first long intervention on *Répliques* makes this argument clearly. In this way, Camus situates himself firmly within the purview of ethnonationalist politicians like Marine Le Pen and Trump, both of whom criticize "globalist" elites who "ship" "our" jobs to Asia.

M. Ty

4. The Myth of What We Can Take In: Global Migration and the "Receptive Capacity" of the Nation-State

The next ship can turn around and go back where it came from because our limit has been reached.
>—Matteo Salvini, deputy prime minister of Italy, as he refused to allow 177 migrants to disembark from a rescue boat recently arrived on European shores[1]

I

THIS CHAPTER DRAWS out affinities between psychoanalytic notions of fortification and contemporary strategies for framing migration as a critical condition requiring national defense. In doing so, these reflections make perceptible the lineaments of a biocultural myth that underlies and (silently) authorizes the discursive construction of the "European refugee crisis"—a catachresis that, improper though it is, nevertheless generates lethal reality-effects.

In order to dissolve the violence that this rubric perpetuates, both practically and epistemically, it is necessary not simply to dismiss it as yet another instance of Eurocentrism but to apprehend the distinctly European coordinates of legibility into which the global displacements of our time are being inscribed—with remarkable consistency. An intransigent lexicon for representing migrants not only de-nationalizes but also de-individualizes them into an uncontrollable natural phenomenon—an aqueous, if not more specifically hydraulic or oceanic, force: the language of influx, flood, inundation, storm, surge, deluge, waves unforeseen; swelling up at checkpoints; tides that must be stemmed; or, as a paradigmatic headline reads, in an involution of natural history, "Refugee Flows Flood the Evros River."[2] How do such image-repertoires and corresponding patterns of cultural anxiety structure the transformation of disparate, collective experiences of dispossession into a scenario of catastrophic engulfment in which Europe is passively overwhelmed and so entitled to take whatever measures it deems necessary for safeguarding its own life? In what ways does the rhetorically realized fantasy of European crisis preserve the latter's unity, even if under the sign of dramatizing the threat to its coherence? What do tropes of ecological disturbance hold, by figuring negatively an order of necessary equilibrium, whose maintenance ideationally coordinates the triangulation of racialized policing, market regulation, and environmental sustainability?

The pervasive image-concept of the West's disintegration, I will argue with the help of Freud, indexes a mythopoetic conception of Life that does not disavow death but topographically contains and strategically incorporates it. The idea of survival derived from such a schema becomes more susceptible to ethnonationalist appropriation the more effectively the relation between its two elements is naturalized: first, a transcendental claim that to live is to have a receptive capacity that can be abstracted from experience and held apart temporally from historical time; second, the mobilization of this proposition as the legitimating ground for bringing under regulation an exteriority that threatens to overload an ontologically given faculty for taking things in. The myth compels—commands the force of intuition—in part because it activates resonances between the individual and the collective subject. As racialization retro-projects differentials of power onto a biological substratum in which a historically contingent order of supremacy can be "discovered" as given, the systemic repression of refugees finds justification in the presumption of a primary receptivity that is assumed to be separable from and prior to political intervention. Under this spell, a death sentence that is decided upon appears as something that had to be done.

II

NEITHER THE FRAMEWORK of political sovereignty nor that of biopolitical governance fully accounts for the regulatory power deployed against "irregular" migrants, although elements of both are routinely deployed, not only to prevent black and brown bodies from being recognized as legitimate subjects of the state but also to keep them on the outer limits of the "population"—inadmissible, even, to demographics. It is true that the structure of sovereign decision is rehearsed in every asylum case. In the culminating stage of the application process, every refugee has a hearing during which she is summoned to perform her vulnerability linguistically—in narrative form—before a representative of the European state. Typically, it is one (often overworked) official who, relying on the labor of an interpreter, judges whether someone has been sufficiently victimized to be eligible for state protection. The decisive scene in which the encounter between law and migrant is transformed into a sentence that can be upheld by force is made with reference to a determination at the level of the state, which not only dictates whom it will (refuse to) take in but also circumscribes the forms of violence for which its law will assume responsibility. Economic and structural oppression are categorically ruled out; and "vulnerability" is formalized so as to discount domestic abuse and unorganized threats of femicide.

And yet the verdict—to let stay or make go—does not map cleanly onto the sovereign power to kill or to spare life. Nor can it be fully assimilated to biopolitical paradigms of social exclusion, such as the foundational division of *bios* from *zoe* that, in Agamben's view, enables bare life to be captured in spaces of exception, or the strategies of immunization that, according to Esposito, constitute community by selectively incorporating the biological contagion attributed to the foreigner.[3] As right-wing populisms polarize dissensus into a rupture between white nationalism and the liberal ideal of *Willkommenskultur*, the question of whether to accept migrants has become increasingly charged as the privileged site of critical attention and political dispute. Yet the Schmittian decision—whom to let in and whom to remove (by force)—is, I am suggesting, epiphenomenal and better understood as a late moment in an operation of state-mediated power whose preconditions have yet to be brought to light.

To do so, this chapter attends to a linguistic echo, a repetition across the century, through which one can discern the animating principle underlying the structural transformation of mass migration into a scenario of *krisis* (from *krinein*, "to decide"). Vital to transnational xenophobic imaginaries, the discursive construction of the "European refugee crisis" is, I will argue, sustained by a relatively new concept—namely, that the nation-state has a finite and objective "receptive capacity" for taking in foreigners, which, when surpassed, sanctions violence against migrants deemed irregular. This notion has pervaded various strata of the public sphere—regularly summoned, for instance, as a truth-discourse in parliamentary debates about asylum policy;[4] trafficking more polemically in populist rhetoric (as exemplified by Salvini's aggressive exasperation in his claim, "our limit has been reached"); and structuring the visual grammar for capturing migrant experience for Western consumption.

During the most intense season of migration to Europe in 2015, mounting anxieties were publicly voiced in similar terms, that is, not directly as an avowed anti-blackness or Islamophobia but as a critical condition of having surpassed the limit of refugees who could be absorbed.[5] This was, for instance, the message of an open letter sent to Angela Merkel by district administrators in southern Westphalia: "The open borders," they wrote in October of that year, "are overtaxing our receptive capacity."[6] In German, *Aufnahmefähigkeit* denotes a faculty for retention, an ability to admit, take in, and absorb. The root of this term, *Aufnahme*, has a number of colloquial usages including assimilation and acceptance; uptake of a force or substance like electricity or water; and admission, for instance, to a school, hospital, or club. *Aufnahme* can also refer to what can be drawn in textually or visually—as in a photograph, inscription, or recording. At play, then, is a limit within the field of perceptual registration, which in turn is a reticulum of governmental registration.

The paradigm in question is transmitted, perhaps even more seamlessly because wordlessly, through photographic images that compose mass migration as an encounter with the visual sublime. The footage that was filmed with drones in Ai Wei Wei's *Human Flow* (2017), for instance, frames refugee experience from a macro-logical perspective in which the limits of perception are made to converge with those of apprehension. In those high-altitude shots, visual repetition borders on mathematical excess: the lifejackets that are metonyms of refugees at sea appear so uncountable that they can only be processed as a color field; the temporary housing in camps, seen with the aerial eye, transforms into a geometric pattern against the flaxen desert. The problem of the inordinate scale of global displacement is translated formally into one of visual saturation—of bodies innumerable pressing against the frame that can scarcely hold.[7]

Claims about the receptive capacities of various cities, nations, regions—and above all "Europe" in general—continue to shape the neoliberal political landscape and have had particularly formidable effects since 2015, as member nations of the EU (fail to) negotiate how many migrants, if any, they are willing to resettle within their borders. Unlike in contestations over territorial sovereignty, the boundary evoked in these instances is not strictly physical but an abstraction, a perceived frontier of an internal capacity.

What's ultimately at issue, I would emphasize, is less any particular resolution concerning immigration—the closing of this or that checkpoint or the barometric shifts in degrees of tolerance—but, more fundamentally, the legitimation of the entire framework that normalizes the subjection of non-European bodies to the infrastructure of knowledge and legal authorization that is administered by the West. The latter includes the paternalistic power to declare unilaterally when a country is safe enough for refugees to return to (by force of deportation). As Harsha Walia discerns, "the primary disagreement between EU States about 'sharing the burden of refugee distribution' is, fundamentally[,] a quarrel over racial imperial management."[8]

Through the trope of overwhelm, Europe represents itself politically as the site of interiority and as a moral Subject endowed with a field of choice. What is newly grafted onto this eidetic legacy of colonization, I am suggesting, is the notion that such a province of decision is bounded by a biomythically defined limit of receptivity for which Europe is not accountable and, further, remains other to economy as its originary condition. This idea of an objective limitation on the capacity for absorption is the conceptual fulcrum that allows states to represent neocolonial forms of brutality and population management as if they were not racially determined and, further, as if their very function were not to reproduce a global division of race that can be exploited as a differential in the value of labor. The crisis of a breached threshold also obscures the perception of border regimes as the continuation of a longer history of anti-black interdictions of free movement. In contrast to legislation like the Negro Act of 1740, the Chinese Exclusion Act of 1882, or the Nuremburg laws, all of which targeted ethnic minorities explicitly, the representation of migrant repression in terms of a critical negotiation with an internal limit provides a distinctly postracial framework of legitimation.[9]

Freud composed *Beyond the Pleasure Principle* (1920) and "A Note upon the 'Mystic Writing-Pad'" (1925) within a decade of his own forced migration from Vienna. In these studies, he theorizes the limits of psychic registration and memory—particularly those induced by traumatic experience. Curiously, the not so common word *Aufnahmefähigkeit* appears in these early documents, where it refers to the "unusual" feature of the psyche—namely, a "receptive capacity" that Freud identifies as astonishingly "unlimited."[10] Rather differently from earlier invocations of the tabula rasa as an image of potentiality (Aristotle) or as an analogy to the blankness that precedes the first mental impressions made by experience (Locke), what emerges across these two texts is the following: identity is established and maintained not only through an articulation of interiority but also through the definition of the interior as the proper place of receptivity; further, the regulation and organization (topographically and via a division of labor) of this potentially infinite capacity are what first inaugurate (psychic) life and, secondarily, not only what will pattern the subject's attempts at self-formation but also what will be experienced in the key of fear or anxiety, as a threat to self-integration.

Listening to this linguistic resonance and so to the mimetic juncture where the resilience of the ego is imagined jointly with that of the body politic, one can ask more pointedly what is meant when a *national* receptive capacity is evoked. What is the basis and history of this abstraction? How is it solicited to act as a reality principle that conjures a bottom line—one that is seemingly not decided upon by any political agent but is the condition that, as it were, structures the structure of decision? What is the difference, in terms of the exercise of power, between selectively prohibiting migration through the force of a ban—as with Trump's executive order to categorically deny refugees entry to the United States—and a declarative statement that posits the breach of a not strictly numerical, but theoretically quantifiable, limit to what a polity can absorb without losing itself? How might the specification of a receptive capacity participate in the consolidation of national sovereignty at a time when the latter has been eroded by neoliberal capital?

III

INSISTING THAT A national receptive capacity has been exhausted does not amount to a direct refusal—a rejection of a particular ethnic or religious group—even if ultimately such statements can be recruited in the service of exclusionary acts. This notion must also be distinguished from quota systems that are more familiar to cultural histories of modern immigration law and its development in relation to war and the legal codification of racial hierarchies. In the United States, the first such regime was established in the 1920s to deter immigration from eastern and southern Europe, and in less equivocal terms, to rule out the assimilation of Asians, whom the law deemed categorically "ineligible" for citizenship.[11] Quite differently from the contemporary allocation of refugees under the Dublin Regulation, these figures were calculated with reference to "national origins," an invented notion derived from incomplete census data on citizens' countries of birth. Such formulas of limited acceptance—x number from y country—purported to reflect existing proportions of the demographic composition but, as Mae Ngai has demonstrated in *Impossible Subjects*, systematically effaced the presence of non-white residents, including "mulattoes" and descendants of slaves.[12] It is these quotas that were in place during the last global refugee movement of this magnitude, following World War II.

The generalization of a receptive capacity to the level of the nation-state marks a relatively new form of governmental reason—one that does not give rise to the comparatively simpler, arithmetical processes of calculation that first put an end to "open" movement and advanced white supremacy by demographically ranking the free Caucasian European as the pinnacle of human desirability. As a signifier, *Aufnahmefähigkeit* has undergone notable semantic fluctuations over the course of the century, transiting as it has across the boundary between Life and non-Life. In Freud's usage, *Aufnahmefähigkeit* has an air of technicality. During his time, the term was largely associated with the applied physical sciences, for instance, in measurements of the magnetic capacitance of machines.[13]

The geographer Nathan Sayre has traced the metamorphosis of its English counterpart, "carrying capacity," from a technic of measurement that facilitated the transnational flow of goods into a concept that, from the mid-twentieth century onward, vitalized neo-Malthusian aspirations for regulating human populations. The phrase first emerged in the 1840s in the context of international shipping, as a way to standardize the measure of how much weight vessels could bear and, consequently, how much they could be taxed. Though originally used to assess objects of human design, the concept was extended in the late nineteenth century to describe natural phenomena—for example, how much moisture the winds could carry or how much water a channel could hold. This broadening in turn gave way to a more figural usage with reference to populations.[14] In a shift that resembles the distinction Foucault makes between disciplinary power, which targets the individual body, and biopower, which addresses itself to the "species," the ambit of "carrying capacity" enlarged considerably with respect to knowledge-production—so as to account, for instance, not only for how many pounds an individual mule could transport but more broadly how much livestock could be supported by a given tract of land.[15]

After studying deer on the Kaibab Plateau in Arizona, the environmental conservationist Aldo Leopold popularized the concept in the domain of wildlife management to describe fluctuations in game populations in terms of variable productivity.[16] Around the time of World War II, he began to analogize the self-regulating dynamics of animal population growth to human patterns of subsistence. Through the academic lecture circuit, he exported the concept to Africa, along with the ideologically laden ethics of sustainability that was its vehicle. Between 1941 and 1949, the British administration of present-day Zambia conducted ecological assessments of the carrying capacity of various subregions within the colony. These studies were subsequently used to justify the forcible resettlement of thousands of Africans—allegedly, to maintain a proper balance between human populations and natural resources.[17] The German *Aufnahmefähigkeit* is likewise deployed in discourses of ecological management, but from the 1970s onward it acquires a more prominent meaning in economics and business administration. Within this literature, it is used synonymously with *Aufnahmekapäzitat* to assess the potential of emerging markets, in distinction from the actual purchasing power within them.[18]

This philological excursion offers a glimpse of the deadly fabrication of market and bioecological restrictions in each other's image. Although Foucault left it undertheorized, anthropocentrically circumscribed, and geographically restricted to Europe, the notion of "environmental power" that he provisionally advances in his lectures on neoliberalism draws near to, without fully perceiving, the degree of collusion among ecological sciences, governmentality, and colonial dispossession. He uses the phrase almost figuratively, to name power and knowledge that, unlike disciplinary regimes, do not enforce the Procrustean transformation of the individual into a normative ideal. Instead, environmental power operates through the creation of a milieu in which (economic) actors are free to play.[19]

The genealogy of *Aufnahmefähigkeit* provokes acknowledgment of the historical complicity between economically sanctioned regimes of racialization and the ethics of environmental conservation. Both deploy *savoir-pouvoir* through the inauguration and holding open of a space of free range, whose boundaries—geospatially and statistically constituted—are regulated and policed. Such a mode of intervention produces a zone of non-intervention, in which its mark tends toward invisibility. With the institution of the Schengen Area as a space of open and free travel—a circumscribed realization of the cosmopolitan ideal—the whole of Europe is reconceived on this model.

The compulsory quotas for relocating asylum seekers indicate a paradigm shift in that they do not directly mark ethnic groups for incorporation or refused recognition. Instead they self-represent the limitations of European states. The rationally calculated, "objective" capacities of absorption—the appraisal of the environmental condition of member nations—are subsequently used to justify forcible restriction of the movement of non-white bodies, which, in relation to such a schema, are primed to appear as a quantitative, then qualitative excess. The "distribution key," an elaborate and baroque mathematical formula for allocating refugees throughout Europe, takes into account four variables, none of which pertain to migrants' country of birth or racial identification.[20] These include the domestic population size; the total GDP; the rate of unemployment; and the average number of asylum applications received in recent years.[21] The fate of non-European bodies, in other words, is determined by the subsumption of the asylum process into a calculus of what the national *oikos*—the root of both economy and ecology—can absorb without dis-equilibration. It is true that Euroskeptics and far-right nationalists have prided themselves on the reactionary and wholesale refusal of the refugee quotas prescribed by the EU. "Here in Poland," insists Prime Minister Mateusz Morawiecki, "it's we who decide who will come to Poland and who will not."[22] But their defense of national sovereignty, whose masculinist aggression toward the Islamic and Black Other is less mediated, nevertheless shares an ideological premise, which binds the threat of destruction with the fear of overtaxing of the receptive capacities of the nation, conceived as a market environment. The bestialization of the (formerly) colonized subject is now neither merely a cultural trope nor a strictly material process of degradation but the suturing together of both in the name of economic management.

IV

DESPITE ITS OMNIPRESENCE, the notion of a national receptive capacity for migrants has largely eluded prevailing representational frameworks for rendering refugee experience visible in the Global North. Humanitarianism, which is supplemented by the exhibition of the refugee as victim, helplessly adrift in a state of oceanic destitution, polarizes the crisis into a dyadic relation in which the suffering refugee is put on display for Western consumption.[23] Elsewhere, critical investigation of border zones has closed in on the tendency toward repressive policing of migrants and the intensified militarization of national boundaries, which increasingly attracts private investment. Dispersed incidents draw themselves together into a pattern of systemic abuse: the arrest and detention of refugees in jails; the show of force at the Serbian border, where riot police deployed water cannons and tear gas against those stranded at a recently sealed point of entry;[24] the French officers who routinely battered refugees in Paris and Calais and confiscated sleeping bags and blankets during the freeze of winter, or drove young women three hours away from the site of their provisional housing and left them to walk back alone;[25] beatings administered by border forces in Croatia, Bulgaria, and Greece, and the countless unreportable injuries that were unable to receive medical attention; the police on Lesbos arresting and breaking the limbs of refugees who were demonstrating against the substandard living conditions where they were forcibly confined;[26] the deliberate starvation of refugees at Hungarian "transit zones" so as to compel them to drop their legal appeals;[27] the illegal "pushbacks" in the Mediterranean, which involve members of the coast guard throwing refugees back into non-European waters, boatless and with diminished chances of survival; in France, the internment of children overnight without food or water, the seizure of their mobile phones, the doctoring of the documents of underage asylum seekers so that technically they would appear old enough to send back to Italy, and the cutting off of child refugees' shoe soles before they were forced to return by foot to the country where they first arrived.[28] The more extreme it is, the more fatally border security hollows into sadism.

The criminalization of refugees risks becoming normalized as the infrastructure of border control becomes increasingly indistinguishable from the prison-industrial complex. Though written before "the refugee crisis" entered public consciousness as such, the central claim of Wendy Brown's *Walled States, Waning Sovereignty*—namely, that the fanatical and masculinist project of wall-building is a compensatory mechanism for the compromised sovereignty of the nation in a post-Westphalian order—resonates with what has since become a more explicitly manic thrill for fabricating infrastructures devoted to migrant repression.[29] In this regard, the carnival Trump generated around the construction of the "great, great wall" along the Mexican border is exemplary but with the important difference that, as with Horst Seehofer's determination to build migrant "concentration" centers along the Austrian border, the physical barriers meant to secure the nation are pursued even at the expense of shutting the government down. Though spoken of as a practical measure of security, defensive fortifications against migrants are gratuitous while simultaneously being made to stand as the sign of the real. As Rob Nixon says of the megadams built during the Cold War era, they are perhaps most accurately thought of as a form of "national performance art."[30] Drawing attention to the extraordinary security apparatus surrounding the Calais refugee camp, Debarati Sanyal has discerned how the "irregular" migrant is arrested in the "unlivable crux of humanitarian compassion and securitarian repression."[31] Dogs, x-ray scanners, carbon dioxide probes, surveillance cameras, twenty-nine kilometers of razor-wire fence—the sheer disproportion in the use of force recalls Walter Benjamin's assertion that the law-preserving use of violence coincides with mythic retaliation.[32]

Both the humanitarian optic and the critical analysis of border militarization turn the gaze toward the realm of hypervisible scenes of defense and injury—to new technologies and weaponized practices of repression. What is liable to fall away from view, however, are the hardly sensational but no less damaging operations of power involved in articulating the nation-state's receptive limit. Similarly, the theoretical paradigms most often summoned to account for the power directed against migrants—as an exercise of sovereignty; as a directive of biopolitical neglect and containment; as a failed politics of hospitality—highlight the question of voluntary exclusion and inclusion (whom and how many to let in). In other words, they funnel attention toward a structure of decision, if not more specifically a Schmittian distinction between friend and enemy.[33] In doing so, they inadvertently eclipse the origins of the internal boundary that such determinations presuppose. What is at play, in other words, is not ultimately the exercise of sovereign power in the classical sense—the performative speech act that consecrates the decision to let a subject live or make him die—nor the biopolitical reversal of the formula, expressive of a power that can make a population live or let a population perish. While indispensable, accounts of power oriented toward the spectacle of weaponized conflict or visible suffering leave untouched what takes place seemingly to the side of the decisive act and its defensive reinforcements—namely, that there is a baseline, a prior knowledge of one's own limits, a quantifiable and bounded capacity for what one can absorb (as a political body).

As suggested earlier, Freud offers a fruitful point of entry for an investigation of this very notion. Particularly salient is the research he pursued during the interwar period, when he moved toward a metapsychological account of the formation of the psychic apparatus and simultaneously attempted to clarify what happens when the perceptual and mnemonic systems that secure identity become damaged. Though better known for its theorization of shock experience as the norm of experience, his work in the early 1920s strikes upon another insight into Western modernity as a condition in which receptivity is no longer, as Kant suggests in *Critique of Pure Reason*, merely one among a set of complementary cognitive faculties.[34] Nor is receptivity, as it appears in Western aesthetics and with a utopic accent in the cultural imaginary of Romanticism, something to be cultivated as a resource of the self.[35] Freud marks, rather, a historical moment in which receptivity is first and foremost a problem that needs to be managed. And he proposes, further, that it is not the expression of an underlying, positive essence but the organization of a given capacity to absorb what comes from without that constitutes the psychic identity of the individual, which, not least in political theory, is often articulated jointly with that of the nation-state. There is, so to speak, no proper site of the proper—no there there—that is not the work of regulation.

Writing in *Beyond the Pleasure Principle* (1920) about traumatic experience, Freud translates the operations of psychic life into the language of the biological sciences in order to elaborate the processes that are set into motion when there is a potentially calamitous "breach in an otherwise efficacious barrier against stimuli."[36] An incursion of force, breaking in from without,

> is bound to provoke a disturbance on a large scale in the functioning of the organism's energy and to set in motion every possible defensive measure. At the same time, the pleasure principle is for the moment put out of action. There is no longer any possibility of preventing the mental apparatus from being

> flooded with large amounts of stimulus, and another problem arises instead—the problem of mastering the amounts of stimulus which have broken in and of binding them in the psychical sense, so that they can then be disposed of. (*BPP* 29; *J* 29–30)

Freud narrates a scene of the lone organism in crisis, a state of exception in which the governing norm of pain-avoidance and satisfaction-seeking is suspended and displaced by the problem of coping with a sudden and involuntary internalization. Reading from and with the historical present, one might hear throughout this passage resonances with the hegemonic framing of the "refugee crisis" as an unexpected affliction of Europe, which calls for a general orientation of necessary management: where and how to bind this not-quite-cognizable force, at checkpoints or at reception centers; at what times and locations to shut the railways down; when to redirect migration routes or allow the perils of the natural landscape to act as a deterrent; how, more bluntly, to suppress entry (with an arsenal of tanks, cannons, tear gas, batons, wire, guns, or with vigilante tactics of intimidation); how to calculate ways to apportion the mass evenly, in the steady *mathesis* of a quota system; and, finally, when to detain and dispose of certain elements or, alternatively, permit those that have already made their way in to occupy a place for a little while.

To emphasize the resemblance between the *topoi* of classical psychoanalysis and the representational structures that confer legibility to contemporary global migration—perhaps the most pronounced being the figuration of outside forces that threaten to overcome the ego as stemming from the oceanic unknown—is not to posit a transparent analogy between the individual and the nation. Nor is the intention here to translate a geopolitically specific problem into a simplified, psychoanalytic schema, sanitized of historical specificity. What this comparative reading discloses, rather, is that heterogeneous experiences of displacement can be made to appear monolithically as a crisis—not only by spotlighting Europe as the fictively unified protagonist engaged in an ordeal of survival but also by repeatedly inscribing events into a framework of traumatic effraction. The work of understanding and dissipating the stronghold of Eurocentrism remains incomplete without deactivating the various image-repertoires for fantasizing about the self qua political body as overwhelmed consciousness—a projected vulnerability that in turn may be used to justify violent patterns of mastery and defense against the foreigner within.

But more than this, Freud cues us into the prehistory of this fraught drama of adjustment.

Freud, I would like to underscore, grounds his account of mental life in the assumption of a primary susceptibility that is unlimited and which psychic structures must work to organize and restrict if they are to resist succumbing to the death-drive. He develops this problematic in the fourth section of *Beyond the Pleasure Principle* (by far the most peculiar of the book), which opens with a thought experiment. "What follows is speculation, often far-fetched speculation," he begins. Freud proceeds to model the human psychic apparatus on a unicellular life form, a protista, which develops a topographical arrangement that in turn gives rise to a primitive division of labor:

> Let us picture [*Stellen wir ... vor*] a living organism in its most simplified possible form as an undifferentiated vesicle of a substance that is susceptible to stimulation. Then the surface turned towards the external world will from its very situation be differentiated and will serve as an organ for receiving stimuli. ... It would be easy to suppose, then, that as a result of the ceaseless impact of external stimuli on the surface of the vesicle, its substance to a certain depth may have become permanently modified. ... A crust [*Rinde*] would thus be formed which would at last have been so thoroughly "baked through" [*durchgebrannt*] by stimulation that it would present the most favourable possible conditions for the reception of stimuli and become incapable of any further modification. (*BPP* 26; *J* 25)

Departing from a scientific mode of exposition, Freud issues a summons—*Stellen wir ... vor*—that marks his own discursive shift into the imaginary. This inaugural image is both the germ and the anchor of the narrative sequence of psychic impingement and formation that follows and will later serve as the (pseudo-biological) basis—the vehicle—for conceptualizing a traumatic experience that is itself resistant to representation. Even if one were ultimately to dismiss this figure as having minimal empirical traction, its rhetorical force in the course of his argument cannot be overstated. The vividness of this peculiar vision—the memorable glimpse of proto-consciousness, crusted through and extending tentative "feelers" into the outside world—translates the complexity of the psycho-perceptual system into the idiom of allegorical simplicity (*BPP* 28; *J* 28). This scene promises to show—with remarkable narrative economy—how things have come to be unchangeable, and how a seemingly invariant structure is formed as a precipitate of hardened accident.

In this section, Freud's whole exposition is set into motion by a single image that seems to emanate its own order of compulsion. It is as though simply holding the vision of the organism before the mind's eye initiates a cascade of necessary developments. Almost as soon as this elemental entity is posited, it undergoes an internal differentiation. The spatial division between what is exposed and what is sheltered from external stimuli immediately generates specialization—as an initially unbounded susceptibility is localized within an "organ" that then becomes an instrument, subservient to the organic whole. As a result of this organization, temporality is implicitly split between an order of contingency and one of permanence—fleeting stimuli against a backdrop of intransigence. Like those improbably long strips of fabric that a magician continues to pull from an upturned hat, a whole chain of necessity emerges from a simple source. *Let us imagine … then … then … then …*—ineluctably, one thing follows upon another, as if Freud is merely helping to unfurl what the image already holds as an internal necessity.

Not unlike in the grand myths of political theory that retrospectively presume the autonomous, violent individual as the starting point of social organization, in Freud's story, life from the very start is closed off from a hostile environment that threatens to annihilate anything that does not develop effective resistance to it. This antagonism is neither human nor strictly agential. The presumption that what is external is life-destroying also means that survival will be equated with fortification, and fortification with a partial deadening that works instrumentally to preserve life, but only for what is safely stationed within the interior:

> This little fragment of living substance is suspended in the middle of an external world charged with the most powerful energies; and it would be killed by the stimulation emanating from these if it were not provided with a protective shield against stimuli. It acquires the shield in this way: its outermost surface ceases to have the structure proper to living matter, becomes to some degree inorganic and thenceforward functions as a special envelope or membrane resistant to stimuli. … By its death, the outer layer has saved all the deeper ones from a similar fate. … Protection against stimuli is an almost more important function than reception of stimuli. The protective

shield is supplied with its own store of energy and must above all endeavour to preserve the special modes of transformation of energy operating in it against the effects threatened by the enourmous energies at work in the external world—effects which tend ... towards destruction. The main purpose of the reception of stimuli is to discover the direction and nature of the external stimuli; and for that it is enough to take small specimens of the external world, to sample it in small quantities. (*BPP* 27; *J* 26–27)

Although Freud is frank in admitting the speculative quality of this imaginative experiment, his fiction, like all literary fictions, is nonetheless governed by an internal logic whose power ranges beyond the hypothetical scenario staged within the text. There is, simply put, something that makes sense about this tale of developmental fortification—or perhaps more accurately, *makes* sense, insofar as the narrative generates an order of causality in which susceptibility and protection are dialectically configured within a broader trajectory of self-preservation. The elements of this rationality are distilled below and accompanied by echoes of their manifestations in contemporary framings of global migration:

1. The account of Life begins with the monadic individual—self-same and bounded—as it is confronted by the undifferentiated, life-destroying forces that emanate from a minimally defined exteriority.

Perspective is concentrated on a unified entity—what is called "Europe," "Hungary," or "America"—whose cohesion is both presupposed and shown to be imperiled by the "influx" from without. The protagonist of this crisis is abstracted from a broader context of (economic) interdependence and from its own history. At the outset, the territorial definition between interior and exterior has already been sufficiently settled in order to be apprehended as undergoing a disturbance.

2. What enables, defines, and sustains Life is the organization of a potentially unbounded receptivity—spatially, so that absorption only occurs in certain zones; and economically, so that the privileged interior remains infinitely capable of registering new phenomena, whereas at the boundaries, reception is subject to a principle of severe economic limitation.

At the Hungarian border, short of banning refugees altogether, officers permit only one or two migrants to enter the reception facility per day.[37] *Border policing and the fixation on repressive infrastructure—walls, (privately operated) detention centers, militarized checkpoints—seek gratification in the topographical containment of foreign intake. Asylum seekers do not "arrive" in Europe until they report to designated "reception centers." And if officials refuse to register their presence because they are personally deemed unwanted, they remain suspended in a precarious state of non-arrival, in which they can neither become citizens nor be legally denied asylum status.*

3. The maintenance of Life requires a desensitization and deadening—or, as Freud puts it, a rendering "inorganic" of the outermost part of the life form. The opposition between death and life is thus reconfigured as an internal structure of Life. To be living, then, is no longer simply to repel death but to have strategically incorporated it—to have subjected life to a principle of sacrifice, precisely in order to conserve Life. Life, in short, must have life at its disposal. The part of Life that has been transformed into a deadened "envelope" or "shield" is designed to protect the vitality of the whole but also makes demands on the energetic resources of the bounded life form.

The state invests (economically, libidinally) in spaces of death—where life can be severely compromised without being said to threaten the livelihood of civil society.

The ANKER centers that Seehofer constructed in Bavaria, to take one representative instance, are the infrastructural incarnation of the armature, the "membrane" whose deadening and cultivated resistance to external forces serves ostensibly to safeguard the integrity of the state. (In expanded form, the acronym—Ankunft, Entscheidung, Ruckführung [Arrival, Decision, Repatriation]—makes explicit how "reception" is schematically reduced to a problem of sovereign disposal.) Such sterile environments—outfitted with weaponized architecture and designed without the aim of provisioning for (social) life—are sequestered from, even while they may be spatially contiguous with, the living fabric of the polity's interior. Informal camps, denied access to basic resources for subsistence, become spaces of dereliction. In many cases, officers employed at migrant holding facilities actively diminish life, through forced starvation or solitary confinement.

4. Survival entails the instrumentalization of receptivity so as to allow for a sampling of homeopathic doses of the external world. A formerly unbounded, non-teleological capacity is profitably installed at the boundary, as an apparatus for reconnaissance. Initially a capacity distributed throughout the whole body and defined broadly as being essential to Life, receptivity is optimized near the border to be discriminating—to take in only certain kinds of stimulation and to "deal only with very small quantities" (J 27). What is other to the life form will subsequently only be taken in as a "sample"—a specimen that is predetermined to be manageable—neither excessive nor overwhelming.

As idiosyncratic as it may sound, Trump's insistence that the barrier to Mexico include little openings—"because you have to see what's on the other side of the wall"—discloses an essential feature of a broader political imaginary in which fortification, in its ideal form, is not absolute but equipped with a specialized apparatus for strategically taking in what is foreign as instrumental knowledge.[38] The "reception" of refugees, aided by transnational agencies like Frontex, euphemistically designates a restrictive process of registration that converts the migrant body into data. All asylum seekers older than six years of age must have their fingerprints entered into the European Dactyloscopy (Eurodac)—a centralized database that was established in 2003 to monitor and facilitate the deportation of "irregular" border crossers. The techno-scientific apparatus for reception—planes, surveillance cameras, motion sensors, infrared imaging, biometrics—transforms the migrant into a manageable specimen of (visual) information, an object of governmental knowledge, that, in turn, can be used to regulate racialized bodies under the aegis of maintaining the life of the polity qua interior.

All of these elements are in place before the narration of any traumatic breach. This mise-en-scène is established prior to any event, antecedent to any episodic irruption of conflict. The story Freud tells, in other words, is one of an originary condition—one that is situated within a temporal order that remains separate from any narratable series of incidents. This formative sequence is prehistorical or, rather, marks itself as the condition of possibility for historical unfolding and subjective experience.

It may seem that at this point in the text Freud goes furthest off the rails into a biological universalism. But it is precisely here that he grasps most incisively that the formative myth of receptivity brought under self-regulation—couched in biological terms—will be very compelling, if not irresistibly intuitive, to the European cultural imaginary of his time. Freud's study is far less illuminating if his excursus on the protista is read as a reductive analogy or an overreaching attempt to legitimate psychoanalytic research by borrowing from the authority of the natural sciences. The great insight of his speculation is precisely that he is able to recognize and mark this logic as mythic—that is, as a set of presumptions that are so powerfully installed in collective structures of belief that they serve as the ground zero of proof, self-evident in their telling.

To underscore: what I am drawing into focus is not simply an affinity between a psychic model of traumatic impingement and the representation of Europe under duress, on account of a critical breach of its interior. My analysis instead restores consciousness to the transcendental proposition of the West that sets the whole logic of management into motion—and, further, makes fortification seem essential to survival. In other words, the question of inclusion or exclusion of the foreign can miss if not entirely occlude how the postulate of an originary, unbounded receptivity props up mythic constructions of necessary protection, which in turn can be variously racialized.

In the blueprint that Freud offers, one can see through to the mythic substrate that organizes historically contingent decisions to shut otherness out or let it in. A naturalized course of "development" moves the individual in the direction of an internal structure of defense. And primary receptivity—at first uncounting, expansive, and non-instrumental—is subject to functional subordination; economic limitation; topographical containment; teleological subsumption under the aim of self-preservation; and organ specialization, including the formation of a sensory apparatus dedicated to one-sided reconnaissance and knowledge-gathering.

What goes by the name of survival, Freud reveals, is a form of incurred damage made strategic, a way of living on that holds death as its shell. The more thoroughly formation and fortification are conflated, the more impoverished the ability to receive non-identity.

One may recall that Freud's theorization of psychic life was contemporaneous with the conceptual genesis of biopolitics, which Thomas Lemke traces back to the organicist conceptions of the state that took hold in Europe during the early twentieth century. Influenced by *Lebensphilosophie*, the reconceptualization of life as the basis of politics gave rise to an understanding of nation-states as "super-individual creatures" rather than as legal constructions.[39] Envisioning the body politic as a living organism, whose vitality or weakness was essentially determined by natural law, lent itself to National Socialism's genocidal ambition for a politically sanctioned genetic enclosure. One sees this fatal synergy at work, for instance, when, in 1934, the president of the Nazi Health Department called for the "recognition of biological thinking as the baseline, direction and substructure of every effective politics."[40] When the empirical tenor of Freud's study bottoms out into the realm of speculative biology, his intervention is not primarily addressed to the clinical realm but instead to the threshold beyond which cultural determination no longer appears as such. He attempts, in other words, to work on the discursive fabric of the life sciences, shot through as it is with political resonances that are latent, if not explicitly charged. It is not merely, then, that the militaristic language of shields, invasions, and barriers that Freud evokes in this primordial scenario of life bears within it the echo, like a ringing in the ear, of wartime experience. He also manages to verbalize the internal logic of the biological fictions that were liable to be taken up as the uncontested basis of political organization—and further, to mark their imaginary dimensions.

PERHAPS EVEN MORE powerful today than the Hobbesian supposition of a mythic state of violence that civil society rises above, the fantasy of necessary self-management potently informs the Western imaginary, heterogeneous as it is. This myth lives on in popular culture—perhaps most conspicuously in the casually defensive affirmation of the therapeutic horizon of "setting healthy boundaries"—as well as in certain expressions of white liberal subjectivity's preference for taking in small quanta of otherness that have already been vetted as not being "too much."

The biocultural myth that Freud delineates survives more lethally as the unspoken kernel of contemporary formations of right-wing populism and is tapped into whenever a "receptive limit" of an imagined community is defensively evoked. Like violence, xenophobia finds a range of expressions scarcely limited to the overtly physical and includes enactments that operate at the level of the epistemic. A critique of xenophobia, then, cannot restrict itself to punctual episodes of conflict—the clash that arises around the militarized wall, the tear gas in the jungle, the standoff at sea. The Schmittian decision of who and how many to admit, how much economic and psychic expenditure to divert to areas where a border has been compromised, how severely to rail against those foreign elements that have come through—all these political contestations remain epiphenomenal expressions of the foundational presumption that survival is only accomplished by strategically deadening one's own affectability. The intransigence of the affective-conceptual paradigm of overwhelmed Europe, to follow this thought through, cannot be dissolved without effecting a lasting de-cathexis from a prevailing notion of Life, which holds that unregulated receptivity, or a breach in the infrastructure that manages it, spells not a transformation of the living but certain death.

If the psychic formation of the individual or the nation is presumed to be inextricable from the effective and profitable regulation of one's own ability to receive non-identity, then the disruption to that organization will be coded with a heightened and hysterical significance of obliteration; the end of fortress Europe will remain ideologically conflated with the end of Europe; and the migrant who approaches the border will, in advance, be marked as the enemy to be disposed of or arrested as a specimen for selective incorporation.

One finds hope, perhaps, in the de-creation of such deadening myths.

Notes

This chapter first appeared as "The Myth of What We Can Take In: Global Migration and the 'Receptive Capacity' of the Nation-State," *Theory & Event* 22.4 (2019): 869–90; it has been lightly revised for inclusion in this volume and is reprinted here with kind permission.

1 Gabriela Saldivia, "Italy's Deputy Prime Minister Investigated After Migrants Kept Aboard Ship for 6 Days," NPR, August 26, 2018, https://n.pr/2Mzo12d.
2 Anthee Carassava, "Refugee Flows Flood the Evros River," *Deutsch Welle*, March 25, 2018, dhttps://p.dw.com/p/2uiAk.
3 Giorgio Agamben, *Homo Sacer: Sovereign Power and Bare Life*, trans. Daniel Heller-Roazen (Stanford: Stanford University Press, 1998); Roberto Esposito, *Communitas: The Origin and Destiny of Community*, trans. Timothy C. Campbell (Stanford: Stanford University Press, 2009).
4 The preamble to the "Migration Masterplan" proposed by Germany's interior minister Horst Seehofer—who claimed that he would go to the border himself to turn refugees away—calls for a stark restriction on immigration on the basis that a society's receptiveness (*Aufnahmebereitschaft*, literally "readiness to receive") requires order and governance, as "no country in the world can take in refugees without limit" (*Kein Land der Welt kann unbegrenzt Flüchtlinge aufnehmen*). Although it was not implemented in full, this docu-

ment compelled Merkel to reverse Germany's commitment to keeping its borders open and prompted the construction of "transit centers" along the Austrian border, where asylum seekers can be "concentrated" in facilities of ambiguous jurisdiction without ever technically entering the EU and its sphere of legal protections. This vision of a masterfully organized program of xenophobia not only indicates a broader ideological shift across North America and Europe—marked, not least, by the expanded presence in the streets and in mainstream electoral politics of far-right parties like the Lega, the AfD (Alternative für Deutschland), and the KKK—but also expresses a line of biomythical reasoning that is the vital nerve of the anti-immigrant racial imaginary. Horst Seehofer, "Verantwortung & Zusammenhalt: Der Masterplan Migration," *Bundesministerium des Innern, für Bau und Heimat*, http://www.bmi.bund.de/SharedDocs/topthemen/DE/topt001hema-masterplan-migration/topthema-masterplan-migration.html?nn=9391320, 2; "Anger at Austria Minister 'Nazi Language,'" BBC News, January 11, 2018, https://www.bbc.com/news/world-europe-42652518.

5   As the far right makes more visible its will to power, it attempts to legitimate its presence by normalizing more frontal expressions of anti-Islamic, anti-Semitic, and explicitly racist speech. One might think of the discourse of surpassed limitations, outlined in this chapter, as one of the fulcrums that tipped a "centrist" position on migration into the xenophobic platform that it already contained latently.

6   Karl Schneider, Eva Irrgang, Thomas Gemke, et al. to Angela Merkel, October 9, 2015, "Möglichkeiten sind begrenzt," *Sauerland Kurier*, October 24, 2015, https://www.sauerlandkurier.de/hochsauerlandkreis/meschede/aufgrund-fluechtlingszustroms-haben-landraete-einen-brandbrief-kanzlerin-merkel-g-5681211.html. Some years later, in a speech calling for the abolition of refugees' rights to family reunification, parliamentary member Alexander Throm cited the same reason, claiming that everywhere in Germany, "the receptive limit has been reached." Alexander Throm, "Wir machen eine fehlerfreie Ermessensentscheidung der Behörden möglich," *CDU/CSU*, June 7, 2018, https://www.cducsu.de/themen/innen-recht-sport-und-ehrenamt/alexander-throm-wir-machen-eine-fehlerfreie-ermessensentscheidung-der-behoerden-moeglich.

7   The film *Purple Sea* (2020) offers a counterpoint to the all-seeing distance of this aerial view. The documentary, whose duration is an unending hour, consists of footage taken by the Syrian artist Amel Alzakout, as she and her fellow passengers capsize en route to Lesbos. The camera remains underwater for most of the film and never lifts away from the body at sea.

8   Harsha Walia, *Border and Rule: Global Migration, Capitalism, and the Rise of Racist Nationalism* (Chicago: Haymarket Books, 2021), 127.

9   Likely the least familiar of these three instances of legal violence, the Negro Act of 1740 prohibited slaves from moving abroad, and also placed restrictions on assembly, growing food, and learning to write in English.

10 Sigmund Freud, "A Note upon the 'Mystic Writing-Pad,'" in *The Standard Edition of the Complete Psychological Works of Sigmund Freud*, vol. 19, *(1923–1925)*, trans. Lytton Strachey (London: Hogarth Press, 1961), 225.

11 Mae M. Ngai, *Impossible Subjects: Illegal Aliens and the Making of Modern America* (Princeton: Princeton University Press, 2014), 7.
12 See, in particular, part 1 of Ngai's *Impossible Subjects* (2014).
13 See, for instance, William Thomson and L. Levy, *Gesammelte Abhandlungen zur Lehre von der Elektrizität und dem Magnetismus* (Berlin: Springer, 1890).
14 Nathan F. Sayre, "The Genesis, History, and Limits of Carrying Capacity," *Annals of the Association of American Geographers* 98.1 (2008), https://www.tandfonline.com/doi/abs/10.1080/00045600701734356?src=recsys&journalCode=raag20.
15 See the first three lectures of Michel Foucault, *Security, Territory, Population*, ed. Michel Senellart, trans. Graham Burchell (New York: Picador, 2009).
16 See Aldo Leopold, *Game Management* (Madison: University of Wisconsin Press, 1986), which was originally published in 1933.
17 Sayre, "The Genesis, History, and Limits of Carrying Capacity," 124–25.
18 Alfred Katz and Claus Köhler, *Geldwirtschaft: Geldversorgung und Kreditpolitik* (Berlin: Duncker & Humblot, 1970), 150.
19 Michel Foucault, *The Birth of Biopolitics: Lectures at the Collège de France, 1978–1979*, trans. Graham Burchell (New York: Picador, 2010), 260.
20 For a detailed analysis of the "distribution key" and the convoluted formula used to calculate the legal fate of refugees, see Martin Altemeyer-Bartscher et al., in which the authors also make reference to the "absorbing capacity of the labour market": "On the Distribution of Refugees in the EU," *EU Intereconomics* 51 (2016): 220–28, here 224.
21 "Communication from the Commission to the European Parliament, the Council, the European Economic and Social Committee and the Committee of the Regions: A European Agenda on Migration," *European Commission*, May 13, 2015, https://ec.europa.eu/home-affairs/sites/homeaffairs/files/what-we-do/policies/european-agenda-migration/background-information/docs/communication_on_the_european_agenda_on_migration_en.pdf.
22 Harvey Gavin, "'We Will Decide Who Enters Our Countries!' Hungary and Poland Reject EU Refugee Quotas," Express.co.uk, May 15, 2018, https://www.express.co.uk/pictures/pics/13817/Migrants-Italy-MOAS-Phoenix-vessel-Crotone-Lampedusa-pictures.
23 Prem Kumar Rajaman, "Humanitarianism and Representations of the Refugee," *Journal of Refugee Studies* 15.3 (2002): 247–64. For a critique of humanitarianism that predates 2015 but remains relevant to the ongoing, see Didier Fassin, *Humanitarian Reason: A Moral History of the Present* (Berkeley: University of California Press, 2011).
24 The duration of detention is perniciously unclear for those who are not technically eligible to gain refugee status but also forbidden from returning to their country of origin. "UN Calls Bulgaria's Jailing and Criminalisation of Refugees 'Inhumane,'" *The Independent*, August 11, 2016, http://www.independent.co.uk/news/world/europe/un-bulgaria-refugee-crisis-inhumane-jailing-prosecuting-a7185501.html.
25 Lizzie Dearden, "Police in Paris Are Tear Gassing Homeless Refugees and Stealing Their Blankets," *The Independent*, February 11, 2017, http://www.

independent.co.uk/news/world/europe/refugee-crisis-paris-migrants-france-police-sleeping-bags-blankets-violence-refugee-rights-data-a7575376.html.

26 Matthew Cassel, "Refugees Seeking Asylum in Europe Are Instead Arrested and Beaten by Police in Lesbos," *The Intercept*, August 9, 2017, https://theintercept.com/2017/08/09/asylum-seekers-face-police-violence-lesbos-greece-moria-camp/.

27 Chase Winter, "Hungary Using Starvation Tactics Against Asylum-Seekers," *Deutsch Welle*, August 22, 2018, https://www.dw.com/en/hungary-using-starvation-tactics-against-asylum-seekers/a-45179267.

28 "French Border Police Regularly Abused Refugee Children: Oxfam," *Al Jazeera*, June 15, 2018, https://www.aljazeera.com/news/2018/06/french-border-police-regularly-abused-refugee-children-oxfam-180615095340502.html.

29 Wendy Brown, *Walled States, Waning Sovereignty* (New York: Zone Books, 2017).

30 Testament among many to such symbolic excess and expenditure is the Great Wall of Calais, the "anti-intrusion wall" that was allegedly built to prevent refugees from clandestinely boarding delivery trucks heading toward the UK. It cost 23 million euros to construct and was completed only after French authorities had razed the refugee settlement to the ground. Rob Nixon, *Slow Violence and the Environmentalism of the Poor* (Cambridge, MA: Harvard University Press, 2013), 156.

31 Debarati Sanyal, "Calais's 'Jungle,'" *Representations* 139.1 (August 1, 2017): 1.

32 Walter Benjamin, "Critique of Violence," in *Selected Writings*, vol. 1 (Cambridge, MA: Harvard University Press, 1996), 248. Elsewhere, I have written about Benjamin's theorization of the border as the ur-phenomenon and paradigmatic instantiation of *Rechtgewalt* (legal violence), while drawing out the mythic dimensions of contemporary border violence: "Benjamin on the Border," *Critical Times* 2.2 (Spring 2019): 306–19.

33 Derrida through Benveniste reminds us that hostility is structured by the ambivalence of its Latin derivation. As *hostis* means both "guest" and "enemy," hospitality, Derrida observes, is always lined with the potential for hostility, its violent contradiction. Jacques Derrida and Anne Dufourmantelle, *Of Hospitality*, trans. Rachel Bowlby (Stanford: Stanford University Press, 2000), 45.

34 See the first part of the "Transcendental Aesthetic," in Immanuel Kant, *Critique of Pure Reason*, trans. Paul Guyer and Allen Wood (Cambridge: Cambridge University Press, 1998).

35 See, for instance, the eighth letter of Schiller's *On the Aesthetic Education of Man* (Oxford: Clarendon Press, 1968), in which he defines culture in terms of bringing the "receptive faculty" in varied contact with the world: "The more facets his Receptivity develops, the more labile it is, and the more surface it presents to phenomena, so much more world does man apprehend" (87).

36 Sigmund Freud, *Beyond the Pleasure Principle*, trans. James Strachey, in *The Standard Edition of the Complete Psychological Works of Sigmund Freud*, vol. 18 (New York: Vintage, 2001), 29 (hereafter cited parenthetically as *BPP*); Sigmund Freud, *Jenseits Des Lustprinzips und Andere Arbiter Aus Den Jahren*

1920–1924, in *Gesammelte Werke XIII* (Frankfurt: Fischer Verlag, 1998), 29 (hereafter cited parenthetically as *J*).

37 Soraya Sarhaddi Nelson, "Hungary Reduces Number of Asylum-Seekers It Will Admit to 2 Per Day," NPR, January 3, 2018, https://www.npr.org/sections/parallels/2018/02/03/582800740/hungary-reduces-number-of-asylum-seekers-it-will-admit-to-2-per-day.

38 Chris Baynes, "Donald Trump Says Mexico Border Wall Must Be See-Through to Stop 'Sacks of Drugs' Landing on People's Heads," *Independent*, July 15, 2017, https://www.independent.co.uk/news/world/americas/us-politics/donald-trump-us-mexico-wall-see-through-sacks-of-drugs-landing-on-peoples-heads-a7842416.html.

39 Rudolf Kjellén, *Grundriß zu einem System der Politik* (Leipzig: S. Hirzel Verlag, 1920), 35, quoted in Thomas Lemke, *Biopolitics: An Advanced Introduction* (New York: New York University Press, 2011), 9.

40 Hans Reiter, *Unsere Biopolitik und das Auslandsdeutschtum*, in *Das Reichsgesundheitsamt 1933–1939: Sechs Jahre nationalsozialistische Führung* (Berlin: Julius Springer Verlag, 1939), 38, quoted in Lemke, *Biopolitics*, 12.

PART II
Ethnostates

Shaul Setter

5. The Return to Exile: Critical Shifts in the Age of Neo-Zionism

IN BEN GURION Airport, on the way from the security checkpoint to passport control, a large photographic installation was presented throughout the year 2017. Its topic was "120 years of Zionism." One hundred twenty meters long, it showed photos of central figures in the history of Zionism together with events that manifested the achievements of Jewish sovereignty and the state of Israel. It ended with a broad inscription: "Zionism is an infinite ideal." Significantly, the show was presented on the way to the departing flights, addressing those who were just about to leave the country. It was then formed as an unrefined lesson in state ideology delivered to the citizens: a crash course in national history, concluding with the promise of a never-ending story. But how can Zionism remain endless if in its very core it is a project of attaining state sovereignty—a political project that is meant to end with the formation of a sovereign state, internationally recognized borders, a solid definition of citizenship, and equality before the law? And even if this project hasn't ended yet, due to a state of war, for instance, shouldn't it at least bear the hope for such an end to arrive? What does it mean to understand Zionism as an infinite project—continuous, constant, ceaseless, unachievable or kept from being achieved, with no imaginary end, without an image of an end, a project that has no end—both as its horizon and at its very core?

This self-proclaimed infinite Zionism may be symptomatic of a paradigm shift within national ideology. This endlessness may indeed mark the end of a certain modality of Zionism and the coming to prevalence of a different one, a discursive political turn in need of articulation. At first, it might seem in sync with the teleological temporality of the modern state; the infinite here might sound like the yet-to-come of a potentially infinite, linear project. Yet endlessness as an ideal—"Zionism is an infinite ideal"—not only indicates a potent continuation of that which cannot but be eventually resumed; it also writes out the end from the project, leaving no perceivable endpoint or any final state of affairs to which to aspire. Read together with the Israeli national anthem, it reveals a convoluted temporality: written in eastern Europe in the 1870s, at the very beginning of the Zionist awakening, the song reads as an emotive plight for a future national liberation: "our hope is not yet lost, the hope that is, two thousand years old, to be a free nation in our land." But adopted as the national anthem without any change to its temporal leaning toward a future liberation, it can be read as an expression of melancholy over a liberation unachieved in times of sovereignty. The endless ideal is then not only directed toward the future but already situated in the past, as what should have happened and did not, and so it becomes an assertion of the unattainable, within the infinite time of the not-yet. In political terms, this means that national sovereignty has not been realized and perhaps is unrealizable; or better, its realization is no longer an end in itself. The expectation and then the melancholy are being replaced with exaltation—of the unrealizable.

I call the current hegemonic political formation "Neo-Zionism," opposing it—analytically and historically—to classical Zionism, while aligning it with various authoritarian and right-wing regimes worldwide.[1] The shift to Neo-Zionism did not happen all at once: it clearly had to do with the occupation of the Palestinian Territories in 1967, and even more so with the movement of religious-national Jewish settlement in those territories from the 1970s onward. It also had to do with the introduction of neoliberalism into the Israeli economy in the mid-1980s, with the heyday of the peace process in the 1990s and its utter collapse at the beginning of the 2000s, the second Intifada, the reoccupation of the Palestinian cities in the West Bank, the siege of Gaza and the deadly bombardments of that city every two or three years, and the strengthening of anti-democratic legislation within Israel. Neo-Zionism is thus a paradigm that has been forming for decades now and has arrived at its point of crystallization, through a rapid acceleration, in the last decade. Yet however different Neo-Zionism is from classical, hegemonic Zionism, it is in no way entirely opposed to it; the relations between the two, both intellectual and political, are up for debate. If the former negates the latter, this is definitely not a simple negation but one that holds affinities to what it negates, and whose seeds are to be found in the negated, mediating it in a shift that is historically determined, not a breakage and an introduction of the entirely new. Consequently, the following discussion is not aimed at affirming classical Zionism, cleansing its image in the face of Neo-Zionism, longing for good old nationalism as if it were a lost lover, once happily forsaken and now bitterly lamented, having offered the last option for decent life. On the contrary, I suggest that to hold onto the image of classical Zionism—either as a villain or as a savior, as an object of critique or an object of attachment—is to miss the political and cultural drama of our age and mistake modes of collaboration for modes of critique. Following the premise of this entire volume of essays, in this age of radical-right resurgence, these are the figures and modes of critique we need to look at anew as some of them have been taken into the core of contemporary hegemonic projects. Instead of holding onto the image of a hegemonic project already past or, on the other hand, holding onto the familiar formulas we use to critique it, we need to narrate the transformation in signification of these critical modalities and the different role they play in this new regime. In this essay I examine how Neo-Zionism has been using critical modalities and tropes to structure a different form of nationalism—a post-sovereign ethnonationalism.

The Movement of Desublimation

SINCE ZIONISM HAS been understood as a statist project, much of the critique of Zionism has been the critique of the state.[2] Yet a formative tendency of Neo-Zionism is the weakening of statism, the undermining of state sovereignty in the face of other entities—the market, the land, the ethnos, or the tribe—showing contemporary Zionism to be something other than a state project. Classical Zionism was understood as a quest for Jewish sovereignty, the ingathering of the many diasporic communities in one place governed through self-rule. From the dispersed existence in exile—a return to the historic homeland. The founding book of the movement was Herzl's *The Jewish State* (1896); the Balfour Declaration referred to "the establishment of a national home for the Jewish people." State building, the state as homeland, was a central, unifying, and collectivist project—and one full of contradictions that was hierarchical, with many victims, Arab and Jewish Arab—a state that rules over territory and is defined by a people. Yet in Neo-Zionism the state is weakened and becomes only the means for a larger project. What seemed to be the anomalies of the Israeli state—that after seventy years there are no defined borders, no unified territory, no equal pattern of citizenship; that there is a discrepancy between outside and inside the body politic (Palestinian citizens are, in many ways, outside of the Israeli *polis*, while Jews from around the globe are in many ways already internal to it)—can be seen as the very stable contours of the Neo-Zionist regime. In this regime, borders are not determined, sovereignty is not settled over all of the territory under Israeli rule (including the Palestinian Territories) nor is land divided (between two states), and citizenship is not the key criterion for participation in the public realm—and all of this is not by mistake. The rule of the state is in decline; the homeland is no longer the horizon.

Novelist David Grossman, an eloquent spokesman for classical Zionism, asserted in a reverberating speech on the occasion of the seventieth anniversary of Israel's independence: "Home is a place whose walls—borders—are clear and accepted; whose existence is stable, solid, and relaxed. ... We Israelis, even after 70 years ... are not there yet. We are not yet at home. Israel was established so that the Jewish people, who have never felt at home in the world, would finally have a home. And now, 70 years later, strong Israel may be a fortress, but it is not yet a home."[3] Great expansionist Israel may indeed resemble a crusaders' fortress on the mountain, expanding its territories without declaring clear statist sovereignty over them, rather than a homeland—a national home—with clear borders and a clear distinction between inside and outside. But this does not mean that it is not *yet* a home. Grossman, a liberal Zionist, portrays the way to home as the only way possible: seventy years for the state, and it is still in the process of becoming a national homeland. Even if this way hasn't ended yet, and its goals haven't been met, the direction is clear; there can just not be a different one. But what if there can be, and contemporary politics walk in it for quite a while, so that the efforts to build a home, to constitute a homeland, have not just not ended yet but are never-ending, endless in their core, so much so that a stable homeland, a recognized sovereign state—either as reality or as fantasy—is not on the horizon? What if this then cleared the way for the construction of a chain of fortresses, defending an expanding Jewish existence, always in the frontier, never at home?[4]

There are good reasons why Grossman does not entertain this possibility—or rather raises it only to shatter it at once. The shift from home to fortress entails one of the greatest fears of classical Zionism, since, as David Ohana writes, "the two most daring and heretical assaults on Israeli-Jewish identity, which are umbilically connected to Zionism, are the Canaanite and the crusaders narratives,"[5] that is, the nativist narrative and the colonialist one. Classical Zionism aimed to distinguish itself from each of these: unlike the Canaanites, it did not wish to cut itself off completely from Jewish tradition but rather to mediate and transform it into sovereignty; unlike the crusaders, it insisted it was not a foreign force in the region but rather a national autochthonous project. These were the ideological limits of the classical Zionist imaginary: beyond them lies an abyss. Yet the expansionist and colonial specter that has hovered over the Zionist enterprise from its inception has been materializing, becoming flesh and blood, in recent years. Neo-Zionist politics, actions, and rhetoric alike are replete with neo-Canaanite and neo-crusader tendencies: the valorization of the Land over the state, of territory over sovereignty, of the actual over the symbolic—of the fortress over the home. The fortress is thus not an embryonic version of home, waiting to mature appropriately; nor is it its perverse version yet to be corrected and normalized. The fortress may be an emblem of the current regime—precisely in that it exceeds the home and homeland paradigm.[6]

The Neo-Zionist movement is therefore one of desublimation—in which the "most daring and heretical assaults" on classical Zionism are being actualized. Once the denied gothic doubles of the regime, they have become its representative figures. The formerly hidden—or negated—is now being revealed. The temporary becomes the everlasting: the not-yet, on the way to transformation and a different state, turns now into the always-not-yet and the never-to-be. Its structure is that of a rupture in dialectics: a halt in the progressive movement of mediation, a break in the course of sublimation. If, following Freud, civilization is based on the suppression of the primal instincts—both sexual instincts and destructive ones—in the continual work for mature, productive life, then, as Herbert Marcuse writes, "the main sphere of civilization appears as the sphere of sublimation."[7] As a civilized and civilizing force, eros is separated from the instincts and becomes desexualized. Yet the sexual and aggressive instincts, unbound from eros, would return and haunt this progressive movement and become a destructive force within civilization itself. Thus, what Freud saw as a necessary process—even if eventually tragic and self-destructive—Marcuse analyzed as marking the ideology of bourgeois capitalist society—aimed at the full rationalization of human life, the maximization of production, and the alienation of social relations. He then suggested, from within the Freudian framework, a different transformation of sexuality to eros, a sublimation based not on restriction and suppression but on expansion and development of libidinal relations.[8] But what he saw in the post–World War II societies in the West was the opposite tendency: instead of a widening sexualized sublimation, a repressive desublimation, a release of instinctual energies that does not take part in emancipatory politics and does not have a liberatory horizon but that accompanies the development of a repressive society and a culture of domination.[9] Marcuse saw this as a distinguishing characteristic of late capitalism: the diminution of the prohibiting superego, the weakening of the antagonism between the pleasure principle and the reality principle, the recourse to libidinal bacchanalia—instead of leading to revolutionary politics, all become its horrifying mirror image, and are integrated into an exploitative society. Wendy Brown has recently mobilized this paradigm to understand current authoritarian neoliberal regimes in which the decline of the demanding superego results in a diminishing conscience and an impoverishing of intellectual comprehension—leading to a relapse into nihilism. Desublimated eros does not serve here as an opening to the kind of experience and knowledge that would oppose regulated society; on the contrary, it is coupled with social forms of aggression.[10]

In both accounts, desublimation is understood as a modality within the libidinal economy of the subject. They sketch the psychic procedures that reveal the cessation or even reversal of what Freud saw as the civilizational movement of sublimation. These procedures are historical, rooted in a certain sociopolitical regime—late capitalism, for Marcuse; right-wing authoritarianism, for Brown. And the subject in question is the leader (the alt-right politician), the citizen (the one-dimensional man), an individual in the mob—and even the mob itself in relation to the leader, and perhaps all of the above.[11] These accounts then take what seems in psychoanalysis as a structural tendency in the life of the subject and discuss the historical conditions under which this tendency comes to the fore and changes the developmental course as such—altering the psychic life of an era. My own account of the current movement of desublimation strives to understand this notion also beyond the psychic economy of the subject, in the register of the sign. Desublimation, in that respect, is first and foremost a rupture in the dialectical process, manifest in the countermovement of literalization. The sublimation of the object into a sign, of the literal meaning into the figurative and symbolic one, is reversed and turns into a regression to unmediated, raw matter as the bearer of meaning. Politically, this means that the rule of law as a symbolic system is weakened and that the nation-state as an institution of symbolic mediation between the citizens is in decline. But this does not lead to a release of egalitarian instincts and emancipative tendencies, on the way to radical democracy. On the contrary, the decline of the regulative symbolic systems occurs due to the rise of forces that literalize institutional aggression and privatize state violence. In Israel/Palestine, ethnic superiority—once veiled in a legal system that made efforts to maintain its liberal facade and adherence to international law—is now openly named in a discriminative law, the 2018 Nationality Law. Jewish superiority has been literalized in recent years; it is literally pronounced, manifest, and celebrated. In classical Zionism, as Raef Zreik has recently argued, the distinction between sovereign Israel, where there is a solid Jewish majority, and the occupied Palestinian Territories, presumably only temporarily under Israeli rule, sanctioned Jewish superiority on the basis of Jewish majority in the sovereign Israel. But with the blurring of the distinction between the sovereign and the non-sovereign parts of Great Israel and the solidification of one territorial unit from the Mediterranean Sea to the Jordan River, Jewish superiority is now sanctioned in an openly discriminatory law.[12] This law replaces a pseudo-liberal conception of citizenship, based on the territorial unit of the sovereign state, with an overtly Volkish distribution of rights, based on ethnonational identity. This transformation is made through the regressive movement of desublimation, an annulment of dialectical negation, and the appearance of the unmediated.

Desublimation—a movement of the sign and of the psyche, of culture and of the subject—is theorized structurally, as the undercurrent of any developmental process, but is portrayed historically, through the specific social phenomena that make it pervasive. In the case of Israel, the political transformation is reinforced by a theological one, since Neo-Zionism is constituted through a different relation to Jewish theology. Gershom Scholem famously warned that "God would not remain silent in the language in which he is invoked back a thousandfold into our life"[13]—that the secularization of a sacred language would leave a residue; that Jewish messianic tendencies, introduced into the structure of a modern state, would leave its mark; that the sovereignty of God cannot be substituted with the sovereignty of the state; that the movement of sublimation is destined to explode. This explosion is now happening. Classical Zionism's process of secularization—secularization and not profanation, following Agamben's distinction, that is, not the reversal of religious power but its transformation into a worldly one—has been ruptured, halted, and to a certain extent reversed.[14] If in earlier stages Jewish theology was processed into state ideology, supplying a mythical justification for a Jewish, sovereign, statist, "secular" existence, it is now the state apparatus that paves the way to a perverse form of Jewish realization—very different from traditional forms of Jewish existence—which is at the core of settler praxis. This is what scholar and poet Haviva Pedaya analyses as the collapse of the symbolic register onto the real—the valorization of the land over the text within the settler movement.[15] And so this is not, as many liberal critics of Neo-Zionism have it, a conflict between religious, ethnocentric, particularist, and exceptionalist Jewish values and the secular, universalist, egalitarian, democratic regime but the introduction of a different relation to Jewish theology. The state was never universalist or fully democratic; but it managed to process Jewish particularism into a modernized structure of sovereignty. Now this exceptionalism has exploded from within, without the modern pseudo-liberal state there to sustain it anymore. In other words, Zionism never ran the course of sublimation and turned into a civic democracy with a fully symbolic rule of law and equal formal rights. The movement of desublimation is then not new (it can never be quite new—since it's the reintroduction of the old). But what managed in the past to remain tamed—sometimes balanced by other forces, sometimes just not fully developed and thus more easily ignored—now erupts grandiosely. The contradictory conditions of the Neo-Zionist political regime manifest themselves.

The movement of desublimation expresses itself nowadays quite literally, literality being its operative mode. The official ceremony celebrating Israel's 70th Independence Day, held in Mount Herzl in April 2018, reveals, in lights and images, this transformation—which can be termed a transformation from *Mamlakhtiyut* back to *Mamlakha*. Ben Gurion, the first prime minister of Israel, coined the word *Mamlakhtiyut*, which could be vaguely translated as statehood, to signify the centralized state as the basis for political rule. The word comes from *Mamlakha*, meaning kingdom, and it marks the transformation of Jewish history (the kingdom of Israel and Judea) into the Israeli state—

since in this late national enterprise also, "all significant concepts of the modern theory of the state are secularized theological concepts."[16] Secularization came in the form of psychoanalytic sublimation and has had its pitfalls. Yet one might say that in recent years statehood has been on the way to turning into kingdom once again. The ceremony therefore started with the imaginary transformation of Mount Herzl, where heads of state are buried, into Mount Sinai, where the Tablets were given to the Israelites; from Herzl, the visionary of the state, to Sinai and Moses. The projection of the Ten Commandments on the mountain marks a reversal movement of desymbolization: the constitutive moment of Jewish history is being resurrected, taking the place of the constitutive moment of the state. In the ceremony, this is done through an audiovisual movement of detextualization as a realization in image: contra the biblical *Bilderverbot*, the prohibition on images, the script becomes an image projected on the territory, spread out on the land. The modern state is eliminated, the mediation of the regime is taken away, and a spectacle of fulfilled realization takes place. Neo-Zionism thus reveals its stylistic modality as spectacular Zionism.

From *Mamlakhtiyut* to *Mamlakha*, from statehood to kingdom: this also means a change in the function of the leader vis-à-vis the law. The Schmittian sovereign who is both inside and outside the juridical order, who can suspend the law—as the basic structure of the modern state—has become the sovereign who mocks the law, the state law, who transgresses it joyously, freely, in the very exercise of (non-)sovereignty. The leader takes the position of the prince surrounded by his own court, or a gangster who circles himself with his own gang, loyal and devoted aides who are there to ensure his reign will last. The formal rule of law, the reign of civil servants, the freedom of the press—these all, until recently, formed part of the decorum of liberal regimes, and as such they were the objects of an ideological critique that sought to unveil their regulative power. Nowadays they are being constantly diminished in the face of a leader who does not rule through them but openly renounces them as instruments of the liberal elite that he opposes, of the "deep state," and instead bypasses them in favor of "unregulated" social media. Corruption becomes an integral part of the new form of sovereignty: the leader is elected, and then praised, not despite his corrupt deeds but also thanks to them. In this populist move, popular resentment is mobilized into individual prince-like acts of resistance to state laws or social norms. The leader is the head of state but at the same time holds the aura of being outside of the state—a maverick, a dissident, a victim of state apparatuses. His illegal maneuvers, his constant change of political positions and abrupt decisions, his unprincipled indecency—all depart from the state and undermine statehood while strengthening his political might. The leader's die-hard supporters imagine a Manichaean struggle between him and the "rotten" state apparatus (a Manichaean struggle many liberals also envision, from the other direction), while others are much more ambivalent about this arrogant rhetoric and disruptive behavior and try to find different rationalizations for what is otherwise seen as a tendency to embrace wholesale destruction. Yet this "tearing up the masks" creates a public sphere in which the "rule of law" as a discursive zero-level and the leader as its eloquent subject (in both senses, speaking in its name while being subjected to it) are being constantly challenged, and the state law is often not only backed with but replaced by other—allegedly prior—concerns: national security, racial supremacy, personal outrageous expression (but also, from the other political pole, historic racial or gender justice). These are all expressions of desublimation—a recourse from the letter of the law to what stands behind it.

The desublimated character describes many of the leaders of the new authoritative right-wing regimes—in Russia, Hungary, India, Turkey, the Philippines, and the United States—as well as Netanyahu's Israel. But Neo-Zionist Israel does not just follow in the footsteps of its much more powerful allies. Israel, which was considered in the past the last post of the democratic West before the East—the Arab Orient, the Middle East—the faraway colony of the white man in the frontier (and so, as things happen in the frontier, white but not quite, always in the endless process of Westernization)—becomes now a point of reference, a paradigm, and an example for the West that has itself changed its character. No longer just the aircraft carrier of the United States but a decisive world player that leads in the global war on terror and on the front against Iran, that exports weapons and security systems and knowledge to many parts of the world, that creates a new international axis of post-democratic countries (with Eurosceptic regimes in Europe, Russia, Trump's United States, Saudi Arabia, and the Emirates). No longer the last of the civilized nations—as nations themselves become less and less civilized—but a start-up nation, a neoliberal nationalist superpower, one that combines high-tech industry, driven by military innovations and put into practice in conflict zones, with a withdrawing liberal democratic ethos, shrinking civil liberties, and intensified security control measures. With the movement of desublimation, at the heart of the current stage of Zionism and widespread around the globe, one could see Israel as one possible avant-garde of a post-democratic world.

Exile Regained

NEO-ZIONIST GREAT ISRAEL is less and less bound to the structure of the sovereign state—to its home-like horizon, legal procedures of citizenship, and linear-teleological temporality. As a result, the relationship between the Israeli state and the Jewish diaspora has changed. In classical Zionism, Israel was meant to be a refuge for a people suffering from ongoing persecutions; Jews were supposed to leave the diaspora behind, cut themselves off from exilic existence, and immigrate into the state, where they could live as citizens in a sovereign body politic of their own. With Neo-Zionism, this ideological structure has changed. Great Israel becomes something other than a state defined as a discrete territorial space with recognized borders and a clear distinction between insiders and outsiders. Israel now exists outside its boundaries and is ever expanding—to Jewish settlements in Palestine but also to wherever Jews live in the world. Greater Israel therefore calls for a maximal definition: its frontier can be found in the secluded Jewish settlements just as it can be found in Paris and London, New York and Johannesburg, wherever there are Jews who fiercely defend the Israeli cause and can be considered potential Israelis.[17] As Hilla Dayan has noted, in the last two decades the Jewish diaspora has undergone a process of Israelization, in position-taking as well as in general positionality, in explicit political views as in habitus:[18] Jews around the globe take part in the war against terror, support the further expansion of Israel through the settlement project, defend Israel in its struggle against BDS (the Boycott, Divestment, and Sanctions movement), and proclaim themselves victims of the supposed anti-Semitism of the BDS movement. Moreover, many of these Jews intimately identify with Israel and see themselves as part of it—not as habitants or citizens but as imaginary participants in the body politic of the nation, adopting some of the most representative attributes of mainstream Israeliness—taking after the army soldier and the high-tech entrepreneur. This is by and large the case in Europe—where an anti-Muslim sentiment is mobilized to recruit Jews to the Israeli, anti-Arab cause; and perhaps to a less extent in America, where Zionism among U.S. Jews has also been on the defensive—in an increasingly polarized political atmosphere, where the U.S. and Israeli administrations so deeply align, and progressive Jews find it hard to cling to their "spontaneous" support for Israel. But in both cases, there are no longer structurally antagonistic relations between the Jewish diaspora and Israel—politically and analytically, the one can be intertwined into the other.

This does not only mean that Jewish diasporic existence is nowadays carved in the image of Israeli existence. It also means that Israeli existence becomes more and more diasporic and that the diasporic has become part of contemporary ideology: post-sovereign, tribalistic, neo-nationalist ideology. For that to happen, its significance has had to change quite dramatically since, as Amnon Raz-Krakotzkin claimed in influential articles published in Hebrew at the beginning of the 1990s, it was the negation of exile that served as a structuring element in Zionist ideology.[19] Within Zionist historical consciousness, modern national sovereignty was tied to the ancient biblical times in which the sovereign Kingdoms of Israel and Judea existed, thus leaping over two thousand years of Jewish exile. Exile was perceived as an intermediary period, "a condition of deficient existence, partial and abnormal," in need of correction through "the return to the Land of Israel" (394). This Zionist negation of exile meant not only the occupation of territory and establishment of a sovereign state. It consisted of a complete transformation—psychic, moral, social—from the exilic condition to the sovereign one: from weak, passive, textual, unworldly existence—ascribed to Jewish diasporic life by Christians and Zionists alike—to active, corporal, realized existence. National statist sovereignty demanded the achievement of a sovereign individual and collective subjectivity. Only then could the Jewish people not only return to the land but, in Gershom Scholem's famous words, return to history. The exilic condition was understood as a long historical hiatus—a parenthesis in the linear development of history—and the sovereign condition demanded a turn to the time of nations. This image of history leaned on a Christian conception of time—the linear-teleological temporality aimed at redemption—secularized into progressivist historiography. Within this course of history, Jewish exilic existence had to be negated—to be dialectically negated and internalized into the advanced, sovereign, indeed historical form of the Jewish nation-state. This turn away from an allegedly scattered, limited, non-autonomous exilic existence was then seen as a necessary precondition for an autonomous national life—entailing constituent power and the ability and right to enforce state violence.

It is thus unsurprising that a major tendency in the critique of Zionism was a critique of the negation of exile. This critique sought to negate the negation, insisting on the virtues of Jewish exilic life on its own terms, before it was incorporated into the dialectical course of national history. This negation of the negation showed how Jewish history is formed on the basis of catastrophe—the destruction of the Temple—and takes a different route than the Christian history of redemption or the secularized-national history of realization. But this does not mean it remains outside of history. Rather, as history, such exilic existence is based on primary loss, on an absent center, and on memory reenacted in time. This negation of the negation valorized pre-sovereign, non-statist, collective existence, Jewish communities dispersed among nations and living under foreign rule, and the modes of cohabitation with the people among whom they lived—paradigmatically in Jewish communities in Muslim countries. It introduced a different notion of power, incommensurable with the sovereign force of the state and based on nonviolence, and it portrayed the horizon of non-statist Jewish life as a critique of Zionism. Judith Butler's *Parting Ways* is but one of the last instantiations of such a negation of the negation.[20] It adds to a long critical trajectory in the twentieth century— from George Steiner's "Our Homeland, the Text" and Adorno's characterization of the intellectual as lacking a homeland to Daniel and Jonathan Boyarin's understanding of diaspora, following the ultra-Orthodox anti-Zionist Neturei Karta, or, at the other end of the spectrum, the non-Zionist socialist Bund.[21] In all of its versions—whether liberal-humanist or Jewish-particularist—this reappraisal of exile stood as a critical stance—opposing the exclusivity of the Zionist narrative of Jewish history, refusing the process of Jewish normalization, and rejecting the Israeli state as the locus of redemption.

Yet from the 1990s onward this negation of the negation of exile has gone through a dramatic transformation within Israel. What started as a critical position in Israeli academia with very few social agents has become widespread in the last two decades and penetrated mainstream politics, in quite an astonishing process of osmosis from critical discourse to social and cultural activism and from here to mass media and state politics. At the same time, its oppositional edge has been diminished if not completely eradicated, and it seems to have been internalized by the new hegemonic ideology: whereas classical Zionism was based on the negation of exile, Neo-Zionism sponsors a revaluation of exile. For the centralized state, sublimated in its political rule, liberal in its aspirations, exile signified a threat: it had to have been overcome in order for the sovereign state to exist, and the possibility that it hadn't been quite overcome, that there were still diasporic lacunas—in ultra-Orthodox Jewish communities or in Mizrahi cultural activities—threatened to destabilize the whole project; like Shylock's "pound of flesh," it might interrupt the dialectical movement negating exile, sublating it into sovereignty. But for the expanded, deregulated state, exile is no longer a threat; it has become integral to this state's operation. The diasporic interruption of dialectical movement has become a diasporic impulse within the opposite movement of desublimation. Thus, the undoing of the strong state with its central sovereign power is often portrayed as a corrective to the modernist agenda of classical Zionism, to its collectivist demands and its melting pot ideology—which, in the name of the general will, allowed for the advancement of only the hegemonic (Jewish Ashkenazi) segment of society. The central state apparatus is weakened in the name of heterogeneity and multiplicity; the unified Zionist narrative is broken into various narratives. State law is disobeyed time and again—by individuals, by social groups (including the Jewish settlers in the Palestinian Territories), by the head of state himself, in the name of a different, perhaps higher, law. Modern general education gives way to the teaching of local traditions—not only of localities within Israel but to a greater extent of local Jewish communities prior to their immigration to Israel: the food and clothes, the songs and prayers, the customs and languages of Jewish diasporic communities, specifically those in North Africa—after having been despised and repressed for decades—are now flourishing in the public sphere, in concerts and exhibitions, in television shows and official ceremonies.[22]

This marks a substantial cultural shift and is often surrounded by the aura of subversion, or of opposition to hegemonic ideology: it seems that the critique of modernist, collectivist, state-centered Zionism has prevailed, and the negation of the negation of exile has become pervasive. But this new appreciation of exile entails a sea change in that term's political significance: exile is aligned with contemporary socioeconomic tendency to dismantle the centralized state and break the population into communities of identities; and it does both of these things while reinforcing an ethnonational ethos. Multiple diasporic narratives are now being celebrated at a time when the unified national master-narrative is in decline—and they move with the multidirectional flows of neoliberal reason. This does not mean that they reject national ideology. Their object of attack has been the anti-diasporic centralized nationalism of classical Zionism—and it remains so also in an era when that is no longer the leading ideological formation. Thus, whereas the negation of the negation of exile in its earlier formations took an oppositional stance toward Zionism, advancing egalitarian even if differential, non-nationalist, and anti-territorial values, its present formation is easily co-opted, whether willingly or not, by contemporary Zionism. This negation of the negation fights against the modernist, collectivist, pseudo-liberal Zionism of past generations and can therefore be subsumed by right-wing, populist, neoliberal Zionism. In its former formations, the diasporic position aimed at bringing out the viability of non-nationalist, diasporic Jewish existence as a bridge to a Jewish-Arab cohabitation not based on colonial rule—one that existed in Arab countries before Zionism, and one that can perhaps exist in the future in Israel/Palestine. This position specifically pointed to a connection between the reclaiming of Mizrahi (or Arab Jewish) social and cultural diasporic forms of life—impoverished by mainstream, Ashkenazi national ideology—and the assertion of Palestinian rights and affirmation of Arab culture in Israel. This critique of Eurocentric, liberal Zionism drew a connection between the Mizrahi cause and the Palestinian one, and between the political subalternity of the "Oriental" subjects in Israel and the cultural eradication of their customs, heritage, and language from the public sphere. In the age of Neo-Zionism, this knot has been untied. The recent affirmation of Mizrahi diasporic culture arrives only after the latter has been rendered discrete, having been separated from a radical movement of Mizrahi political emancipation, from Palestinian culture, and most emphatically from the Palestinian politics of liberation. The diasporic turned into a mode expressed only entirely in the cultural field.

Relevant to this analysis is Nancy Fraser's famous distinction between the politics of recognition and the politics of redistribution and her argument about the focus on the politics of recognition—liberal rights, symbolic achievements, status hierarchies—in the Western politics of the last decades.[23] Yet this politics takes an interesting turn here, since the inclusion of formerly marginal social groups in mainstream society and the insistence on difference have been aligned in Israel not only with progressive politics. Difference has been a central trait in the political language reclaiming the diasporic—where it is mobilized against the unifying politics of classical Zionism, allowing the multiple voices of different communities, once repressed and silenced, to be expressed, letting attachments to their places of origin and their customs and habits be explicitly manifest. Yet this is a special form of difference—difference within the Jewish national ethnos, formed as a rejection of pseudo-universalist modern "European values" and ruling out Palestinians as a native community or a diasporic one. This is a non-liberatory difference, and almost entirely symbolic, within a cultural field. This new difference is at the same time postcolonial, since it is based on arguments against the universalist civilizing mission of the Western Ashkenazi elite, and neocolonial, since it is aligned with chauvinist-nationalist values and anti-Palestinian politics. And it makes use of the language of equal opportunities, of strengthening the periphery, of cultural multiplicity, and of social affirmative action—to strengthen the national body politic, going beyond liberal democratic categories of citizenship and the apparatus of the state. In this vein, the recognition in formerly repressed voices and social groups would only be within the ethos and would involve no apparent antagonism to Israeli expansionist politics; the cherished periphery would be found in the frontier of Jewish settlements in Palestine; and multiplicity of traditions would apply to an Jewish-Arab culture already divorced from Arab countries, Arab politics, and Arab subjects.

Three images from the ceremony commemorating Israel's 70th Independence Day can serve as expressions of this move—in which cultural difference is being celebrated as part of the new national ethos, detached from all politically emancipatory impulses. Within the historical narrative portrayed in the ceremony, the scenes shown come just after the giving of the Torah at Mount Sinai. The first image shows the different tribes, populating the biblical land of Israel, Great Israel, on the two banks of the Jordan River (greater than it is today). The second shows a pre-state Jewish school in one of the Arab countries; on the board, the map of Israel is accompanied by the words "the land of Israel" written in Arabic. And the third shows an enormous Menorah, just being lit by an officer in the Israeli army.

Such tribalistic imagery of Jewish history exemplifies the current ideology of tribalistic ethnonationalism. It emerges from an exilic-national nexus meant to sustain the movement of actualization. The twelve tribes—no longer making up a central unified state but instead a multiple and heterogeneous body politic—give shape to Greater Israel in a massive, expansionist manifestation of territoriality. The seven-lamp Menorah, an ancient Jewish symbol, once a sanctuary object in the Temple and later a figure of Jewish diasporic existence, is now portrayed anew, lit and highlighted at the very moment of the

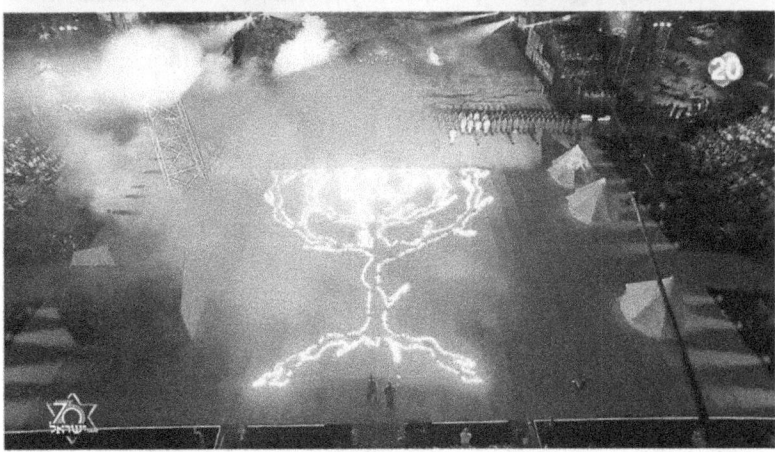

Figs. 10a–c. "The full 2018 Torch-lighting ceremony." YouTube video, 22:12, 27:28, 48:49, April 19, 2018.

ceremony as a national symbol. And the Arab Jew, once a volatile critical category that undid the nationalist antagonism between Arab and Jew, a spectral character haunting the presumably European character of the Israeli state, is here miraculously recovered as part and parcel of a decentralized nationalist agenda. And so in the national ceremony, the most ideological document of all, Jewish diaspora in Arab counties is celebrated, and the Arabic language is invoked, but only to signify that the land of Israel, written in Arabic letters, belongs to the Jewish people. The Arab Jews materialize as they are pitted against the Palestinians—in what turns out to be Arabic without non-Jewish Arabs, without present-day Arabs, without contemporary Arab politics and without any horizon of reconciliation let alone of Palestinian emancipation. Exile thus ceases to be a locus of unrealized potential, an obstacle to normalized existence, and an impulse to imagine a different one. It is the already fulfilled state of dispersed, post-democratic nationalism, an abnormal tendency within hegemonic abnormality: from a critical category formed against exclusive Jewish nationalism, it has turned into a mark of post-sovereign Jewish exceptionalism.

Afterword: Out of History

THE CLASSICAL ZIONIST hope to leave exile behind and return to history has been replaced with an actualized, however distorted, Neo-Zionist return to exile. This form of return reveals the temporal modality of the present moment and the critical challenges it introduces. The modernist "return to history" expressed an aspiration to join the supposedly linear-teleological course of historical development, in which exile was a cipher for a different temporality—that of unlocalized remembrance and circular reenactment.[24] The escape from such temporality and belated admission to history presupposed a project, an intention and progression toward its realization, and a future in which this movement could be fulfilled. It had a direction, it wanted to leave things behind, it carved a horizon. The return to exile is of a different kind. It is a return to the return—to a circular endless movement. But this time it is formed without history in sight, in a world that has lost its own sense of history, that has been robbed of the future. As Franco "Bifo" Berardi has famously stressed, at the beginning of the twenty-first century—after a whole century spent formulating the myth of the future, as the basis of individual life as well as of collective emancipatory action—we have lost hold of the future, which is now over for us.[25] This return to exile occurs then not as a recourse to progressive history but rather as an exemplary instantiation of a global state of realized exile. It is an expression of the new nationalist tendency in the neoliberal era. The Neo-Zionist modus vivendi settles into this "no future"—not subversive nowadays but hegemonic—and carves a new political credo out of its elements: the temporal occupation of the Palestinian lands is de facto eternal; the two-state solution has collapsed and together with it any sense that there might be a "solution"; cultural heterogeneity is co-opted by the market and subsumed under its aegis; and the undoing of formal-official institutions, the undermining of state law, and transgressive-regressive politics have become omnipresent.

This puts a different pressure on critical discourse. Formerly faced with efforts to return to history, the critical task was to show how this teleological path was marked by fissures; how historical fulfillment was haunted by ghosts; how sublimation had its cost and we could always expect the return of the repressed; and how the decisive turn was also a circular, endless return. But now, when this critical task has been devilishly successful, and the objects of such critique—historical time, the liberal project, the state apparatuses and formal civil rights—are collapsing, the call for its retooling is urgent. Some politely ignore this call and continue to hold to the orthodoxy of critique, enjoying the aura of subversion while supporting, whether knowingly or not, the new regime. Others engage the current state of affairs through recourse to a lesser evil, trying to rehabilitate the former object of critical endeavor—liberal politics or state-sanctioned citizenship—in a nostalgic move that has little validity in social reality. But the more interesting responses are two opposite ones: the resurgence of a strong universalist claim—for radical democracy or for a socialist transformation—which, in times of desublimation and exilic realization, insists on a sovereign, all-encompassing, grown-up position; and, on the other hand, being swept away in a contemporary bacchanalia, abiding by its course and allowing it to be fully realized, while messianically waiting for an inversion to happen, recovering sparks from the husks, generating redemption through sin.

Notes

1   The term "Neo-Zionism" has had, by now, a long career and a wide range of signification—indicating, in Tom Segev, *Elvis in Jerusalem: Post-Zionism and the Americanization of Israel* (New York: Metropolitan Books/Henry Holt), the influence of a U.S.-leaning globalization on Zionism, and, in Ilan Pappé,

The Idea of Israel: A History of Power and Knowledge (New York: Verso, 2014), the new nationalistic tendencies. The most comprehensive account is to be found in Hilla Dayan, "Neozionism: Portrait of a Contemporary Hegemony," *Settler Colonial Studies* 9.1 (2018): 22–40, where she addresses Neo-Zionism as a hegemonic project that has managed, from the 2000s onward, to bridge classical Zionist approach and the accelerated privatization processes—in a neoliberal Zionist order.

2   See, for example, Oren Yiftachel, *Ethnocracy: Land and Identity Politics in Israel/Palestine* (Philadelphia: University of Pennsylvania Press, 2006); Ariella Azoulay and Adi Ophir, *The One-State Condition: Occupation and Democracy in Israel/Palestine* (Stanford: Stanford University Press, 2012); Jacqueline Rose, *The Question of Zion* (Princeton: Princeton University Press, 2007); and Judith Butler, *Parting Ways: Jewishness and the Critique of Zionism* (New York: Columbia University Press, 2013).

3   David Grossman, "Israel Is a Fortress, but Not Yet a Home," *Haaretz*, April 18, 2018, https://www.haaretz.com/israel-news/2018-04-18/ty-article/full-text-speech-by-david-grossman-at-alternative-memorial-day-event/0000017f-e98a-dea7-adff-f9fb41180000.

4   On the concept of home—specifically from the perspective of the Hebrew language, in which the same word signifies home, house, and household and connotes the national homeland—see Hagar Kotef, "Ba'it" (Home/Household), *Mafteakh* 1e (2010): 1–22.

5   David Ohana, *The Origins of Israeli Mythology: Neither Canaanites nor Crusaders* (Cambridge: Cambridge University Press, 2012), 1.

6   And see David Ohana's more recent book, in which he examines the neo-Canaanite and neo-crusader tendencies in contemporary Israel: *A Land of Stones* (Tel Aviv: Hakibbutz Hameuchad, 2017).

7   Herbert Marcuse, *Eros and Civilization: A Philosophical Inquiry into Freud* (New York: Routledge, 2005), 83.

8   Ibid., 211–12.

9   Herbert Marcuse, *The One-Dimensional Man* (New York: Routledge, 2002), 75–77.

10 Wendy Brown, "Neoliberalism's Frankenstein: Authoritarian Freedom in Twenty-First Century 'Democracies,'" *Critical Times* 1.1 (2018): 60–79.

11 This last option is the object of Freud's analysis in his *Group Psychology and the Analysis of the Ego* (New York: W. W. Norton, 1949).

12 Raef Zreik, "The New Governmental Discourse of the Settler Right," *Hazman Haze*, April 2019, https://hazmanhazeh.org.il/zreik/.

13 Gershom Scholem, "Confession on the Subject of Our Language," in Jacques Derrida, *Acts of Religion*, ed. Gil Anidjar (New York: Routledge, 2002), 226–27. And see Derrida's reading of this letter, "The Eyes of Language: The Abyss and the Volcano," focusing on the undecidable locus of this explosion.

14 Giorgio Agamben, "In Praise of Profanation," in *Profanations*, trans. Jeff Fort (Brooklyn, NY: Zone Books, 2007), 73–92.

15 Haviva Pedaya, *Space and Place: An Essay on the Theological and Political Unconscious* (Tel Aviv: Hakibbutz Hameuchad, 2011).

16 Carl Schmitt, *Political Theology: Four Chapters on the Concept of Sovereignty*, trans. George Schwab (Cambridge, MA: MIT Press, 1985), 36.

17 At the same time, the definition of the Jew has been expanding. A governmental committee recently published a report declaring that some sixty million people worldwide have an affinity to Judaism or to Israel, and suggesting ways to make good use of them for Israeli interests—that is, for propaganda. See Sue Surkes, "Ministry: Israel Should Woo 60 Million People Who Have Jewish Links to Aid State," *Times of Israel*, March 28, 2018, https://www.timesofisrael.com/60-million-people-with-affinity-to-israel-should-be-tapped-ministry-report/.

18 Dayan, "Neozionism: Portrait of a Contemporary Hegemony."

19 Amnon Raz-Krakotzkin, "Exile Within Sovereignty," *Theoria u-vikoert* 4 and 5 (1993, 1994) [in Hebrew]. These articles were translated into English only lately: "Exile Within Sovereignty: Critique of 'The Negation of Exile' in Israeli Culture," in *The Scaffolding of Sovereignty*, ed. Zvi Ben-Dor Benite, Stefanos Geroulanos, and Nicole Jer (New York: Columbia University Press, 2017), 393–420.

20 In her book, Butler formulates exile as a counterprinciple to Zionism and nationalist chauvinism—and as a path to egalitarian cohabitation. "I am writing this book to understand how the exilic or the diasporic is built into the idea of the Jewish, not analytically but historically, that is over time. In this sense, to be a Jew is to be departing from oneself, to be cast out in a world of non-Jews, within a world of irreversible heterogeneity" (*Parting Ways*, 15).

21 Daniel Boyarin and Jonathan Boyarin, "Diaspora: Generation and the Ground of Jewish Identity," *Critical Inquiry* 19 (Summer 1993): 693–725. In the Hebrew version of this article, the last section is titled "Toward a Diasporic (Multicultural) Israel," and there they write: "We argue that an Israel that re-imports a diasporic consciousness, that of a Jewish community that shares its living space with others and is free of ruling power, is the only Israel that can answer Paul, Lyotard, and Nancy's calls for care for the entire human race, without having to cut off cultural difference." Daniel Boyarin and Jonathan Boyarin, "No Homeland for Israel," *Teorya u-vikoret* 5 (1994): 100–101.

22 On the flourishing of the diasporic elements of the largest North African community in Israel, see Orit Ouaknine Yekutieli and Yigal Shalom Nizri, "'My Heart Is in the Maghrib': Aspects of the Cultural Revival of the Moroccan Diaspora in Israel," *Hesperis-Tamuda* 51.3 (2016): 165–92.

23 Nancy Fraser and Axel Honneth, *Redistribution or Recognition?: A Political-Philosophical Debate* (New York: Verso, 2003); Nancy Fraser, *The Old Is Dying and the New Cannot Be Born* (New York: Verso, 2019).

24 On Jewish remembrance standing in opposition to historiography, see Yosef Hayim Yerushalmi, *Zakhor: Jewish History and Jewish Memory* (Seattle: University of Washington Press, 1996).

25 Franco "Bifo" Berardi, *After the Future*, trans. Arianna Bove et al., ed. Gary Genosko and Nicholas Thoburn (Baltimore: AK Press, 2011).

Melinda Cooper

6. The Alt-Right: From Libertarianism to Paleolibertarianism and Beyond

FEW THINKERS HAVE had a more profound influence on the American alt-right than the libertarian Murray Rothbard. Paul Gottfried, the paleoconservative scholar who is credited with coining the term "alternative right," counted Rothbard as a close friend and enduring influence on his thinking.[1] Richard Spencer, founder of the *Alternative Right* website, cut his teeth on Rothbard's screeds against central banking and was once an enthusiastic supporter of Ron Paul.[2] Mike Enoch (Peinovich), the creator of the infamous *Daily Shoah* podcast, embarked on his journey towards the alt-right by imbibing the work of Ayn Rand, Murray Rothbard, and Ludwig von Mises.[3] As *Counter-Currents'* Gregory Hood remarks, for many on the alt-right, libertarianism is a "gateway drug."[4] Wherever they have ended up, almost every leading figure on the alt-right started out as an acolyte of Murray Rothbard.

Yet just a few years ago, Rothbard might have seemed an unlikely candidate for such posthumous fame. Throughout his lifetime, Rothbard remained faithful not only to Austrian economics, the most marginal of currents in American neoliberalism, but also to the most abstruse and unfashionable of methods within this current, the deductive apriorism of Ludwig von Mises.[5] A trained mathematician, Rothbard was nevertheless convinced by his mentor that mathematical models and statistical evidence were irrelevant to economic reasoning and developed, instead, an intricate, almost scholastic philosophy of market exchange, which derived economic freedom and property rights from natural law. From this foundation, he built up an uncompromising and (in the eyes of many) unrealistic vision of libertarian politics, which would tolerate nothing less than the complete dismantling of the state, the abolition of central banking, and the return to so-called honest money, that is, the commodity-money of gold and silver.

Rothbard's American references were no less arcane. Just as the American right was turning decisively in favor of Cold War militarism, Rothbard chose to align himself with a now largely forgotten group of early twentieth-century libertarians who had opposed the foreign interventionism of leaders such as Woodrow Wilson and decried the inexorable buildup of the administrative state under the influence of the Progressive movement.[6] Not only were these "old right" libertarians viscerally hostile to the New Deal, they wished to repeal both the Federal Reserve Act, which had established the United States' first central bank, and the Sixteenth Amendment, which authorized the federal government to collect income tax. In their eyes, all taxation was theft and any attempt by government to manage the money supply was a ruse to confiscate the public's savings through the dark arts of inflation. After World War II, these anti-progressive isolationists retreated to the margins, as Cold War paranoia and big-state militarism became the dominant position on the American right. Rothbard was one of the few to remain true to the cause.

From this vantage point of self-imposed exile, Rothbard developed a relentlessly paranoid theory of power that saw the state as the instigator of all violence and the market as a space of perfectly consensual relations, where violence is only ever legitimately exercised in defense of my person and property.[7] Rothbard imagines the primitive world of market exchange is one in which all property is freely acquired, hence sanctioned by natural law, and money is always honest, a transparent veil through which the solidities of precious metal can be lucidly discerned. From his Austrian mentors Ludwig von Mises and Carl Menger, he inherits the idea that the subjective determination of value—a key insight of the marginal counterrevolution to which Menger contributed—must nevertheless be counterbalanced by the absolute stability of the money-token. As the most primitive medium of exchange and a token whose origins appear to lie entirely outside of the state, commodity money plays an exemplary role in Rothbard's vision of the free market, guaranteeing the honesty of transactions and the justice of any given distribution of wealth.[8] As long as it is firmly anchored in the scarce commodities of gold and silver, money can't help but express the real, underlying value of economic relations and so can never distort the natural distribution of wealth and income that prevails under pure free-market conditions. The sheer hard work of discovering and mining new reserves keeps money honest, always tethered to its telluric origins in precious metal and always constrained by the law of scarcity.

The state, by contrast, is incapable of producing anything of real economic value and always tempted to distort the legitimate distribution of wealth ordained by the market's primitive state of nature. Despite his obvious debt to Locke's theory of natural rights, Rothbard is adamant that the state was born of a violent act of dispossession, not a peaceable social contract, and so can only sustain its existence through the continuous theft of other people's property.[9] The state is thus an essentially parasitic institution that feeds off the productive labor of others and transfers its misbegotten gains to its various dependents: the businesses that live off state monopolies and subsidies, the trade unions, and the non-productive welfare class.[10] Taxation is the most obvious form of appropriation exercised by the state; indeed, Rothbard follows the nineteenth-century Southern senator John C. Calhoun in claiming that the dividing line between tax producers and tax consumers is the first and only salient class distinction.[11] But far more dangerous, he believes, because less visible to the public, is the method of inflation, a form of taxation by stealth which subtly redistributes wealth and income from creditors to debtors and from savers to consumers, thereby upsetting the natural distribution of property that prevails in the state of nature.[12] Honest money is the guarantee of natural inequality and its inevitable reflection in the unequal distribution of wealth and income. But this spontaneous order of distribution is always threatened by the ability of the state to seize control of money creation and divorce it from the underlying value of precious metal. Unleashed from the discipline of hard money, the state is all too easily tempted to live beyond its means and to fund itself through the extortionary instruments of public borrowing, always ultimately paid for in taxes, and the inflation of the money supply, a monetary sleight of hand that completely reshuffles the distribution of income, turning natural winners into losers and vice versa.[13]

Few of the innovations of modern banking escape Rothbard's suspicion. From legal tender laws to paper money and fractional reserve banking, Rothbard perceives any departure from the pure gold standard as a descent into fraudulence and legalized counterfeiting.[14] But his paranoia is extreme when it comes to central banking, an institution, he is convinced, that was created with the sole aim of inflating the money supply and defrauding producers and savers of their hard-earned wealth. In his voluminous writings on money and banking, Rothbard imbues the Federal Reserve with all the malign powers of action-at-a-distance that far-right conspiracy theorists more often ascribe to international financiers and the Jews. The Fed, he writes, is "by far the most secret and least accountable operation of the federal government," far more secretive than the CIA or any other intelligence organization.[15] Where money in its primitive state is all transparency and honesty, a mere veil through which the solidities of precious metal can be clearly discerned, the Federal Reserve's money-issuing operations are shrouded in mystery, its behind-the-scenes machinations deliberately concealed from the eyes of an unwitting public. If "the public knew what was going on, if it was able to rip open the curtain covering the inscrutable Wizard of Oz," Rothbard intones, "it would soon discover that the Fed, far from being the solution to the problem of inflation, is itself the heart and cause of the problem."[16] The accusation strains credulity given that central banks have spent the last half century attempting to suppress inflation, whatever the political costs to incumbent leaders. Yet Rothbard remains steadfast in his conviction that the Federal Reserve is an immense "socialist" machine for inflating the money supply and thus engineering a "criminal" redistribution of wealth from deserving producers and creditors to undeserving consumers and debtors.[17] Together, inflation and progressive taxation are the leading instruments through which the modern fiscal state feeds off the hard work of unwitting citizens, draining the producers of their lifeblood and transfusing it into the veins of a parasitic welfare class.

Having established the essential criminality of its methods, Rothbard will settle for nothing less than total insurrection against the state. His absolutist (and to many on the right, near treasonous) opposition to American imperial power led him to form a tactical alliance with the New Left in the 1960s, with whom he shared the minimal desire to "smash the state."[18] But whereas Rothbard's Marxist and anarchist allies saw the state as inextricably tied to capitalism and nurtured an ideal of egalitarian and collectivist social relations against the state, Rothbard opposed the state because it disrupted the free market, which he saw as a source of natural inequalities. Rothbard's relationship with the New Left reached a breaking point in the early 1970s when he explained that inequality was not only natural but ethical because it reflected the biological variation in individuals' ability to produce wealth (as perfect a fusion of meritocratic and determinist arguments as one could find).[19] "The great fact of individual difference and variability (that is, inequality)," he insists, "is evident from the long record of human experience. ... Socially and economically, this variability manifests itself in the universal division of labor, and in the 'Iron Law of Oligarchy'—the insight that, in every organization or activity, a few ... will end up as leaders, with the mass of the membership filling the ranks of the followers. In both cases, the same phenomenon is at work—outstanding success of leadership in any given activity is attained by what Jefferson called a 'natural aristocracy'—those who are best attuned to that activity."[20] As enthused as he was by the New Left's animus against the state, Rothbard had nothing but scorn for their sentimental egalitarianism.

Rothbard is similarly contemptuous of the Chicago and Virginia school neoliberals who preach market freedom but inexplicably lose courage when it comes to the state's most vital functions: control of the money supply, security, and the law.[21] In lieu of Friedman's monetarist rule instructing the central bank to curb inflation, Rothbard calls for pure and simple abolition of the Federal Reserve and a return to a 100 percent metallic standard, with silver and gold coins minted to strict weight requirements and all notes backed by equivalent warehouse reserves of precious metal.[22] Only such an extreme measure, he believes, will prevent the state from resorting to counterfeit and fraud. But Rothbard goes one step further still—further than most libertarians even—in calling for the complete privatization of defense and police forces, to be supplanted by mercenaries and militia, and the replacement of the legal system by privately contracted law courts.[23]

Rothbard's preferred strategy vis-à-vis state power is one of radical secession. Here again he invokes the work of John C. Calhoun, who relentlessly championed the right of Southern states to secede from the union and thus escape the unjust tax burdens imposed by the North. But why stop short at the state, Rothbard asks? Why not push the strategy of secession to the limit and grant every municipality, neighborhood, school, church, family, and indeed individual the right to defect from government rule?[24] This is not simply a pacifist solution, since Rothbard simultaneously recognizes that the state has transgressed on the natural rights of individuals and has therefore triggered the right of every individual to arm himself in self-defense. Indeed, Rothbard's thought process seems to lead to the logical conclusion that productive citizens should take up arms not only against the state but also against the many parasites who feed off the largesse of the state—the non-producers and the welfare recipients. For aren't they the inheritors of the special privileges and unearned income once reserved for the feudal elite?[25]

It is impossible to read Rothbard's reflections on anti-state violence without being aware of the relentless identification between state parasitism, black welfare queens, and undocumented migrants in right-wing American political discourse. And is difficult to read his repeated invocations of John C. Calhoun without also hearing the states' rights and white supremacist arguments that Calhoun's name has so often justified. The studiously neutral language Rothbard uses to denounce the state doesn't make the threat less legible or menacing. Yet remarkably, in his earlier work, Rothbard does stop short of translating his indictment of the welfare state into a call for racial terrorism and instead calls for a rigorous questioning of the economic status quo, to determine whether the origins of any given property title are legitimate or not. Rothbard is so conscientious in his pursuit of this task that he goes so far as to call for a restitution of American Indian lands to their original owners and reparations for the heirs of former slaves.[26] In much of his early work, in fact, Rothbard appears to be torn between the idea that libertarian principles should apply universally—independently of gender, race, and class—and the belief that the unequal distribution of wealth and income is ordained by natural law. This tension leads him to affirm on the one hand, that libertarianism must break with all inherited privileges and all hierarchies of social status,[27] and on the other, to assert with equal conviction that "inequality ... is rooted in the biological nature of man" and hence (one must assume) inheritable.[28] The contradiction is flagrant. Does the acquisition of wealth cease to be illegitimate when it is authorized by a biological rather than a political order of privilege and heredity? Isn't Jefferson's natural aristocracy simply another way of defending established hierarchies of wealth and status, on biological rather than political grounds?[29] Rothbard simply transfers the privileges of inheritance from the political to the biological realm. But arguably the contradiction is at work in all philosophies of the free market that claim to reconcile property and meritocracy while at the same time upholding the sanctity of inheritance. (Rothbard attempts to resolve *this* particular contradiction by defending inheritance in terms of the freedom to bequeath rather than the unearned privilege of the heir).[30] But it takes on a peculiar intensity in the work of someone like Rothbard who is otherwise so unforgiving of any departure from the principle of economic freedom.

The stubbornness of this contradiction—its insolubility within the terms of economic libertarianism—no doubt accounts for the extreme flightiness of Rothbard's alliances, which saw him career back and forth across the political spectrum, from the traditionalist new right of William F. Buckley's *National Review* in the 1950s, to the anti-war countercultural New Left in the 1960s and 1970s, and back to the paleoconservative far right in the 1990s. When Rothbard distanced himself from the *National Review* in the late 1950s it was not only on account of their imperialist and nationalist tendencies (all nationalism representing a deference to state power, in Rothbard's eyes) but also because of their obsession with "the preservation of tradition."[31] It was under the influence of the New Left that Rothbard wrote his most excoriating denunciations of American state power, extending his sights from America's imperial ventures and war crimes in Southeast Asia to the state's violations of civic freedom at home—from the war on drugs to censorship laws and the criminalization of abortion. But as Rothbard moved on to a new institutional home, the Koch-funded Cato Institute, in 1977, he became less tolerant of his erstwhile friends on the New Left and began to look askance too at the free-market cultural libertarians who were being courted by the Cato Institute and Libertarian Party.[32] After being fired from the Cato Institute in 1981, and welcomed into the Ludwig von Mises Institute by his long-time friend, the traditionalist libertarian Llewellyn H. (Lew) Rockwell Jr., Rothbard swung decisively to the right and over the following years dedicated countless articles to attacking the positions of his former allies.[33]

The fact that these allies were guilty of professing many of the same opinions that Rothbard himself had once defended was irrelevant. Absolutism was Rothbard's one constant. The same Rothbard who had decried the mindless traditionalism of Buckley's *National Review* and saw libertarianism as hostile to all forms of cultural conservatism was now advising his fellow libertarians not to assume that "individuals are only bound to each other by the nexus of market exchange" since "everyone is necessarily born into a family, a language, and a culture" with its specific "traditions" and customs.[34] And the same Rothbard who had railed against the Cato Institute's ambivalence on the question of free migration would soon be convinced that economic freedom required strong borders.[35]

Tellingly, Rothbard's take on the right to self-defense now descended into outright racism. In a 1994 review of Charles Murray and Richard Herrnstein's book *The Bell Curve*, Rothbard notes approvingly that the authors' "recognition of inheritance and natural inequalities among races as well as among individuals knocks the props out from under the welfare state system."[36] The apparent inequities of our economic status quo are not the result of historical injustices but of the natural inferiority of certain races. Any attempt to redress this inequality amounts to a criminal extortion of fairly acquired wealth by the state. The productive citizen therefore has every right to strike back in self-defense, not only against the state but also its dependents. The "racialist science is properly not an act of aggression or a cover for oppression of one group over another, but, on the contrary, an operation in defence of private property against assaults by aggressors."[37]

Paleolibertarianism

BEGINNING IN THE early 1990s, Rothbard and Rockwell joined forces to call for a new alliance between libertarians and paleoconservatives, in the hopes that this fusion would be vindicated by Patrick J. Buchanan's campaign for the Republican Party presidential nomination. The hybrid term "paleolibertarianism" was first coined by Lew Rockwell in 1990, in an article calling on free-market radicals to cast off their countercultural friends and retrieve an "older," more culturally conservative libertarianism.[38] The term "paleoconservatism" was itself a neologism—it referred to a splinter movement on the American right that had gained self-consciousness in opposition to the rising fortunes of the neoconservatives in the 1980s and, in the process, projected itself backward into an imagined prehistory of American conservatism.[39] Gathered together around the magazine *Chronicles*, the self-identified paleoconservatives saw themselves as the defenders of an older, more authentic right, one that they variously identified with the protectionist nationalism of the nineteenth-century Republican Party or the antebellum nostalgia of Southern Democrats.

This they contrasted with the relative progressivism of the neoconservatives, who in their eyes had made far too many concessions to the victories of the left to call themselves true conservatives.[40] As sons and daughters of Jewish and Irish immigrants, the neoconservatives had no problem with the melting pot of American multiculturalism and saw the civil rights movement (but not black power or affirmative action) as necessary steps toward American progress. Their critique of the welfare state as an agent of moral decadence was welcome but insufficiently attuned to the specific racial grievances of the South. Their commitment to democracy was internationalist and increasingly belligerent: as the paleocons rightly sensed, the alliance between Israel and the United States would commit the United States to reckless imperialist wars long after the fall of the Berlin Wall and the natural death of anticommunism.[41] The paleoconservatives, by contrast, were obsessively insular.[42] At the national level, they called for a stricter imposition of border controls, stronger trade protections, and military isolationism. At the state and local level, they readily retreated into paranoid self-defense mode, convinced that their right to cultural difference was under permanent threat of attack from a meddling federal government.

Unceremoniously brushed aside by the neoconservative modernizers, shunned even by the more hard-line exponents of the postwar new right represented by William F. Buckley and the *National Review*, the paleoconservatives tended to their wounds as outsiders and extremists. Their sense of group identity was based on a history of slights: their members had been expelled from the *National Review*, shafted by the neoconservatives during the Reagan presidency, uniformly ejected from polite society.[43] "Conservatism," they argued, was too quiescent a word to capture the full force of their ambition.[44] More than simple conservatives, the paleocons were reactionaries and revolutionaries: their willful archaism a spur to grand insurrectionist fantasies against the overbearing power of the state. This was bound to be congenial to the notoriously contrarian Murray Rothbard, who had been expelled from almost every organization he took part in, from the *National Review* to Ayn Rand's inner circle and the Cato Institute, and who nursed similar fears of persecution at the hands of the state.

By his own admission, Patrick J. Buchanan was more of a paleoconservative than a libertarian. But Rothbard and Rockwell hoped that the connection between the two movements would prove adhesive enough to form a durable alternative to the neoconservative-neoliberal alliance that had come to dominate the Republican Party in the 1980s. The alliance signaled a move to the extremes on both sides. The libertarianism of Murray Rothbard and Ron Paul was much more vehement in its distrust of the state than any of the neoliberal ideologies that were then influential in the Republican Party (monetarism, supply side economics, and public choice theory), while the paleoconservatives stood at the far edge of the American right, deeply entrenched in the white supremacist and Christian reconstructionist traditions that neoconservatism had always eschewed.

The fusion between the two movements was by no means self-evident and, as Rothbard himself acknowledged, required more concessions on the part of libertarians than paleoconservatives. For the alliance to stick, libertarians needed to abandon the belief that economic freedom could be straightforwardly translated into cultural freedom and that cultural freedom applied to all, men and women, whites and blacks. Specifically, libertarians would have to give up their support for abortion rights, homosexuality, and any notion of equal freedom among races.[45] They also needed to abandon their commitment to the free movement of peoples. This was a position that was already familiar to Lew Rockwell, who had long occupied the borderlands between traditionalism and libertarianism, and who is credited with ghostwriting a series of viciously racist, misogynist, and homophobic texts for Ron Paul during the 1980s.[46] But it was a new stance for Rothbard, who embraced it with all the zeal of the recent convert.

The paleoconservatives saw themselves as the political heirs to the Southern Agrarians, the writers and literary critics who infamously "took a stand" on behalf of Southern states' rights in the 1930s and went on to flirt with European fascism.[47] Like their forefathers, the paleoconservatives romanticized the pre–Civil War South, which they perceived through the mists of European feudalism, and lamented the loss of benevolent hierarchies in public and private life. In 1981, fifty years after the publication of the manifesto *I'll Take My Stand*, the paleoconservatives came together in a collective volume to reflect on the continuing relevance of the Southern Agrarians to American political life. Here they reiterated their forefathers' sense that the American South—with its "difference and intransigence"—had "something to say to a troubled nation" and something unique to offer the Western conservative tradition as a whole.[48] The "social fragmentation and demoralization that the Agrarians sought to combat" had "become much more evident and menacing" since the manifesto was first published.[49] But almost alone among American regions, the American South had "retained an unselfconscious relationship with some of the ancient values of Western civilization that [were] increasingly attenuated elsewhere" and so offered a beacon of hope to cultural conservatives throughout the United States and Western world.[50]

The contributors to this volume included several leading academics from the University of South Carolina. Thomas Fleming, a traditionalist Catholic who blamed racial desegregation and secularism for the loss of American community; Clyde N. Wilson, editor of the collected works of John C. Calhoun, the nineteenth-century Southern senator who has long served as an intellectual figurehead to the states' rights and white supremacist movements; and the writer Samuel T. Francis, one of the most important disseminators of paleoconservative ideas. Each of these was involved with the *Southern Partisan*, a journal that espoused a revisionist history of the Civil War (tax burdens rather than slavery, it was alleged, were the true source of conflict between North and South) and defended white Southerners in civilizational terms as a distinct ethnos whose traditions and customs had been subject to a form of "cultural genocide."[51] *Southern Partisan* laid the intellectual foundations for the so-called neo-confederate movement in the 1980s, which called on all states and local communities to follow the example of the South in seeking an exit route from the overbearing weight of the federal government and Supreme Court.[52] Appealing to Calhoun, the paleoconservatives argued for the continuing legality of the doctrines of nullification and secession: the idea, that is, that any state has the right to invalidate federal law it considers unconstitutional and to separate from the union on those grounds. If they would only avail themselves of these dormant constitutional arms, urged the paleoconservatives, local governments, communities, and ultimately families would be free to practice segregation without punishment from the state; free also to run their own institutions, in keeping with traditionalist Christian rules of morality and gender difference; and free to defend themselves from both unwanted outsiders and the federal government.

Along with libertarianism, the neo-confederate movement has served as a powerful source of inspiration for the many experiments in far-right institution-building that proliferate in the United States today: the white supremacist enclave, the home school, and the private militia.[53] This, if nothing else, is the glue that unites libertarians and paleoconservatives: so convinced are they of the fraudulence of state power that they are willing to bear arms *against the state* if it threatens their independence in any way. Indeed, they are persuaded that the government is secretly intent on waging warfare against *them*—a conviction that gained widespread currency in the 1990s, when local and state law enforcement agencies inherited surplus military equipment from the federal government and undertook a number of disastrous counterinsurgency operations against non-law-abiding white citizens.[54] Both movements are fascinated with the possibilities of decentralized institution-building—the creation of militias, private law courts, and home-schooled families that will resist the overbearing power of the federal bureaucracy.[55] Together they define a style of militancy that turns treason into virtue: a permanent readiness for civil war that takes the old South's resistance to the North as a general model for resistance on both the local and national scale. But while libertarians define their resistance in purely negative terms—as simple freedom from the state—and sometimes extend this right to freedom into the realm of gender and race relations, for paleoconservatives, freedom from the state is only a necessary prelude to building new forms of unfreedom in the private sphere. This was the tension that had to be resolved before libertarians and paleoconservatives could forge a durable alliance.

For Rothbard and Rockwell, the alliance between paleoconservatives and libertarians made sense on both strategic and logical grounds. Rockwell complained that radical economic libertarians such as those organized around the Libertarian Party had condemned themselves to political insignificance by ignoring the instinctive cultural conservatism of Middle America. By confusing economic with sexual libertarianism, the countercultural wing of the Libertarian Party had alienated the great mass of Americans who could have been natural allies, so instinctively distrustful were they of the state.[56] Rothbard, for his part, castigated the libertarians for their strategic tone-deafness when it came to public communications. Although they "have often seen the problem plainly," he observed, "as strategists for social change they have often missed the beat."[57] Although Rothbard himself had been a staunch advocate of Leninist avant-gardism during his time at the Cato Institute, he now accused his former colleagues of investing too much faith in the Hayekian credo that political change could best be fomented from above by a select cadre of intellectuals and militants.[58] This had left the libertarians without a people to reach out to, and too readily associated with the very elites they should be condemning. The solution must be "to tap the masses directly, to short-circuit the dominant media and intellectual elites, to rouse the masses of people against the elites that are looting them"[59] and the parasitic underclasses they were playing host to. The solution, in short, was right-wing populism. But since any populism must single out some group to stand in as the true representative of the "people," Rothbard immediately adds the proviso: "we must concentrate strategically on those groups who are most oppressed and who also have the most social leverage."⁶⁰ In other words, what was needed was not only objective grievance but also relative privilege: to be aggrieved was too mundane and democratic a condition to ignite a far-right populism; what was also required was the specific conviction among the aggrieved that they had been dispossessed of something that was once rightfully theirs. The Koch brother libertarians of the Cato Institute had made the fatal mistake of catering to the educated and well-to-do whites—constituencies who cherished their freedom from state interference but were too upwardly mobile to feel any acute sense of resentment against the state and its alleged beneficiaries. The paleolibertarians, by contrast, would reach out to the "rednecks"[61]—the white working and lower-middle classes whose experience of economic uncertainty and lost privilege had made them suitably "disgruntled" and the most "likely to nurse a deep grievance against the State."[62]

But beyond these strategic concerns, the alliance between paleoconservatives and free-market radicals also promised to resolve some of the logical inconsistencies that plagued the pure economic libertarianism of Rothbard's early work. As noted by Rockwell, libertarians painted themselves into a corner by refusing all forms of coercion—private as well as public—and deluded themselves when they argued that a free-market order could be sustained by purely voluntary contractual relations. As long as it implied the protection of private property, a free-market order needed some recognition of law and some institution capable of administering violence—a point that libertarians implicitly conceded when they turned to the solution of private militias and private law courts. Paleoconservatives offered libertarians a way out of this conundrum by acknowledging the fact that freedom from the state implied radical unfreedom in the social or private sphere, where rigorous gender and race hierarchies must hold sway. "Conservatives," he wrote, "have always argued that political freedom is a necessary but not sufficient condition for the good society, and they're right. Neither is it sufficient for the free society. We also need social institutions and standards that encourage private virtue, and protect the individual from the State."[63] Libertarians were "wrong to blur the distinction between State authority and social authority, for a free society is buttressed by social authority. Every business requires a hierarchy of command and every employer has the right to expect obedience within his proper sphere of authority. It is not different within the family, the church, the classroom."[64] The salient distinction was between two forms of authority—the "natural authority" that "arises from voluntary social structures" and the "unnatural authority" that is "imposed by the State."[65]

Rothbard and Rockwell may have miscalculated with Pat Buchanan. But their sense of long-term political strategizing was uncanny. With the Alabama-based Mises Institute as its headquarters, the alliance between paleoconservatives and libertarians continued to gain influence throughout the 1990s. The alliance was consummated in 1995, when the Mises Institute held a conference titled "Secession, State and Economy" in which the libertarian principle of freedom from federal government intrusion was stitched together with neo-confederate demands for states' rights, racial segregation, and a literal interpretation of Christian law.[66] In the following years, the institute would become a hothouse for paleolibertarian scholars such as Hans-Hermann Hoppe, the German American student of Rothbard who combines Austrian economics with the "blood and soil" imagery of European fascism, and Thomas E. Woods, a founding member of the white supremacist League of the South and a leading exponent of the neo-confederate philosophy of nullification and secession.[67] Despite the Mises Institute's libertarian origins, it was now regularly exchanging ideological positions and personnel with paleoconservative organizations such as *Southern Partisan*, *Chronicles*, and the League of the South.[68] Their collective message, radiated outward across a network of publications such as *VDare*, the *Right Stuff*, and *Taki's Magazine*, would come to define the movement we now know as the "alt-right."

Today, the role of paleolibertarianism in giving shape to this palpably new configuration of the American far right is undeniable. Almost all of the figures who self-identify as part of the alt-right are former supporters of Ron Paul, raised on a diet of Rothbardian diatribes against the Federal Reserve and neo-confederate calls to militia warfare. Almost all have been associated with the Mises Institute or its satellite organizations at some stage or another.[69] Murray Rothbard's comment that the paleolibertarian movement needed a presidential nominee who would "take the fight to the Republican convention" and explode the GOP from within may have been premature when it came to Pat Buchanan.[70] But it is eerily prescient when it comes to the rise of Trump and the utterly disintegrative role he has played within the Republican Party establishment.

Post-Libertarianism on the Alt-Right

THIS IS NOT to say that the fault lines between libertarians and paleoconservatives have been completely extinguished. In fact, they are widening—not in spite of but precisely because of Trump's success in translating paleolibertarian ideas onto the national stage. It is remarkable in this regard how many of the key figures on the alt-right have begun to mark their distance from libertarianism. These include Matthew Heimbach, whose now defunct Traditionalist Worker Party claimed allegiance to the twenty-five-point program of the early Nazi party; Richard Spencer, who in recent interviews claims that he "is not a libertarian" ("I grew out of that phase")[71] (2019); Mike Enoch (Peinovich), host of the *Daily Shoah*, who has renounced his earlier libertarianism in favor of anti-Semitic "anti-capitalism";[72] and the editor-in-chief of *Counter-Currents*, Greg Johnson, who sees his publishing agenda as that of promoting the "rich tradition of critiques of capitalism from the right."[73] The key reference points for these militants could not be further removed from the libertarian intellectual sphere: they include Gottfried Feder, the national socialist economist who first inspired Hitler; the social credit theories of C. H. Douglas; Kerry Bolton, a far-right theorist of money and banking based in New Zealand; Father Charles Coughlin, the fascist sympathizer who criticized FDR's New Deal for not going far enough; and Alain de Benoist, the leading intellectual of the French New Right and an ardent critic of capitalism from the far right. These new intellectual horizons have ushered in a dramatic change in political-economic strategy: while the paleolibertarians associated with Rothbard and the Mises Institute hew to a radically secessionist position, seeking ultimately to demolish the Federal Reserve and to restore a world of entirely private money creation based on a pure gold standard, the national socialist elements on the far right are intent on taking over the government and central bank as key institutions of a white ethnostate to come.

At first glance, the sudden conversion of so many alt-right figures from paleolibertarianism toward a national social or "anti-capitalist" far right, unthinkable only a few years ago, may appear difficult to fathom. Yet it is clearly foreshadowed in the work of key paleoconservative thinkers who were always more ambivalent about the free market than their libertarian brethren and who always had their own distinct sense of the strategic long-game. Samuel F. Francis in particular foresaw the tensions to come. In an essay on the prospects of a right-wing populism, published at the time of Buchanan's first campaign for the Republican presidential nomination, Francis was at pains to stress the selective character of white middle America's opposition to welfare state capitalism: the paleoconservative "resentment of welfare, paternalism and regulation," he writes, "is not based on a profound faith in the market but simply a sense of injustice that unfair welfare programs, taxes and regulation have bred."[74] Although it might look indistinguishable from libertarianism from the outside, he suggested, middle American opposition to welfare was entirely defensive and reactive—inspired by a sense of helplessness before the perceived racial favoritism of the "managerial" welfare state—hence liable to change in unexpected ways. If it ever got a whiff of power, it was "doubtful that the MAR [Middle American Radical] coalition ... [would] continue to focus on the classical liberal principle" of market freedom. It was more likely that "MAR-Sunbelt interests [would] require a strong governmental role in maintaining economic privileges for the elderly and for unionized labor (where it now exists)," that is to say, a welfare state selectively oriented toward the interests of the white working and lower-middle classes.[75] If the far right was truly committed to seizing power, Francis observed, it would benefit from the "frank recognition that the classical liberal idea of a night watchman state is an illusion and that a MAR elite would make use of the state for its own interests as willingly as the present managerial elite does."[76] Once in power, paleoconservatives would cast off their erstwhile libertarian allies and instead become economic nationalists and protectionists.

This was a position that Pat Buchanan had championed from the very start. Although he was a fellow traveler of the paleoconservatives, Buchanan was never won over by their secessionist fantasies and sought instead to reconcile the utopia of political and cultural decentralization with an overarching vision of national renewal. Indeed, Buchanan saw the neo-confederate will to secede as a symptom of defeat—an admission that nationhood had become impossible in the face of a relentlessly globalizing, homogenizing elite: "The deconstruction of the United States can be seen in resegregated student dorms, ethnic gangs, a revival of ethnic and racial politics, secessionist movements in the Southwest, all the way over to the white militias and the Southern League."[77] Taking issue with the Southern Agrarian and neo-confederate romanticization of Calhoun and all that he represents—the strategy, that is, of nullification and secession—Buchanan appeals to an alternative conservative tradition that includes the national mercantilism of Alexander Hamilton and the conservative national-populism of Andrew Jackson.[78] His twentieth-century heroes are Theodore Roosevelt, the Republican president turned Progressive, and the industrialist Henry Ford, both of whom championed a conservative corporatism founded on high wages for male workers, strict workplace and industrial regulations, consumer and environmental protections, punishing import tariffs, and maternalist welfare policies designed to subsidize women's labor as reproducers of the nation.[79] As Buchanan never tires of repeating, the free-trade and open borders position of the late twentieth-century Republican Party is a historical anomaly: up until the 1930s, the Republicans were relentlessly protectionist and it was only in the 1980s, with the personal about-face of Ronald Reagan, that the GOP unambiguously embraced the cause of free trade.[80] In so doing, he laments, they betrayed middle America and sapped the very foundations of American nationhood and family life. As corporations outsource jobs to the free-trade zones of China, Mexico, and elsewhere, American workers are placed in impossible competition with low-paid workers from around the world, while lax migration controls and the influx of workers from south of the border put further downward pressure on wages. The America of today is a "land of middle-class anxiety, down-sized hopes and vanished dreams, where economic insecurity is a pre-existing condition of life."[81] And "when company towns become ghost towns, when wives with young children are forced into the job market to make up the lost family income, America pays. Broken homes, uprooted families, vanished dreams, delinquency, vandalism, crime—these are the hidden costs of free trade. And if not families and neighbourhoods, what in heaven's name is it that we conservatives wish to conserve"?[82] Buchanan was concerned not only with a loss of principle among conservatives but also with a failure of strategic common sense. If it continued in this direction, Buchanan warned, the Republican Party risked losing the allegiance of the culturally conservative "Reagan Democrats" who had kept them in power for so long.[83] What was to be done? Buchanan's economic program called on the GOP to withdraw from all international free-trade deals, to deport all non-legal migrants and limit future migration intakes, to oversee "a deeper, wider distribution of property and prosperity" premised on the return of high-paying manufacturing jobs, and to redistribute the tax burden from income on labor and production to tariffs on imported consumer goods.[84]

Yet however unorthodox his ideas might appear when juxtaposed with the instinctive neoliberalism of the late twentieth-century Republican Party, Buchanan's economic nationalism remains legible as part of a once mainstream Republican tradition that sought to reconcile the interests of domestic free trade with national protectionism. As his invocation of the German ordoliberal, Wilhelm Röpke, might suggest, Buchanan is intent on containing market freedom within the bounds of the "organic nation" and its local communities of family, faith, and tradition, not abolishing it altogether.[85] Crucially, his economic nationalism stops short at the all-important question of money creation, which he thinks should be kept as far as possible in private hands and, in the case of the Federal Reserve, quarantined from the interventionist hand of government. Thus, he represents a fusion of paleoconservative, nationalist, and classical liberal positions.

The more recent exponents of anti-capitalism on the alt-right belong to a different tradition altogether, one that has never hesitated to infringe on market freedom—even and especially when it comes to the crucial question of money creation. The most extreme example of this alternative lineage can be found in the political program of the now defunct Traditionalist Worker Party, which resurrected the ideas of the German National Socialists to call for the cancellation of all "usurious" interest-bearing debt, including student loans, the abolition of the Federal Reserve as a semi-private entity independent of government, and the complete nationalization of banking and money creation in the service of a (white) worker's state: "The clearest way the globalist elites control America is through the Federal Reserve and the current banking system. As it stands, a private bank, the Federal Reserve, controls the money supply of the United States. The Traditionalist Worker Party believes that the nation, not international globalist bankers, should control the money of a nation."[86] The Traditionalist Worker Party has now closed shop, but such ideas have widespread currency on the "post-libertarian" margins of the alt-right. The work of New Zealand–based scholar Kerry Bolton has played a particularly important role in disseminating the "anti-capitalist" economics of fascist thinkers such as Gottfried Feder, Hjalmar Schacht (Hitler's central banker), and Father Charles Coughlin, each of whom was interested in the possibilities of a fully politicized system of state money creation, liberated from the whims of private financiers and international credit markets. This represents an extreme departure from the libertarianism of Murray Rothbard: although it is wedded to the sanctity of private property, national socialism as an economic doctrine has no respect at all for market (that is to say, contractual) freedom. Its vision of the ideal economic sphere is one that is totally reabsorbed in the non-contractual, organic hierarchies of race, gender, and tradition.

Trump, inevitably, has disappointed—he stands accused of being too soft on Wall Street financiers and migrants, of falling prey to the machinations of his Jewish son-in-law Jared Kushner[87]—but he has also sharpened the dividing lines within the alt-right and arguably triggered a deep shift in the alt-right's center of equilibrium, from paleolibertarianism to a new, post-libertarian, paleo-national socialist position. Now that President Donald Trump has improbably brought paleo ideas into the broad light of day, openly mouthing the words of Pat Buchanan—"America first" and "build the wall"—the secessionism of the paleolibertarian movement is beginning to appear redundant. Why revile the state and its social welfare institutions when they can be taken over? Without renouncing any of the paleoconservative positions espoused by Rothbard and his ilk—the visceral hatred of blacks, Jews, Muslims, women, gays, and trans people—younger militants such as Spencer and Heimbach have been less enthusiastic about his libertarianism. As Richard Spencer complained in a recent interview, "I would have preferred universal health care, I would have been more enthusiastic with Trump if instead of ending Obamacare and cutting taxes and all this kind of stuff, if he had said we are going to have an FDR style social programs. We are going to rebuild infrastructure, we are going to put people to work, building the wall but also doing other things."[88] Trump has disappointed then, but he has also emboldened. Now that the far right has a sense of what it can achieve on the national scale, it wants to go further.

This does not mean that the alt-right has completely abandoned the secessionist experiment. As explained by *Counter-Currents*' Gregory Hood, the enclave spaces and institutions created by the American Patriot movement and various other militia groups remain absolutely necessary as the building blocks of a new social order.[89] The home school, the militia, and the rural enclave are experimental prototypes that can tell us how social hierarchies will be organized and enforced in the future. They are sleeper cells ready to be mobilized as an army of militias and a conglomerate of fit-for-purpose social institutions. When the time is ripe, these secessionist forces will be waiting in the sidelines, ready to be enrolled in a larger cause. The national social turn expresses a new triumphalism on the radical right—a hope that the purified social orders which for many years have been nurtured in miniature, in various enclave spaces, can now become the model of a white ethnostate to come.

Notes

This chapter first appeared as "The Alt-Right: Neoliberalism, Libertarianism and the Fascist Temptation," *Theory, Culture & Society* 38.6 (2021): 29–50, https://doi.org/10.1177/026327642199944. It has been lightly revised for inclusion in this volume and is reprinted here with kind permission.

1. Paul Gottfried, "What I Learned from Rothbard," LewRockwell.com, https://www.lewrockwell.com/1970/01/paul-gottfried/what-i-learned-from-rothbard/.
2. Elliot Gulliver Needham, "Adam Smith to Richard Spencer: Why Libertarians Turn to the Alt-Right," *Medium*, February 23, 2018, https://medium.com/@elliotgulliverneedham/why-libertarians-are-embracing-fascism-5a9747a44db9.
3. Andrew Marantz, "Birth of a White Supremacist," *New Yorker*, October 9, 2017, https://www.newyorker.com/magazine/2017/10/16/birth-of-a-white-supremacist.
4. Gregory Hood, "Review: 'Right Wing Critics of Conservatism' by George Hawley," *Radix*, May 4, 2016, https://radixjournal.com/2016/05/2016-5-4-review-right-wing-critics-of-conservatism-by-george-hawley/.
5. Mark Skousen, *Vienna and Chicago: Friends or Foes? A Tale of Two Schools of Free Market Economics* (Washington, DC: Capital Press, 2005), 107–9, 113–14; Brian Doherty, *Radicals for Capitalism: A Freewheeling History of the Modern American Libertarian Movement* (New York: Public Affairs, 2007), 9–10, 247.
6. Justin Raimondo, *An Enemy of the State: The Life of Murray N. Rothbard* (Amherst, NY: Prometheus Books, 2000), 45–48; Gerard Casey, *Murray Rothbard* (New York: Continuum, 2010), 4–6. The "old right" libertarians included such figures as Frank Chodorow, H. L. Mencken, Garet Garrett, Robert Taft, and Alfred Jay Nock. Rothbard's own perspective on this alternative rightist tradition can be found in Murray N. Rothbard, *The Betrayal of the American Right* (Auburn, AL: Ludwig von Mises Institute, 1991/2007).
7. On this point, Rothbard deferred to the insights of the German Jewish sociologist Franz Oppenheimer, who distinguished between two diametrically opposed ways of acquiring wealth and power: the economic means, which involved the peaceable trade of legitimately produced goods and services, and the political means, which involved the organized theft of the goods and services produced by others. See Franz Oppenheimer, *The State* (New York: Free Life Editions, 1908/1975); and Murray N. Rothbard, *For a New Liberty: The Libertarian Manifesto* (Auburn, AL: Ludwig von Mises Institute, 1973/2006), 61–62.
8. Murray N. Rothbard, *The Case Against the Fed* (Auburn, AL: Ludwig von Mises Institute, 1994), 12, 20.
9. Rothbard, *For a New Liberty*, 78.
10. Rothbard, *The Case Against the Fed*, 86.
11. Rothbard, *For a New Liberty*, 64.
12. Murray N. Rothbard, *What Has Government Done to Our Money?* (Auburn, AL: Ludwig von Mises Institute, 1963), 50, 86.
13. Ibid., 52; Rothbard, *The Case Against the Fed*, 145.

14 Rothbard, *What Has Government Done to Our Money?* 64–81; Rothbard, *The Case Against the Fed*, 27.
15 Rothbard, *The Case Against the Fed*, 3.
16 Ibid., 11.
17 Rothbard, *What Has Government Done to Our Money?* 86.
18 Raimondo, *An Enemy of the State*, 151–77; Doherty, *Radicals for Capitalism*, 336–41.
19 Murray Rothbard, "Egalitarianism as a Revolt Against Nature," in *Egalitarianism as a Revolt Against Nature and Other Essays*, ed. R. A. Childs Jr. (Auburn, AL: Ludwig von Mises Institute, 1974/2000), 1–20.
20 Ibid., 8.
21 Rothbard, *What Has Government Done to Our Money?* 2; Murray Rothbard, "The Anatomy of the State," in *Egalitarianism as a Revolt Against Nature and Other Essays*, ed. R. A. Childs Jr. (Auburn, AL: Ludwig von Mises Institute, 1974/2000), 79.
22 Rothbard, *The Case Against the Fed*, 146.
23 Rothbard, *For a New Liberty*, 267–99.
24 Rothbard, "The Anatomy of the State," 75–78.
25 Rothbard, *For a New Liberty*, 12–13.
26 Murray N. Rothbard, *The Ethics of Liberty* (New York: New York University Press, 1982/1998), 63–76 and cf. Doherty, *Radicals for Capitalism*, 339.
27 Rothbard, *For a New Liberty*, 10, 17.
28 Rothbard, "Egalitarianism as a Revolt Against Nature," 8.
29 For a related problematization of Jefferson's understanding of "natural aristocracy," see Brian Steele, "Jefferson's Legacy: The Nation as Interpretative Community," in *A Companion to Thomas Jefferson*, ed. Francis D. Cogliano (Malden, MA: Wiley-Blackwell, 2012), 532–33.
30 Rothbard, *For a New Liberty*, 28, 44–45, 49–50.
31 Murray N. Rothbard, "Confessions of a Right-Wing Liberal," *Ramparts* 6.4 (1968): 50.
32 Raimondo, *An Enemy of the State*, 235–41, 263–66; Doherty, *Radicals for Capitalism*, 411–18.
33 Raimondo, *An Enemy of the State*, 257–301; Doherty, *Radicals for Capitalism*, 558–65.
34 Murray N. Rothbard, "Nations by Consent," *Journal of Libertarian Studies* 11.1 (1994): 1.
35 Doherty, *Radicals for Capitalism*, 417.
36 Murray N. Rothbard, "Race! That Murray Book," *Rothbard Rockwell Report* 5.12 (1994): 8. I am indebted to John Ganz for drawing attention to this publication. See John Ganz, "The Forgotten Man: Murray Rothbard and the Alt Right," *The Baffler*, December 15, 2017, https://thebaffler.com/latest/the-forgotten-man-ganz.
37 Rothbard, "Race! That Murray Book," 10.
38 Llewelyn H. Rockwell Jr., "The Case for Paleolibertarianism," *Liberty* (January 1990): 35.

39 For an insider perspective on paleoconservatism, see Joseph Scotchie, "Paleoconservatism as the Opposition Party," in *The Paleoconservatives: New Voices of the Old Right*, ed. Joseph Scotchie (New York: Routledge, 2017), 1. And for an outsider perspective, see Peter Kolozi, *Conservatives Against Capitalism: From the Industrial Revolution to Globalization* (New York: Columbia University Press, 2017), 170–71.
40 Scotchie, "Paleoconservatism as the Opposition Party," 5.
41 For a revealing insight into the paleoconservative perspective on neoconservatism and its faults, see Paul Gottfried and Thomas Fleming, *The Conservative Movement* (Boston: Twayne, 1988), 59–76. Fleming and Gottfried (the son of a Jewish refugee) are particularly interesting on the specificity of neoconservatism as a right-wing movement shaped by the Jewish migrant experience, hence instinctively inclined to distrust the Southern Agrarian tendencies on the American right.
42 Scotchie, "Paleoconservatism as the Opposition Party," 7–8.
43 Ibid., 4–5.
44 Ibid., 2.
45 On the necessity for compromise on the part of libertarians in particular, see Murray N. Rothbard, "Right-Wing Populism: A Strategy for the Paleo Movement," *Rothbard Rockwell Report* (January 1992): 9. It should be acknowledged that Rothbard ultimately had trouble accepting some of these concessions. He was, for example, deeply disturbed by Pat Buchanan's hostility to his mentor, Ludwig von Mises, on the question of free trade. See Raimondo, *An Enemy of the State*, 281.
46 Edoardo Saravalle, "Lew Rockwell, the Man Behind Ron Paul," *Penn Political Review*, January 21, 2012, https://pennpoliticalreview.org/2012/01/lew-rockwell-the-man-behind-ron-paul/.
47 The Southern Agrarians were a group of twelve poets, novelists, and critics, many of them based at Vanderbilt University, who developed a romantic and reactionary critique of industrialism from the point of view of the South. In 1930, they published a manifesto, *I'll Take My Stand: The South and the Agrarian Tradition* (New York: Harper, 1930), using the collective authorial name of "Twelve Southerners." For an analysis of the Southern Agrarian flirtation with European fascism, via their involvement with the magazine *American Review*, see Robert H. Brinkmeyer Jr., *The Fourth Ghost: White Southern Writers and European Fascism, 1930–1950* (Baton Rouge: Louisiana State University Press, 2009), 24–70.
48 Clyde N. Wilson, "Introduction: Should the South Survive?" in *Why the South Will Survive by Fifteen Southerners*, ed. Clyde N Wilson (Athens: University of Georgia Press, 1981), 2, 3.
49 Ibid., 3.
50 Ibid., 4.
51 Michael Hill and Thomas Fleming, "New Dixie Manifesto: States' Rights Will Rise Again," *Washington Post*, October 29, 1995, C03.
52 Euan Hague and Edward H. Sebesta, "Neo-Confederacy and Its Conservative Ancestry," in *Neo-Confederacy: A Critical Introduction*, ed. Euan Hague, Edward H. Sebesta, and Heidi Beirich (Austin: University of Texas Press, 2008), 29.

53 On the recent evolution of far-right militia movements in the United States, see Lane Crothers, *Rage on the Right: The American Militia Movement from Ruby Ridge to the Trump Presidency*, 2nd ed. (Lanham, MD: Rowman and Littlefield, 2019). According to Crothers, the 1990s militia movement experienced a lull in the early 2000s but underwent a rapid expansion after the election of Barack Obama and the rise of the Tea Party and Birther movements. A number of new militia movements have proliferated alongside the rise of the alt-right and have taken active part in their public demonstrations. In contrast to their forerunners in the 1990s, these new militias are much more openly white supremacist.
54 Robert H. Churchill, *To Shake Their Guns in the Tyrant's Face: Libertarian Political Violence and the Origins of the Militia Movement* (Ann Arbor: University of Michigan Press, 2010), 188–89.
55 Matthew N. Lyons, *Insurgent Supremacists: The U.S. Far Right's Challenge to State and Empire* (Oakland, CA: PM Press, 2018), 144–60.
56 Rockwell, "The Case for Paleolibertarianism," 35–36.
57 Rothbard, "Right-Wing Populism," 7.
58 Ibid. On Rothbard's Leninism, see Daniel Bessner, "Murray Rothbard, Political Strategy, and the Making of Modern Libertarianism," *Intellectual History Review* 24.4 (2014): 448–49.
59 Rothbard, "Right-Wing Populism," 8.
60 Ibid.
61 Ibid., 12.
62 Ibid., 10.
63 Rockwell, "The Case for Paleolibertarianism," 34.
64 Ibid., 36.
65 Ibid.
66 Hague and Sebesta, "Neo-Confederacy and Its Conservative Ancestry," 33.
67 Rachel Tabachnik, "Nullification, Neo-Confederates, and the Revenge of the Old Right," *Political Research Associates*, November 22, 2013, https://www.politicalresearch.org/2013/11/22/nullification-neo-confederates-and-the-revenge-of-the-old-right/.
68 Hague and Sebesta, "Neo-Confederacy and Its Conservative Ancestry," 33.
69 Lyons, *Insurgent Supremacists*, 150.
70 Rothbard, "Right-Wing Populism," 14.
71 "Is Richard Spencer a Socialist?" YouTube, February 15, 2018, 2:30–2:35.
72 "Michael 'Enoch' Peinovich," Southern Poverty Law Center, https://www.splcenter.org/fighting-hate/extremist-files/individual/michael-enoch-peinovich.
73 Georges Feltin-Tracol, "Interview on White Nationalism with Greg Johnson," *Counter-Currents*, December 30, 2016, https://www.counter-currents.com/2016/12/interview-on-white-nationalism/.
74 Samuel Francis, "Message from Mars: The Social Politics of the New Right," in *Beautiful Losers: Essays on the Failure of American Conservatism* (Columbia: University of Missouri Press, 1994), 72. I am indebted to Peter Kolozi for drawing attention to this text. See Kolozi, *Conservatives Against Capitalism*,

183–84. It should be noted that other paleoconservative figures, most notably Paul Gottfried, remained much more faithful to the paleoconservative-libertarian alliance.

75 Francis, "Message from Mars," 71.
76 Ibid., 72.
77 Patrick J. Buchanan, *The Great Betrayal: How American Sovereignty and Social Justice Are Being Sacrificed to the Gods of the Global Economy* (New York: Little, Brown, 1998), 113. For a profoundly insightful analysis of Buchanan's anti-libertarianism, see Kolozi, *Conservatives Against Capitalism*, 178–83.
78 Buchanan, *The Great Betrayal*, 145–46.
79 Ibid., 93, 288.
80 Patrick J. Buchanan, *Day of Reckoning: How Hubris, Ideology, and Greed Are Tearing America Apart* (New York: Thomas Dunne Books, 2007).
81 Buchanan, *The Great Betrayal*, 7.
82 Ibid., 285.
83 Buchanan, *Day of Reckoning*.
84 Buchanan, *The Great Betrayal*, 289.
85 Ibid., 288–89, 285.
86 Traditionalist Worker Party, "25 Points," September 11, 2017, https://web.archive.org/web/20171206221203/https://www.tradworker.org/points/.
87 For an insight into alt-right grievances against Trump, see "Richard Spencer: The Five Stages of Trump," YouTube, June 9, 2018, https://www.youtube.com/watch?v=E2KGwWs3C1A.
88 "Is Richard Spencer a Socialist?" YouTube, February 15, 2018, 3:43–3:53. Interestingly, the Mises Institute has responded to Spencer's change of political outlook by publicly disowning him. See "Tho Bishop: The Alt-Right in Auburn," *The Human Action Podcast: Mises Weekends with Jeff Deist*, April 21, 2017, https://mises.org/library/tho-bishop-alt-right-auburn.
89 Gregory Hood, "The Solution Is State Power," *Counter-Currents*, December 24, 2012, https://www.counter-currents.com/2012/12/the-solution-is-state-power/.

Rahul Rao

7. Nationalisms By, Against, and Beyond the Indian State

ON JANUARY 26, 2020, thousands of people cheered as four women hoisted the Indian flag in Shaheen Bagh, a predominantly Muslim locality in New Delhi, which had become the epicenter of protests against the highly controversial Citizenship (Amendment) Act (CAA) that was passed in December 2019. Three of the women referred to as the dadis (grandmothers) of Shaheen Bagh—Bilkis (82), Asma Khatoon (90), and Sarvari (75)—were leading figures in the sit-in protest in this locality that began soon after the law was passed and that has inspired scores of similar protests in other cities. The fourth, Radhika Vemula, is the mother of Rohith Vemula, a Dalit student whose suicide in January 2016 triggered widespread protests against caste discrimination. The flag hoisting, accompanied by the singing of the national anthem and other patriotic songs, marked India's 71st Republic Day, which commemorates the promulgation of the Indian Constitution.[1] It offered a popular counterpoint to the annual state-orchestrated military parade in the center of New Delhi that is typically the focus of public attention. On the same day in the southern state of Kerala, seven million people formed a 620-kilometer-long human chain stretching from one end of the state to the other and took a mass oath to defend the Constitution against what they saw as the CAA's "attempts to subvert and destroy it."[2]

The demonstrations in Shaheen Bagh and Kerala were two of thousands that rocked India for nearly three months after the CAA was passed in December 2019. The Act offers a fast track to citizenship for non-Muslims fleeing religious persecution in predominantly Muslim Pakistan, Afghanistan, and Bangladesh. Its opponents argue that in introducing a religious qualification for Indian citizenship for the first time, it strikes at the root of the Constitution's commitment to secularism. The Act followed on the heels of an effort to compile a National Register of Citizens (NRC) in the northeastern state of Assam, responding to long-running protests by the state's majority ethnic Assamese population against immigration from neighboring Indian states as well as from Bangladesh.[3] This registration exercise, justly described as "one of the largest purges of citizenship in history," required all people in the state to demonstrate proof of their citizenship.[4] While the Assamese agitation has historically been directed at all non-Assamese immigrants regardless of religion, India's ruling Hindu supremacist Bharatiya Janata Party (BJP) has championed the demand for the NRC (and has promised to conduct it on a countrywide basis) on the assumption that the exercise would disenfranchise mostly Muslims. It did not bargain for the possibility that many of the 1.9 million people (in a state with a population of 33 million) who failed to meet the onerous documentary requirements of the Assam NRC would be Hindus. The CAA is widely believed to be an attempt to offer a safety net for non-Muslims who fail to demonstrate proof of citizenship in the NRC exercise, putting in place a legal regime that will target primarily Muslims for detention and deportation.[5]

Numbers cannot adequately convey the scale or ferocity of the agitation against the NRC/CAA, which has drawn people from all communities and which commentators have described as the most significant upheaval since the Emergency of 1975–77. Within three weeks of the passage of the CAA, protests had taken place in 94 of India's 732 districts across 14 of its 29 states. Thousands of people were arrested, and 31 were killed in an initial wave of police repression mostly in BJP-ruled states.[6] Events took a darker turn in February 2020 after the sit-in at Shaheen Bagh had inspired scores of similar protests in other cities. When one of these sprang up in Jaffrabad in northeast Delhi, local BJP leader Kapil Mishra invited his followers to clear the protesters off the streets if the Delhi police did not do so within three days.[7] His ultimatum was widely seen as a call to violence to which Hindu mobs responded with a brutality not seen in the city since the anti-Sikh pogrom of 1984.[8] Fifty-three people, mostly Muslims, were killed, and Muslim-owned properties and mosques vandalized, while the police looked on and by some accounts even participated in the violence.[9]

Throughout this period, protests against the CAA continued, drawing thousands of people onto the streets in marches and sit-ins and into conversations on social media where protest memes offered a running commentary on the intricacies of the law as well as the state's response to the movement that it had brought into being. The protests were remarkable as much for their peacefulness as for their earnest deployment of a repertoire saturated with symbols of national identity, which is the subject of this chapter. Protesters wrapped themselves, quite literally, in the national flag. Images of leaders in the struggle for independence from British rule such as Gandhi, Bhagat Singh, and especially B. R. Ambedkar—the foremost Dalit leader and chairperson of the Drafting Committee of the Indian Constitution—became talismans of the movement. Mirroring the leading role that Muslim and oppressed caste women have played in the anti-CAA protests, the pavement library that sprang up at Shaheen Bagh was named after Fatima Sheikh and Savitribai Phule, both pioneering nineteenth-century social reformers and educationists from these communities.[10] Protesters sang the national anthem and embraced the Constitution of India on a scale and with an affective intensity that were unprecedented, engaging in mass readings of its Preamble and lingering over its promise to constitute India into a "sovereign socialist secular democratic republic." Much of this came as a surprise even to seasoned analysts of Indian politics. Until recently it was thought that India did not have a tradition of constitutional patriotism akin to that of the United States.[11] In contrast to the aural ubiquity of the pledge of allegiance and the visual omnipresence of the stars and stripes, until 2002 the Flag Code of India prohibited the use of the flag by private citizens except on national holidays, and until 2005 the flag could not be displayed on clothes. Commentators have remarked on the alacrity with which pious Muslims have adopted secular nationalist symbols to affirm their belonging alongside visible markers of religious identification.[12] In this chapter, I want to try to make sense of the reasons for the widespread adoption of a nationalist repertoire of protest in the current moment, before turning to a critical evaluation of its potentials and limits.

Nationalism By the State

THE FRISSON INHERENT in the protesters' take-up of nationalist symbols derives in part from a recognition that they were being seized back from a Hindu Right that has deployed them as a stick with which to beat its opponents. The coercive imposition of a state-authorized nationalism has been central to the BJP's wider political and cultural agenda since its return to power at the federal level in 2014. The Shaheen Bagh sit-in was initiated by women who were outraged by the police brutality unleashed on students protesting on the campuses of the historically Muslim Jamia Millia Islamia and Aligarh Muslim University in mid-December 2019, immediately after the CAA had been passed. In early January 2020, masked members of the Akhil Bharatiya Vidyarthi Parishad (ABVP), the student wing of the BJP, physically attacked students and faculty at Jawaharlal Nehru University (JNU) in retaliation for their protests against the CAA, while the police looked on. Long considered the intellectual bastion of the left, JNU has over time become a microcosm of national politics, with the rise of the ABVP on its campus mirroring that of the BJP on the national stage.[13] The ABVP attacks were reminiscent of similar provocations in 2016, which triggered widespread student resistance. On that occasion, ABVP harassment in collusion with authorities at the University of Hyderabad drove Dalit activist Rohith Vemula to take his life. Around the same time, ABVP activists accused communist student leader Kanhaiya Kumar, then president of the JNU students' union, of sedition in connection with a Kashmir solidarity event that he had helped organize and demanded that the Delhi police file charges against him. The state has made enthusiastic use of the draconian sedition law to crack down on dissidents of all stripes.

In addition to invoking the full wrath of the law, the state also responded to the 2016 protests on university campuses in an emphatically symbolic register. At a meeting with the minister of Human Resources Development, whose portfolio includes the governance of universities, the vice-chancellors of 42 central (federal) universities agreed to fly the national flag from 207-foot-high masts to counter what they perceived as a rising tide of anti-nationalism sweeping across their campuses.[14] (So there was a poignant irony in Radhika Vemula hoisting a flag of her own four years later.) In 2017, the vice-chancellor of JNU—widely perceived to be sympathetic to the Hindu Right and to have facilitated the latest round of ABVP violence—requested the government to install a battle tank on the JNU campus as a way of inculcating in students a spirit of patriotism and an appreciation for the sacrifices made by soldiers.[15] Between 2016 and 2018, as a result of a Supreme Court ruling that was subsequently reversed, the playing of the national anthem was made compulsory in every cinema before a film was screened. It was not uncommon during this period to read news stories reporting vigilante attacks against people who were unable or unwilling to stand for the anthem.[16]

In her account of the visual politics of Indian nationalism, Srirupa Roy argues that "the reproduction of the nation-state rests not on the existence of individuals who identify with the nation but rather on their ability to identify the state as the nation's authoritative representative."[17] She suggests that this ability is acquired through repeatedly encountering rather than necessarily believing in the official imagination of nationhood. As she explains, "the sights and sounds of the nation-state clutter public space, and it is their familiarity or pervasiveness rather than their persuasiveness that engenders public recognition."[18] Recognition of the state as the authoritative representative of the nation is a complex affective transaction shot through with fear of state violence, gratitude for its benevolence, enchantment at its spectacle, and boredom with its familiarity. Importantly, Roy's account of the institution of nation-statist ideology in India focuses not on its most recent iteration under the Hindu Right but on the early postcolonial decades of what is typically referred to as the "Nehruvian" state. This begs the question of what might have changed given the intensification of the deployment of this ideology as a disciplinary apparatus under the current ruling dispensation. How are the emotional valences of symbols transformed in a context in which the state seeks to saturate public space with them in an attempt to repair what it sees as a deficit in public recognition of its ability to represent the nation? What happens to the affective and political capital of symbols when the state cares more about their pervasiveness than their persuasiveness?

One answer is suggested by Lisa Wedeen's landmark study of the cult of Hafez al-Assad in Syria, which, she argues, engendered a politics of public dissimulation in which subjects behaved as if they revered the leader even if they patently did not.[19] Importantly, Wedeen argues that the spectacles that constitute the authority of the cult anchor politically significant ideas that ground political thinking and frame the way people see themselves as citizens, even if their claims are not taken literally, providing a visual and aural language for *both* complying with and contesting the regime.[20] Separately, Lacanian psychoanalysts have developed the notion of overidentification to describe how people living under authoritarian regimes might attack the norms by which they are governed not with a direct and straightforward critique but rather through a rabid and obscenely exaggerated adoption of them.[21] As Slavoj Žižek argues, by taking the norms of the system more seriously than the system itself does, overidentification lays bare the hollowness of regnant ideologies and their claims to obedience.[22]

Neither of these scenarios for living under authoritarianism fully describes what is unfolding in India. Anti-CAA protesters appear deeply invested in the very symbolic apparatus that has been used to discipline them. At one level this can be explained quite straightforwardly: the protesters wrap themselves in national symbols to obviate the state's all-too-predictable charge of anti-nationalism. Yet the deployment of these symbols is far from simply instrumental and defensive. The exuberant profusion of their creative reconfiguration, the evident sincerity with which they are invoked, the febrile pitch of contemporary public discourse, and the sheer scale on which all of this is unfolding suggest that the protesters retain a faith in the power of these symbols to shield them from the violence of the state even when they patently do not. (A widely circulated video from the Delhi violence shows policemen beating a group of protesters, one of whom subsequently died, and taunting them by forcing them to sing the national anthem.[23]) This begs the question of how national symbols have managed to retain a degree of subversive critical potential despite their deployment as a disciplinary apparatus by the state.

Nationalism Against the State

I SUGGEST THAT the protests against the CAA are better understood as an instance of what David Lloyd has called "nationalisms against the state."[24] Lloyd reminds us that even as they seek to saturate the field of subject formation, anticolonial nationalisms are articulated in a variety of ways with social movements organized around other logics such as class and gender. When nationalism becomes annexed to the territorial state, the processes of articulation that maintain nationalism as an element of broader, more complex and internally antagonistic social fields are brought to an end. Yet these other movements are never fully absorbed into state-oriented nationalisms, persisting as a potentially disruptive excess over the nation and its state. As Lloyd explains, "the possibility of nationalism against the state lies in the recognition of the excess of the people over the nation and in the understanding that that is, beyond itself, the very logic of nationalism as a political phenomenon."[25] This "excess" grows in those historical conjunctures in which the state becomes increasingly unmoored from the nation or at least from key constituents of it, as is evident in the BJP's unwillingness to consider Muslims a part of the nation and in its determination to subordinate and/or expel them from a reimagined Hindu nation-state.[26] In such moments, nationalisms against the state marshal the symbolic repertoire of nationalism to shame the state for its betrayal of the nation, with a view to repairing the disconnect between state and nation.[27]

This seems precisely to be the import of, for example, Varun Grover's defiant poem that in the few short weeks since it was composed at the start of the protests went viral, mutating into song and graffiti.[28] One stanza reads:

> Hum samvidhan ko bachaenge,
> Hum kagaz nahin dikhaenge,
> Hum jan gan man bhi gaenge,
> Hum kagaz nahin dikhaenge.
>
> We will save the Constitution,
> We will not show [NRC] papers,
> We will sing Jan Gan Man [the national anthem]
> We will not show papers.

Participants in the leaderless movement against the NRC/CAA have taken on the pedagogical task of reminding both the people and the state of the nation's founding ideology. Musicians have resurrected the less well-known verses of the longer poem by Rabindranath Tagore from which the national anthem is extracted, poignantly drawing attention to lines that affirm the national belonging of Hindus, Buddhists, Sikhs, Jains, Parsis, Muslims, and Christians—as if to underscore the betrayal inherent in the CAA in singling out one community for removal from the nation that the anthem sings into being.[29] It is an enduring irony that the man who wrote the anthem (as well as the song that became the national anthem of Bangladesh) was, for much of his life, a fierce critic of nationalism. In his 1917 lectures on nationalism, Tagore describes the idea of the nation as "one of the most powerful anesthetics that man has invented," under the influence of which "the whole people can carry out its systematic program of the most virulent self-seeking without being in the least aware of its moral perversion—in fact feeling dangerously resentful if it is pointed out."[30]

The trope of "saving the constitution," literalized in the names of political action groups such as the Samvidhan Suraksha Samiti and the Dastoor Bachao Committee that have sprung up recently, likewise represents the Constitution as endangered by the state and therefore requiring the protection of the nation. In his book *A People's Constitution*, the legal historian Rohit De attempts to unsettle the conventional view of the Indian Constitution as the discursive preserve of state and civil society elites. He opens the book with an image of the Constituent Assembly being "flooded with telegrams, postcards, and petitions from schoolboys to housewives to postmasters, staking claims, making demands, and offering suggestions" while it went about its work of drafting the Constitution.[31] The story he tells about the Constitution in its first decades of existence is one of a document produced through elite consensus but enlivened by the use made of it by ordinary litigants, many from unpopular minorities whose rights were not always assured by the majoritarian institutions of the state. But it is still a story about litigants invoking the Constitution before a court that they hope will rule in their favor. The CAA's critics, in contrast, do not sound like they are waiting for a court ruling, convinced as they are of the incompatibility of the CAA with the Constitution and indeed of its potential to undermine it. It is as if the people have sought a direct relationship with the text of the Constitution, insisting on their right to interpret it unmediated by the authority of a secular clergy whose recent judgments have not always inspired confidence.

The Supreme Court is, at the time of writing, considering over 140 petitions challenging the constitutionality of the CAA. While it would be imprudent to anticipate its conclusions, it is sobering to recall that the Court has often chosen not to restrain the executive's majoritarian excesses, notably in three recent cases that implicate central elements of the Hindu Right's vendetta against Muslims. First, in November 2019, the Court brought to a conclusion the long-running dispute over the Babri Mosque that had been demolished in 1992 by Hindu mobs claiming that the sixteenth-century mosque had been built on the ruins of a temple that marked the birthplace of the Hindu god Ram. After decades of litigation, the Court awarded the disputed site in its entirety to the Hindu parties despite acknowledging that the demolition of the mosque was illegal.[32] Second, in August 2019, the Modi government drastically altered the position of India's only Muslim-majority province, the disputed state of Jammu and Kashmir, by revoking the autonomy guaranteed to it by article 370 of the Constitution and downgrading its status to that of a territory ruled directly by the federal government in New Delhi. The move was accompanied by draconian measures including curfews, the incarceration of virtually the entire political class, and the longest internet shutdown ever imposed in a democracy. In January 2020, the Court ruled that the indefinite suspension of the internet violated fundamental rights but inexplicably declined to pass any specific orders mandating relief.[33] Third, the NRC exercise in Assam—the results of which, recall, provided the impetus for the CAA—was conducted after much stonewalling by politicians as a result of the zealous oversight of a Supreme Court bench headed by then Chief Justice Ranjan Gogoi, who is himself Assamese. Indifferent to the obvious conflicts of interest at play, Gogoi's political views as an Assamese nationalist heavily shaped decisions about the constitutionality and conduct of the NRC.[34]

Faced with a fascist executive that commands a supermajority in the legislature and is unrestrained by a supine judiciary, the anti-CAA movement's nationalism against the state seeks to reiterate and protect an endangered vision of the moral values of the nation and ultimately to persuade or force state institutions to uphold those values. Unreliable as it has been as a guardian of minority rights, the Supreme Court has shown itself to be attentive to public opinion—for better and worse. For example, the outcry that greeted the Court's 2013 judgment upholding India's colonial-era anti-sodomy law may have played some role in persuading it to change its mind five years later.[35] In quite a different vein, upholding the death sentence awarded to Afzal Guru, a Kashmiri convicted for his alleged involvement in an attack on the Indian Parliament in December 2001, the Court justified its decision on the ground that "the collective conscience of the society will only be satisfied if capital punishment is awarded to the offender."[36]

Beyond Nationalism Against the State

NATIONALISM AGAINST THE state aspires to strengthen the hyphen between nation and state to make the state representative of the nation from which it has become unmoored. This is the source of both its power and limits. Because it looks forward to a re-hyphenated nation-state, it cannot in good faith be accused of anti-nationalism or even anti-statism, even if it throws the full weight of its anger at the current incumbents of the state apparatus. Yet the presumption of "good faith" in the debate over the CAA itself betrays a naive Habermasian faith in the possibility of consensus on the rules of communicative reason. Nothing in the nationalism of the anti-CAA protesters protected them from the viciousness of the bad faith accusations of anti-nationalism that were hurled at them by the state and its acolytes. The most popular slogan of the Hindu mobs rampaging through northeast Delhi was "desh ke gaddaron ko, goli maro salon ko" (shoot the traitors). In the face of such murderous disingenuousness, the imperative of solidarity with the victims and survivors of this pogrom and with their demands for justice is clear. What follows is offered less in the register of critique of the normative imaginary of a movement that could not *not* have appealed to a certain kind of nationalism in its struggle against the state and more in the spirit of a search for what lies beyond this imaginary, circumscribed as it is by the telos of the idealized nation-state. If the very possibility of nationalism against the state lies in the recognition of the excess of the people over the officially constituted nation, then the performance of this nationalism generates excesses of its own. In this section, I offer some illustrations of such "excesses" whose claims are difficult to advance even within the more capacious imaginaries enabled by nationalisms against the state.

First, the question of Kashmir brings the limits of this discourse into stark relief. While the struggle for self-determination in Kashmir has been ongoing for decades—since the late 1980s in some reckonings and the inception of independent India in others—it has taken on a particular urgency since August 2019 in the wake of the repeal of article 370, the abrogation of which fulfills the BJP's cherished ambition of integrating this Muslim-majority state more firmly into the Indian Union. In this regard, calls to defend the Constitution can be construed as a demand to restore the constitutional status quo ante vis-à-vis article 370. Yet to demand this is not to demand very much at all: by the time the provision had been formally abrogated, it had become a shell of its former self, hollowed out by successive Congress and BJP governments in New Delhi. There is something disingenuous in the sudden resurgence of left-liberal interest in Kashmir, newly rediscovered as a weapon with which to attack the BJP, given the historically bipartisan insistence on its status as an "integral part of India." Many Kashmiris resent how Kashmir has been drawn into the anti-CAA protests (if it is remembered at all) as one issue among many with which to criticize the government, bristling at the manner in which their demand for azadi (freedom) has been appropriated and resignified to express a plurality of other demands in the slogans of the current movement.[37] The tension arises from the fact that the desires of those protesting their forced inclusion in the nation (in places like Kashmir) are fundamentally different from those protesting their forced exclusion from it (in places like Assam), even if both processes are manifestations of the BJP's coercive nation-building. Calls to protect the Constitution cannot mean much to those who do not wish to be governed by it—unless the Constitution can contemplate a process by which it will no longer be applicable to unwilling subjects. But this is typically where law ends and politics begins.

Second, not enough attention has been paid to how adivasis (indigenous peoples), who constitute 8.6 percent of the Indian population, are likely to be disproportionately and differentially impacted by the NRC-CAA. While the politics of indigeneity—specifically the "fear" of powerful ethnic groups of being reduced to minorities in their homelands—has underwritten the NRC, the demand for documentary proof of citizenship that it has entailed will be especially difficult for adivasis to meet given the greater likelihood of their being poor, rural, landless, and nomadic and/or displaced.[38] The CAA is unlikely to function as a safety net for adivasis given that many do not identify as belonging to the major religious groups to which it promises citizenship. Indeed the combined effect of these exercises in governmentality might be to incentivize adivasis to become Hindus, a process that the Hindu Right already encourages through campaigns of coercive inducement that it calls "ghar wapsi" (return home). Some of the most powerful moments in the protests against the CAA have arisen from gestures of everyday fraternity between religious groups—as when Hindus have formed protective cordons around Muslim protesters offering prayers, or when Sikhs have set up langars (community kitchens serving free meals typically at gurudwaras). Moving as they have been, the very ontology of these gestures—in which communities divided by something that can be identified as "religion" nonetheless make common "political" cause—can feel analytically incommensurate with what Alpa Shah calls the "sacral polities" of adivasi lifeworlds in which distinctions between religion, politics, and economics have never been very meaningful.[39] In such lifeworlds, the constitutionalism of the current nationalism against the state can seem presumptuous. In recent years, a movement known as Pathalgadi has spread particularly through adivasi villages in the state of Jharkhand. Responding to the threat of dispossession posed by land acquisition legislation, the movement has made itself visible through the erection of gigantic stone plaques quoting extracts from the Constitution that protect adivasi rights at the entrances to villages. Yet Pathalgadi evinces a paradoxical constitutionalism, asserting the exclusive sovereignty of gram sabhas (village assemblies) while in the same breath denying the sovereignty of other levels of government.[40] As some participants in the movement explained to journalists: "We have all descended from nature and we worship it. We don't believe in the Indian Constitution, nor do we recognize government officials."[41]

Third, the reference to nature invites us to think beyond the humanist discourses of liberal constitutionalism to consider how relationships between people and the environment have produced the current conjuncture. In the preparation of the Assam NRC, a xenophobic and arbitrary adjudication process has conspired with the paucity of record-keeping by people who are poor and illiterate, and have often had to move frequently as a result of war, partitions, and environmental displacement, to deprive nearly two million people of citizenship.[42] As Arundhati Roy writes, the very impermanence of the nearly 2,500 shifting, silty "char" islands in the river Brahmaputra on which many of the most marginal farmers live has meant an absence of land deeds and other documentation that might establish their connection to the land as demanded by the NRC.[43] Whatever fences and border regimes are put in place, if current projections of climate-induced displacement in the region are correct, we must expect migration only to grow. It is estimated that by 2050, one in seven people in Bangladesh will be displaced by climate change, with up to 18 million people having to move because of a rise in sea level.[44] This will offer grist to the mill of the Hindu Right, which for decades has used the specter of "illegal migration" from Bangladesh to whip up anti-Muslim hysteria in India.

Nowhere in the world are the forms of international cooperation necessary for better management of land and water resources or indeed the mitigation of the global climate crisis adequate to the scale of the task that they face. But these processes are particularly deficient in South Asia, which remains one of the least integrated regions in the world thanks to the bitter legacies of Partition, war, contested borders, a lack of complementarity between economies, and the mistrust that comes from the sheer disparity in size between India and its neighbors.[45] There has been little consideration, even within the anti-CAA movement, of the international effects of an Indian law that presumptively declares the country's Muslim-majority neighbors to be persecuting states while setting itself up as a refuge for the non-Muslim victims of such persecution. In February 2020, a twenty-year-old woman named Amulya Leona took to the stage at an anti-CAA rally in Bengaluru and attempted to lead the crowd in a chant that began with the words "Pakistan Zindabad!" ("Long live Pakistan!"). It was unclear where she was going with this because she was violently taken off the stage by event organizers and police before she could finish; we hear her repeat the Pakistan slogan several times interspersed with cries of "Hindustan Zindabad!" ("Long live India!").[46] A Facebook post by her from several days earlier suggests that she was trying to articulate a position of pan–South Asian fraternity.[47] Such views cannot easily be accommodated even within the discursive and affective realm of nationalism against the state. The Hyderabad MP Asaduddin Owaisi, who was on the stage at the time and has been a leading Muslim political voice in the anti-CAA protests, immediately distanced himself from Leona, undoubtedly mindful of the portrayal of Indian Muslims in Hindu right-wing propaganda as fifth columnists sympathetic to Pakistan. The police filed charges of sedition against Leona, Hindu vigilantes offered a bounty for her murder, and even her own father was publicly critical of her actions.[48] And yet, in the fraught international context produced by the NRC-CAA, the politically naive slogans of a young woman with a terrible sense of timing may be the thing we most need to hear.

Nationalism in the Time of Covid-19

WHAT THREATS, LITIGATION, and even the Delhi pogrom could not do, Covid-19 accomplished. A hundred days and nights after it first began, the sit-in at Shaheen Bagh and other anti-CAA protest encampments in New Delhi and elsewhere were cleared by police as part of the lockdown imposed by the government in the wake of the spread of the coronavirus. As Raghu Karnad put it, political togetherness had yielded to the inexorable logic of social distancing.[49] Popular responses to the pandemic were sometimes troubling, featuring racist anti-Chinese tropes and caste supremacist claims about the putative superiority of the traditional Namaste as a form of greeting that does not involve touching. The state's initial response tilted heavily in the direction of securitization (curfews and lockdowns) with rather less consideration given to the welfare of people disadvantaged by these measures.[50]

Leading these responses has been the figure of the prime minister himself, whose own discourse has been heavy on symbolism and citizen duty rather than state responsibility.[51] In what seems to have been a trial run for a subsequently ordered twenty-one-day lockdown, Narendra Modi asked people to observe a fourteen-hour curfew on March 22, 2020, as part of which he urged them to beat on pots and pans to demonstrate their gratitude for the efforts of medical and emergency workers. Many appear to have ignored, forgotten, or misunderstood the instructions on physical distancing, congregating on balconies and in streets to participate in the moment with enthusiasm. Whatever superficial resemblance the gesture might have borne to spontaneous demonstrations in Italy, Spain, and elsewhere, many who witnessed the moment firsthand described it as evoking the soundscapes of Hindu ritual especially as people also took to blowing the horn-like conches commonly used in temple worship. The Leader had ordered and the People had obeyed. The last Indian able to stage such impressive shows of symbolic conformity might have been Gandhi.

Notes

This chapter first appeared as "Nationalisms By, Against and Beyond the Indian State," *Radical Philosophy* 2.07 (2020): 17–26; it has been lightly revised for inclusion in this volume and is reprinted here with kind permission.

1 "In Photos: Republic Day at Shaheen Bagh," *The Wire*, January 27, 2020, thewire.in/rights/in-photos-republic-day-at-shaheen-bagh.
2 Siddharth Premkumar, "Kerala Forms 620 Km Human Chain Against CAA, NRC on Republic Day," *Outlook*, January 26, 2020, https://www.outlookindia.com/website/story/india-news-kerala-forms-620-km-long-human-chain-against-caa-nrc-on-republic-day/346282.
3 For an account of how the politics of Assam has shaped successive amendments to Indian citizenship law, see Anupama Roy, *Mapping Citizenship in India* (New Delhi: Oxford University Press, 2010), chap. 2.
4 Rohini Mohan, "Inside India's Sham Trials That Could Strip Millions of Citizenship," *Vice News*, July 29, 2019, news.vice.com/en_us/article/3k33qy/worse-than-a-death-sentence-inside-indias-sham-trials-that-could-strip-millions-of-citizenship.
5 Arundhati Roy, "India: Intimations of an Ending," *The Nation*, November 22, 2019, thenation.com/article/archive/arundhati-roy-assam-modi.
6 Sumant Sen and Naresh Singaravelu, "Data: How Many People Died During Anti-CAA Protests?" *The Hindu*, January 6, 2020, thehindu.com/data/data-how-many-people-died-during-anti-caa-protests/article30494183.ece.

7   Sukirti Dwivedi, "'We'll Be Peaceful Till Trump Leaves,' BJP Leader Kapil Mishra Warns Delhi Police," NDTV, February 24, 2020, ndtv.com/delhi-news/bjp-leader-kapil-mishras-3-day-ultimatum-to-delhi-police-to-clear-anti-caa-protest-jaffrabad-2184627.
8   Hannah Ellis-Petersen, "Delhi Protests: Death Toll Climbs amid Worst Religious Violence for Decades," *The Guardian*, February 26, 2020, theguardian.com/world/2020/feb/26/delhi-protests-death-toll-climbs-amid-worst-religious-violence-for-decades.
9   Jeffrey Gettleman, Sameer Yasir, Suhasini Raj, and Hari Kumar, "How Delhi's Police Turned Against Muslims," *New York Times*, March 12, 2020, nytimes.com/2020/03/12/world/asia/india-police-muslims.html.
10 Sneha Bhura, "The Story Behind the Library at Shaheen Bagh," *The Week*, February 18, 2020, theweek.in/news/india/2020/02/17/the-story-behind-the-library-at-shaheen-bagh.html.
11 Srirupa Roy, *Beyond Belief: India and the Politics of Postcolonial Nationalism* (Durham: Duke University Press, 2007), 6.
12 Rajeev Bhargava, "The Return of the Secular," *The Hindu*, December 26, 2019, https://www.thehindu.com/opinion/op-ed/the-return-of-the-secular/article30397647.ece; Rahul Rao, "Test of Faith," *The Caravan*, January 29, 2020, https://caravanmagazine.in/politics/caa-protests-shake-old-bounds-indian-secular-morality.
13 Ankita Pandey, "Keeping India's Universities for the Rich," *Jacobin*, January 27, 2020, https://jacobinmag.com/2020/01/jawaharlal-nehru-university-india-fee-hike; Samanth Subramanian, "How Hindu Supremacists Are Tearing India Apart," *The Guardian*, February 20, 2020, theguardian.com/world/2020/feb/20/hindu-supremacists-nationalism-tearing-india-apart-modi-bjp-rss-jnu-attacks.
14 Anuradha Raman, "National Flag to Fly at All Central Universities," *The Hindu*, February 18, 2016, thehindu.com/news/national/hoisting-of-tricolour-to-be-made-mandatory-in-all-central-universities/article14086309.ece.
15 Staff Reporter, "JNU VC Asks Govt. to Install a Battle Tank on Campus," *The Hindu*, July 24, 2017, thehindu.com/news/cities/Delhi/jnu-vc-ask-govt-to-install-a-battle-tank-on-campus/article19341486.ece.
16 BBC News, "India National Anthem No Longer Compulsory in Cinemas," January 9, 2018, bbc.co.uk/news/world-asia-india-42618830.
17 Roy, *Beyond Belief*, 14.
18 Roy, *Beyond Belief*, 18.
19 Lisa Wedeen, *Ambiguities of Domination: Politics, Rhetoric, and Symbols in Contemporary Syria* (Chicago: University of Chicago Press, 1999), 6.
20 Wedeen, *Ambiguities of Domination*, 19–24.
21 Stevphen Shukaitis, "Overidentification and/or Bust?" *Variant* 37 (Spring/Summer 2010): 26, nictoglobe.com/ new/articles/V37overident.pdf.
22 Slavoj Žižek, "What the Hell Is Laibach All About?" last modified March 11, 2009, youtube.com/watch?v=1BZl8ScVYvA.
23 Anumeha Yadav, "Ground Report: Delhi Police Actions Caused Death of Man in Infamous National Anthem Video," *Huffpost*, March 1, 2020, https://www.

huffingtonpost.in/entry/delhi-riots-police-national-anthem-video-faizan_in_5e5bb8e1c5b6010221126276.

24 David Lloyd, "Nationalisms Against the State," in *The Politics of Culture in the Shadow of Capital*, ed. Lisa Lowe and David Lloyd (Durham: Duke University Press, 1997), 173–97.

25 Lloyd, "Nationalisms Against the State," 192.

26 The most authoritative exposition of this ideological worldview remains V. D. Savarkar, *Hindutva: Who Is a Hindu?* (1923; New Delhi: Bharti Sahitya Sadan, 1989).

27 For an argument along similar lines, see Pheng Cheah, *Inhuman Conditions: On Cosmopolitanism and Human Rights* (Cambridge, MA: Harvard University Press, 2006), 38–40.

28 The full text of the poem can be found at https://lyricsraag.com/hum-kagaz-nahi-dikhayenge-varun-grover/.

29 Moushumi Bhowmik, "The Art of Resistance: Unsung Verses of India's National Anthem Shine a Light on the Idea of India," *Scroll*, January 7, 2020, https://scroll.in/article/948836/the-art-of-resistance-unsung-verses-of-indias-national-anthem-shine-a-light-on-the-idea-of-india.

30 Rabindranath Tagore, *Nationalism* (London: Macmillan, 1917), 42.

31 Rohit De, *A People's Constitution: The Everyday Life of Law in the Indian Republic* (Princeton: Princeton University Press, 2018), 2.

32 *M. Siddiq (D) Thr Lrs v. Mahant Suresh Das and others*, Civil Appeal Nos. 10866–10867 of 2010, sci.gov.in/pdf/JUD_2.pdf.

33 "Status Quo SC Likely to Continue in Kashmir; SC Avoided Primary Responsibility of Judicial Review," *Firstpost*, January 10, 2020, firstpost.com/india/article-370-jammu-and-kashmir-supreme-court-verdict-on-restrictions-petitions-updates-latest-news-today-foreign-envoys-visit-7885211.html.

34 Arshu John, "Sealed and Delivered: Ranjan Gogoi's Gifts to the Government," *The Caravan*, February 2020, 26–55.

35 Compare *Suresh Kumar Koushal v. Naz Foundation* (2014) 1 SCC 1, and *Navtej Singh Johar v. Union of India*, WP (Crl) No. 76 of 2016.

36 *State (NCT of Delhi) v. Navjot Sandhu @ Afsan Guru*, Appeal (Crl) 373–75 of 2004, https://indiankanoon.org/doc/1769219/.

37 Listen especially to Mehroosh Tak, "Hindutva and the University," teach-in at Queen Mary University of London, January 22, 2020, thepolisproject.com/hindutva-and-the-university.

38 Ananya Singh, "How Will CAA and NRC Affect India's Tribal Population?" *The Citizen*, December 31, 2019, thecitizen.in/index.php/en/NewsDetail/index/9/18101/How-Will-CAA-and-NRC-Affect-Indias-Tribal-Population; Jawar Bheel, "Citizenship Amendment Act (CAA), and the Tribal Community (Adivasi)," *Round Table India*, December 18, 2019, roundtableindia.co.in/index.php?option=com_content&view=article&id=9773.

39 Alpa Shah, "Religion and the Secular Left: Subaltern Studies, Birsa Munda and Maoists," *Anthropology of This Century* 9 (2014), http://aotcpress.com/articles/religion-secular-left-subaltern-studies-birsa-munda-maoists/.

40 Nandini Sundar, "Pathalgadi Is Nothing but Constitutional Messianism So Why Is the BJP Afraid of It?" *The Wire*, May 16, 2018, https://thewire.in/

rights/pathalgadi-is-nothing-but-constitutional-messianism-so-why-is-the-bjp-afraid-of-it.

41 Amarnath Tewary, "The Pathalgadi Rebellion," *The Hindu*, April 14, 2018, https://www.thehindu.com/news/national/other-states/the-pathalgadi-rebellion/article23530998.ece.

42 Mohan, "Inside India's Sham Trials."

43 Roy, "India: Intimations of an Ending."

44 Environmental Justice Foundation, "Climate Displacement in Bangladesh," ejfoundation.org/reports/climate-displacement-in-bangladesh.

45 P. V. Rao, "South Asia's Retarded Regionalism," in *Indian Ocean Regionalism*, ed. Dennis Rumly and Timothy Doyle (London: Routledge, 2016), 37–53; Pratap Bhanu Mehta, "SAARC and the Sovereignty Bargain," *Himal Southasian* 18.3 (November/December 2005): 17–21.

46 Amulya Leona speech, February 20, 2020, https://www.youtube.com/watch?v=fUOcHVw9Evg.

47 Rohini Swamy, "Student Who Shouted 'Pakistan Zindabad' on Owaisi Stage Had Praised Modi Hours Before," *The Print*, February 21, 2020, theprint.in/india/student-who-shouted-pakistan-zindabad-on-owaisi-stage-had-praised-modi-hours-ago/368917; K. P. Sasi, "Sedition for Peace! The Curious Case of Amulya Leona," *Countercurrents*, February 25, 2020, https://countercurrents.org/2020/02/sedition-for-peace-the-curious-case-of-amulya-leona.

48 D. P. Satish, "Let Her Rot in Jail, Says Father of Amulya Leona, Arrested for Raising Pro-Pakistan Slogans," *News18*, February 21, 2020, news18.com/news/india/let-her-rot-in-jail-says-father-of-amulya-leon-arrested-for-raising-pro-pakistan-slogans-2509445.html; Manu Kaushik, "If Released, We Will Kill Her in Encounter: Ram Sena Man Offers Rs 10L Bounty for Amulya's Head," *Times Now*, February 22, 2020, timesnownews.com/india/article/if-released-we-will-kill-her-in-encounter-ram-sena-man-offers-rs-10l-bounty-for-amulyas-head/556634.

49 Raghu Karnad, "Farewell to Shaheen Bagh, as Political Togetherness Yields to Social Distance," *The Wire*, March 24, 2020, thewire.in/politics/farewell-to-shaheen-bagh-as-political-togetherness-yields-to-social-distance.

50 Pranav Kohli and Prannv Dhawan, "Covid-19 and India's Hindu-Fascism Outbreak," *Newsclick*, March 22, 2020, newsclick.in/index.php/covid-19-and-indias-hindu-fascism-outbreak.

51 Vidya Krishnan, "High on Talk, Low on Substance: Modi's Speech Showed India Is Ill-prepared for COVID," *The Caravan*, March 20, 2020, caravanmagazine.in/health/high-on-talk-low-on-substance-modi-speech-showed-india-ill-prepared-covid.

Julian Göpffarth

8. Giving the Heimat a New Home: National Belonging and Ethnopluralism on the German Far Right

FOLLOWING THE SO-CALLED refugee crisis in 2015, the concept of "Heimat" (homeland) has once again emerged as a powerful symbol for national belonging in German public debates. The idea of a Heimat threatened by immigration as a trigger for a renewed German nationalism has not only become a concept propagated by Germany's populist far-right party Alternative für Deutschland (AfD). A diffuse but pervasive feeling of national identity crisis reached its climax in 2018, with rising support for the AfD, an increased political polarization and far-right violence, a number of murders committed by refugees, political chaos in centrist parties, an exacerbating housing crisis, the threat of an economic downturn, and, last but not least, a disastrous performance of Germany's national soccer team in the 2018 World Cup. In this context, major news outlets and political magazines such as *Der Spiegel* used their cover pages to symbolically show a white country beleaguered my non-white immigrants, a formerly strong nation in decline and, represented by a so-called "Gartenzwerg," the garden gnome, representing the average German who, in face of an increasing visibility of Islam, asks, "Is this still my country?" (Fig. 11).

Figure 11. *Left*: "Who can come in? The right refugee policy—a plaidoyer," April 2018. *Center*: "Football, politics, economy. There once was a strong country," June 2018. *Right*: "Is this still my country? Legitimate concerns, exaggerated angst—the facts around the debate on Islam and Heimat," August 2018. Photos of the covers taken by the author.

The feeling of a loss of control, political chaos, and a threatened Heimat captured on these covers was not only pushed by the far-right AfD, which made the Heimat and national belonging the central element in its political campaigning. In an unprecedented move and a desperate attempt to counter the AfD's rise, Chancellor Angela Merkel's center-right Union parties decided to rename the Federal Ministry of the Interior the Federal Ministry of the Interior, Building, and Heimat.

Likewise, centrist and far-left politicians explored the possibility of a "leftist reading" of the Heimat. Green Party co-leader Robert Habeck started a "summer tour" through rural Germany visiting places that link a local imagery of the Heimat to national and nationalist history, for instance the Hambach Castle.[1] Located in southwest Germany, the castle symbolizes German liberal nationalism. It was here where in 1832 the so-called Hambach Festival, a liberal-bourgeois revolt against German monarchies and for national unity, took place. By invoking it, Habeck and the Green Party tried to put forward a "patriotism from the left."[2] Following Habeck's example, Germany's Federal president, the center-left social-democrat Frank-Walter Steinmeier, proposed to draw on the image of a liberal-democratic Heimat represented by the Hambach Castle to establish a "democratic patriotism."[3] Beyond the liberal and centrist left, the far-left party Die Linke called for reclaiming the Heimat from the far right.[4]

In view of the diffuse mixture of regional homeland aesthetics, nineteenth-century history, and "democratic nationalism" represented by the Hambach Castle, it should come as no surprise that Germany's far-right party, AfD, also embraced the castle in its effort to locate the party within a tradition of "patriotic democrats" rising up for a national renewal and the defense of cultural diversity threatened by a homogenizing globalization (Fig. 12). The Heimat is a central concept to the far right's ideology of ethnopluralism. Merging right-wing ethnic exclusion and left-wing regionalism, ethnopluralism calls for ethnoculturally homogeneous regions and nations that coexist peacefully but do not mix. German mainstream media presented the AfD's attempts to incorporate the Hambach Castle and, more generally, notions of the Heimat linked to it in its ethnopluralist ideology as a "hijacking of history." Centrist and leftist attempts to embrace the Heimat and the castle's mythology were, on the other hand, justified by the claim that one cannot leave questions of belonging to the far right.[5]

In this chapter I show that attempts by the center and the far left to reclaim the Heimat from the far right obscure and reproduce the myriad ways conventional visions of the Heimat are interwoven with widely shared symbolic repertoires of white identity. This goes hand in hand with, as the German historian Fatima El-Tayeb has argued, the externalization of racism onto the far right,[6] ignoring the structural racism that, as studies by Oliver Decker and Rita Chin have shown, continues to pervade German culture and politics.[7] The compatibility of the far right's ethnopluralist conception of the Heimat with East and West German mainstream visions of the Heimat, I argue, brings out the unmarked, racialized notions of German culture and identity inherent in these visions. Reclaiming the concept of the Heimat from the far right thus also means mainstreaming the far right's ideology of ethnopluralism.

The (Pre-)Politics of the Heimat

REFERRING TO NATIONAL identity politics, anthropologist Michael Billig distinguishes a "hot nationalism" from what he calls "banal nationalism."[8] The latter describes unquestioned symbols of nationhood and collective belonging, such as national dishes or omnipresent national flags, that make the answer to the question of who is included in

Figure 12. *Left*: "Off to the castle, patriots!" AfD's advertising of the New Hambach Festival. *Center*: Green Party leader Robert Habeck visiting the Hambach Castle in 2018. *Right*: German president Frank-Walter Steinmeier visiting the Hambach Castle in 2018.

the collective identity appear as uncontested and self-evident to the majority population. In times of perceived national crisis, Billig argues, these references can become mobilizing symbols for a "hot nationalism" when political groups claim to be the sole legitimate representatives of the nation by directly linking symbols of nationhood to their political ideology.[9]

By defining the specificity of "hot nationalism" through its link to an explicit political ideology, Billig implies that banal forms of nationalism are apolitical and based on politically irrelevant and acceptable contents. Yet, as I argue, the difference between "hot" and "banal" is less one of content but one of form. If one takes the Heimat as a symbol for German nationhood, Billig's argument would mean that the far right's use of the Heimat was a mere appropriation of an otherwise unproblematic concept. Yet the invisibility and acceptability of the exclusive politics of class and race *inherent* in the Heimat depend on its perceived self-evidence and the apolitical character of its definition among Germany's white majority.

As I will show, in Germany these seemingly apolitical understandings of the Heimat are deeply entangled with an exclusive white identity politics that is widely shared by political actors beyond the far right. As the example of the Hambach Castle reveals, it is not the content of the politics of the Heimat of the far right that is criticized by mainstream politics and media but rather the different populist forms in which the Heimat is expressed by the German far right. In fact, both far-right and mainstream visions of the Heimat represent neither a biological fact nor an illusion but what sociologist Matthew Hughey has called a "real social classification that supplies a meaningful worldview and set of strategies" to the white majority population that embodies that category.[10] Following Hughey, the qualitative claiming and definition of a meaningful Heimat is a way to construct "a collective white identity" that is based on seemingly self-evident shared cultural symbols, that is, "supposedly common traits, experiences, and a shared sense of belonging."[11] Instead of appropriating "innocent" banal visions of the Heimat, the far right's "hot Heimat" thus makes visible the politics of exclusion inherent in "banal" notions of the Heimat. Drawing on these shared and unmarked symbols of white identity allows the far right to introduce its principle of ethnopluralism into the mainstream.

The Heimat as a Local Metaphor for the Nation

IN THE LATE nineteenth century, in a young country full of small-scale state and denominational differences, the Heimat was defined as what cultural historian Alon Confino has called a "local metaphor of the nation," allowing the national community to be imagined through a regionally colored sense of community.[12] As in postwar Germany, the concept of nation was negatively affected by Nazism; the concept of the Heimat was put forward in both East and West Germany as a substitute, a positive symbol of national identity untainted by the Holocaust and unrelated to Germany's colonial past.

However, as German historians Marianne Bechhaus-Gerst and Ozan Zakariya Keskinkılıç have shown, this vision omits that in the nineteenth century the Heimat was constructed as a regional identity that was put in contrast to exotic distant German colonies and a non-white and non-Christian colonized "other."[13] These visions of the Heimat were part of literary productions such as Karl May's "adventure novels" and transmitted in school curricula, emerging *Heimatmuseums* (Heimat museums), and associations such as the *Heimatschutz* (Heimat protection movement). German regions became signifiers of both the essential distinctiveness of the local and the oneness of the German nation.[14] Contrasted with the non-white exotic colonies, the Heimat was constructed as what Anthony Smith has called an "ethno-scape" of a superior European nation that sees terrain, culture, and people in a symbiotic relationship.[15]

In postwar Germany, the entanglement of the Heimat with European nineteenth-century colonial and white supremacist narratives and its focus on regional identity made it a useful concept and semantic figure to perpetuate a white regionalism. The Heimat avoided the open embrace of nationalism as an ideology that, after Nazism and World War II, was largely ostracized in German politics and society. Both in the socialist German Democratic Republic (GDR) and the capitalist German Federal Republic (FRG), the Heimat stood as a welcome symbol for the regional construction of a white German identity.

Following the myth of the GDR as an antifascist state,[16] the concept of a guilt-free Heimat untainted by the Nazi past was promoted to legitimize the socialist regime.[17] As a result, after the fall of the Berlin Wall, East and West Germans idealized the GDR's cultural politics for having preserved a positive national identity that was undermined in the FRG by an overly critical coming-to-terms with the Nazi past. As the anthropologist Jason James has shown in his ethnographic study of heritage activism in East Germany in the 1990s, the Heimat played a central role in local heritage activism in the East German federal states long before far-right parties and the AfD embraced Heimat-activism.[18] James's study explores how activism advocating for the preservation of historical townscapes in postwar Germany reflects a local cultural struggle for monuments as symbols of a German past "unspoiled" by the GDR and Nazi dictatorships. These activists perceived the Heimat as threatened by West German investors, modern architecture, and the critical assessment of the Nazi past at the local level.

Today, far-right intellectuals such as Vera Lengsfeld, Monika Maron, and Sigmar Faust show how former GDR dissidents once again set themselves up as defenders of the Heimat, this time against a cultural decay ostensibly promoted by "left-wing liberal totalitarianism," "universalism," and "fascist Islam."[19] The connection between an activism that seeks to defend the Heimat and anti-socialist opposition proves to be useful for the far right in the present context in that it allows far-right movements to simultaneously mobilize for a renewed "resistance" against an emerging "socialism" while designing a sanitized version of the national past, freed from guilt.[20]

Historical studies have shown that the Heimat was equally central to West Germany's post-fascist process of self-legitimation,[21] where it allowed for a form of white national identity detached from the Nazi past by shifting the focus from nationalism to regional attachment.[22] As German historian Gaëlle Fisher has argued, the Heimat acquired an explicit racial charge, particularly in the context of the integration of displaced persons in West Germany.[23] In this context the concept of the Heimat was interwoven with that of a Christian-influenced Western world and a superior European civilization.[24] A central element in this process of regionalist identity formation were so-called "Heimatfilme," popular movies in regional settings representing the Heimat that dominated German film productions especially in the 1950s. These movies facilitated the imaginary overcoming of feelings of guilt linked to the Nazi past while reproducing narratives of colonial racism and anti-Semitism in the attempt to reconstruct a sanitized vision of Germanness.[25] These Heimat movies projected images of landscapes as apolitical symbols of a white national belonging, sidestepping the notion of "nation" because this concept was seen as intrinsically linked to Nazism. The Heimat was thus a key element of the avoidance of contentious politics that was fundamental to West Germany's early postwar society.[26]

These entanglements of banalized Heimat narratives with visions of white supremacy not only remained central to the politics of national belonging in both German postwar states. Traditions of white regionalism also spanned across German political parties and movements. As German historian Sven Reichardt demonstrated in his study of Germany's postwar New Left, the left tried to establish the Heimat as a symbolic carrier of popular authenticity, community, and local resistance against the "alienation" caused by "soulless" capitalism and globalization.[27] In the 1980s, New Left activists appropriated postcolonialist discourses to portray Germany as colonized by Western powers and subscribed to an ethnoculturally homogeneous Germany.[28] The Heimat narratives developed in this context had an impact on the early Green Party as well as center-left politicians and continue to be influential for contemporary German environmental protection politics. For example, the 2007 "Vilmer Theses" of the Federal Agency for Nature Conservation aim to normalize and democratize the Heimat in order to place it in the "service of nature conservation."[29] According to the document, the preservation of the concept of the Heimat is necessary because nature conservation cannot only be justified by ecological or economic factors but also requires a justification in ethical, aesthetic, and cultural-historical terms.

The continued use of the Heimat on the left as well as in the context of environmental protection has gone hand in hand with ignoring and reproducing the Heimat's racial dimension. While the "Vilmer Thesen" claim that "in view of globalization and the anonymity of industrial mass society" the attachment to the Heimat expresses the resistance to a capitalist-globalist "system,"[30] a critical examination of the Heimat itself, as well as the ways it continues to be underpinned by notions of a white racial identity, is absent. Racism, according to a common argument, is a residue only on the far-right margins, not the mainstream or the left. This lack of critical engagement with commonly used visions of the Heimat enables the far right to easily connect to mainstream and leftist discourses of environmental protection in its white identity politics.

Attempts to critically assess majority white visions of the Heimat and their exclusionary character have been made only recently by a new generation of German writers and intellectuals such as Fatma Aydemir and Hengameh Yaghoobifarah. In *Eure Heimat ist unser Albtraum* (Your Heimat Is Our Nightmare), a collection of essays written by minority intellectuals, the unmarked white identity politics inherent in German mainstream visions of the Heimat are dissected from different angles. At the same time, some of the authors attempt a subversive appropriation of the Heimat as a concept defined by minorities and their struggle to shape German culture.[31] Interventions like "Your Heimat Is Our Nightmare" have largely been marginalized in the wider public debates. Here the focus continues to lie on the Nazi past while the white identity politics underpinning mainstream visions of the Heimat are not only neglected but reasserted through centrist and leftist attempts to reclaim the Heimat from the far right and, as I argue, with the far right's ideology of ethnopluralism.

The Heimat in Far-Right Thought

IN GERMANY, THE far right uses various levels of mobilization beyond party politics to gain broader support, especially at the local level.[32] As the far right's intellectual network, the so-called New Right ideologically and structurally connects conservatism and right-wing extremism.[33] Unlike the establishment right, the far right in Germany and other countries embraces what U.S. political scientist David Art has called an "alternative" language and subcultural political positioning.[34] Central to this "alternativeness" is the explicit and shared embracing of white supremacy and nativism by the various currents within the far right.[35]

The New Right's loose and flexible networks connect the far right's explicit white identity to the mainstream by moving away from the biological racism of the "old right" toward what Étienne Balibar and Immanuel Wallerstein have called a "cultural racism" that is compatible with mainstream visions of a secular liberal democracy.[36] Following this strategy widely shared values such as the support of democracy, constitutional rights, and pluralism are presented as essential components of Western civilization and white culture.[37] As the German historian Yasemin Shooman has argued, following this cultural racism and construction of a white identity enables the far right to racialize notions of culture and religion shared by the majority population and to give them a similar position as the far right's older eugenic notion of race.[38] In this process, the concept of the Heimat enables the linkage of notions of Western civilization and white supremacy to an ethnically inflected understanding of the nation through the prism of the local.

Reflecting the role of the Heimat as a metaphor for the German nation, far-right nationalism emphasizes an ethnoregionalism, which tracks currents on the New Left in Germany and beyond.[39] Better known as ethnopluralism, this ideological merger of right-wing ethnic exclusion and left-wing regionalism is based on the notion of ethnoculturally homogeneous regions that coexist peacefully but do not mix. The concept emerged in the 1970s as part of an anti-imperialist nationalism that resonated with both left and right. Here parts of the New Left embraced nationalism as a way to realize a liberation from an Eastern communist and a Western capitalist totalitarianism.[40] Former New Left intellectual Henning Eichberg developed the concept of ethnopluralism, claiming that the New Left's 1968 student movement had rediscovered the need for a national cultural identity in the fight against alienation driven by "big business and bureaucrats."[41] In 1978 he asked: "Are we Germans or 'citizens of the FRG' with an Americanised language (...)? Identity or alienation, this is the new main contradiction, Imperialism or our *Volk*."[42] Following the example of Eichberg, embracing ideological elements and vocabulary (like "anti-imperialism," "alienation," or "pluralism") from the left enabled the far right to incorporate a neo-Marxist discourse of anti-hegemony into its racist ideology.[43] Analyzing the French Nouvelle Droite, French sociologist Pierre-André Taguieff has called this incorporation "retorsion," that is, the effort to delegitimize the political and/or cultural other in order to legitimize the political self by taking up the other's discursive semantics and filling them with new meaning.[44] Inscribed in this strategy, ethnopluralism has become a central concept in the far right that has been opposed to multiculturalism as an ideology that aims to impose an artificial egalitarianism and totalitarian globalism in the name of an uprooted cosmopolitan elite.

The aims followed by the ideology of ethnopluralism are by no means as new as the term "New Right" suggests. In Germany, they can be traced back to the Romantic movement of the late nineteenth century and especially the "Conservative Revolution" in the 1920s.[45] The label "Conservative Revolution" was coined by the German New Right to legitimize itself as an intellectual current distinct to National Socialism. The key works of the 1920s attributed to the so-called Conservative Revolution, particularly Oswald Spengler's *The Decline of the West* and Carl Schmitt's political theory, have today become central elements in not only the German New Right but the far right in Europe and the United States more generally.[46] Then as now, the non-Western and the foreign are invoked to conjure the white political self.[47] Then as now, as U.S. literary scholar Donna Jones argues, the fear of an imminent decline of the Occident expresses an anxiety about a historicity that is not dominated by white Europeans with increasingly visible political demands by non-white and non-Christian minorities.[48] Then as now, the far right mobilizes against the threat of global uprooted elites and the end of white supremacy by offering an "alternative" aesthetic or symbolic redescription of the white national self that speaks to the different historical and sociopolitical contexts in which the far right operates.

On the contemporary German far right, the Heimat is embedded in an ethnopluralist "right to be different"[49] as proclaimed by the central thinker of the French New Right, Alain de Benoist. Opposed to a "multicultural mixing," the Heimat symbolizes a "communitarian racism"[50] seemingly dissociated from a biological understanding of race while racializing the vision of a Western civilization and secular democracy rooted in a "Judeo-Christian tradition" as essential elements of a white European cultural identity. In turn, non-white immigration and Islam are styled as threats not only to an ethnocultural homogeneity but equally to democracy itself as a cultural mixing would lead to the "dissolution of the *Staatsvolk*," the national people constituting the basis for a democratic statehood.[51] The old right's narrative of racial impurity gives way to the claim that multiculturalization and an increasing ethnocultural diversity undermine not only traditional culture but democracy as a whole.

By explicitly embedding such an ethnocultural understanding of the Heimat in its claims to defend European nations against globalization and multiculturalism the far right can blur the borders between cultural and biological definitions of race and racialize supposed cultural differences between white and non-white, European and Muslim cultures. U.S. alt-right activists such as Jared Taylor have here become increasingly influential on the German far right. Taylor, who attempts to scientifically relegitimize the concept of race, has been able to expand his influence in both public and scientific discourse during the Trump presidency.[52] The self-described "race realist" is the author of *White Identity*,[53] a bestseller among the American alt-right. The book's cover features a painting symbolizing Heimat by German nineteenth-century artist Caspar David Friedrich. In 2018 Taylor gave a lecture at a conference organized by Germany's leading far-right think tank, Institut für Staatspolitik (IfS).[54] In his presentation Taylor called on Europeans to make sure that "Europe remains Europe":

> You still have the chance to remain the majority in your country, to preserve your culture, to avoid the deep and unbridgeable trenches that exist in the US. You have to encourage your co-Europeans to say: "This Heimat was built by our ancestors for us, not for you! Our culture reflects our way of life, not yours!"[55]

Taylor shows how easily the Heimat can be embedded in a discourse of white supremacy using the Heimat as the key vehicle for making white identity meaningful and charged with exclusionary cultural meaning.

Equally central to the far right in Germany, Europe, and beyond[56] is the philosophy of Martin Heidegger, one of the few philosophers who has elaborated the concept of the Heimat and integrated it in his notion of the essential historical rootedness of the *Volk*, the national people.[57] Rejecting a "rationalist" biological definition of race in favor of a "spiritual" or cultural essentialism, Heidegger's philosophy has been highly influential on French Nouvelle Droite's mastermind Alain de Benoist's anti-biological, ethnospiritual concept of national peoplehood. In Germany, Heidegger's anti-modern philosophy and his critique of technology have also made him a fundamental influence on far-right environmentalism. Since 2020 *Die Kehre* (The Turn), a new far-right "magazine for environmental protection" with links to the Identitarian Movement, has been published in Dresden.[58] Its title and content are directly inspired by Heidegger's *Die Technik und die Kehre* (Technology and the Turn),[59] a work that, as is claimed on the magazine's website, shows how technology is the "the highest danger" for "our human being."[60] Supported by Thurigian AfD leader Björn Höcke, the magazine aims to establish an understanding of environmental protection that overcomes a "narrow focus of ecology on climate change" and that, echoing the abovementioned Vilmer Thesen, includes the "teaching of the environment as a whole, including cultural landscapes, rituals and customs."

Heidegger's concept of the Heimat as a native soil has to be contextualized within the *völkisch* tradition that was central to the thinkers of the 1920s Conservative Revolution. Similar to the more contemporary ideology of ethnopluralism, the *völkisch* tradition links biology, culture, and religion to define "the national community" (*Volksgemeinschaft*) and its racial identity.[61] For Heidegger, as for the Nazis, "the Jew" represented a racialized other embodying liberalism, capitalist modernity, and rationalism that were "contaminating" the Volk while he styled himself as an authentic thinker "rooted in our native soil."[62] The focus on Nazi biological racism in both the public debate and the scholarship has often veiled the more acceptable, but equally racializing, forms of cultural racism put forward by Heidegger. As U.S. historians Robert Bernasconi and Jonathan Judaken have shown, Heideggerian cultural, anti-eugenic racism was just as central to Nazism as biologist ideas of racial purity and eugenics[63] and "legitimated Nazi state policy on the Jewish question."[64] For Heidegger, the Heimat was an identity-forming alternative to a technologized and uniform modern world civilization[65] and essential to forward-looking and self-affirming meaningful existence.[66] He defined the Heimat as a social and natural environment that gives meaning to a collective being and that opposes a destructive, nihilistic, and purely quantitative modern world.[67]

By making the Heimat's political and exclusive character explicit and by offering an exclusive cultural understanding of race that opposes the biological racism of the Nazis, Heidegger offers a useful ideological resource for a contemporary far right, which searches to dissociate itself from Nazism. In a 2013 program of a summer academy on the topic of the Heimat organized by the IfS that took place in a small village in Saxony-Anhalt, the Heimat is described through reference to Hegel as an unquestionable place where "I do not have to explain myself" and to which I feel a prepolitical emotional bond.[68] In the program Heidegger's philosophy is celebrated as producing a way of thinking that is rooted in the Heimat and that should serve as a guiding principle for a strengthened regionalism and a Heimat protection movement. Such a movement should prevent the "relationship between nature and culture [essential to the concept of the Heimat] [from getting] out of joint" and the Heimat, through globalization and multiculturalism, from changing its character to such an extent that it is "no longer recognisable."

Beyond the far right's intellectual circles, the Heimat has become a central term for the Identitarian Movement and its white resistance activism. On its website,[69] the movement takes up the danger of a uniform "One-World" and connects it to the idea of a "Great Replacement," a popular far-right conspiracy theory that claims that Europe is undergoing a "population exchange," replacing white Europeans with non-white Muslims.[70] Following Heidegger's diagnosis of the destructive effects of the modern, uprooted concept of "culture," the Identitarian Movement argues that immigration destroys the Heimat and, following the theory of ethnopluralism, insists that every people has the right to its own particular Heimat. Immigration is presented as a danger and threat that helps to define the Heimat as the signifier for an ahistorical, homogeneous, and static entity owned by an ethnic group.

In a similar manner, Frank Böckelmann, a New Left activist in the 1960s and 1970s and today the editor of the Dresden-based far-right magazine *Tumult*, proclaimed in the widely read center-right *Focus* magazine that people live today on a "largely borderless planet," in a unified world, in which a growing longing for the Heimat is "not a return to dull nationalism, but resistance to an existence everywhere and nowhere."[71] Here, too, the "catastrophe of mass immigration" appears as the "overwhelming problem" threatening the Heimat. Karlheinz Weißmann, a former member of the IfS, is a leading figure in the Berlin-based Library of Conservatism, a far-right think tank close to the AfD. Along with Götz Kubitschek, Weißmann is arguably the most influential far-right intellectual in Germany. Weißmann has dealt in detail with the concept of the Heimat in an article for the far-right magazine *Cato*.[72] Framed by the column "What Is German?" as well as a detailed glossy report on the "New Hambach Festival," Weißmann's text describes the Heimat as a familiar space of meaning that is closely interwoven with rural life. He develops an image of the Heimat reminiscent of Heidegger's, evoking a sensory experience bound to the rhythms of nature whose increasing mechanization and industrialization lead to a dissolution of roots and allow an uprooted and interchangeable form of humanity to develop.

Weißmann sees movements fighting for the protection of the Heimat as the expression of a resistance against a growing homogenization of cultural differences. He sees himself as standing up for the "preservation of the 'peculiarities' of the landscape" and trying to "correct what ... has led to man's alienation from everything that had determined his existence until then." He strongly supports the subject of "Heimatkunde" (local history and geography) in schools, which he believes was introduced in the twentieth century to promote "Heimatliebe," the love of one's homeland through education. In this context, Weißmann's vision of the Heimat is linked to a contradictory reading of the East German GDR. He praises the GDR for having recognized the importance of teaching a prepolitical bond to one's Heimat, implying that this was neglected in West Germany. While he rejects the socialist economic system, Weißmann celebrates "the people" and culture of the GDR as "more German" since they have been spared from a West German "left-liberal brainwashing."[73]

Weißmann's idealization of the GDR as a state in spite of its socialism, keeping a national pride and local rootedness alive, is often seen in the German far right. Yet, this highly selective idealization contradicts the equally popular comparison of the GDR with Germany's contemporary politics and "dissidence" against the return of a new totalitarian socialism. In the same *Cato* issue as well as in the AfD's 2019 election campaigns in East Germany, Germany's present political system is described as a "GDR 2.0,"[74] arguing that current German politics are marked by a leftist totalitarianism similar to East Germany's former socialist regime. The Heimat is positioned as the basis for countercultural activism against this "totalitarianism," linking the idealization of local communities to the strength of the so-called German *Mittelstand*, the small and medium-sized businesses that have often strongly benefited from an economic globalization dominated by Western countries.

The romanticized image of the GDR as a political system that has preserved a notion of the Heimat neglected in the capitalist West also surfaces in the preference of the far right for rural East Germany as a place to live and work.[75] Isolated regions like the area surrounding Schnellroda, a little village in East Germany that is home to the IfS, are perceived as places where an authentic Germanness can still be experienced and where people are still rooted in their Heimat. Here, too, a continuity with more widely spread and less explicitly political narratives of the Heimat is evident. After the German reunification in 1990 the discovery of East Germany also represented the "revelation" of an authentic Germany that was seen as lost in the West not only in the West German far right around Kubitschek and Weißmann but for many West Germans in general.[76] As anthropologist Jason James shows, the territory of the former GDR emerged here as a symbolic space where prewar and pre–Nazi Germany could still be experienced. This Heimat shaped by a landscape, culture, and architecture became the imaginary for a national identity "untainted" by Nazism,

World War II, West German capitalism, leftist politics of coming to terms with the past, non-white and Muslim immigration, and modern urban development.[77]

Thinkers of the far right such as Weißmann also refer to the visions of the Heimat expressed in the 1970s and 1980s by the New Left social movements as exemplary because they were opposed to "large-scale industrial projects" of globalizing capitalism.[78] Yet the New Left failed, Weißmann claims, because it was an elitist project organized by "spoiled youth" imposing leftist visions of the Heimat on ordinary people from above.[79] Today, Weißmann sees the chance to use the Heimat to mobilize for the far right from below. The so-called refugee crisis, he claims, would have triggered a new attachment to the Heimat, this time expressed as a "feeling of the common man," who sees himself betrayed by the political class while his country is left to "foreigners."[80] Following Heidegger, Weißmann sees the preservation of the Heimat as incompatible with a globalist order, which inhumanly regards "people only as atoms or as disposable masses" and which makes any possibility of an "organic construction" of the local belonging impossible.

The interweaving of left and right Heimat narratives exemplified by Weißmann enables the far right's pitch for a Heimat-based conservatism[81] that is also directed toward parts of the left. Both in the past and more recently, the far right in Germany and beyond has engaged in an aesthetic embracing of nature and the environment that easily connects to more widely shared notions of the Heimat.[82] Some of the central figures of Germany's contemporary far right have their origins in the Green movement. One example is Thomas Hoof, the founder of the publishing house Manuscriptum and Manufactum, a popular company that produces sustainable furniture. While Hoof has sold Manufactum, he has turned Manuscriptum into one of the central German far-right publishers responsible for books by leading AfD politicians such as Alexander Gauland and Björn Höcke. Another example is Rolf Peter Sieferle, who became known through his books on the preservation of German forests and later authored the book *Finis Germania* that warned of a self-destruction of a German culture that, in his eyes, had submitted to leftist self-hate and immigration.[83]

The Heimat in Far-Right Politics

HOW IS THE concept of the Heimat, developed by far-right intellectuals, translated into the realm of party politics and activism? As it points out in its party newspaper, Germany's far-right AfD understands its task to be giving the growing need "to return to one's immediate surroundings, to one's region and Heimat a political representation."[84] The Heimat is officially defined by the party as a "geographically, linguistically and mentally determined space that gives identity, meaning, and value to existence." The knowledge of one's origin, culture, and identity gives, according to the party, *"the necessary orientation in the globalizing world. It enables our children to appreciate their own culture and foreign cultures. Moreover, it has great integrative power for the foreigners who come to us."*

To strengthen the attachment to the Heimat, the party follows Weißmann's call for the introduction of "Heimatkunde" into school education and tries to present it as part of a modern approach to teaching: "The AfD wants to free the term Heimat from its antiquated and sentimental connotations by offering modern and age-appropriate local history lessons." The subject "Heimatkunde" should be conceived "as an invitation to students to actively and consciously explore their immediate region, the nature and history of their Heimat." Local history in schools is, the party claims, a "contribution to more equal opportunities and an important contribution to the cohesion of our modern society, which is characterised by migration." The concept of the Heimat formulated here has, it seems, little to do with the ethnopluralism outlined above. Embedded in the argument for the appreciation of other cultures, for more social cohesion and a greater equality of opportunity in a society shaped by migration, is an effort to formulate a concept of the Heimat that is clad in the political vocabulary of tolerance and diversity that is often employed left-liberal mainstream—a vocabulary that the AfD tends to ridicule and denounce in less official statements yet that is used here to make its Heimat policy resonate with broader audiences.

However, the article in the official party newspaper leaves unclear what a concrete Heimat-based policymaking would look like. Here, it is worth taking a look at the "government program" of the AfD in Saxony and the policies it proposes. The program was published in 2019 prior to the regional elections for Saxony's state parliament. Given that polls anticipated the AfD as a potential winner of the election,[85] the party set up a program to prepare for actually being in power and translating the party's abstract notion of the Heimat into concrete policy. In the program, the state of Saxony is presented as a Heimat under threat. In the preamble, the AfD depicts itself as the political force that "will make Saxony what it once was: a proud, family-friendly, and secure Heimat."[86] The dichotomy between an organically grown Heimat and a "system" imposed from the outside is conjured up when a "naturally grown Heimat that shapes a secure Saxon and German identity" is contrasted with an "artificial European identity that does not and cannot exist in this form" and an "egalitarian and patronising zeitgeist."[87] In line with the European far right's racialization of a liberal-democratic and secular democracy, the Heimat is defined as the bearer of an enlightened and democratic German identity threatened by leftist totalitarianism, a technocratic EU, and an Islam that "does not belong to our identity."[88] The party has also sought to integrate elements of environmental protection. For example, the party's Saxon leader Jörg Urban is the former director of the so-called Grüne Liga (Green League), a union of local environmental associations. Furthermore, in the so-called Dresden Declaration,[89] the party links notions of the Heimat to the protection of the regional natural heritage.

While the AfD presents itself as modern in public statements and its official programs, a look into the party's social media statements and campaign posters reveals that its "Heimat" is a codeword for a white nation defined against immigration, leftist parties, and the EU. For example, the Junge Alternative Dresden, the AfD's local youth organization, used Twitter to celebrate a report that claimed that refugees want to leave East Germany because of a possible AfD victory in the upcoming state elections. "More AfD," the post says, means "less 'refugees.'" In other posters that were circulated on social media as well as in election campaign posters, the Heimat is presented as a rural space that allows for the safe upbringing of children and that must be protected against Brussels and the EU. This assertion of Heimat implies the deportation of refugees and asylum seekers, celebrates the cultivation of the forest as part of the cultural heritage, opposes the Green Party's aim to build more wind turbines, and understands itself to represent a "European culture and Freedom" that is threatened by Islam. Another post claims that the "love of Heimat is no crime." It is modeled on the antiracist and pro-asylum activist symbol "no human is illegal" (Fig. 13). This visual version of what Taguieff calls "retorsion" combines the alt-right symbol Pepe the Frog with both Smurfs and garden gnomes, which symbolize not only Weißmann's ordinary white German's love for the homeland but also mainstream visions of typical Germanness as presented in *Der Spiegel*'s cover page (see Fig. 11).

The centrality of the Heimat in far-right ideology is mirrored in how the AfD and its supporting milieus have used local and regional aesthetics in its activism. Since the foundation of the AfD in 2013, two

Figure 13. "No human is illegal." Source: Wikipedia Commons.

major events have been established that explicitly seek to symbolize the connection between white national identity and the Heimat: in East Germany, the Kyffhäuser Meeting of the radical right-wing party Der Flügel (The Wing), which is known to be close to Kubitschek's IfS and the PEGIDA movement; and in West Germany, the New Hambach Festival. As a counterevent to the Kyffhäuser Meeting, the New Hambach Festival is organized by an elitist milieu of professors and economists around AfD leader and economics professor Jörg Meuthen and Max Otte, equally a professor of economics—a milieu that is closer to Weißmann, *Cato*, and the Library of Conservatism. Both festivals demonstrate the similar narratives employed across inner-party differences to ritualize an alternative version of national identity through the prism of the Heimat.[90]

The East German Kyffhäuser Meeting follows the tradition of a spiritual understanding of the Heimat and nation and takes place at the so-called Kyffhäuser Memorial, built as one of a number of national memorials in the late nineteenth century to forge a German national spirit. In the Kyffhäuser Meeting, the Heimat is constructed as the bearer of a mythical, timeless past and a sacralized national tradition that Der Flügel claims to represent and continue. In his speech at the Kyffhäuser Meeting in 2017,[91] Thuringia's AfD leader, former teacher from West Germany, and Flügel protagonist Björn Höcke describes why this specific place had been chosen. As a mythical place, it is the starting point for a restrengthening community and a new tradition, opposing "an unprecedented migration" that would result in a "cultural and civilizational break of historical dimensions." Höcke portrays other parties as part of a homogenizing cultural hegemony, "which wants to overcome everything that has grown" organically. In order to counter this, Höcke calls for a return to the "three great myths that have shaped our cultural identity ... as Germans": the Song of the Nibelungen as a symbol of self-sacrificing struggle, the Faust saga as the epitome of the German hunger for knowledge, and the Kyffhäuser saga, according to which the "old, kind and just emperor in the mountain ... will one day return to raise the glory of the empire," an emperor "who would strike down enemies and remove injustice." These myths are indispensable, Höcke claims, as sources of inspiration for Germany's struggle for sovereignty.

Although the mythical is more central here than at the West German New Hambach Festival, Höcke also draws parallels to modern democracy and the secular constitutional state. Here, too, the main enemy is migration, defined by Höcke as a "weapon in the hands of the one-world ideologues" that threatens democracy and seeks to dissolve the constitutional rights of the German people and the secular state. Höcke rejects the critical questioning of the Heimat and nation as destructive. Instead, he wants to promote an ethnodemocratic understanding of the Heimat to create an "unquestionable being with oneself ... nourished by the attachment to the native landscape, thinking in one's mother tongue and belonging to a historically grown culture."

The New Hambach Festival in West Germany reflects an equally mythical understanding of politics. However, given a West German audience that is more skeptical of forms of explicitly mythical nationalism, the festival clads this mythical understanding in the language of a rational liberal-democratic tradition. The festival was established by Max Otte, a central figure of the so-called Werte Union, a lose network inside German chancellor Merkel's governing CDU with close ties to both the New Right and parts of the AfD.[92] In speeches by Thilo Sarrazin, Vera Lengsfeld, Imrad Karim, and Jörg Meuthen, Germany as a Heimat is portrayed as the epitome of progress and civilization. As in the Kyffhäuser saga, an awakening is to be celebrated here as well. In the abovementioned issue of *Cato*, the event is described as the awakening of democracy from its "Sleeping Beauty slumber."[93] A photograph of the "master of the castle," Max Otte, looking out over the landscape from the castle, adorns the cover of the glossy magazine, in which—introduced by Weißmann's treatise on the Heimat and a section titled "What Is German? Culture Has a Heimat"—speeches from the festival are reprinted.

More than at the Kyffhäuser Meeting, Islam plays a central role in most of these speeches. For example, for Sarrazin, a member of Germany's center-left social democratic party and former senator in Berlin, it embodies an "immigration foreign to our culture"[94] as Muslims are "uncomprehending, foreign, and largely hostile to our culture."[95] Sarrazin avoids openly racist terms such as "great replacement" or "population exchange" that are more readily used by AfD politicians and far-right activists, but he makes clear that he sees himself as a rational defender of a white, culturally homogeneous Germany.[96] While Germany is celebrated as the bearer of a "technical civilisation," any responsibility for Germany's involvement in the history of colonialism is swept aside.[97] Sarrazin's speech largely repeats the claims he has presented in his 2011 bestseller *Deutschland schafft sich ab* (Germany Abolishes Itself)[98] as well as his more recent *Feindliche Übernahme* (Hostile Takeover), which focuses on "how Islam impedes progress and endangers society."[99]

Sarrazin acknowledges Germany's coming to terms with its Nazi past but denies that migration can play any role in the emergence of a more open and inclusive society: "Germany's spiritual recovery did not require immigrants from the Middle East and Africa."[100] Any contribution to Germany's prosperity made by immigrants is ignored. Instead, Sarrazin conjures the spirit of resistance of the liberal nationalist, anti-monarchic movements that gathered at the Hambach Castle in the nineteenth century. He sees the New Hambach Festival in the tradition of a democratic nationalism that today needs to rise up a political establishment which "together with the left-wing mainstream media implements a universalist agenda ... that irrevocably changes the character of Germany and Europe by letting in immigration foreign to our culture."[101] While Sarrazin uses the imaginary of the Heimat to idealize a German identity as inherently democratic and progressive, Islam is demonized as essentially premodern and regressive, backward-looking and inefficient.[102]

In the speech of AfD leader Jörg Meuthen,[103] the concept of the "nation" is avoided. Instead the Heimat takes on a central role as a local metaphor for the nation. The Heimat is presented as threatened by an ideology of multiculturalism imposed in a totalitarian way onto the German people.[104] Although Meuthen claims to embrace a more inclusive nationhood that is open to immigrants, he nevertheless portrays the German people as a force of greatness resisting the "one-world ideology" of multiculturalism.[105] The Heimat is designed as a territorially located as well as spiritually idealized possession that must not be abandoned. By referring to the far right's ethnopluralist right of cultural difference, he argues Islam has its place in the world—but not in Germany as it is incompatible with German culture. He claims that marking the critique of Islam as racist would be the attempt to veil the imminent threat of a civil war with and a submission to Islam.[106] He refers to Samuel Huntington's thesis of a "clash of civilisations,"[107] a discourse which, as Fatima El-Tayeb has shown, has been the dominant framework for the debates on migration and Islam in Europe at least since 9/11, within and beyond right-wing contexts.[108] The Heimat is here—as in postwar West Germany—recast not only as the bearer of the German nation but also as a local metaphor of a West, this time not threatened by totalitarian communism but a totalitarian Islam.

Both events and their use of the Heimat reflect the two faces of the German far right: on the one hand, an East German movement that refers to an anti-rational, spiritual, and communitarian understanding of the nation; and, on the other hand, a primarily West German movement that constructs the German nation as an epitome of Western rational progress and liberalism in the tradition of the Enlightenment. Both currents embody the two forms of racialized mobilization for white German identity: a more explicit and crude East German version and a more subtle and liberal-bourgeois West German one.[109] Both use Heimat narratives established in West and East Germany mystifying the link of a racial identity, its territory, and its culture as the expression of the respective political ideals they propagate. To do so, both designate globalization, a left-liberal technocracy, Islam, and "mass immigration" as the main enemies and regard attempts to critically assess Germany's history as well as the concept of the Heimat as expressions of self-hate.[110] Despite their differing rational and spiritual conceptions of the Heimat, both use the Heimat as a metaphor for a white, civilized, democratic, and Christian Germany and Europe, constructed by the explicit exclusion of an Islam that is alien to culture and democracy.[111] Finally, both events show different ways of turning banal visions of the Heimat into Heimat activism by making explicit Heimat's implicit political and racial dimensions.

Conclusion

THE ABOVE ANALYSIS shows how widely spread white German visions of the Heimat are entangled with the racialized concept of the Heimat developed by far-right intellectuals, turned into policy in AfD programs, and enacted by AfD political activism. The Heimat emerges as a utopia and place of longing that resonates with narratives of the white national self and its local embeddedness beyond classical far-right audiences and the economically left-behind. As a sanitized homeland, it is imagined as an ahistorical ideal and a supposedly prepolitical expression of a profoundly human need for belonging and community. The unmarked political dimension of the Heimat lies in the fact that, in the context of contemporary Germany, it is intended to be a political metaphor for all of "German" society and thus also an ideal image of the white political community that underlies the far right's vision of democracy. The German far right's understanding of the Heimat is thus the expression of the political ideal of a white national identity based on a guilt-free past and an Islam-free future. While the "other" is constructed as an uprooted and technocratic liberalism as well as an essentially alien Islam and non-white immigration, the Heimat appears as the carrier of a rooted democracy and ethnically homogeneous culture.

With its concept of the Heimat, the German far right offers a new political home to the current renaissance of solidarity, social belonging, and the "imagination of equality"[112] within a defined, ethnoculturally homogeneous group.[113] The political quality here lies in the combination of this principle of solidarity and sense of belonging with a widespread longing for an immaculate white myth of origin.[114] The anti-pluralistic shadows of the past are projected onto a "totalitarian" left and onto an Islam that is portrayed as premodern, anti-democratic, and fascist.[115] By drawing on mainstream visions of the Heimat and widely shared anxieties about immigration and economic globalization, the far right can turn the Heimat into a symbol for an alternative far-right future. As the example of Jared Taylor shows, the political ambiguity of the Heimat enables the far right to use a discourse of essential cultural differences rooted in local descent to construct a shared white identity. By bringing together East and West German as well as left and right narratives of the Heimat in the principle of ethnopluralism, the far right can racialize cultural differences without resorting to an explicitly eugenic concept of race.[116]

What thus remains is answering the question of whether the Heimat is a concept that should inform inclusive and future-oriented politics. On the one hand, given the structural racism inherent in the concept of the Heimat, any progressive use of the concept appears compromised.[117] Yet, the use of the Heimat in German everyday language by white and non-white Germans as well as the ways it is critiqued and rethought by feminist, queer, and non-white intellectuals such as Sharon Dodua Otoo and Fatma Aydemir points to the possibility of Heimat as a complex performative identity instead of a marker of a racialized cultural essence. As a marker of belonging that resonates with a widespread human need for solidarity and local community, it may have a unifying force if it productively integrates a critical, reflective view of the past and a subversive use of white majority symbols of Heimat by marginalized groups. One example of how this could work is the YouTube channel "Germania" that is produced by the public broadcaster *funk*. Playing with Heimat aesthetics such as known local historical landmarks, gothic letters, and traditional German Christmas songs in the introduction to its videos, the channel presents known minority-background Germans and the meaning Heimat bears for them. Bringing together stories of exclusion and of how they embrace their local belonging in different German cities, it critically assesses traditional accounts of Heimat while opening the possibility for more inclusive and diverse stories of local belonging in Germany.

For the Heimat to become an inclusive category of collective belonging, however, implicit racialized narratives of the Heimat in the mainstream need to be exposed, questioned, and deconstructed. Instead of externalizing the racial dimensions of the Heimat to the far-right margins, the fact that the far right can seamlessly connect with widespread visions of the Heimat should point to the enduring racial dimensions in mainstream visions of German identity. As long as such exclusive understandings of the Heimat are not fundamentally reassessed they can be politically used to shut off a critical engagement with Germany's and Europe's colonial past—according to U.S. political theorist Barnor Hesse, a precondition for a serious fight against contemporary structural racism.[118] Banalizing its political and racial dimensions instead of making them explicit means using the Heimat to naturalize racial power structures and, as Fatima El-Tayeb puts it, to categorize as not-European all those who violate Europe's implicit but normative whiteness, thus allowing dominant society forever to consider the "race question" as externally (and by implication temporarily) imposed from the outside. The result is an image of Europe as self-contained and homogenous in which racialized minorities permanently remain outsiders.[119]

As long as the Heimat and other forms of national belonging in and beyond Germany can be and are used to reproduce this image, they remain concepts of the past, not the future. Instead of paving the way for inclusive local societies, such uses of the Heimat make visible the identity politics inherent in widespread visions of white national belonging not through a critical assessment but by showcasing, embracing, and wearing as a "badge of honor" the white identity politics that have long remained unmarked in mainstream tropes of the Heimat.

Notes

1   Katrin Keller, "Neustadt: Grünen-Chef Habeck im Hambacher Schloss," *Die Rheinpfalz*, July 19, 2018, https://www.rheinpfalz.de/lokal/neustadt_artikel,-neustadt-gr%C3%BCnen-chef-habeck-im-hambacher-schloss-_arid,1219724.html.
2   Miriam Scharlibbe, "Grünen-Chef Robert Habeck auf Heimatsuche am Hermannsdenkmal," *Neue Westfälische*, July 12, 2018, https://www.nw.de/nachrichten/zwischen_weser_und_rhein/22190393_Gruenen-Chef-Robert-Habeck-auf-Heimatsuche-am-Hermannsdenkmal.html.
3   Frank-Walter Steinmeier, "Deutsch und frei," *Zeit Online*, March 13, 2019, https://www.zeit.de/2019/12/demokratie-nationalismus-tradition-gedenktage-geschichtsunterricht.
4   Peter Porsch, "Muss denn Heimat übel sein? Anmerkung zu einer immer wieder aufflammenden linken Debatte," *Neues Deutschland*, January 12, 2019, https://www.neues-deutschland.de/artikel/1109809.linke-debatte-muss-denn-heimat-von-uebel-sein.html.
5   For example, Melanie Amann, "Wie sich das AfD-Milieu die deutsche Geschichte zurechtbiegt," *Spiegel Online*, March 23, 2018, https://www.spiegel.de/spiegel/neues-hambacher-fest-wie-sich-die-afd-die-deutsche-geschichte-zurechtbiegt-a-1204211.html; Margarete van Ackeren, "Grünen-Chef will republikanische Symbole nicht der AfD überlassen," *Focus*, July 24, 2018, https://www.focus.de/politik/deutschland/robert-habeck-in-leipzig-von-einem-gruenen-der-auszog-schwarz-rot-gold-zu-entdecken_id_9302990.html.
6   Fatima El-Tayeb, "'The Forces of Creolization': Colorblindness and Visible Minorities in the New Europe," in *The Creolization of Theory*, ed. Francoise Lionnet and Shu-mei Shih (Durham: Duke University Press, 2011), 239.

7   Oliver Decker and Elmar Brähler, *Flucht ins Autoritäre: Rechtsextreme Dynamiken in der Mitte der Gesellschaft* (Gießen: Psychosozial-Verlag, 2018); Rita Chin and Heide Fehrenbach, "What's Race Got to Do with It? Postwar German History in Context," in *After the Nazi Racial State: Difference and Democracy in Germany and Europe*, ed. Rita Chin, Heide Fehrenbach, Geoff Eley, and Atina Grossmann (Ann Arbor: University of Michigan Press, 2009), 1–29.
8   Michael Billig, *Banal Nationalism* (London: Sage, 1995).
9   Alon Confino, "The Nation as a Local Metaphor: Heimat, National Memory and the German Empire, 1871–1918," *History and Memory* 5.1 (1993): 75.
10 Matthew Hughey, *White Bound: Nationalists, Antiracists, and the Shared Meanings of Race* (Stanford: Stanford University Press, 2012), 5.
11 Ibid.; Bethany Bryson, *Making Multiculturalism: Boundaries and Meaning in U.S. English Departments* (Stanford: Stanford University Press, 2005).
12 Confino, "The Nation as a Local Metaphor," 50.
13 Marianne Bechhaus-Gerst, "Decolonize Germany? (Post)Koloniale Spurensuche in der Heimat zwischen Lokalgeschichte, Politik, Wissenschaft und 'Öffentlichkeit,'" *Werkstatt Geschichte*, no. 75 (2017): 53; Ozan Zakariya Keskinkılıç, *Die Islamdebatte gehört zu Deutschland: Rechtspopulismus und antimuslimischer Rassismus im (post-)kolonialen Kontext* (Berlin: AphorismA, 2019).
14 Confino, "The Nation as a Local Metaphor," 54.
15 Anthony Smith, *Ethno-Symbolism and Nationalism* (Abingdon: Routledge, 1991), 50.
16 Mary Fulbrook, *German National Identity After the Holocaust* (Cambridge: Polity Press, 1999); Jenny Wüstenberg and David Art, "Using the Past in the Nazi Successor States from 1945 to the Present," *The Annals* 617.1 (2008): 72–87.
17 Peter Pfeiffer, "The National Identity of the GDR: Antifascism, Historiography, Literature," in *Cultural Transformations in the New Germany: American and German Perspectives*, ed. Frederike Eigler and Peter Pfeiffer (Columbia: Camden House, 1993), 23–41; Alon Confino, *Germany as a Culture of Remembrance: Promises and Limits of Writing History* (Chapel Hill: University of North Carolina Press, 2006); Jan Palmowksi, *Inventing a Socialist Nation: Heimat and the Politics of Everyday Life in the GDR, 1945–1990* (New York: Cambridge University Press, 2009).
18 Jason James, "Retrieving a Redemptive Past: Protecting Heritage and Heimat in East German Cities," *German Politics and Society* 27.3 (92) (2009): 1–27.
19 Vera Lengsfeld, "Der deutsche Herbst 2015 ist nun Alltag," *Achse des Guten*, March 21, 2019, https://www.epochtimes.de/meinung/gastkommentar/vera-lengsfeld-der-deutsche-herbst-2015-ist-nun-alltag-a2829889.html?print=1; Monika Maron, "Links bin ich schon lange nicht mehr," *Neue Züricher Zeitung*, June 30, 2017, https://www.nzz.ch/feuilleton/bundestagswahl-links-bin-ich-schon-lange-nicht-mehr-ld.1303513; Sigmar Faust, "Die totalitäre Welteroberungsideologie im Namen Allahs?" *The European*, February 20, 2018, https://www.theeuropean.de/sigmar-faust/13522-die-totalitaere-demokratie.
20 Julian Göpffarth, "Activating the Socialist Past for a Nativist Future: Far-right Intellectuals and the Prefigurative Power of Multidirectional Nostalgia

in Dresden," *Social Movement Studies* (2020), https://www.tandfonline.com/doi/full/10.1080/14742837.2020.1722628.

21 Norbert Frei, *Vergangenheitspolitik: Die Anfänge der Bundesrepublik und die NS-Vergangenheit* (Munich: Beck, 1996).

22 Neil Gregor, *Haunted City: Nuremberg and the Nazi Past* (New Haven: Yale University Press, 2013); Jeremy De Waal, "The Turn to Local Communities in Early Post-war West Germany: The Case of Hamburg, Lübeck, and Bremen, 1945–1965," in *Reconstructing Communities in Post-war Europe, 1918–1968*, ed. Stefan Couperus and Harm Kaal (London: Routledge, 2017), 130–50.

23 Gaëlle Fisher, "Heimat Heimstättensiedlung: Constructing, Belonging in Postwar West Germany," *German History* 35.4 (2017): 568–87.

24 Jeremy De Waal, "Heimat as Geography of Postwar Renewal: Life After Death and Local Democratic Identities in Cologne, 1945–1965," *German History* 36.2 (2018): 247.

25 Maja Figge, *Deutschsein (wieder-)herstellen: Weißsein und Männlichkeit im bundesdeutschen Kino der fünfziger Jahre* (Bielefeld: Transcript, 2015), 13; Julia Anspach, "Antisemitische Stereotype im deutschen Heimatfilm nach 1945," in Heinz Ludwig Arnold and Matthias N. Lorenz, *Juden.Bilder* (Munich: Edition Text & Kritik, 2008).

26 Barbara Schrödl, "Heimatfilme und die Neuordnung des Nationalen," *Frauen Kunst Wissenschaft/Zeitschrift für Geschlechterforschung und visuelle Kultur* 35 (2004): 32–33. For a similar role of "Heimat" movies in the constitution of an East German national self, see Sebastian Heiduschke, "The Gegenwartsfilm, West Berlin as Hostile Other, and East Germany as Homeland: The Rebel Film Berlin—Ecke Schönhauser (Berlin Schönhauser Corner, Gerhard Klein, 1957)," in *East German Cinema: DEFA and Film History* (New York: Palgrave Macmillan, 2013), 61–68.

27 Sven Reichardt, *Authentizität und Gemeinschaft: Linksalternatives Leben in den siebziger und frühen achtziger Jahren* (Berlin: Suhrkamp, 2014), 60–66.

28 Hans-Georg Betz, "Deutschlandpolitik on the Margins: On the Evolution of Contemporary New Right Nationalism in the Federal Republic," *New German Critique*, no. 44 (1988): 129–33; Jan-Werner Müller, *Another Country: German Intellectuals, Unification and National Identity* (New Haven: Yale University Press, 2000), 215; Chin and Fehrenbach, "What's Race Got to Do with It?" 111.

29 Franz August Emde, "Vilmer Heimatthesen und ihre Kritiker," in *Symposium zur Beziehung von Heimat und Naturschutz erschienen* (2007), published October 18, 2007, https://idw-online.de/en/news230962; Reinhard Piechocki, Konrad Ott, Thomas Potthast, and Norbert Wiersbinski, "Vilmer Thesen zu Grundsatzfragen des Naturschutzes," *Vilmer Sommerakademien 2001–2010* (2010), https://www.bfn.de/fileadmin/MDB/documents/service/Skript_281.pdf.

30 Piechocki et al., "Vilmer Thesen," 12.

31 Fatma Aydemir and Hengameh Yaghoobifarah, eds., *Eure Heimat ist unser Albtraum* (Berlin: Ullstein, 2019), 68.

32 Pierto Castelli Gattinara and Andrea Pirro, "The Far Right as Social Movement," *European Societies* 21.4 (2018): 447–62; Bert Klandermans and

Nonna Mayer, *Extreme Right Activists in Europe: Through the Magnifying Glass* (London: Routledge, 2005); Manuela Caiani, Donatella della Porta, and Claudius Wagemann, *Mobilizing on the Extreme Right: Germany, Italy, and the United States* (Oxford: Oxford University Press, 2012); Julian Göpffarth, "Between the 'Street' and the 'Salon', the Local and the National: Mediating Intelligentsia and the German New Right in Dresden," *Europe Now Journal*, no. 21 (2018), www.europenowjournal.org/2018/10/01/between-the-street-and-the-salon-the-local-and-the-national-mediating-intelligentsia-and-the-german-new-right-in-dresden/.

33 Wolfgang Gessenharter, "Die 'Neue Rechte' als Scharnier zwischen Neokonservatismus und Rechtsextremismus in der Bundesrepublik," in *Gegen Barberei: Essays Robert M. W. Kempner zu Ehren*, ed. Rainer Eisfeld and Ingo Müller (Frankfurt am Main: Athenäum, 1989), 424–52.

34 David Art, *Inside the Radical Right: The Development of Anti-Immigrant Parties in Western Europe* (Cambridge: Cambridge University Press, 2011), 11.

35 Cas Mudde, *Populist Radical Right Parties in Europe* (Cambridge: Cambridge University Press, 2007), 19.

36 Étienne Balibar and Immanuel Wallerstein, *Race, Nation, Class: Ambiguous Identities* (London: Verso, 1991); Riem Spielhaus, "Media Making Muslims: The Construction of a Muslim Community in Germany Through Media Debate," *Contemporary Islam* 4.1 (2010): 11–27.

37 Rogers Brubaker, "Between Nationalism and Civilizationism: The European Populist Moment in Comparative Perspective," *Ethnic and Racial Studies* 40.8 (2017): 1191–1226.

38 Yasemin Shooman, *"… weil ihre Kultur so ist": Narrative des antimuslimischen Rassismus* (Bielefeld: Transcript, 2014), 81.

39 Alberto Spektorowski, "The New Right: Ethno-regionalism, Ethnopluralism and the Emergence of a Neo-fascist 'Third Way,'" *Journal of Political Ideologies* 8.1 (2003): 112.

40 Rudi Dutschke, "Zur Nationalen Frage," in *Die Linke und die nationale Frage: Dokumente zur deutschen Einheit seit 1945*, ed. Peter Brandt and Herbert Ammon (Hamburg: Rowohlt, 1981), 350–51.

41 Henning Eichberg, "National ist Revolutionär," in *Die Linke und die nationale Frage*, ed. Brandt and Ammon, 352.

42 Ibid., 351.

43 Günter Bartsch, *Revolution von rechts? Ideologie und Organisation der Neuen Rechten* (Freiburg: Herder, 1984).

44 Pierre-André Taguieff, "Le néo-racisme differentialiste: Sur l'ambiguité d'une évidence commune et ses effets pervers," *Langage et société*, no. 34 (1985): 75.

45 Mark Sedgwick, ed., *Key Thinkers of the Radical Right: Behind the New Threat to Liberal Democracy* (Oxford: Oxford University Press, 2019).

46 David Engels, "Oswald Spengler and the Decline of the West," in *Key Thinkers of the Radical Right*, ed. Sedgwick, 22–35; Reinhard Mehring, "Carl Schmitt and the Politics of Identity," in *Key Thinkers of the Radical Right*, ed. Sedgwick, 36–53.

47 Barnor Hesse, "Symptomatically Black: A Creolization of the Political," in *The Creolization of Theory*, ed. Francoise Lionnet and Shu-mei Shih (Durham: Duke University Press, 2011), 45.

48 Donna Jones, "The Ambiguous Promise of European Decline: Crisis, Aesthetic Possibilities and the Re-Alignment of Power in the Wake of the Great War," presentation for the symposium "Plotting Internationalism," Duke University, November 15, 2013.
49 Spektorowski, "The New Right," 115–17; Jean-Yves Camus, "Alain de Benoist and the New Right," in *Key Thinkers of the Radical Right*, ed. Sedgwick, 76–78.
50 Pierre-André Taguieff, *La force du préjugé: Essai sur le racisme et ses doubles* (Paris: La Découverte, 1988).
51 "Der Große Austausch als Auflösung des Staatsvolkes," Identitäre Bewegung (blog), February 25, 2017, https://blog.identitaere-bewegung.de/der-grosze-austausch-als-aufloesung-des-staatsvolkes/.
52 Angela Saini, *Superior: The Return of Race Science* (Boston: Beacon Press, 2019), 111–33; Russell Nieli, "Jared Taylor and White Identity," in *Key Thinkers of the Radical Right*, ed. Sedgwick, 137–54.
53 Jared Taylor, *White Identity: Racial Consciousness in the 21st Century* (Oakton, VA: New Century Books, 2011).
54 The conference was attended by the author and took place in the East German city of Magdeburg on April 14, 2018. For the conference program, see Institut für Staatspolitik, "Staatspolitischer Kongreß 'USA unter Trump—wie weiter, Europa?' April 14, 2018, in Magdeburg," March 5, 2018, https://staatspolitik.de/staatspolitischer-kongress-am-14-april-2018-in-magdeburg/.
55 Jared Taylor, "Warum ethnische Bruchlinien in den USA ein Thema sind," presentation at the Staatspolitischer Kongress of the Instituts für Staatspolitik, Magdeburg, April 14, 2018.
56 Heidegger is a core influence in the thought of panrussian far-right ideologue Aleksander Dugin. In the United States, Steve Bannon claimed that Heidegger "is my man." See Christoph Scheuermann, "Searching in Europe for Glory Days Gone By," *Spiegel Online*, October 29, 2018, https://www.spiegel.de/international/world/stephen-bannon-tries-rightwing-revolution-in-europe-a-1235297.html.
57 Julian Göpffarth, "Rethinking the German Nation as German Dasein: Intellectuals and Heidegger's Philosophy in Contemporary German New Right Nationalism," *Journal of Political Ideologies* 25.3 (2020), http://dx.doi.org/10.1080/13569317.2020.1773068; Camus, "Alain de Benoist and the New Right," 80; Ronald Beiner, *Dangerous Minds: Nietzsche, Heidegger, and the Return of the Far Right* (Philadelphia: University of Pennsylvania Press, 2018).
58 Andreas Speit, "Den Grünen den Naturschutz nehmen," *TAZ*, June 2020, https://taz.de/Rechtes-Oeko-Magazin-Die-Kehre/!5690299/.
59 Martin Heidegger, *Die Technik und die Kehre* (Pfullingen: Neske, 1962).
60 *Die Kehre*, website presenting the concept of the magazine, https://die-kehre.de/konzept/.
61 Jonathan Judaken, "Heidegger's Shadow: Levinas, Arendt and the Magician from Messkirch," in *The Routledge Companion to Philosophy of Race*, ed. Paul C Taylor, Linda Martín Alcoff, and Luvell Anderson (London: Routledge, 2017), 63.
62 Heidegger quoted in ibid., 63–64.

63 Robert Bernasconi, "Heidegger's Alleged Challenge to the Nazi Conception of Race," in *Appropriating Heidegger*, ed. James E. Faulconer and Mark A. Wrathall (New York: Cambridge University Press, 2000), 50–67; Sonia Sikka, "Heidegger and Race," in *Race and Racism in Continental Philosophy*, ed. Robert Bernasconi and Sybol Cook (Bloomington: Indiana University Press, 2003), 87–88.
64 Judaken, "Heidegger's Shadow," 66.
65 Kai Hammermeister, "Heimat in Heidegger and Gadamer," *Philosophy and Literature* 24.2 (2000): 313; Martin Heidegger, *Denkerfahrungen, 1910–1976* (Frankfurt: Klostermann, 1983), 187.
66 Martin Heidegger, *Nur noch ein Gott kann uns retten*, interview in *Der Spiegel*, no. 23 (May 31, 1976): 209, 219.
67 Pieter Tijmes, "Home and Homelessness: Heidegger and Levinas on Dwelling," *Worldviews* 2.3 (1998): 201–13.
68 "Sommerakademie 'Heimat,'" Institut für Staatspolitik, September 20–22, 2013. Call published July 24, 2013, https://sezession.de/40048/sommerakademie-heimat-jetzt-anmelden.
69 "Politische Forderungen: Erhalt der ethnokulturellen Identität," Identitäre Bewegung website, https://www.identitaere-bewegung.de/forderungen/erhalt-der-ethnokulturellen-identitaet/.
70 Caterina Froio, "Race, Religion, or Culture? Framing Islam Between Racism and Neo-Racism in the Online Network of the French Far Right," *Perspectives on Politics* 16.3 (2018): 696–709.
71 Frank Böckelmann, "Sehnsucht nach Heimat," *Focus Magazin*, January 7, 2016, https://www.focus.de/magazin/archiv/politik-und-gesellschaft-sehnsucht-nach-heimat_id_5229084.html.
72 Karlheinz Weißmann, "Herkunft Kennt Keine Reue," *Cato: Magazin für Neue Sachlichkeit*, no. 4 (2018): 33–37.
73 Ibid., 36.
74 Max Otte, "DDR 2.0," *Cato: Magazin für Neue Sachlichkeit*, no. 4 (2018): 17.
75 Stephan Trüby, "Right-wing Spaces," *E-flux Architecture*, September 1, 2016, https://www.e-flux.com/architecture/superhumanity/68711/right-wing-spaces/.
76 Günter Kowa, "Niemand ist eine Insel: Was der ICE Erfurts historischem Bahnhof anzurichten droht," *Frankfurter Allgemeine Zeitung*, October 10, 1995.
77 James, "Retrieving a Redemptive Past," 18–19.
78 Weißmann, "Herkunft Kennt Keine Reue," 35.
79 Ibid.
80 Ibid., 36.
81 "Naturkonservatismus bedeutet Umkehr zu traditionellen Werten wie Familie und Heimat," presentation by Volker Kempf in the Library of Conservatism, July 4, 2018, https://www.bdk-berlin.org/veranstaltungsberichte/naturkonservatismus-als-umkehr-zu-traditionellen-werten-wie-familie-und-heimat/.
82 Bernhard Forchtner, "Nation, Nature, Purity: Extreme-right Biodiversity in Germany," *Cultural Imaginaries of the Extreme Right*, special issue of *Patterns*

of Prejudice 53.3 (2019): 285–301; Bernhard Forchtner, ed., *The Far Right and the Environment: Politics, Discourse and Communication* (New York: Routledge, 2020).

83 Rolf Peter Sieferle, *Finis Germania* (Schnellroda: Antaios, 2017).
84 Alternative für Deutschland, "AfD-Fraktionen setzen sich für Rückkehr des Fachs 'Heimatkunde' an Schulen ein," *AfD Kompakt*, June 7, 2018, https://afdkompakt.de/2018/06/07/afd-fraktionen-setzen-sich-fuer-rueckkehr-des-fachs-heimatkunde-an-schulen-ein/.
85 In the final result the AfD came in second with 27.5 percent of the vote behind the center-right CDU, which had 32.1 percent, and ahead of the far-left Die Linke (10.4 percent), the Green Party (8.6 percent), the center-left SPD (7.7 percent), and the liberal FDP (4.5 percent).
86 Alternative für Deutschland, *Trau Dich Sachsen: Regierungsprogramm der Alternative für Deutschland zur Landtagswahl Sachsen 2019* (2019): 7, https://www.afdsachsen.de/files/afd/landesverband-sachsen/download/LTG2019/RWP_190618.pdf.
87 Ibid.
88 Ibid., 36–37.
89 Susanne Götze, "Grünes Blatt, brauner Boden: Umwelt-Erklärung der AfD," *Spiegel Online*, July 28, 2019, https://www.spiegel.de/wissenschaft/mensch/dresdner-erklaerung-das-nationalistische-umweltverstaendnis-der-afd-a-1279206.html.
90 Fabian Virchow and Dennis Zuev, "Performing National-Identity: The Many Logics of Producing National Belongings in Public Rituals and Events," *Nations and Nationalism* 20.2 (2014): 192.
91 Björn Höcke, "Rede auf dem Kyffhäusertreffen 2017," YouTube, September 11, 2017, https://www.youtube.com/watch?v=7ALZpg3gIGk.
92 Julian Göpffarth, "Radicalising the Establishment from Within? The CDU and the Werte Union," *CARR Blog*, November 25, 2019, http://www.radicalrightanalysis.com/2019/11/25/radicalising-the-establishment-from-within-the-cdu-and-the-werte-union/.
93 Andreas Lombard, "Standing Invitation," *Cato: Magazin für Neue Sachlichkeit*, no. 4 (2018): 38.
94 Thilo Sarrazin, "Es Steht Viel Auf Dem Spiel," *Cato: Magazin für Neue Sachlichkeit*, no 4 (2018): 40–46.
95 Ibid., 41.
96 Ibid., 42–43.
97 Ibid., 44.
98 Thilo Sarrazin, *Deutschland schafft sich ab* (Stuttgart: DVA, 2010).
99 Thilo Sarrazin, *Feindliche Übernahme: Wie der Islam den Fortschritt behindert und die Gesellschaft bedroht* (München: Finanzbuch Verlag, 2018).
100 Sarrazin, "Es Steht Viel Auf Dem Spiel," 41.
101 Ibid., 44.
102 Ibid.
103 Jörg Meuthen, "Unser schönes, unser einziges Land," *Cato: Magazin für Neue Sachlichkeit* 4 (2018): 54–59.

104 Ibid., 56.
105 Ibid., 57.
106 Ibid., 57–59.
107 Samuel Huntington, *The Clash of Civilizations and the Remaking of World Order* (London: Free Press, 2002).
108 El-Tayeb, "'The Forces of Creolization,'" 236.
109 Lucia Muriel, "Wir wurden angestarrt wie im Zoo," *Zeit Online*, July 21, 2019, https://www.zeit.de/gesellschaft/2019-07/rassismus-lucia-muriel-ddr-brd-ecuador.
110 Sarrazin, "Es Steht Viel Auf Dem Spiel," 42.
111 El-Tayeb, "'The Forces of Creolization,'" 238.
112 Virchow and Zuev, "Performing National-Identity," 4.
113 Stephan Lessenich, "Heimat lässt sich nur in einem sozialen Zusammenhang denken," in *INDES: Zeitschrift für Politik und Gesellschaft* 4 (2018): 18.
114 El-Tayeb, "'The Forces of Creolization,'" 242.
115 Esra Özyürek, "Muslim Minorities as Germany's Past Future: Islam Critics, Holocaust Memory, and Immigrant Integration," *Memory Studies* 15.1 (2019): 139–54.
116 Chin and Fehrenbach, "What's Race Got to Do with It?" 4.
117 Samuel Salzborn, "Heidegger für Halbgebildete—Identitäre Heimatideologie zwischen Fiktion und Propaganda," *Wissen schafft Demokratie* 3 (2018): 164, https://www.idz-jena.de/fileadmin/user_upload/PDFS_WsD3/Text_Salzborn.pdf.
118 Hesse, "Symptomatically Black," 58.
119 El-Tayeb, "'The Forces of Creolization,'" 233.

PART III
Counterrevolutions and Culture

Benjamin Noys

9. Planetary Technology and Reactionary Accelerationism

THE CURRENT REACTIONARY, white supremacist, and fascist movements exploit technology, particularly the internet, to achieve their ends. While stressing racial hierarchy, tradition, and a vehement rejection of forms of abstraction and modernity, these movements embrace the emblematic form of what Heidegger called the reign of "planetary technology,"[1] the internet. Certainly, these movements are heterogeneous and plural, but they all constitute socio-technical assemblages. In their most violent forms these assemblages include the internet manifesto, the assault rifle, livestreamed video, leaderless resistance, and a verbal and physical iconography that is designed to signal intent across the mediascape. Paul Virilio had noted that, deprived of a territory, Palestinian struggles of the 1970s were left to the international space of the airport before being left only with the space of the media.[2] These current forms of reactionary violence take a different form. They are not deprived of a territory but aim to expand or create a territory. In this assemblage forms of separatism, individual and communal physical territories, violently appear in the media to terrorize and destroy territories that embody what they see as mixing or sites that defy the hegemonic aims of reactionary movements.

None of this should be taken as paradoxical or contradictory, at least in any simple sense. Instead, as I will explore here, the reactionary right has its own thinking of technology that is not simply one of rejection or one of temporary use. The reactionary right does not have to be anti-technological nor does it have to treat technology simply as a means to an end. Certainly, it does find itself in a tense and antagonistic relationship with technology. Technology, as a force of abstraction and as a force of global uprooting, finds itself in conflict with claims to autochthony and forms of ethnonationalism. The anti-Semitism that runs through reactionary thought often associated this global form of abstraction with Jewishness, in a conspiratorial rejection of cosmopolitanism. For all that, however, as Jeffrey Herf has tellingly detailed, we also have a reactionary modernism,[3] which can be traced from the Italian Futurists through Weimar Germany, and today we find such instances as Guillaume Faye's Archeofuturism, or the feudal technocratic fantasies of the Neoreactionary Movement (NRx).[4] While different in aims and forms, these movements actively celebrate the fusing of technology with ethnonationalist claims to overcome the abstraction of technology by integrating it with ethnic and hierarchical characteristics. They also tend to celebrate the hardness of technology as, precisely, a form.[5] It is the masculine violence of technology as a mode of organizing the world that promises the hierarchical reordering of life demanded by reactionary currents.

To analyze these currents of the reactionary embrace and engagement with technology I begin with Martin Heidegger, who is usually taken as an emblematically anti-technological reactionary thinker. Instead, I will argue that Heidegger's thinking of technology, from his positive engagement with Nazism to the postwar turn, is consistent in trying to accept and engage with technology as a mode of thinking. Within this thinking we will see a struggle to retain a privilege for certain sites of thinking and a certain ethnonational privileging of Germany and a particular vision of Germany. While often a kind of feudal pastoral, in its celebration of the Black Forest and the work of the farmer, Heidegger also engages with the desire to traverse technology into new and enigmatic forms of thinking and politics. Certainly, these modes remain reactionary and problematic, but they suggest the necessity of technology as something to be surpassed to generate new articulations of place and politics.

I then turn to Heidegger's friend and fellow thinker Ernst Jünger, who reflects on the intimate relation between technology and war. Jünger both galvanized Heidegger's thinking on technology and took a different path in celebrating the possibilities of technological nihilism. Originally articulated in the 1930s, I particularly trace Jünger's thinking of technology during World War II and in the postwar period. Jünger's technological naturalism, his fusion of nature and technology, is curiously prescient of contemporary cyberpunk celebrations of digital technology. The importance of Jünger is that he indicates differences of emphasis in relation to the reactionary right engagement with technology, offering a much more positive sense of technology compared to Heidegger. Jünger is also important in his stress on the military dimensions of technology, especially as the military continues to operate as a breeding ground for the contemporary right. For all these reasons Jünger is a resonant figure for grasping contemporary reactionary thought.

Finally, I want to consider contemporary currents of right or reactionary accelerationism, which emphatically demand the melding of the human with the technological and with capitalism to achieve a post-humanist vision of racial and social hierarchy. Accelerationism has proved a controversial and plural term, subject to repeated appropriations and revisions.[6] While not trying to identify accelerationism as a whole with the reactionary right, it is important to trace the reactionary iteration of accelerationism. Reactionary accelerationism condenses elements of the arguments of Heidegger and Jünger in its desire to traverse technology and to fuse with technology as a process of dissolution that also produces new hierarchies. In fact, the test of reactionary accelerationism becomes the test of the capacity to embrace technology as a vector of dissolution, which creates the hierarchy between those able to pass this test and those who do not. The thinker who has done most to develop this mode of vision is Nick Land, but Land's work engages with a broader milieu of desires to meld or fuse with technological and social forms of acceleration.

In all these cases my aim is a critical analysis that grasps how racist and reactionary politics tries to traverse and engage planetary technology as the condition of its own project. I do not aim to dignify such a politics, but I do aim to take it seriously as an object of critique. This critique is a speculative genealogy or constellation of particular reactionary right engagements with the technological, especially in its planetary form. The analysis is concerned with not only direct influences and engagements, such as between Heidegger and Jünger, but also the suggestion of a range of positions that occupy different reactionary perspectives on the form of technology. It is a matter of affinities and common assumptions, as well as changing and shifting alliances and disagreements. In this way I hope to take an initial measure of the thinking of technology on the reactionary right.

The Supreme Danger

IT IS HEIDEGGER who might seem to stand as the thinker who is most anti-technological and furthest from any reactionary modernism, let alone any reactionary accelerationism. In the postwar essay "The Question Concerning Technology" (1954),[7] Heidegger relentlessly connects technology to danger, to "supreme danger," and even to "danger as such" (26). This is what gives rise to the image of the anti-technological Heidegger, who contrasts a hydroelectric plant on the Rhine with a sawmill secluded in a valley of the Black Forest (5).[8] The former is forcing the Rhine into work that perverts and disrupts the very form of the river into a device for generating power, while the latter, still technological, is at least to scale and relatively hidden. Heidegger also contrasts the same hydroelectric plant with "the old wooden bridge that joined bank with bank for hundreds of years" (16). Again, we have the contrast of an inhuman technological domination for a more human-scale technology that serves to join rather than sunder or alienate, in Heidegger's reading. Finally, this is the same Heidegger who contrasts the Rhine dammed *up* into the power works with the Rhine uttered *out* of the art work (the reference being to Hölderlin's hymn "The Ister").[9] The Rhine has gone from being spoken out poetically to "an object on call for inspection by a tour group ordered there by the vacation industry" (16). The final abject fate of the Rhine is to be reduced to not only a source of power but also a source for tourism. In all these instances we can see the obvious anti-technological drift, or certainly an instance of manageable and human-scale technology that serves a real use.

Heidegger, however, wants to resist the usual narrative of being either pro- or anti-technology. Technology is not just a particular means to achieve an aim and a particular form of human activity. Instead, if we are to pursue the essence of technology then, for Heidegger, we must go beyond technology. The essence of technology is not, according to Heidegger, anything technological (4).[10] Instead, technology goes beyond tools and means, beyond instrumentality, to become a particular way of revealing the world and Being. Technology is a mode of revealing, a form of philosophy, and a kind of regime of seeing and understanding. It belongs to the history of Western metaphysics, which is a history of various ways of revealing and understanding Being.[11] For Heidegger, this history is also one of the forgetting and misunderstanding of Being. We have fallen further and further from understanding Being and, we could say, furthest of all with technology. Technology is the reign of a particular mode of revealing that is the limit of revealing Being. This is why technology is the supreme danger. It threatens the complete forgetting of Being and all other dangers are merely local versions of this threat.

What then is the essence of technology? "The essence of technology lies in Enframing [*Ge-stell*]" (26). It "frames" or "enframes" the world and Being in a particular way. What technology reveals to us is a world in which everything is a "standing-reserve," ready for potential use. Alain Badiou offers a useful summary: "the essence of technology is to mobilize Being, brutally treated as a simple reserve of availability for willing in the latent and essential form of nothingness."[12] Again, enframing is not itself technological, but enframing orders and produces the world as standing-reserve. This is also not simply a human activity. It is not simply something we do to the world by subjecting it to instrumental treatment. While it might seem technology places humans as lords of the earth, in fact we become another standing-reserve and subjected to enframing as a mode of revealing. It is this that places technology, whose essence is enframing, as a form of danger (26). The danger is we cannot grasp this revealing as we become standing-reserve and so we lose all relationship to revealing. The world simply is what we take it for—a stock of potential resources. As Heidegger puts it in the essay "What Are Poets For?" "the earth and its atmosphere become raw material. Man becomes human material, which is disposed of with a view to proposed goals."[13] Even if we conceive of these resources as finite or endangered we remain within seeing them as a set of resources.

So far then this appears as another reactionary lament on the forces of technology instrumentalizing the world, even if one given a particular metaphysical or cosmic hue. Certainly, this is not an incorrect way of reading Heidegger. This technological enframing seems contrasted with the moments of resistance to be found in poetry. It is poetry as a mode of revealing, as it is practiced by Hölderlin and others, which could shift us away from enframing into a new mode of dwelling on the earth, or what Badiou calls "a resacralization of the earth."[14] This reading would confirm the usual reactionary conservative lament at technology and seem to place Heidegger at a distance from planetary technology. It would also seem to confirm the narrative that reactionary thought is antithetical to technology. This is not all that Heidegger says, however. Technology is not only the supreme danger but also the possibility of saving. It is for this reason he quotes Hölderlin: "But where danger is, grows / The saving power also" (28). This saving involves the traversal of technology. It is the fact, if we like, that technology is so bad, such a danger, that it starkly offers the possibility of reversal into saving. In Heidegger's words, "the closer we come to the danger, the more brightly do the ways into the saving power begin to shine and the more questioning we become" (35).

Of course, this saving is left quite vague or even messianic, as "only a God can save us," according to Heidegger in a later interview.[15] The turn to the poetic seems designed to be another anti-technology of founding or making beyond the calculable.[16] Again, this would seem to refute engagement with technology as the site of calculation, even more so today since the rise of digital technologies. The digital, in the form of the binary rendering of language as code, would appear to be furthest from the poetic, as Heidegger conceives it. Yet, this turn to the poetic is also a traversal of technology, a movement through it that does not simply deny its existence. The dominance of technology, its saturation of Being, also reveals the possibility of "a surpassing of the technical."[17] Heidegger traces this possibility in the reversal of danger and saving, as well as in Rilke's invocation of the "Open." In this moment, according to Heidegger, the human enters into the danger of losing the self to technical objectification. This venturing into danger is what makes possible a transition or another possibility that surpasses technology. Poetry opens an interiority of consciousness and an invisibility that moves beyond the calculability of technology.[18]

Again, we seem to have a resolute rejection of technology, but we should also note the retention of human-scale technologies, evident in the invocations of the old wooden bridge, and the stress on the need to think and exhaust technology to the end.[19] In this particular and peculiar way, we could regard Heidegger as an accelerationist: in the contemporary sense that does not simply refer to the desire to speed up technology but in the sense of the necessity to engage and redeploy the horizon of technology that confronts us.[20] Heidegger is far from the tropes of speed and the frenzy of technology, something much more present in Ernst Jünger. No doubt Heidegger would regard such celebrations as instances of technological nihilism. Heidegger does, however, aim at a traversal of technology into new modes of use, into new forms of making, even if those remain associated with the poetic. While calling Heidegger an accelerationist may seem to be a deliberately provocative gesture, my aim is to insist on the surprising degree to which Heidegger can be read as a thinker engaged with the technological.

This traversal of technology also requires a particular formation of the ethnonational within the technology. We can return to Heidegger's notorious remarks in *An Introduction to Metaphysics* (1935), where he states:

> This Europe, in its ruinous blindness forever on the point of cutting its own throat, lies today in a great pincers, squeezed between Russia on one side and America on the other. From a metaphysical point of view, Russia and America are the same; the same dreary technological frenzy, the same unrestricted organization of the average man.[21]

Here we see the trope of the "land of the middle" that was central to German national identity somewhat disguised within European identity.[22] While this seems to belong to a more typical discourse of anti-technological lament, we can again see how it can be integrated with a traversal of technology. Only some, those of the correct spirit, can make a use or questioning of technology that can traverse planetary technology.

This can be reinforced by the later, even more notorious remark in the same book, that "the works that are being peddled about nowadays as the philosophy of National Socialism ... have nothing whatever to do with the inner truth and greatness of this movement (namely the encounter between global technology and modern man)."[23] Again, a claim to inner truth is made not only for Nazism but for its particular ability to grasp this encounter with technology. Much ink has been spilled about the continuities or discontinuities between pre- and postwar Heidegger. What concerns me here is more the notion that the global or planetary is not necessarily a blockage to a particular and local articulation of technology and its traversal. Within the seemingly most anti-technological mode of twentieth-century reactionary thought we can see that technology persists as something to be engaged with and surpassed. In fact, and in line with Heidegger's own anti-Semitism, this surpassing is predicated on a return to the local and concrete through the traversal of global and abstract technology.

What all this suggests is that Heidegger articulates an integration of a conception of a rooted place with the uprooting that characterizes technology as a planetary force. This integration may be politically toxic and also extremely fragile, hence the turn to a more messianic discourse of saving in the postwar period. It does, however, remain an engagement with the technological. This engagement appears as anti-technological while retaining the necessity of the technological as a site to be traversed, in the same manner in which Nietzsche suggested the necessity to traverse global nihilism.[24] Its reactionary form lies in the aim to control and delimit the abstract force of technology to a national or transnational political or poetic engagement delimited by notions of ethnicity and place. This is most explicit in the invocation of Germany as the "land of the middle," a kind of metaphysical nationalism, as the place in which technology can be thought and surpassed. There is no doubt, however, that Heidegger still retains a distance from technology, which is what justifies his image as an anti-technological or even ecological thinker. I now want to turn to, or return to, Ernst Jünger, as a symptomatic figure of the reactionary embrace and celebration of technology. We move from the studied distance of Heidegger, which aims to manage the engagement with technology, to an ecstatic immersion.

Insect War

ERNST JÜNGER WAS the German writer and thinker whose work was most important to Heidegger for his thinking of nihilism and technology, especially Jünger's book *The Worker* (1932).[25] Jünger's speculations on the planetary future as one dominated by the figure of the worker were obviously influential on Heidegger's understanding of planetary technology as the fulfillment of nihilism (one volume of Heidegger's writing consists of notes and work on Jünger, especially *The Worker*).[26] Heidegger also, it should be noted, took a distance from Jünger, regarding him as a symptom of the technological nihilism he diagnosed.[27] Jünger, however, also remains an interesting thinker in his own right, one whose more active embrace of technology and its possibilities is predictive of contemporary currents of reactionary accelerationism. It is Jünger's embrace of technology, in a more unequivocal sense, as a hardening form, a gestalt, which prefigures contemporary reactionary interests in the fusion of the human and the technological. In this sense, Jünger presents another facet of the debate to Heidegger, one in which we can see a less quietist and more activist, if still aristocratic, radicalism around the question concerning technology.

To undertake this reading of Jünger on technology, who is a notoriously evasive thinker writing across the prewar, wartime, and postwar period, I will initially focus on some remarks by Jünger from his wartime diaries on technology that further flesh out the dangers of technology. During the war years Jünger's brother, Friedrich-Georg Jünger, was writing a book, *The Failure of Technology: Perfection with Purpose* (published in 1949). Therefore, in his diaries, Jünger was already in dialogue with this work and the question of technology. Jünger's warning about technology will turn out to be highly equivocal and also foretell possibilities of traversal and integration with the technological. It will be in Jünger's postwar fiction that we will see a turn toward an integration with technology that is less martial and focused on the new appearance of technology as a form of second nature. In this sense Jünger forms a bridge between a reactionary celebration of technology as hardening form of war and violence to a modulation of this celebration into a postwar cybernetic culture that has often been portrayed as neutral or emancipatory. In this way Jünger complicates the narrative of cyberculture as counterculture in ways that unlock the configurations of contemporary reactionary accelerationism.

Jünger's analysis of technology is bound up with war. He is probably best known for his World War I memoir, *Storm of Steel* (1920), and Jünger's writing on the worker has already predicted the transformation of the warrior into the worker. Therefore, war is the focus of Jünger's speculations on technology.[28] This is what Jünger reports about the images he sees, in 1941, of the German Blitzkrieg:

> During the newsreel, the room remained illuminated to prevent any demonstrations. Our offensives in Africa, Serbia, and Greece were shown. The mere glimpse of weapons of annihilation produced screams of fear. Their automated nature, the way the steel plates of the tanks glide, the way the ammunition belts with their bright projectiles are swallowed as they fire. The rings, hinges, armor, observation slits, sections of the tank, the arsenal of life-forms that harden like crustaceans, toads, crocodiles, and insects—Hieronymus Bosch had already envisioned them.[29]

Jünger was a proficient amateur naturalist and entomologist and this cold observant gaze on nature and the destruction wrought by war is something that runs through the diaries and his other writings. This cold gaze has become a critical commonplace of writing on Jünger.[30]

Here the technology of war is prefigured by an art that reinscribes the fusion of technology and nature in what Jünger calls, in *The Worker*, an "organic construction."[31] War machines become the mutant monsters with which Bosch had peopled his vision of hell.

Jünger's other intermittent comments on technology often record the notion that human beings are now submitting to technology. The implication is that war is driven by technology. This is something suggested, in a different way, by Thomas Pynchon's novel *Gravity's Rainbow* (1973).

> It means this War was never political at all, the politics was all theatre, all just to keep the people distracted ... secretly, it was being dictated instead by the needs of technology ... by a conspiracy between human beings and techniques, by something that needed the energy-burst of war.[32]

In Pynchon's reading the war is at the service of technological acceleration. This also informs Heidegger's assertion that technology is about not only the human domination of nature but the domination of the human by technology. In a similar vein, writing in his diary in 1942, Jünger reflects on the role of the German generals on the Eastern front:

> I am driving around with the generals and observing their metamorphosis into workers. One has to abandon the hope that any traits of a Sulla or Napoleon might develop from this class. They are specialists in the area of command technology and as interchangeable and expendable as the next best worker at a machine. (142–43)

The thesis of the worker suggests that the general becomes another worker or technician, a mere cog in the machine. It is this thesis that Jünger had already outlined in *The Worker*. It should be noted that the diaries do not extend this analysis to Hitler, who remains a malign figure driving the Germans to catastrophe (Jünger refers to Hitler as Kniebolo in the diaries).[33] What remains, however, is a still a troubling thesis that the violence of the Eastern front and the military-led campaigns of extermination should be treated as the mere functioning of a machine.

While Jünger may appear celebratory he is similarly equivocal to Heidegger about technology, which is both absolute danger and the reality that we confront. For Jünger we cannot escape technology:

> Technology has now been so profoundly implemented that even after the domination of the technicians and their major premises has been broken, we are going to have to deal with the remnants. The terrible fate of its victims is built into this system. (87)

This concern with the fate of the victims of technology is left as a remarkably abstract category considering the industrial dimension of the Holocaust.[34] Technology is a world-historical force for Jünger, one literally driving development, and the issue becomes the containment or management of that force by a particular form or gestalt. Hence Jünger's thinking is dominated by the necessity of thinking types and a type of character mimetic enough of technology to master its hardness with their own. This concern with the mastery of technology through typology and through a mimetic relationship with technology continues in Jünger's postwar writing.

Jünger's novel *The Glass Bees* (1957) is another meditation on the dangers of technology that also sees the passage through technology as the only way in which we can be saved. The novel concerns the interactions of the narrator, a former cavalryman named Captain Richard, with his prospective employer, the mysterious techno-industrialist Zapparoni (something like a more malign iteration of a Walt Disney figure). Zapparoni is successful due to his construction of humanoid robots and the robotic glass bees are his latest success in mimicking nature. In some ways the novel records the encounter between different modalities of technology. Richard has made the transition from horse-mounted cavalry to tanks with some difficulty. Now he encounters a new miniature technology that extends into everyday life. In the 1930s Jünger had written of "total mobilisation" and its "extension to the deepest marrow, life's finest nerve."[35] Now that technology is realized in the new forms of the prescient imagination of the future of the micro-technologies of computing.

For Jünger, like Heidegger, the point is to traverse technology, although, unlike Heidegger, Jünger's vision does not seem so quietist or couched in the mode of a new poetic thinking. Instead, Jünger is concerned to engage technology as a form and with giving a form to technology. In the case of the robotic glass bees and the air of violence that hangs over Zapparoni's projects, which imply the replacement of the human by the technological, the narrator Richard tries to grasp this fusion of the natural and the technological as a form. We can see here the fusion of technology with nature, especially in the form of the insect, which runs through Jünger's speculations. This includes both the hardened carapace of the beetle, the focus of Jünger's entomological attentions, and the softer hive organization of the bee. Technology is imprinted with a form through its mimicry of nature, which places it within the systems of classification characteristic of Linnaeus. Jünger becomes the entomologist of a new technological reality, which itself takes the form of a fusion with the natural world.

This melding of techno-nature also places Jünger in a strange sympathy with those writings that would later be known as cyberpunk and makes Jünger resonant for contemporary reactionary appropriations of technology. The introduction to the English translation of *The Glass Bees* is written by the cyberpunk writer Bruce Sterling.[36] While this might be a contingent reference, we can also note that Andreas Huyssen suggests Jünger's "flight" into "cyborg science fiction."[37] I would stress this is not a flight, in the sense of simple evasion, but a continuation of Jünger's project of the reactionary appropriation of technology. Jünger's techno-naturalism is also reflected in the foundational novel of cyberpunk, William Gibson's *Neuromancer* (1984), and especially the techno-nihilist subculture of the Panther Moderns:

> Dark eyes, epicanthic folds obviously the result of surgery, an angry dusting of acne across pale narrow cheeks. The Hosaka released the freeze; the boy moved, flowing with the sinister grace of a mime pretending to be a jungle predator. His body was nearly invisible, an abstract pattern approximating the scribbled brickwork sliding smoothly across his tight one piece. Mimetic polycarbon.[38]

Here the mutant subcultures of the near future integrate advanced technology in a portrait of subversion. Widely read as celebrating the hacker and disruptor of corporate power, *Neuromancer* takes on a more complex and troubling tone when read against Jünger's mode of reactionary science fiction.

Certainly, the complexity of cyberpunk needs attention, and Joshua Clover has identified the neoliberal dynamics at work on Gibson's fiction.[39] My aim is not simply to accuse Gibson of reactionary politics to add to this but rather to trace certain potential equivocations in cyberpunk and in its subcultural portraits of subversion. Certainly, the reactionary line of cyberpunk is fully played out in the work of Nick Land and the Cybernetic Culture Research Unit, as we will shortly see.[40] What Jünger's work predicts in advance is the melding of the techno-natural in a fusion that also aims at the mastery and traversal of technology. While apparently celebrating fusion and the fluid, evident in the flowing movement of Gibson's Panther Moderns, what Jünger is interested in is a parallel project of freezing and giving form. It is as if the enframing that technology undertakes, according to Heidegger, has itself to be enframed in turn to develop a reactionary politics.

In Jünger's postwar writing these possibilities of traversal shift from the figure of the worker to the figure of the "anarch."[41] The worker was the figure who would give form, an international figure but one Jünger tried to delimit to the national as he feared the internationalist communist worker. Form was a nationalist type or structure that imprinted the worker and gave form to the global dimension of technology while avoiding any transnational working-class solidarity. The anarch now performs a similar function in managing the global force of technology. If the worker permitted new modes of national identification, and new possibilities of ethnonationalism, the anarch is now the exceptional figure who does not identify with a particular nation, who remains above struggles and conflicts, observing them with the cold gaze of the entomologist. In the collapse of wartime belligerence into the uneasy and static conflict of the Cold War, the anarch is a deliberately individual and international figure, in contrast to the collective and national figure of the worker. The anarch, as *The Glass Bees* demonstrates, is also very close to the transnational figure of the techno-entrepreneur, which we are now familiar with in those who flirt with reactionary and alt-right notions, such as Elon Musk. Once again, Jünger is trying to capture a particular type or form, through precision or hardening, that also threatens to dissolve into other competing figures or into what it mimics. Here we have the shift to the transnational ruling class and its flunkies, figured as court philosophers and anarchic thinkers, all prescient of configurations of the reactionary accelerationists.

This is the equivocation of Jünger's writing, between a hardening that tries to give form to technology and a dissolution into a fusion or mimicry with technology. From the worker to the anarch we see the struggle to impose form and to delimit technological integration into ethnonational or ethno-trans-national forms. Jünger, while a peripheral or minor figure, in fact demonstrates the key mode of reactionary engagement with technology as a fusion that aims to integrate form and nation within the technological. In this way the planetary dominance of technology is countered by the nomadic figure of the transnational anarch, haunted by their uncanny double the techno-entrepreneur, suggesting a new reactionary configuration. The violence of mass warfare, figuring a reactionary collective, is now traded for the seemingly withdrawn individual, who, in fact, remains a figure of aristocratic mastery and domination. This is why we have focused on Jünger as another perspective on technology, one far more welcoming of technology than Heidegger and one still concerned in a mastery of abstraction for a certain political will. While unacknowledged, and probably unknown and unrecognized, Jünger is a vital transitional figure that helps us grasp contemporary reactionary accelerationism.

Speed as Politics

THE CONVERGENCE OF the themes and attitudes I have discussed is visible in the various currents and forms of contemporary reactionary accelerationism. Heidegger's melding of danger and saving, Jünger's melding of technology and nature, are speculative resources, even if largely disavowed, for accelerationism in its reactionary forms. Certainly, as I have repeatedly argued, accelerationism is heterogeneous and a term that often lacks historical specificity or weight.[42] Since my coining of the term as a critical concept referring to the so-called philosophies of desire of the early and mid-1970s, found in the work of Deleuze and Guattari, Lyotard, and Baudrillard,[43] the term has been inflated, adopted, contested, and, often, abandoned since then.[44] Despite this, it remains a clarifying optic for certain claims made for the engagement with technology, including the fusion with technology.

Accelerationism is a broad term referring to the desire to embrace or engage with forms of technology and abstraction to achieve a post-capitalist or hyper-capitalist future. The claim has been made by left accelerationism that the existing left is mired in a folk politics that rejects the global and the technology.[45] In its most extreme form this folk politics would be represented by the anti-civilization or primitivist currents that desire a return to a pre-technological, pre-agricultural, or even pre-language society.[46] In contrast, left accelerationism claims to embrace the future and rejects left tendencies to resist technology, perhaps best summed up with the notion of the machine-breaking Luddite. One difficulty here can be the flattening of history, in which Luddism offered a rich moment of opposition to "all Machinery hurtful to Commonality."[47] The Luddites also grasped a different mode of working and of "task-scapes" to that imposed by the new forms of agricultural machinery.[48] This is one example of the flattening of history that can take place under the banner of accelerationism, but from within left accelerationism the desire has been to nuance and complicate notions of speed and the future.[49]

Right and reactionary accelerationism abandons the nuances and cautions of left accelerationism around acceleration and, obviously, the aim of universal emancipation. While articulated in very different and explicitly antagonistic forms there are areas of overlap and shared commitments.[50] One of the major resources of contemporary accelerationism has been the work of Nick Land, Sadie Plant, and the Cybernetic Culture Research Unit (CCRU) at the University of Warwick (UK) in the 1990s. That work was often equivocal, in political terms, and posed an accelerationism that aims to accelerate capitalism into a hyper or purified form. In the telling phrase of Nick Land, it offered an acceleration "in the opposite direction to socialistic regulation; pressing towards ever more uninhibited marketization of the processes that are tearing down the social field."[51] While anti-socialist, this mode of acceleration could also appear anarchistic or, perhaps better considering Land's writing on Georges Bataille, acephalic or headless. It also echoes Jünger's anarch, as the figure of a particular aristocratic radicalism, a radicalism which can also be found in Bataille.[52]

Land's celebration of meltdown into a post-capitalist existence could be read in different ways, although in retrospect it appears more consonant with neoliberal modes of justification for capitalism. Land, however, went on to engage with the reactionary right and found the Neoreactionary movement. Now, accelerationism was not simply a term for debate on the left but also on the extreme right. Land articulated an accelerationism that accelerated capitalism to shred through the forms of human solidarity and create an inhuman or post-human world of cyber subversion that would re-found racial and social hierarchy in the name of realism and science against liberal goodwill.[53]

This is a brief history of a current that has emerged and receded, appropriately, across the social and technological landscape of social media. After all, the recent iteration of accelerationism began in a hashtag form: #accelerationism. The historical grasp of this current has also been weak, with various attempts to develop or construct a canon of accelerationism. Certainly, however, the currents I have traced of reactionary embraces and engagements with technology are in close and dangerous proximity to accelerationism and especially reactionary accelerationism. This has been partially occluded as, philosophically, accelerationists have often taken Heidegger and phenomenology (with its stress on human meaning) as their primary targets of criticism and rejection; charges include: Heidegger adopts a fatalistic attitude to technology,[54] Heidegger retreats into authenticity as he cannot cope with the mutations of capitalist modernity,[55] and Heidegger's critique of metaphysical voluntarism disables a Promethean engagement with technology.[56]

What I have suggested is that Heidegger's anti-humanism and its traversal of technology are close to accelerationism, especially in its reactionary forms. In fact, accelerationists often adopt something like Heidegger's model of technology as a site of danger and saving, as technology must be adapted, accelerated, and repurposed to new ends. Instead of Heidegger's poetry, letting be, or intimations of other modes of thinking Being, for accelerationists the saving is to be found in the repurposing or selection (and then acceleration) to achieve the desired ends. For all the in-, anti-, and post-humanism of these currents, they remain within an infusion of human will into technology to dictate its ends. Also, while Heidegger claims to reject a politics of will his messianic moment of saving becomes a site of decision and acceleration into another mode of Being. While we should retain the differences between Heidegger and reactionary accelerationism we can see esoteric and obscure connections, in which initial premises about the dominance of technology result in different conclusions as to the mastery of that technology.

The left accelerationist attitude, it seems to me, finds much of its source in Alain Badiou's scorn at these nostalgic and reactionary moments in Heidegger. Badiou, in his *Manifesto for Philosophy*, remarks that Heidegger's "meditations, calculations and diatribes about technology, ... are nonetheless uniformly ridiculous."[57] Heidegger, as Badiou notes, inhabits this pathos of "the 'timber trail', the clear-eyed peasant," and so forth. Badiou's rejoinder is that the problem of technology is it is so timid and mediocre: "Just look at planetary exploration, energy through thermo-nuclear fusion, flying machines for everyone, three-dimensional images [VR]. ... We must indeed say: 'Gentlemen Technicians, one more effort if you are truly working towards the planetary reign of technology!'"[58] This is a position enthusiastically adopted by accelerationists. Certainly, these formulations suggest a decisive break with Heidegger. What I have been suggesting, however, is a more complex position in which alternative reactionary forms of accelerationism are possible that integrate technology. While Heidegger remains largely implicitly suggestive of such forms, Ernst Jünger's work can be read as a powerful precursor by the integration of the transnational domination of technology into a new reactionary gestalt. The transition is from the ethnonational celebration of German exceptionalism, found in Heidegger, to a transnational grasp of accelerating technology as an operator of new forms of domination and differentiation.

In its reactionary form, accelerationism embraces capitalist technologies, notably the technologies of digital money, such as Bitcoin,[59] to serve the ends of establishing hierarchies based on technological competence. The purification of capitalism, which supposedly opens a flattened field of immanence and the reign of intensities traversing various techno-natural hybrids, also reinstates modes of domination and distinction based on supposedly natural competencies in technological manipulation. Therefore, the ethnonationalism of reactionary accelerationism, at least in Land's form, can embrace or be sympathetic to China, for example. The cyberpunk imagery of China and Japan—visible in the opening of *Blade Runner* (1982), William Gibson's Sprawl trilogy, or the popularity of the manga and anime *Akira*—was recoded by Land through the celebration of "neo-China," which "arrives from the future" in his earlier work.[60] Land's celebration of neo-China persists in his reactionary turn, but it is now coded within a global conception of technological competence and unleashed experimentation that codes new modes of racialization and exclusion.

Land's past cyberpunk celebration of neo-China or, more negatively, his cyberpunk Orientalism is now retrofitted to a reactionary framing of racialized science that regards "natural" differences as reflected in technological ability. While not aligning simply with nationalist racisms, in which racial coding matches national identities, we have a transnational racism in which technological competence and ability is racialized.[61] In particular, this transnational racism embraces a strongly anti-black racism, by the exclusion of African Americans from forms of technological competence and engagement. Rather than technology being an abstraction that threatens identity and the rooting of racist schemas, the ability to use and engage with planetary technology itself becomes a naturalized marker of worth and value. Not surprisingly, considering its history, this is another iteration of the racialization of intelligence. The fusion of technology with nature is not only that of the cyberpunk mutant but also that of racial classification treated as a matter of natural competences. What reactionary accelerationism makes explicit is a fusion and melding of reactionary thought with technology that actively deploys that technology to structure relations of dominance.

This reactionary turn, of course, already gains support in the rapid development of forms of electronic domination, from drones to facial-recognition software. The neutral technologies of the present are not so neutral, and the technologies of so-called liberal democracies often involve technological filtering and discrimination (on both senses). This has been especially evident in terms of border control and the forms of biopolitical monitoring by state agencies that often deploy racialized modes of understanding in the cause of exclusion from national spaces. These technologies of regulation present themselves as merely neutral instruments but operate a particular enframing of the "other." While the currents of reactionary accelerationism decry nearly all contemporary government regimes as part of the "Cathedral," supposedly structured as a left hegemony of antiracism, in fact reactionary accelerationism draws on and exacerbates the illiberal common sense at the heart of the liberal present.

This revelatory sense of reactionary accelerationism, its revelation of the forms of racial domination that emerge in the engagement with technology in a transnational form, should not be taken as implying that it has an inner truth or greatness, as Heidegger claimed of Nazism's relation to technology. Instead, I have argued that we regain a critical genealogy of the relation of technology to reactionary forms of thought that moves beyond the image of reactionary thought as simply and always opposed to technology. The danger of technology that Heidegger proclaims is certainly real, but that danger does not simply lie in calculability or the application of reason and science to the world. It is not a matter of the forgetting of Being, so much as the forgetting of reactionary engagements with technology that deploy forms of melding and fusion with the technological to produce and sediment forms of domination and exploitation. As we have seen, the ability to use and deploy technology, to become part of the planetary reign of technology, takes on a reactionary and naturalized form. What contemporary reactionary accelerationism reveals are the modes of this fusion, in which danger and saving, technology and nature, and the planetary with the ethnonational and ethnotransnational take on malign configurations. In this sense, as the broader notion of accelerationism identifies, technology is a site of contestation and conflict. The difficulty lies in the ways in which accelerationism risks occluding the forms and modes of this conflict, which become reduced to positions of being pro- or anti-technology. Instead, what is required is the careful critical analysis of modes of fusion as well as the interrogation of the ways in which domination and exploitation are embedded in technological forms in new transnational forms of reaction.

Notes

1. Martin Heidegger, *The Question Concerning Technology and Other Essays*, trans. and intro. William Lovitt (New York: Garland, 1977).
2. Paul Virilio, *Popular Defense & Ecological Struggles*, trans. Mark Polizzotti (New York: Semiotext(e), 1990), 56.
3. Jeffrey Herf, *Reactionary Modernism: Technology, Culture and Politics in Weimar and the Third Reich* (Cambridge: Cambridge University Press, 1984).
4. Guillame Faye, *Archeofuturism: European Visions of the Post-Catastrophic Age* (London: Arktos, 2010); Mencius Moldbug, "A Gentle Introduction to Unqualified Reservations," January 8, 2009, https://www.unqualified-reservations.org/2009/01/gentle-introduction-to-unqualified/.
5. Andreas Huyssen, "Fortifying the Heart: Ernst Jünger's Armoured Texts," *New German Critique* 59 (1993): 3–23.
6. See Benjamin Noys, *Malign Velocities: Accelerationism and Capitalism* (Winchester: Zero Books, 2014); and Robin Mackay and Armen Avanessian, eds., *#Accelerate: The Accelerationist Reader* (Falmouth: Urbanomic, 2014).
7. Heidegger, *The Question Concerning Technology*. Further references in text.
8. This nostalgia, especially for the Greeks, or more specifically the pre-Socratics, is evident in Heidegger's note on a comment by Ernst Jünger that Greek aqueducts are a prototype of modern technology: "Roman, but never Greek!" in Wolf Kittler, "From Gestalt to Ge-Stell: Martin Heidegger Reads Ernst Jünger," *Cultural Critique* 69 (Spring 2008): 79–97, here 90.
9. Gilbert Simondon notes that in contrast to folk customs, "technical ensembles are true networks attached to the natural world; a dam cannot be built just anywhere, nor can a solar furnace … an artisanal custom, like a regional costume, can, by simple influence, be transported from one place to another; it is only rooted in the human world; conversely a technical ensemble is profoundly rooted in the natural milieu." Gilbert Simondon, *On the Mode of Existence of Technical Objects*, trans. Cecile Malaspina and John Rogove (Minneapolis: Univocal Publishing, 2017), 228.
10. For Derrida this claim allows Heidegger to protect philosophy from any contamination by technology. Jacques Derrida, *Of Spirit: Heidegger and the Question*, trans. Geoffrey Bennington and Rachel Bowlby (Chicago: University of Chicago Press, 1991), 10.
11. For a reading of Heidegger's history of these regimes, see Reiner Schürmann, *Heidegger on Being and Acting: From Principles to Anarchy* (Bloomington: Indiana University Press, 1987).
12. Alain Badiou, *Manifesto for Philosophy*, trans., ed., and intro. Norman Madarasz (Albany: State University of New York Press, 1999), 49.
13. Martin Heidegger, *Poetry, Language, Thought*, trans. Albert Hofstadter (New York: Harper Colophon Books, 1971), 111.
14. Badiou, *Manifesto*, 51.
15. Martin Heidegger, "Only a God Can Save Us: The *Spiegel* Interview (1966)," trans. W. Richardson, in *Heidegger: The Man and the Thinker*, ed. Thomas Sheehan (Abingdon: Routledge, 2017), 45–67.

16 Heidegger, *Poetry, Language, Thought* and *On the Way to Language*, trans. Peter D. Hertz (New York: Harper & Row, 1982).
17 Heidegger, *Poetry, Language, Thought*, 112.
18 Heidegger, *Poetry, Language, Thought*, 128.
19 Bernard Stiegler, *Technics and Time, 1: The Fault of Epimetheus*, trans. Richard Beardsworth and George Collins (Stanford: Stanford University Press, 1998).
20 Patricia Reed, "Seven Prescriptions for Accelerationism," in *#Accelerate*, ed. Mackay and Avanessian, 521–36.
21 Martin Heidegger, *An Introduction to Metaphysics*, trans. Ralph Manheim (New Haven: Yale University Press, 1987), 37.
22 Philippe Lacoue-Labarthe, *Heidegger, Art and Politics: The Fiction of the Political*, trans. Chris Turner (Oxford: Basil Blackwell, 1990).
23 Heidegger, *An Introduction to Metaphysics*, 199.
24 Friedrich Nietzsche, *The Will to Power*, trans. Walter Kaufmann and R. J. Hollingdale, ed. Walter Kaufmann (New York: Vintage, 1968).
25 Ernst Jünger, *The Worker: Dominion and Form*, ed. Laurence Paul Hemming, trans. Bogdan Costea and Laurence Paul Hemming (Evanston, IL: Northwestern University Press, 2017).
26 Kittler, "From Gestalt to Ge-Stell."
27 Kittler notes that Heidegger considers Jünger's work as a description of technology and not a questioning of technology ("From Gestalt to Ge-Stell," 85). Kittler also reads Heidegger's essay on technology as an attack on Jünger (and Lenin) (93).
28 In a different political framework, comparison could be made with the work of Paul Virilio.
29 Ernst Jünger, *A German Officer in Occupied Paris: The War Journals, 1941–1945*, trans. Thomas S. Hansen and Abby J. Hansen (New York: Columbia University Press, 2019), 9. Further page references in text. On the experience of the soldier in the tank Jünger's narrator, in his novel *The Glass Bees*, states:
    In the tanks it was close, hot, and noisy, as if one sat on a boiler on which steamfitters hammered. It smelled of oil, gasoline, rubber, scorched insulating tape, asbestos and—should we come into the firing zone—of powder, which puffed out of the cartridges. We felt concussions in the soft ground, then sharper and nearer impacts, then direct hits. These were not the great days of the cavalry, which Monteron had described to us, but hot machinework, obscure and without glory, always accompanied by the prospect of death by fire. I was repulsed by the thought that the spirit should in this manner submit itself to the power of flame—a deep-seated natural feeling.
    Ernst Jünger, *The Glass Bees*, trans. Louise Bogan and Elizabeth Mayer, intro. Bruce Sterling (New York: NYRB Books, 2000), 58. On the intimate relation of spirit and fire, see Derrida, *Of Spirit*.
30 The best account is Herf, *Reactionary Modernism*. See also Andreas Huyssen, "Fortifying the Heart: Ernst Jünger's Armoured Texts," *New German Critique* 59 (1993): 3–23.
31 Kittler, "From Gestalt to Ge-Stell," 84.
32 Thomas Pynchon, *Gravity's Rainbow* (London: Picador, 1975), 521.

33 This is related to Jünger's barely coded allegorical novel about the rise of Nazism, *On the Marble Cliffs*, trans. Stuart Hood (Harmondsworth: Penguin, 1983).
34 Zygmunt Bauman, *Modernity and the Holocaust* (Oxford: Polity, 1989).
35 Ernst Jünger, "Total Mobilization," in *The Heidegger Controversy: A Critical Reader*, ed. Richard Wolin (Cambridge, MA: MIT Press, 1993), 126–27.
36 Jünger, *The Glass Bees*, vii–xii.
37 Huyssen, "Fortifying the Heart," 9.
38 William Gibson, *Neuromancer* (London: Grafton, 1985), 74.
39 Joshua Clover, "Remarks on Method," *Film Quarterly* 63.4 (2010): 7–9.
40 See Nick Land, *Fanged Noumena* (Falmouth: Urbanomic, 2011); and CCRU, *CCRU: Writings, 1999–2003* (Time Spiral Press, 2015), e-book. For a retracing of accelerationism (see below) to the 1920s and 1930s, including the figure of Jünger, see Landon Frim and Harrison Fluss, "Back to the Futurists: On Accelerationism Left and Right," in *Anti-Science and the Assault on Democracy: Defending Reason in a Free Society*, ed. Michael J. Thompson and Gregory R. Smulewicz-Zucker (Amherst, NY: Prometheus Books, 2018), 177–202.
41 Ernst Jünger, *Aladdin's Problem*, trans. Joachim Neugroschel (London: Quartet Books, 1993).
42 See Noys, *Malign Velocities*; and Mackay and Avanessian, *#Accelerate*.
43 Benjamin Noys, *The Persistence of the Negative* (Edinburgh: Edinburgh University Press, 2010), 3–9.
44 Benjamin Noys, "Accelerationism: Adventures in Speed," in *The Palgrave Handbook of Critical Posthumanism*, ed. Stefan Herbrechter, Ivan Callus, Manuela Rossini, Marija Grech, Megen de Bruin-Molé, and Christopher John Müller (London: Palgrave, 2022).
45 Alex Williams and Nick Srnicek, "#Accelerate: Manifesto for an Accelerationist Politics," in *#Accelerate*, ed. Mackay and Avanessian, 347–62.
46 John Zerzan, *Elements of Refusal* (Columbia, MO: Columbia Alternative Library, 1999).
47 Peter Linebaugh, *Ned Ludd & Queen Mab: Machine-Breaking, Romanticism, and the Several Commons of 1811–12* (Oakland, CA: PM Press, 2012), e-book.
48 Katrina Navickas, "Luddism, Incendiarism and the Defence of Rural 'Task-Scapes' in 1812," *Northern History* 48.1 (2011): 59–73.
49 Nick Srnicek and Alex Williams, *Inventing the Future: Postcapitalism and a World Without Work* (London: Verso, 2016).
50 For a critical discussion, see Benjamin Noys, "Accelerationism as Will and Representation," in *The Future of the New: Artistic Innovation in Times of Social Acceleration*, ed. Thijs Lijster (Amsterdam: Valiz/Antennae, 2018), 83–97.
51 Nick Land, *Fanged Noumena: Collected Writings, 1987–2007*, intro. Ray Brassier and Robin Mackay (Falmouth: Urbanomic, 2013), 340.
52 Jean Baudrillard, "When Bataille Attacked the Metaphysical Principle of Economy," in *Bataille: A Critical Reader*, ed. Fred Botting and Scott Wilson (Oxford: Blackwell, 1998), 191–95, here 192.
53 Nick Land, "The Dark Enlightenment," 2013, https://www.thedarkenlightenment.com/the-dark-enlightenment-by-nick-land/.

54 Robin Mackay and Armen Avanassian, introduction to *#Accelerate*, 1–46, here 6.
55 Sadie Plant and Nick Land, "Cyberpositive," in *#Accelerate*, ed. Mackay and Avanassian, 303–14, here 306.
56 Ray Brassier, "Prometheanism and Its Critics," in *#Accelerate*, ed. Mackay and Avanassian, 467–88, here 471.
57 Alain Badiou, *Manifesto for Philosophy*, trans., ed., and intro. Norman Madarasz (Albany: State University of New York Press, 1999), 53.
58 Badiou, *Manifesto for Philosophy*, 54.
59 David Golumbia, *The Politics of Bitcoin: Software as Right-Wing Extremism* (Minneapolis: University of Minnesota Press, 2016); Benjamin Noys, "Stable Dematerialisations: The Dialectics of Bitcoin," *Australian Humanities Review* 66 (May 2020): 210–14, http://australianhumanitiesreview.org/wp-content/uploads/2020/05/AHR66_16_Noys.pdf.
60 Land, *Fanged Noumena*, 442.
61 This is very close to the "transversal" racism of Nietzsche, identified by Domenico Losurdo, in which racial difference is treated as global and related to an aristocratic caste of rulers; see Domenico Losurdo, *Nietzsche, the Aristocratic Rebel*, intro. Harrison Fluss, trans. Gregor Benton (Chicago: Haymarket Books, 2021), 782–85.

Bruno Perreau

10. "The New Conservative Humanism": Reflections on a New Ethnonational Counterrevolution

Translated by Patsy Baudoin

"NATIONAL CONSERVATISM. GOD, Honor, Country: President Ronald Reagan, Pope John-Paul II, and the Freedom of Nations." This was the banner under which several conservative European, American, Israeli, and far-right leaders met at the Grand Hotel Plaza in Rome on February 4, 2020.[1] Among the most notable guests were Newt Gingrich, former Republican Speaker of the U.S. House of Representatives; Giorgia Meloni, president of the openly fascist group Fratelli d'Italia; Viktor Orbán, Hungary's prime minister; Marion Maréchal-Le Pen, a rising figure on the French far right and the granddaughter of the founder of the Rassemblement national;[2] and Yoram Hazony, an Israeli intellectual and author of *The Virtue of Nationalism* as well as the chairman of the Edmund Burke Foundation, one of the co-sponsors of the event.[3] The conference set for itself the goal of rethinking conservatism along the lines of both Reagan and John Paul II, whose alliance, according to the organizers, is said to have led to the fall of Europe's communist regimes. As journalist Jean-Marc Four notes, this meeting is the umpteenth attempt to bring together "European conservative or even traditionalist Catholics, right-wing Zionist Jews, and finally American Evangelical Christians."[4] They all claim to have in common their rejection of economic liberalism, immigration, supranational legal norms, and progressive values in matters of family and sexuality. Their rallying cry is the disintegration of Western nations. But this message conceals important differences: some conference participants reject their country's political system, others play an electoral game,[5] while still others hesitate between rejecting and accepting representative democracy.[6] Some operate under the hierarchical authority of a leader; others belong to more autonomous local groups.[7] Their anti-globalization positioning has also varied widely during the past decades: the Rassemblement national defended liberal economic policies during the 1980s and 1990s before presenting itself as an alternative to global capitalism;[8] in matters of gender and sexuality, Jean-Marie Le Pen, throughout his career, alternated between stigmatizing sexual minorities and displaying indifference toward them in the name of respecting their "privacy."[9] Such different outlooks and arrangements necessarily make it difficult to build a lasting coalition. The challenge of the Rome meeting was therefore to shape a program for a renewed conservatism built not merely on condemning the social and political transformations underway in Western countries. Marion Maréchal's speech during this event left no doubt:

> Our grand idea is that conservatism is not a norm; it is not a fixed doctrine. It is above all a cast of mind. This is why there are so many national expressions of conservatism. The genius of each people has in its own way translated the universal need for the conservation of society. The peculiarity of present-day conservative movements is that they do not simply want to slow down the march of progressivism. It's not just a "yes, but." They offer a radically different path. We have beautiful examples of these different national paths here, today, and in the world: Donald Trump's national conservatism, Viktor Orbán's illiberalism, Boris Johnson's sovereignism, Polish national Catholicism, Austrian and Czech liberal-conservatism. Behind our differences, we can all accept this word, "conservative," because we all support a common vision of humanity and its natural extensions: communities of different kinds,

more specifically a national community. We are the new humanism of this century.[10]

In this chapter, I wish to present several fronts on which the idea of "new conservative humanism" is taking shape. This form of ethnonationalism is still uncertain and its means of expression remain very variable according to the places where it is expressed and according to the themes it embraces (gender, environment, economy, law, immigration, etc.).[11] Ethnonationalism is, moreover, a transcendental thought, capable of affirming simultaneously a thing and its opposite in the name of an instance (whether it be God, tradition, nature, the nation, etc.), which cannot contradict it.[12] Finally, political platforms are never decided once and for all: they are adjusted in situ, depending on the winds of public debate and the surrounding political atmosphere. To take just one example, there is, at the heart of some movements of the alt-right in the United States, both a desire to bring the nation down by replacing it with a white transnational community and, at the same time, an attachment to American identity through the "transposition" of the civic patriotism that all political life of the United States is bathed in.[13]

In this context, trying to reveal what the essence of ethnonationalism would be today is bound to fail. There are as many motives as there are movements[14] and even personalities.[15] I wish, however, to explore their modes of operation. If it is disparate and often contradictory, contemporary ethnonationalism is deployed according to very specific discursive strategies: stigmatization of all forms of minority subjectivation, embezzlement of human rights and environmental activists' references, instrumentalization of antidiscrimination law and attempts to appropriate discourses produced by mass protests. Studying these strategies is essential. It is a matter of capturing the dynamic at work in the expectations of a population looking for new ways to understand the social world and the way in which ethnonationalist movements manage to capture these expectations.[16] My goal here is to bring to light, using several examples of public interventions (speeches, legal proceedings, legislative proposals, and advertising campaigns), the ideological register that, in France and in Europe, often with the United States as counterpoint, hides behind the rhetoric of "new conservative humanism." This archaeological approach is intended to help better understand how very different movements can collaborate and, from there, how these collaborations redefine the contours of ethnonationalism today. I am interested in discursive registers because, by producing categories of thought and fueling belief in these categories, they constitute one of the cornerstones of power relations.[17] This approach is in no way blind to the sociohistorical challenges that shape the constitution of ethnonationalist movements.[18] Ethnonationalist activists pursue class and bodily interests. But that is not all. It is precisely because they are fighting for their own interests that social agents create a set of references and strategies that inscribes them in a long history—a history that, in turn, validates them. As a result, the analysis of these references and strategies, as long as it does not seek to be totalizing, also sheds light on the motives of the social agents.[19]

Today, ethnonationalist ideology claims to be both a majority and a minority. While it conceives of itself as the voice of the silent majority, subjected to laws controlled by active minorities, it also claims legal protection under the right of freedom of expression and the necessary protection of minority opinions, in this case, its own. It makes no bones about adopting references that are those used in the struggle for the rights of minorities, such as equality, antiracism, pacifism, humanism, and environmental protection. In the following pages, I intend to demonstrate one thing: because contemporary ethnonationalist thought relies on a paradoxical legitimization strategy, to try to respond to it, term to term, is to fall into the trap of moral relativism. I will first show that the "new conservative humanism" claimed at the Rome conference is akin to counterrevolutionary thinking and structured around the notion of order. In a second step, I will explain why this school of thought unfolds around questions of gender, sexuality, race, and ecology, in Europe and in France. Third, I will analyze its main strategic moves, notably the use of antidiscrimination law and the attempts to seize mass protests, such as the Yellow Vests. Finally, I will argue for inventing new ways of theorizing social bonds. This work is the condition of a real resistance to the ethnonational trope that is unfolding today in Europe and on the American continent.

An Ethnonational Counterrevolution

THE TERM "NATIONALISM" appears in Europe during the eighteenth century when the first nation-states begin to take shape. At that time, it designates an exalted belief in the ideal of a nation both to define the boundaries of its community and to allow for it to exercise its rightful political sovereignty. It therefore differs from patriotism in that it also constitutes a principle of government. Eric Hobsbawm showed how this belief in the nation was first perceived as an obstacle to international economic liberalism before being theorized as its ally, starting at the end of the nineteenth century.[20] Today, the meaning of "nationalism" is broader since the word designates both an ideology and the movements that claim it. That is why, in 1973, political scientist Walker Connor introduces the concept of ethnonationalism. He considers that "nationalism" is so broadly used that it is important to specify its object. According to him, the idea of self-determination is foundational to nationalist aspirations. Nationalists believe in the ability of each nation to determine its borders and its population and to entrust a state apparatus with the task of ensuring full control. Nevertheless, Connor highlights the paradox of the principle of self-determination:[21] How does one affirm this right for oneself and deny it to others? How do we legitimize the fact that nationalism grants the nation what it refuses to give regional and transnational minorities?[22] The sociohistorical work that Connor undertakes leads him to the following conclusion: the only way to resolve the paradox of self-determination is, for nationalists, to base the feeling of belonging on more or less homogeneous and exclusive ethnic criteria. According to him, even birthright citizenship always ends up being based on the valorization of national cultural traditions and thus submitting will to heritage. The invention of the figure of the foreigner is an essential part of how this works. The non-self makes it possible to define the self.[23] In this sense, "new conservative humanism" matches the definition of ethnonationalism perfectly: the figure of the foreigner acts as a specter that threatens the nation from inside and from outside and makes it possible to circumscribe—and carve away—what constitutes it. An enemy from elsewhere threatens the nation because it is weakened by minorities with confusing behaviors and divided loyalties. Foreignness makes the foreigner's bed. In her speech in Rome, Marion Maréchal provides a good overview of what constitutes ethnonationalism today in France:

> There is a specific French spirit of freedom and reason. But what remains of this French spirit in the era of ideological delusions such as postcolonial studies? What remains in a time of restricted freedom of expression and intellectual terrorism? France for centuries was considered "the eldest daughter of the Church." What remains when my country turns into a back room of Salafist ideology, at a time when one hundred

and fifty French districts are in the hands of the Islamists? Every day in France, Christian churches and cemeteries are ransacked as the media indifferently watches on. France is the country of gallantry and the emancipation of women. What remains, in the era of gender theory, of inclusive writing and neo-feminism? France is also known as the nation-state *par excellence*. What remains, in these days of European technocrats and judges who ignore the will of the people? ... What remains, at a time when minority lobbies take the law into their own hands?[24]

The "new conservative humanism" is embedded in a counterrevolutionary dynamic, in that it rejects the ideal of individual emancipation that revolutions brandish as a standard against an established order, whether it be religious, natural, or autocratic. The "new conservative humanism" believes, to the contrary, in the destiny of individuals: "We reject the relativism by which each individual creates his own values. We believe in natural law, in a universal ethics. We believe that individual will cannot be society's sole compass. ... Edmund Burke already detected in the French Revolution the roots of the evil that gnaws at us: an abstract citizen of the French Revolution, detached from his land, his parish, his profession, is a matrix of the citizen of the world!"[25] More precisely, a counterrevolutionary movement rejects the idea that individuals be their own guide, that is, can determine their own choices according to values they have acquired. This sort of speech permeates public debates broadly, and far beyond the far right. Thus, in France, in 1998–99, some leftist intellectuals mobilized against the creation of civil union contracts for homosexual couples in the name of the world's anthropological order,[26] or, in a Lacanian vein, in the name of the symbolic order of sexual difference.[27] Once the text was adopted, a number of them had to face the facts and even ended up joining the movement to open up marriage and adoption to same-sex couples. Now they think homosexual couples can be a part of the world order, whose foundation is presumed to be a desire for marriage and family. They are thus moving their cursor to a different place than far-right movements do, but they continue to share with these movements the belief in a transcendental order. Sociologist Irène Théry protests: "certain solutions proposed by transgender identities sometimes give the impression of refining [the logic of identity] in an increasingly desperate way, in the hope, in the end, of dissolving in its own logic: each individual would be a class unto himself."[28] What these counterrevolutionary arguments fail to grasp is that sexual minorities are not aspiring to create their own order but to question the notion of order itself.

Gender Disorder

IN 1995 AT the Beijing conference of the United Nations, the notion of gender, widely used in the humanities and social sciences as an analytical category, seems to prevail in public policies. The mainstreaming of gender was already of real interest to member states since the Nairobi conference in 1985, but in 1995 gender as a category is introduced as a way to broaden the definition of discrimination.[29] The Vatican, whose doctrine stresses that the sexes complement each other, realizes that gender, thanks to its plasticity, might help to redefine the traditional family.[30] It establishes several committees to monitor gender research programs and public policies.[31] Thus members of the Vatican's networks are among those who, in 2010–11 in France, mobilize against publishing biology textbooks that refer to homosexuality as one sexual orientation among others.[32] Such is the case with Opus Dei and its representative, Christine Boutin, a Catholic antiabortion representative.[33] The leaders of this movement, supported by the upper hierarchy of the French Catholic Church, and in particular the bishop of Lyon,[34] meet to ready their weapons on the eve of the debate about the bill that would allow homosexual couples to marry and adopt jointly. They then organize several major street demonstrations made up of diverse Catholic groups.[35] The argument they put forward is about disorder: the male/female and, hence, father/mother, binary is, in their eyes, the cornerstone of civilization but also of the nation. Rather than drawing on a theological arsenal—an ineffective strategy in a country that thinks of itself as secular—these Catholic activists speak of saving France, whose symbol, Marianne, they use at each of their demonstrations. According to them, there is a risk of losing one's cultural identity in the context of the globalization of sexuality, where an individualistic philosophy reigns, one based on consumption, pleasure, and individual rights. This philosophy is supposed to have come straight from American university campuses. Judith Butler, in their eyes, is a veritable antichrist because she is not only the spokesperson for "gender theory" so called but also its impure embodiment, through her very gender. By contrast, the fantasy of the cis body's purity is borne by two militant groups. On one hand, Antigones, young women who call themselves feminine, not feminist, and who wear diaphanous white clothing as they claim to be fighting an unjust law. On the other, Hommens, a direct response to the Ukrainian feminist Femens group, intervene in public spaces—all white, of slim build, with exposed torsos covered in slogans against the "marriage-for-all" law, in an effort to assert the protective strength of the male body.

The law is nevertheless voted on in the National Assembly and promulgated on May 17, 2013. The movements that are hostile to it (the main one being the Manif pour tous)[36] then focus more directly on what they call gender theory. They fear that school will teach children to deconstruct gender categories to the point where children will no longer be able to tell the difference between women and men and will therefore more easily become homosexual or transgender. Their struggle pays off: on June 30, 2014, the socialist government withdraws its educational programs for equality between girls and boys, the ABCDs of Equality.[37] People fighting against gender theory paradoxically grant considerable power to minority sexualities, which would be irresistible, these people claim, if they were no longer blocked by stigmatizing social norms and repressive, or at least unequal, legal norms. Their fight against medically assisted procreation for all women[38] is part of their fantasy of a homosexual and transgender society that could replace heterosexual society, with its bases in procreation by natural means and religious faith.[39] Such an alternative society could even become autonomous by having its own children. These movements, which have become movements against "fatherless, medically assisted procreation," wield new anti-marriage-for-all posters that cry out: "She doesn't need a man. They don't need a father?" We see here the fear of a symbolic castration of heterosexual men by powerful women, feminists, and/or lesbians.[40] The second register mobilized objectifies children: other posters depict a baby on all fours surrounded by vegetables and ask: "We have GMO vegetables, do we want children with a single parent?" The law has for a long time recognized single-parent families, for example in the context of adoption, since the (French) law of July 11, 1966. It is thus the symbol of a right, stripped of its naturalistic trappings, that is problematic here because the French Catholic Church, currently facing the desertion of its faithful en masse, could do nothing other than play the role of exegete of the natural order before public authorities.[41] Through the fantasy of converting children to homosexuality and trans identities, a counterprojection of the ideal of religious conversion is also at work.

This phenomenon is very apparent in the anti-gender mobilizations, which have grown in Poland, Italy, and Romania but which have had less impact in Europe's Protestant countries.[42] Likewise, evangelists are the ones attacking Judith Butler in South America. When she arrived in São Paulo in November 2017 to give a series of lectures, Butler was met with hostile protests, starting at the airport. During her presentations, demonstrators burned an effigy, a likeness of her as a witch, in the middle of the street. On February 23, 2020, in the Croatian village of Imotski, carnival participants burned effigies of a male couple with their child right in the middle of the street. The organizers explained, "We are a conservative society and follow tradition. Give a child to a mother, as the saying goes. We think it's the right thing to do."[43] Gender transforms the social gaze by moving it from a binary and hierarchical mode to a plural mode. It is therefore unbearable for many religious and conservative activists: it destabilizes their often single-sex and/or homosocial arrangements, transforms representations of ethnonational bodies whose heirs and guardians they claim to be, and finally calls the hegemony of their own standards and practices into question.[44] These activists fear being dismantled, decommissioned, and replaced, respectively.

Human Ecology

THE FEAR OF erasure is strongly expressed in terms of race. Some opponents of same-sex marriage explained that it would lead to marrying animals.[45] They were not shy about circulating leaflets depicting a chimpanzee with the slogan, "Marriage for all. Why not with him?" Such bestiality associated with homosexuality was projected onto Christiane Taubira, the French Minister of Justice and a black woman of Guyanese origin, who had already written the law of May 21, 2001, that recognized slavery as a crime against humanity. Taubira was caricatured many times as an ogress, as a monkey, and even as being pro-slavery. Children threw bananas at her during a trip to Angers in November 2013. Bestiality, according to this logic, means the end of humanity. Posters displaying mammoths and snails circulated in demonstrations to emphasize the risk of returning to a primitive and sexually confused stage (snails are a hermaphroditic animal). The racist register also made it possible to underscore how homosexual marriage "perverts" white Catholic national tradition. This is an old register where minorities are placed on the side of the foreign forces with which they are allegedly colluding.[46] At the turn of the twentieth century, homosexuality was a German vice in France, an English vice in Germany, and a French vice in England.[47] This register is also strongly inflected by anti-Semitism.[48] A Jew is an enemy within, prone to betrayal, whose gender is perverted: Jewish men are said to be effeminate (they thus weaken a virile nation facing an enemy without), and Jewish women are represented as masculine and castrating.[49] Butler was attacked as both a Jew and a lesbian by activists against marriage for all.[50] Fear of an Islamist invasion was also mobilized: several images circulated online depicting Taubira veiled in a French flag, with a chyron that read "terrorist alert"; Minister of National Education Najat Vallaud-Belkacem, who was behind the ABCDs of Equality, was attacked by the Catholic and far-right press in a similar way. On September 3, 2014, shortly after her appointment, the newspaper *Minute* featured the headline: "A Muslim Moroccan Woman in *Éducation nationale*: The Vallaud-Belkacem Provocation"; the next day, *Valeurs Actuelles* followed suit: "The Ayatollah: Investigation of the Minister of National Reeducation." Associating social change with the foreign makes it possible to protect certain majority practices that have thus become custodians of national cultural tradition. This tropism is now expressed on a new front, that of intersectionality. Coined by legal scholar Kimberlé Crenshaw in 1989 and 1991,[51] the notion of intersectionality has become the narrative of choice for minority rights movements in the United States. Intersectionality refers to the fact that some individuals are at the intersection of several identities and that the multiple discriminations they experience are mutually reinforcing. This framework has brought greater visibility to those who are most vulnerable. This social theory has been gaining ground in France for the last ten years, particularly among decolonial associations. While some, such as the Indigènes de la République, tend to use one form of discrimination against another,[52] the fact remains that they deeply question the persistence of colonial thought patterns in the idea of belonging to the French nation. Ethnonationalists have seen this as a new manifestation of the threat posed by minorities to the French and European tradition. In April 2019, the magazine *Marianne* denounced "the offensive of the obsessed with race, sex, gender, identity." In May 2019, the *Revue des deux Mondes* titled: "Intellectual terrorism. After Sartre, Foucault, Bourdieu ... Indigenist ideology enters the university" then in April 2021 "Cancel culture tyranny of minorities. The new media order." In November 2021, the conservative newspaper *Le Figaro* announced: "School: how we indoctrinate our children. Antiracism, LGBT+ ideology, decolonialism. ... Investigation into a well-organized drift." The government took up this ethnonational reading of minority struggles. Minister of National Education Jean-Michel Blanquer declared in the *Journal du dimanche* on October 25, 2020, "There is a fight to be waged against an intellectual matrix coming from American universities and intersectional theses, which want to essentialize communities and identities. This matrix is the antithesis of our republican model, which postulates equality between human beings, regardless of their characteristics of origin, sex, religion. This matrix is the breeding ground for a fragmentation of our society and a vision of the world that converges with the interests of Islamists. This reality has affected a significant part of the French social sciences."

Ethnonationalist ideology took on another inflection during public debates about marriage. Here it was a matter of not only defending the nation but protecting its very territory, its soil, its *terroir*. The Vatican had put forth the idea of human ecology to resist what it considered the empire of gender: it was protecting family as modeled in nature. Especially since St. Thomas Aquinas, Christian theology has set natural acts against unnatural acts.[53] Because the use of theological arguments in public debates could prove counterproductive, recourse to the rhetoric of environmental risk made it easier to accept a doctrine long supported by the Church. The Second Vatican Council had indeed promoted the idea of Christian humanism, based on the vocation of women, bearing children.[54] John Paul II took up this doctrine in two texts: *Theology of the Body* (1979–84) and "Letter to Women" (1995). He created the Pontifical Council for the Family in 1981 and the Pontifical Academy for Life in 1994. It was in this context that the concept of human ecology was born. Benedict XVI focused more particularly on gender and "ideologies that promote, for example, putting the family in question, with its natural two-parent (that is to say, consisting of a father and a mother) as well as putting homosexuality and heterosexuality on the same level, in a new model of polymorphic sexuality."[55] In 2008, he compared homosexuality to the destruction of the equatorial forest.[56] Pope Francis takes up this rhetoric by comparing gender theory to nuclear weapons,[57] and then "transgender teachings" to "ideological colonization."[58] In keeping with this ideology, the Manif pour tous depicted Taubira, chainsaw in hand, cutting down the family tree of the nation and metaphorically destroying nature itself. In her speech in Rome, Marion Maréchal gives a more detailed overview of the way in which human ecology and ethnonationalism are intertwined: "This anthropological revolution is just beginning. Eugenics is already reappearing and transhumanism is taking shape."[59] Nature would therefore assign a destiny to humans, who should not become demiurges. Human ecology would consist in finding a right, balanced relation to Nature. A nation becomes the ready-made framework, a sort of second nature: "Even in the 'ecological' world, we find the root 'eco,' which means 'home' in Greek. Preserving our territories, our biodiversity, our landscapes should be conservatives' natural fight. Let us not allow the defense of nature to be robbed by cynics of the far left or madmen who make love to trees. I don't want to choose between Greta's followers, hysterical doomsayers, or climate change deniers, who are all equally ideological and who deny the damage caused by an ultra-productive model and planned obsolescence."[60]

Reverse Discrimination

FACED WITH THE emergence of new gender categories and the use of new reproductive technologies, ethnonationalist groups seem to be moving full speed ahead. In this context, they aren't shying away from developing fallback strategies. These strategies consist in reversing power relationships by posing as victims of minority policies. This rhetoric is not new: it can be seen working against the civil rights movement in the United States and against decolonization in France, a rhetoric of victimization aimed at ensuring the "heroic redemption"[61] of majority culture. This culture now borrows from the lexicon of antidiscrimination law itself. This reversal was evident in movements against gay marriage. The reactionary Catholic group Le Printemps français defined their battle as follows: "Against an unfair bill serving minority privileges that [they] seek to violently impose upon us, we are expressing our personal refusal to be accomplices of the Taubira project or any program that targets the weak, the poor, and those without rights." Many people denounce this "tyranny of minorities." Essayist, "national preference" theorist in the Rassemblement national, and former activist of the Parti républicain Jean-Yves Le Gallou does, for instance: for him, ethnic, parliamentary, sexual, and media minorities "hold and help each other."[62] Another expression of the need to be protected from sexual minorities is offered by the conservative Polish newspaper *Gazeta Polska*, which disseminated stickers that read: "LGBT-free Zone."[63] Today, more than eighty communities have taken part in this initiative, representing almost a third of the country.

The United States faces a similar battle against the rights of sexual minorities. This is taking place in the judiciary and in the name of freedom of expression and religious freedom.[64] In 2012, the CEO of the Chick-fil-A fast food chain, Daniel Truett Cathy, spoke out vigorously against gay marriage. The media quickly revealed that his (company-founder) father's foundation was funding several anti-LGBT organizations, especially organizations supporting conversion therapy. Several LGBT organizations called for a Chick-fil-A boycott, and in response conservative leaders including Mike Huckabee called for supporting the company. The latter reoriented its philanthropic donation policies but continued to financially support the Salvation Army, whose policy openly discriminates against LGBT people. In response, the Texas Senate drafted legislation on April 3, 2019, that stipulated that "sincere religious beliefs" could not be used to withdraw the licenses of state-certified professionals (doctors, electricians, teachers, etc.).[65] This draft legislation, in contrast, authorized all kinds of discriminatory treatment in matters of service. The Texas Senate had explicitly rejected an amendment that included a non-discrimination clause against LGBT people. Promoted by Lieutenant Governor Dan Patrick, it was sent the following day to the House of Representatives, which postponed deliberations. It was taken up in another form by the Texas Senate. On June 9, 2019, Texas governor Greg Abbott promulgated the law and declared: "Discrimination is not tolerated in Texas. No business should be discriminated against simply because its owners donate to a church or the Salvation Army or other religious organization. ... The 'Save Chick-fil-A' legislation that I'm about to sign is a victory for religious liberty in Texas."[66]

On June 4, 2018, a Colorado baker's refusal to make a wedding cake for a gay couple was validated in a 7–2 U.S. Supreme Court decision (*Masterpiece Cakeshop v. Colorado Civil Rights Commission*). On the basis of Colorado's antidiscrimination law, the Colorado Civil Rights Commission found that there had indeed been discrimination and ordered the pastry chef to provide the service requested by his customers. The Colorado Civil Rights Commission mentioned, in its review of the case, the ideologies of hatred that had led to slavery and the Holocaust. The Supreme Court found that the Colorado Civil Rights Commission, by relying on such arguments, had failed to fulfill its duty of religious neutrality. The Court quashed the decision. The organization representing the pastry shop, the Alliance Defending Freedom, commented: "Tolerance and respect for good-faith differences of opinion are essential in a society like ours."[67] Several cases followed in which state courts recognized discrimination in similar cases where hostility to religious belief had not been established. The *Masterpiece Cakeshop v. Colorado Civil Rights Commission* decision was also used by Supreme Court Justice Sonia Sotomayor in *Trump v. Hawaii*, a case decided on June 26, 2018. In her dissenting opinion, Sotomayor considered that Trump's decision to prevent the issuance of visas to citizens of Muslim countries was a sign of religious hostility. The Court did not side with her, making the paradoxical claim that the religious neutrality argument risked destroying antidiscrimination law.

On February 24, 2020, in *Fulton v. City of Philadelphia*, the Supreme Court agreed to consider the constitutionality of some adoption agencies' refusals to accept applications from gay couples. The Department of Human Services of the City of Philadelphia is responsible for collecting and finding a home for abandoned children and for children subjected to abuse or neglect. To do this, it works with field organizations, a number of which are Catholic. After learning that one of them (Catholic Social Services [CSS]) systematically rejected gay couples, the city broke its contract with the organization. The latter sued the city in the name of freedom of expression and religion guaranteed by the First Amendment. On appeal, the court found that these freedoms had not been violated, and the agency therefore decided to appeal to the Supreme Court. In its petition, it argued that "as a Catholic agency, CSS cannot provide written endorsements for same-sex couples which contradict its religious teachings on marriage. The mayor, city council, Department of Human Services, and other city officials have targeted CSS and attempted to coerce it into changing its religious practices."[68] In a unanimous decision, the Supreme Court found that the City of Philadelphia had placed undue control over the Catholic agency that denied adoption to homosexuals.[69] The Court first held that private child placement arrangements did not fall within the scope of the 1990 case *Employment Division, Department of Human Resources of Oregon v. Smith*, which held that no general, neutral statute could be challenged on the basis of religious freedom. Since it was a private agency, its decisions could not be neutral and general. Therefore, the Catholic agency was entitled to raise the First Amendment religious freedom argument against the City of Philadelphia. Justice Roberts also noted that the city had the ability to exempt its service providers from some of the constraints of its antidiscrimination provisions through its human relations officer. Therefore, the city was not justified in terminating its contract with Catholic Social Services on the basis that the agency refused to accept same-sex couples. The decision does not proclaim a right to discriminate, but neither does it preclude it.[70]

On November 20, 2020, the 11th Federal Circuit Court of Appeals overturned a Palm Beach County and Boca Raton, Florida, ordinance that had banned conversion therapies in 2017.[71] These therapies treat homosexuality as a mental illness that can be eliminated through rehab, brutal physical activities, and the intervention of spiritual and religious guides. The decree in question prohibited all conversion therapies, including those limited to talking sessions. Two family therapists and marriage counselors appealed on the basis that their patients were volunteers and that none of their promotional materials claimed to be able to change sexual orientation but simply to induce new behaviors that enabled adolescents to resist their sexual desires and to overcome confusion about their gender identity. The county and the city pointed to the health risks to young patients, including suicide, which had been highlighted by numerous professional associations such as the American Pediatric Association and the American Psychiatric Association. However, the court found that these risks were not proven in this case and that, therefore, the restriction on freedom of expression as set forth in the First Amendment to the U.S. Constitution was not justified. The judges, Britt C. Grant and Barbara Lagoa, the authors of the majority opinion, were appointed by President Donald Trump. The Supreme Court has repeatedly refused to consider the prohibition of conversion therapy. In 2017, it ruled against the state of California's ban, which had been in place for five years.[72] By refusing to intervene, the Supreme Court thus allowed this ban to remain legal but refused to generalize it. This refusal to intervene is quite frequent. However, Donald Trump's nomination of Amy Coney Barrett as Supreme Court Justice in September 2020 and her subsequent confirmation significantly shifted the political balance on the Supreme Court: conservative justices now have a 6–3 majority. The Court's silence no longer has the same meaning. While the Washington State Supreme Court had unanimously ruled that refusing to sell flowers to gay and lesbian clients for their weddings was illegal,[73] the Supreme Court refused to rule, therefore not putting an end to the antidiscrimination law battle once and for all.[74] The Supreme Court's hesitations are therefore double-edged: they can be both a step toward extending minority protection (as evidenced by the *Obergefell v. Hodges* decision, which opened marriage to gay couples a few months after the Court refused to intervene on this topic)[75] and an obstacle to recognizing the discriminatory nature embedded in some claims for free expression. This tension is tempered by the existence of other legal protections, such as Title VII of the Civil Rights Act of 1964, which protects against discrimination on the basis of race, sex, color, ancestry, and religion (extended on June 15, 2020, by Supreme Court decision to include gender and sexual orientation).

However, the freedom of speech argument remains one of the spearheads against minorities in the United States.[76] American constitutional law was indeed born of the protection of religious freedom.[77] French public law also recognizes freedom of belief, but it was essentially built at the turn of the twentieth century in a context where the state sought to withdraw from the influence of religions. The strategies developed by ethnonational groups and activists on both sides of the Atlantic are therefore not exactly the same: in Washington, they use religious freedom and play the card of moral relativism; in Paris, they seek to avoid the argument of religious freedom in order to fit into a universalist and secular framework in which social harmony and therefore the interests of the nation are at stake. It is also, for French Catholic militants, a way of not taking the risk of having to recognize other religions on an equal footing, starting with Islam. From this point of view, ethnonationalist discourses in France tend to lean on the nation through collective identity, whereas in the United States they do so more through personal identity and intimate, heartfelt convictions. Behind these singular strategies, a similar reversal of power relations between minorities and the majority is taking place. While ethnonationalist movements have long refused any moral equivalence between their values and those of minority groups (by denying them, for example, the status of "family"),[78] they are now mobilizing this equivalence argument to their advantage. This movement could attest to a loss of power on their part; they would be left, as it were, with the rhetorical resources of minorities in a world that would no longer recognize their values. However, the greater visibility of certain minority groups does not necessarily imply a retreat from majority values. Minority groups gain recognition only insofar as they pledge allegiance to these values.[79] What the new reactionary rhetoric indicates, then, is not so much a retreat from majority domination as a change of scale, from a fairly general discourse of rejection to local strategies of appropriation of minority references and symbols.

Using "Minority" Status as a Strategy

IN ALL OF the cases I have just presented, a rhetorical reversal of power relationships occurs. This strategy is coupled with another: taking the place of minorities in the public sphere by appropriating their modes of action and their references. This is how Le Printemps français (French Spring) chose its name, in reference to the Arab Spring revolutions, as it sought to combat gay marriage. During demonstrations against marriage-for-all, slogans claimed parity (referring to the law of June 6, 2000, promoting equal representation of women and men in elected office), chanting, "Parity, first in marriage."[80] Manif pour tous also used a whole visual arsenal inspired by the student revolution of May 1968 as well as workers' union fights for paid holidays and for protecting employment in industrial zones devastated by relocations; these included references to abandoned factories, raised fists, the color red, tools, and so on. Some Manif pour tous posters proclaimed: "Our priority is Aulnay [an industrial site closed owing to relocation], not gay marriage"; "We want work, not gay marriage"; "*Fraternité* for growth." The children of the demonstrators were dressed as Gavroche, the orphan in Victor Hugo's novel *Les Misérables*, a symbol of a poor children in nineteenth-century Paris. Manif pour tous systematically used the expression "Touche pas à" (Get your hands off) (as in "Touche pas à nos gosses" [Get your hands off our kids]; or "Touche pas au mariage" [Get your hands off marriage]), echoing the antiracist movement SOS racisme, founded in 1984, whose slogan was "Get your hands off my friend." In 2016, Manif pour tous called for demonstrations using posters that represent whole groups of people: a heterosexual couple with two children (placed at the top and center of the image), an elderly man with a cane, a young boy with a skateboard, an overweight person, a gay couple, and so forth. Their slogan, "Demonstrate as you are" (Manifestez comme vous êtes), thus took up the imaginary of political struggles for diversity. Manif pour tous's latest advertising campaign, whose posters plastered the streets of Paris in November 2019, talks about defending social progress as long as there is respect for fatherhood, motherhood, and difference (here they show a young woman with multiple disabilities in a motorized wheelchair). During anti-marriage-for-all demonstrations, the Catholic group Les Veilleurs organized street prayers: participants recited texts by Arendt, Aristotle, Einstein, Gandhi, King, Aragon, Apollinaire, Camus, and others. Éric Lemaître, an activist with the Veilleurs group in the city of Reims, explained: "The new slaves are those individuals who go beyond their limitless desires. Who are prisoners of themselves. ... This is why we quoted Martin Luther King, and this is why we also sing the Negro spiritual 'Let my People Go.'"[81] Following George Floyd's death, the Adama Traoré committee (Traoré was a young black man killed by the French police without any light being shed on the circumstances of his death by choking)[82] organized a demonstration at Place de la République in Paris on June 13, 2020. Ethnonationalist activists from Génération identitaire took advantage of the occasion to display a banner that stated: "Justice for the victims of anti-white racism." In this context, President Emmanuel Macron accused the social sciences of stirring up conflict by using critical categories that would divide the nation. He declared in *Le Monde* on June 10, 2020, "The academic world has been guilty. It has encouraged the ethnicization of the social question in the belief that this is a good way to go. But the outcome can only be secessionist. This amounts to breaking the Republic in two." Macron thus placed himself on the side of ethnonational movements by taking up the idea of the weakening of the nation by its minorities, with the support of critical intellectuals. He thus took up the counterrevolutionary anti-intellectualism that has marked the entire history of the Republic in France, and whose favorite fields are gender, sexuality, race, and religion.[83]

By appropriating the tools, concepts, and visual aids of movements defending minorities, ethnonationalist ideology refuses to recognize the specificity of minority experiences and, in so doing, reinforces stigmatization. This phenomenon is heightened by the fact that ethnonationalist movements also do not shy away from calling themselves allies in certain struggles against discrimination in order to better reject others. During discussions around the second round in the 2017 presidential election, Marine Le Pen embraced the causes of women, Jews, and gays and lesbians, while her party was regularly singled out for anti-Semitic remarks and its presidential program attacked freedom of choice for women—Le Pen spoke of "convenience abortions"—and gays and lesbians (to whom she refused equal rights, particularly when it came to access to marriage and parenting). Le Pen argued that the Islamization of the country put minorities at risk, thus strategically fitting them into her imaginary of the nation. She even played on gender roles, claiming political strength by being a woman and by valuing the presence in her entourage of gay men (including some among the candidates for legislative elections), starting with Florian Philippot, her campaign manager. Her father, Jean-Marie Le Pen, then criticized his daughter's entourage for having weakened and even feminized her, and he made fun of the decadent role of *gestapettes* (the little Gaystapo boys, a reference to Abel Bonnard, a collaborationist minister under Vichy and an alleged homosexual).

In this kind of environment, rethinking the very notion of minority is essential. Minority is not in fact a simple question of numbers (fewer than 50 percent according to a given criterion) or identities (recognizing oneself as a minority) but a matter of injustice insofar as this experience can be correlated with a number and an identity. This difference is difficult to establish, but it is nevertheless fundamental in order for minority policies not to become confused and thus not lose all legitimacy.

Coming Out as a Majority

U.S. LAW IS rooted in the defense of religious freedom.[84] To be sure, French public and constitutional law also recognizes freedom of conscience and religion, but it was essentially structured at the turn of the twentieth century, at a time when the state sought to free itself from the grip of religion. Minority strategies developed by conservative groups and activists on both sides of the Atlantic are thus not exactly the same: in Washington, their minority strategies involve religious freedom and play the relativism card (my way of life as opposed to yours); in France, they try to avoid arguing for religious freedom in order to conform to a universalist and secular framework where social harmony and thus the interest of the nation are at stake. For French Catholic conservatives, this is also a way of not having to risk recognizing other religions, including Islam, on an equal footing. From this perspective, anti-gender struggles in France lean on an ethnonationalist rhetoric that invokes collective identity, whereas American conservative groups and activists tend to invoke personal identity. In both cases, the notion of identity is the object of renewed interest. The very need to react to minority cultures and identities brings the majority out of the closet. This phenomenon played a key role during the debates against marriage-for-all in France. Many demonstrators spoke of Catho Pride—which Sara Garbagnoli and Massimo Prearo call "Catholics' identity revenge."[85] France is also the subject of regular controversies about the use of foreign flags at sporting events, when the national team faces the teams of other citizens' countries of origin. The potential expression of minority identities helps reinforce the perception of one's own identity and the need to assert it in response.

Calling oneself a member of the silent majority is no longer just a self-definition by default. It's an element of one's identity that ties one to a language, a territory, and ancient cultural practices. Citizens of majority cultures used to embody the nation de facto; they didn't have to affirm who they were. With major demographic shifts in the United States and the diversification of the French population, majority identities announce themselves as such.[86] This is particularly the case with white identity, which has become, for American white supremacists, a real social project rooted in the feeling of being the object of a new form of racism.[87] They think of white identity as an endangered race that must reclaim its natural space. The fallback strategy mentioned earlier suits such a novel crusade. Protests against marriage-for-all were no exception. There we saw, on February 2, 2014, demonstrators dressed as crusaders, ready to liberate an ungodly and racially mixed France. This context explains the success of the "great replacement theory," according to which French and European populations would be replaced by Arab, Maghrebian, and sub-Saharan African populations with the complicity of perverted elites. This thesis, inherited from Maurice Barrès's national right wing, was first formulated by the writer Renaud Camus in his work, *L'Abécédaire de l'In-nocence* (2011). In 2019, he argued for "remigration" and ran as a candidate in the European elections.[88] His thesis was taken up by Jean-Marie Le Pen and Maréchal but rejected by Marine Le Pen.[89] It comes up on a regular basis in public debates, notably in the writings of the columnist Éric Zemmour, who, despite being convicted for provoking racial hatred,[90] ran for office in the 2022 presidential race. The Christchurch shooter in New Zealand also believed the great replacement thesis, as did the shooter in the El Paso massacre.

Finally, it should be stressed that the idea of an ethnonationalist resurgence is not only a project for society; it is also a mode of socialization.[91] A new societal endogamy is brought into being, with its references, its values, and its learned experiences. This explains why Maréchal founded a new school, which she also heads: the Institute of Social, Economic and Political Sciences in Lyon's Confluence neighborhood, founded in 2018. This institute's mission is to train the ethnonationalist elite; and her Rome speech is the product of this expertise. The institute also functions as a place for ethnonationalist circles to meet through corporate partnerships and student tutoring.

Populism and Hegemony

ETHNONATIONALIST MOVEMENTS ALSO seek bridges of influence into mass movements in order to connect the national and popular registers. The Yellow Vests are a good example of an attempt to rally popular protest to the ethnonationalist cause, an attempt that did not really succeed. The Yellow Vests movement appeared in France during the month of October 2018. It amounts to a spontaneous mobilization of citizens against a plan to increase the "carbon" share of the internal consumption tax on energy products. This carbon component was created in 2014 under the presidency of François Hollande, but President Emmanuel Macron planned to increase the amount. The Yellow Vests movement therefore opposed the fight against global warming, if it was to the detriment of the poorest people—among them in particular those who live in the countryside and cannot go without a car. On November 4, President Macron said: "The same people who gripe about a rise in fuel costs also demand that we fight [to reduce] air pollution because their children are suffering from illnesses."[92] The Yellow Vests, however, were not mobilized against environmental protection policies as such but rather against the fact that financial stress weighed more heavily on the poorest people. They were demanding taxes on high income and on financial transactions. By wearing a safety vest, which every car must have by law, and gathering at roundabouts, they drew attention to the vulnerability of a whole section of the population. The Yellow Vests were thus protesting against social inequality, and their protest crossed traditional political lines. The government organized heavy police crackdowns on the weekly street protests, resulting in several deaths and many injuries, and people struck by rubber bullets. Thugs also infiltrated the Yellow Vests and anti-Semitic, racist, and homophobic activists were among the demonstrators. Ethnonationalist parties including the Rassemblement national therefore sought to side with the Yellow Vests but without directly claiming to do so, since their authoritarian framework is at odds with the movement's spontaneity and its supposed absence of leadership. Still, after several months of demonstrations, the Yellow Vests' demands gradually changed: a demand for direct participation and a general hostility to the representative regime overrode the aim to defend the most disadvantaged. This characterizes the transition from a popular movement to a populist one.[93] Direct participation is in fact not a guarantee of democracy if its practice is not framed by fundamental principles. Thus, in 2013, Manif pour tous demanded a referendum to do away with the law that allowed homosexual couples to marry. In December 2018, the government instructed the Economic, Social and Environment Council to open an online consultative site to address the expectations of the Yellow Vests and thus prepare for the great national debate organized throughout France starting on January 15, 2019. Manif pour tous then bombarded the site with contributions calling for the abrogation of marriage-for-all, pushing their demands to the top.[94]

Populism is characterized by a rejection of elites, a valorization of direct experience, and a monolithic vision of the people. Its protest dimension most often takes precedence over its ideological framework.[95] This is how populism crosses political lines and avoids nostalgic attachments to tradition, of the kind associated with ethnonationalism. In France, the Rassemblement national has long been a party hostile to the Fifth Republic; its organization is elitist; and it is heir to the Poujadist movements, which supported small traders and artisans. This is why it was never shy about demonstrating in the streets[96] but did so by inserting populist references into its main frame of reference, that of the nation. The Rassemblement national has always strived to capture and structure populism at the same time. To this end, it went ahead with advancing its authoritarian claims: its attachment to security, social conformity, and obedience.[97] A displacement occurred when control was handed off from Jean-Marie Le Pen to his daughter, Marine Le Pen. The Front's electorate is now more rural[98] and includes more women.[99] The party has also established itself strongly locally, particularly in the north of France, an industrial region with a high unemployment rate. It wants to be the voice of the people rather than its armed wing. The notion of a people, however, remains difficult for it to claim because, unlike the very abstract idea of the nation, the people refers to social trajectories that do not always match party strategies. The notion of a people is also the object of a nostalgic attachment within left-leaning political movements, which feel they are its custodians.[100] To put it another way, ethnonationalism finds it difficult to rally popular movements to its cause but more easily draws on the support of populist movements because its authoritarian structure resonates with their "anti-system" views.[101] The counterrevolutionary ideology that Maréchal is pushing works at legitimizing the bridge between populism and ethnonationalism by inflecting it with spiritualism:

> Everyone here still has these terrible images in mind of Notre-Dame de Paris up in flames. Eight centuries of civilization

almost vanished before our eyes. ... Facing such a blaze, the French felt this intense need to preserve. ... Miraculously, all that was essential was saved: relics, statues of saints, stained glass windows. Even the proud Gallic rooster, symbol of our nation, was found almost intact after the steeple collapsed. Some saw the event as symbolic, symbolic of our dying society. Others saw a warning signal about the vulnerability of our heritage. I prefer to see in it the promise of hope: that our civilization's foundation still stands despite the dangers of the times. And a call to rebuild this roof that protects us and this steeple that connects us to the sky.[102]

Rethinking Minority Policies

THE ANALYSIS THAT I have outlined here highlights a whole set of ethnonationalist references and strategies that explicitly reconnect with a counterrevolutionary horizon. I have chosen to speak of ideology because these elements seek to form a system. At the beginning of the French Revolution, Burke wrote:

> Thanks to our sullen resistance to innovation, thanks to the cold sluggishness of our national character, we still bear the stamp of our forefathers. We have not (as I conceive) lost the generosity and dignity of thinking of the fourteenth century, nor as yet have we subtilized ourselves into savages. We are not the converts of Rousseau; we are not the disciples of Voltaire; Helvetius has made no progress amongst us. Atheists are not our preachers; madmen are not our lawgivers. We know that we have made no discoveries, and we think that no discoveries are to be made in morality, nor many in the great principles of government, nor in the ideas of liberty, which were understood long before we were born, altogether as well as they will be after the grace has heaped its mold upon our presumption and the silent tomb shall have imposed its law on our pert loquacity. In England we have not yet been completely embowelled of our natural entrails; we still feel within us, and we cherish and cultivate, those inbred sentiments which are the faithful guardians, the active monitors of our duty, the true supporters of all liberal and manly morals. We have not been drawn and trussed, in order that we may be filled, like stuffed birds

in a museum, with chaff and rags and paltry blurred shreds of paper about the rights of men.[103]

THE ECHOES OF Burke in Maréchal's speech in Rome are obvious. However, her new counterrevolutionary horizon shows several important changes with respect to Burke's. First, a change of scale: the new counterrevolutionaries deploy a universalist rhetoric in defense of the land (*terroir*) and the environment. Second, they are perfectly willing to strategically use the law that they would otherwise fight against, by passing as minorities and oppressed people. Finally, they are no longer fully satisfied with flattering the virile and noble values of the national spirit, and they are actively trying to redefine the human against all forms of minority subjectivation. According to these counterrevolutionaries, humans cannot be their own measure without detaching themselves from their humanity, without becoming strangers to themselves.

This resistance to subjectivation is all the more powerful in that, as Walker Connor has already noted, the fantasy of the foreigner at the heart of ethnonationalism requires no direct experience:

> Though knowledge of the aliens and their foreign ways is essential to national consciousness, first-hand is not. Awareness of the existence of other cultures can be acquired by way of the spoken or written word, or the telecommunication media, as well as by actual contact. The rapid spread of literacy, the greater mobility of man made possible by dramatic developments in the form and expanse of transportation, and the even more revolutionary strides in communications have rapidly dissipated the possibility of cultural isolation, and correspondingly have rapidly propagated national consciousness.[104]

I would, however, like to qualify this thesis: on one hand, geographic mobility and access to information are very unequally distributed within a society; on the other hand, the resulting hyperconnection and saturation of images can produce as many cultural fantasies as digital isolation does. The figure of the stranger is as much a fantasy of the unknown as it is blind to what seems, at first sight, known. Guy Debord rightly noted that "the spectacle reunites the separate, but reunites it *as separate*."[105] The spectacle of cultural interdependence and the acceleration of exchanges have paradoxically reinforced a feeling of helplessness among those whose mobility is restricted by strong social segregation (sedentary lifestyles, exclusions from school, debt, limited time availability, and so on), and it has simultaneously compounded the anxiety of disappearing among those whose social mobility is greater and who thus confront the limits of their capacity to act in a world that is changing before their eyes.[106] Discussions about the "great replacement" of Western civilization expose, depending on the context, the reversal of colonial power relations, the indigenization of whites, the destruction of the Christian faith, and diversity. They stem from the resonance between feelings of helplessness and a fear of disappearing across various social spaces. Social stratification therefore plays an essential role in advocacy for the return of the traditional nation-state.[107]

This is why it is more necessary than ever to analyze the dissemination and the impact of counterrevolutionary ideology in public policies.[108] What remains of minority policies if the movements that are against them also lay claim to them? What impact do counterrevolutionary movements have on the political representation of minorities even as these movements are sometimes espoused by women, gay men, and the descendants of migrants? These questions can only be answered by reexamining the very notion of minority.[109] Counterrevolutionary movements instrumentalizing the apparatus of minority protections are indeed also a consequence of the uncertainties weighing on minority policies today. First, population movements make traditional legal categories more questionable: this is how, in most American universities, affirmative action policies benefit African Americans but not Asian Americans, even though racism affects both of them, differently.[110] Second, protections against discrimination have extended into so many areas during the past several decades that what defines a minority in one area is not necessarily applicable in another. Thus, in higher education, Asian Americans do not enjoy any preferential treatment, given their high performance in admission procedures.[111] They are nonetheless minorities and face stereotyping and discrimination during their years in school. Both in the media and in politics, moreover, populist rhetoric that opposes social and cultural struggles alike tends to create competition among minorities.[112] Finally, the demand for more fluid identities causes the law to confront its own limits when it comes to grasping complex discriminations.[113] Some writers have responded to this challenge by invoking the convergence of social struggles toward a common ideal of justice,[114] by defending "liberal *political* consciousness" against "liberal *identity* consciousness,"[115] or even by advocating that different "tribes" of the liberal left and nationalist right reconcile, as if they were compatible.[116]

On the contrary, I am arguing that what truly enables us to rethink minority policies is the way in which different experiences of injustice resonate and can, in doing so, open up an ethics of responsibility for others. The Yellow Vests movement was an opportunity to move in this direction.[117] Several student unions, the defense committee for Adama Traoré, railway workers, and queer and feminist organizations came together around the Yellow Vests' fight, not only to support the movement but also to guide it toward more solidarity.[118] Pierre Creton's film *Le Bel Été* (*The Beautiful Summer*), released in 2019, reflects on hospitality toward other minority people through a meeting of several migrants and the rural world of the Pays de Caux. More recently still, on January 17 and 18, 2020, the Queer Liberation and Autonomy Committee (Comité de Libération et d'Autonomie Queer) organized a whole series of events to support the "chambermaids" at the Ibis Batignolles hotel in Paris, who were starting the sixth month of their strike. These few examples invite us to put forward other ways of theorizing social bonds. This task is crucial today; without it, minority policies are doomed to be driven by counterrevolutionary strategies, such as the rhetoric of "new conservative humanism."

Notes

1. https://www.eventbrite.com/e/god-honor-country-national-conservatism-conference-tickets-86695694155#.
2. Le Rassemblement national was called Front national until 2018. The party was founded by Jean-Marie Le Pen in 1972; he directed it until 2011, when his daughter, Marine Le Pen, succeeded him.
3. Yoram Hazony, *The Virtue of Nationalism* (New York: Basic Books, 2018).
4. "Les droites radicales cherchent à s'unir autour d'un corpus idéologique," *La Chronique de ... Jean-Marc Four*, France Inter, February 3, 2020, https://www.franceinter.fr/emissions/la-chronique-de/la-chronique-de-03-fevrier-2020.
5. On the distinction between radical-right politics and radical-right parties, see Cas Mudde, *On Extremism and Democracy in Europe* (New York: Routledge, 2017), 47–49.
6. See Clarence Y. H. Lo, "Astroturf v. Grassroots: Scenes from Early Tea Party Mobilization," in *Steep: The Precipitous Rise of the Tea Party*, ed. Lawrence Rosenthal and Christine Trost (Berkeley: University of California Press, 2012), 98–130.
7. Ami Pedahzur and Avraham Brichta, "The Institutionalization of Extreme Right-wing Charismatic Parties: A Paradox?" *Party Politics* 8.1 (2002): 31–49.

8   Cécile Alduy and Stéphane Wahnich, *Marine Le Pen prise aux mots: Décryptage du nouveau discours frontiste* (Paris: Seuil, 2015), 149.
9   Bruno Perreau, *Queer Theory: The French Response* (Stanford: Stanford University Press, 2016), 117–18.
10 Le Pen's entire speech is available on the extreme right wing's website, *Boulevard Voltaire*. Marion Maréchal, "Discours de Rome," *Boulevard Voltaire*, February 4, 2020, https://www.bvoltaire.fr/marion-marechal-nous-conservateurs-voulons-a-nouveau-lhomme-comme-sujet-de-lhistoire-et-leconomie-comme-outil-et-non-comme-ordre-lui-meme.
11 Protectionism in the United States; anti-Americanism in France; neofascism in Austria, Germany, and northern Italy; anti-Europeanism in Central and Eastern Europe; religious proselytizing in schools in Brazil; and so on. See, for example, Sabine Hark and Paula-Irene Villa, eds., *(Anti-)Genderismus: Sexualität und Geschlecht als Schauplätze aktueller politischer Auseinandersetzungen* (Bielefield: Transcript, 2015); Sarah Bracke and David Paternotte, "Unpacking the Sin of Gender," *Religion and Gender* 6.2 (2016): 143–54; Alexandra Minna Stern, *Proud Boys and the White Ethnostate: How the Alt-Right Is Warping the American Imagination* (Boston: Beacon Press, 2019); Monique de Saint Martin, "Extrémisme politique et extrémisme religieux évangélique au Brésil," *Raison Présente* 212 (2019): 23–32.
12 This is what the political scientist Jacques Lagroye called a "regime of revealed truth." Jacques Lagroye, *La Vérité dans l'église catholique: Contestation et restauration d'un régime d'autorité* (Paris: Belin, 2005), 147.
13 Daniel Martinez Hosang and Joseph E. Lowndes, *Producers, Parasites, Patriots: Race and the New Right-Wing Politics of Precarity* (Minneapolis: University of Minnesota Press, 2019), 107–11.
14 Pippa Norris has demonstrated that no single or multifactorial explanation is enough to understand the radical right, whether regarding class, downward social mobility, the psychology of authoritarian personalities, resentment, geographic isolation, contingent events (including terrorist attacks), economic factors (including debt, unemployment, and dependence), party dealignment, electoral regulations, the ideological distance between parties, or migratory phenomena. Pippa Norris, *Radical Right: Voters and Parties in the Electoral Market* (Cambridge: Cambridge University Press, 2005), 11–19.
15 The work of historian Laurent Kestel can serve as a model for studying the individual trajectories of contemporary ethnonationalist figures. See Laurent Kestel, *La Conversion politique: Doriot, le PPF et la question du fascisme français* (Paris: Seuil, 2012).
16 Norris, *Radical Right*, 23–25.
17 Michel Foucault, "La naissance d'un monde," in *Dits et Écrits I, 1954–1975* (Paris: Gallimard, 2001), 814.
18 Just as sociology, except when it is reductionist, cannot deny the role of ideologies in social interactions, ideology itself being a way of apprehending the social world. Gilles Houle, "L'idéologie: Un mode de connaissance," *Sociologie et Sociétés* 11.1 (1979): 123–45.
19 Charles Tilly, "The Analysis of a Counter-Revolution," *History and Theory* 3.1 (1963): 57–58.

20 Eric J. Hobsbawm, *Nations and Nationalism Since 1780: Programme, Myth, Reality* (Cambridge: Cambridge University Press, 1990).
21 Walter Connor, "Self-determination: The New Phase," *World Politics* 20.1 (1967): 30–53.
22 See also Vernon Van Dyke, "Self-Determination and Minority Rights," *International Studies Quarterly* 13.3 (1969): 223–53.
23 This immunological conception of identity and belonging is itself a wrong understanding of diachronic biological individuality. See Thomas Pradeu, *The Limits of the Self: Immunology and Biological Identity*, trans. Elizabeth Vitanza (Oxford: Oxford University Press, 2012), 228–37.
24 *Boulevard Voltaire.*
25 Ibid.
26 Françoise Héritier, "Aucune société n'admet de parenté homosexuelle," *La Croix*, September 11, 1998.
27 Irène Théry, "Le contrat d'union sociale en question," *Esprit* 236 (October 1997): 159–87.
28 Irène Théry, *La Distinction de sexe* (Paris: Odile Jacob, 2007), 255.
29 *Report of the Fourth World Conference on Women*, Beijing, September 4–15, 1995, 162, https://www.un.org/womenwatch/daw/beijing/pdf/Beijing%20full%20report%20E.pdf.
30 Mary Anne Case, "The Role of the Popes in the Invention of Complementarity and the Vatican's Anathematization of Gender," *Public Law and Legal Theory Working Papers* 565 (2016): 1–17.
31 Pontifical Council, *Lexicon: Ambiguous and Debatable Terms Regarding Family Life and Ethical Questions* (Front Royal, VA: Human Life International, 2006).
32 See Odile Fillod, "Genre et SVT: Copie à revoir," *Allodoxia* (blog), August 15, 2012, http://allodoxia.blog.lemonde.fr/2012/08/15/genre-svt/.
33 Opus Dei was created in 1924 to evangelize through education. In 1982 it was put under the direct authority of the pope.
34 "Mgr Barbarin contre le mariage gay: 'Le Parlement n'est pas Dieu le Père,'" *Le Progrès*, August 14, 2012.
35 Sylvain Mouillard et Kim Hullot-Guiot, "Manif pour tous: La vraie photo de famille," *Libération*, September 13, 2013, https://www.liberation.fr/societe/2013/09/13/manif-pour-tous-la-vraie-photo-de-famille_931667.
36 Le Rassemblement national opposed opening up marriage to gay couples without officially supporting the protests over which it had almost no political grasp. Several of its leaders, including Marion Maréchal, still participated in demonstrations and street prayers.
37 Ministère de l'Éducation nationale, "Outils Égalité: Filles-Garçons," Réseau-Canopé.fr, http://www.reseau-canope.fr/outils-egalite-filles-garcons.html; "Égalité des sexes à l'école: Machine arrière, toute!" *Les Invités de Mediapart* (blog), January 16, 2015, http://blogs.mediapart.fr/edition/les-batailles-de-legalite/article/160115/egalite-des-sexes-l-ecole-machine-arriere-toute.
38 The bioethics laws of 1994 restricted medically assisted procreation in France to situations of medical infertility, in this case heterosexual couples married or living together for more than two years. The 1994 laws also prohibited surrogacy in the name of the unavailability of human bodies.

39 I hypothesized that studies on gender compete with the doctrine of the Catholic Church (a large part of which deals with the regulation of relations between men and women), its single-sex organization, and its symbolism (that of procreation without a biological father). Bruno Perreau, "Genre: Ne renonçons pas trop vite à la théorie!" *Libération*, October 20, 2016, https://www.liberation.fr/debats/2016/10/20/genre-ne-renoncons-pas-a-la-theorie_1523265. See also Michael Stambolis-Ruhstorfer and Josselin Tricou, "Resisting 'Gender Theory' in France: A Fulcrum for Religious Action in a Secular Society," in *Anti-Gender Campaigns in Europe: Mobilizing Against Equality*, ed. David Paternotte and Roman Kuhar (London: Rowman & Littlefield, 2017), 79–95.

40 See the Manif pour tous arguments against medically assisted procreation (PMA) for all women, "La PMA sans père," Manifpourtous.fr, https://www.lamanifpourtous.fr/nos-combats/pma-sans-pere.

41 "Denis Pelletier: La vraie nature des catholiques français," *Le Point*, November 23, 2019, https://www.lepoint.fr/histoire/denis-pelletier-la-vraie-nature-des-catholiques-francais-23-11-2019-2349112_1615.php.

42 See the special issue edited and with an introduction by Mieke Verloo and David Paternotte: "The Feminist Project Under Threat in Europe," *Politics and Governance* 6.3 (2018).

43 Sam Dashenas, "Croatian Town Cheers and Dances After Setting Fire to Effigy of Gay Couple," GayTimes.co.uk, February 24, 2020, https://www.gaytimes.co.uk/community/132885/croatian-town-cheers-and-dances-after-setting-fire-to-effigy-of-gay-couple.

44 Sophie Rétif, "Ringards, hypocrites et frustrés? Les militants des associations familiales catholiques face à la réprobation," *Politix* 106 (2014): 85–108.

45 On April 19, 2013, Senator Colette Giudicelli (from the Union pour un mouvement populaire party) explained, in the Chamber, that marriage-for-all "will open the way to other claims which this time will be completely fanciful but which already exist: marriage with objects. In the United States an American woman married the Eiffel Tower; marriage with oneself, also in the United States always; three people married together as in Brazil; marriage with animals like in Australia."

46 Sandrine Sanos, *The Aesthetics of Hate: Far-Right Intellectuals, Antisemitism, and Gender in 1930s France* (Stanford: Stanford University Press, 2013), 124.

47 On this question, see Norman Domeier, *The Eulenburg Affair: A Cultural History of Politics in the German Empire* (Rochester, NY: Camden House, 2015).

48 Carolyn J. Dean, *The Frail Social Body. Pornography, Homosexuality, and Other Fantasies in Interwar France* (Berkeley: University of California Press, 2000), 88.

49 Florence Tamagne, "Caricatures homophobes et stéréotypes de genre en France et en Allemagne: La presse satirique, de 1900 au milieu des années 1930," *Le Temps des Médias* 1.1 (2003): 42–53.

50 Thus extreme right-wing essayist Claude Timmerman could declare: "Gender theory is an ethnic theory that seeks to legitimize homosexuality. Period. It is the fruit, and only the fruit, of American Jewish lesbians." "Théorie du genre: qui est derrière?" YouTube video, 6:23, from a lecture delivered for

the Centre d'Études et de Prospectives sur la Science on October 1–2, 2011, February 2, 2014, https://www.youtube.com/watch?v=nYdLL5Hjjfc

51 Kimberlé Crenshaw, "Demarginalizing the Intersection of Race and Sex: A Black Feminist Critique of Antidiscrimination Doctrine, Feminist Theory and Antiracist Policies," *Chicago Legal Forum* 1.8 (1989): 139–67; Kimberlé Crenshaw, "Mapping the Margins: Intersectionality, Identity Politics, and Violence Against Women of Color," *Stanford Law Review* 43.6 (July 1991): 1241–99.

52 On this contradiction, see Perreau, *Queer Theory*, 125–34.

53 Daniel Borrillo and Dominique Colas, *L'Homosexualité de Platon à Foucault* (Paris: Plon, 2005), 114–23.

54 Susan A. Ross, "The Bride of Christ and the Body Politic: Body and Gender in Pre–Vatican II Marriage Theology," *Journal of Religion* 71.3 (1991): 345–61.

55 "Letter from Cardinal Joseph Ratzinger, Prefect, Congregation for the Doctrine of the Faith, to the Bishops of the Catholic Church on the Collaboration of Men and Women in the Church and in the World," May 31, 2004, http://www.vatican.va/roman_curia/congregations/cfaith/documents/rc_con_cfaith_doc_20040731_collaboration_en.html.

56 "Homosexuality Is as Great a Threat as Rainforest Destruction Says Pope," *Daily Mail Reporter*, December 23, 2008.

57 Joshua McElwee, "Francis Strongly Criticizes Gender Theory, Comparing It to Nuclear Arms," *National Catholic Reporter*, February 13, 2015.

58 John Newsome, "Pope Warns of 'Ideological Colonization' in Transgender Teachings," CNN.com, October 4, 2016, https://www.cnn.com/2016/10/02/world/pope-transgender-comments/index.html.

59 *Boulevard Voltaire*.

60 Ibid.

61 See James Aho, *Far-Right Fantasy: A Sociology of American Religion and Politics* (New York: Routledge, 2016), 43.

62 In French, "se tiennent et se soutiennent," *Polemia*, April 14, 2013, http://www.polemia.com/la-radicalite-contre-la-dictature-des-minorites.

63 "Conservative Polish Magazine Issues 'LGBT-Free Zone' Stickers," Reuters, July 23, 2019, https://www.reuters.com/article/us-poland-lgbt/conservative-polish-magazine-issues-lgbt-free-zone-stickers-idUSKCN1UJ0HE.

64 See Wendy Brown, *In the Ruins of Neoliberalism: The Rise of Antidemocratic Politics in the West* (New York: Columbia University Press, 2019), 1–14.

65 Texas Senate Bill 17, 86th Legislature, 2019–2020, Legiscan.com, https://legiscan.com/TX/text/SB17/id/1983006.

66 Hannah Denham, "Texas Governor Signs 'Save Chick-fil-A' Bill into Law," *Washington Post*, July 19, 2019, https://www.washingtonpost.com/business/2019/07/19/chick-fil-a-inspires-new-texas-law-focused-protecting-religious-freedom.

67 Adam Liptak, "In Narrow Decision, Supreme Court Sides with Baker Who Turned Away Gay Couple," *New York Times*, June 4, 2018, https://www.nytimes.com/2018/06/04/us/politics/supreme-court-sides-with-baker-who-turned-away-gay-couple.html.

68 *Sharonell Fulton et al. v. City of Philadelphia et al.*, Petition for a writ of certiorari granted, 1, https://www.supremecourt.gov/DocketPDF/19/19-123/108931/20190722174037071_Cert Petition FINAL.pdf.
69 *Fulton et al. v. City of Philadelphia*, 19-123, June 17, 2021, https://www.supremecourt.gov/opinions/20pdf/19-123_g3bi.pdf.
70 James Esseks, "At End of SCOTUS Term, Where Are We on LGBT+ Rights?" American Civil Liberties Union, July 12, 2021, https://www.aclu.org/news/lgbtq-rights/at-end-of-scotus-term-where-are-we-on-lgbtq-rights/?fbclid=IwAR3U_oFPPRuDEGMEkRon4iVwjVi0rngzuIfW06sv6VB7i-YzKfGJX7nSaNFI.
71 Court of Appeals, 11th Circuit, 19-10604, November 20, 2020, https://media.ca11.uscourts.gov/opinions/pub/files/201910604.pdf.
72 Andrew Chung, "U.S. Top Court Rejects 'Gay Conversion' Therapy Ban Challenge," Reuters, May 1, 2017, https://www.reuters.com/article/us-usa-court-gayconversion-idUSKBN17X1SJ.
73 *State of Washington v. Arlene's Flowers*, Washington State Supreme Court, 91615-2, June 16, 2019.
74 SCOTUS, July 2, 2021, https://www.supremecourt.gov/search.aspx?filename=/docket/docketfiles/html/public/19-333.html.
75 Amy Howe, "Today's Orders: Same-Sex Marriage Petitions Denied (updated)," *SCOTUSblog*, October 6, 2014, https://www.scotusblog.com/2014/10/todays-orders-same-sex-marriage-petitins-denied/.
76 Jeannine Bell, "Pour faire barrage à ceux qui n'ont pas de cœur: Expressions racistes et droits des minorités," in *La Liberté d'expression aux États-Unis et en Europe*, ed. Élizabeth Zoller (Paris: Dalloz, 2008), 56–65.
77 Caroline Winterer, *American Enlightenments: Pursuing Happiness in the Age of Reason* (New Haven: Yale University Press, 2016), 171–95.
78 Kenneth L. Karst, *Visions of Power in the Politics of Race, Gender, and Religion* (New Haven: Yale University Press, 1993), 59–60.
79 This is why Serge Moscovici distinguished between compliance to minority views and acceptance (which is only possible if mediated by the majority). Serge Moscovici, *Social Influence and Social Change* (London: Academic Press, 1976). See also Melanie Trost, Anne Maass, and Douglas Kenrick, "Minority Influence: Personal Relevance Biases Cognitive Processes and Reverses Private Acceptance," *Journal of Experimental Social Psychology* 28.3 (1992): 234–54.
80 *Brush & Nib Studio v. Phoenix*, Arizona Court of Appeals, June 7, 2018; *State of Washington v. Arlene's Flowers*, Washington Supreme Court, June 6, 2019.
81 Henrik Lindell, *Les Veilleurs: Enquête sur une résistance* (Paris: Salvator, 2014), 39.
82 Assa Traoré and Geoffroy de Lagasnerie, *Le Combat Adama* (Paris: Stock, 2019).
83 Perreau, *Queer Theory*, 148–57.
84 Winterer, *American Enlightenments*, 171–95.
85 Sara Garbagnoli and Massimo Prearo, *La Croisade "anti-genre": Du Vatican aux manifs pour tous* (Paris: Textuel, 2017), 96.

86 Lars Rensmann, "The Noisy Counter-Revolution: Understanding the Cultural Conditions and Dynamics of Populist Politics in Europe in the Digital Age," *Politics and Governance* 5.4 (2017): 123–35.
87 Ashley Jardina, "Celebrating Whiteness," in *White Identity Politics* (Cambridge: Cambridge University Press, 2019), 136–44.
88 "Renaud Camus, tête de liste aux européennes," *Valeurs Actuelles*, April 9, 2019, https://www.valeursactuelles.com/politique/renaud-camus-tete-de-liste-aux-europeennes-105724.
89 Ivan Valerio, "Pour Marine Le Pen, la théorie du 'grand remplacement' relève du 'complotisme,'" *Le Figaro*, November 2, 2014, https://www.lefigaro.fr/politique/le-scan/citations/2014/11/02/25002-20141102ARTFIG00145-pour-marine-le-pen-la-theorie-du-grand-remplacement-releve-du-complotisme.php.
90 "Éric Zemmour définitivement condamné pour provocation à la haine raciale," *Le Monde*, September 20, 2019, https://www.lemonde.fr/societe/article/2019/09/20/eric-zemmour-definitivement-condamne-pour-provocation-a-la-haine-raciale_6012389_3224.html.
91 This is what Kathleen Belew demonstrates about supremacist, paramilitary groups: there are no "lone wolves." Each person is linked to the others by all kinds of references and spaces of exchange, real or virtual. Kathleen Belew, *Bringing the War Home: The White Power Movement and Paramilitary America* (Cambridge, MA: Harvard University Place, 2018), 55–76.
92 "Carburants: Macron 'assume parfaitement' la hausse de la taxation," *Capital*, November 4, 2018, https://www.capital.fr/economie-politique/macron-assume-parfaitement-la-hausse-de-la-taxation-sur-le-diesel-1314239.
93 Nadia Urbinati, "The Populist Phenomenon," *Raisons Politiques* 5.3 (2013): 138–40.
94 "Gilets jaunes: La Manif pour tous truste la consultation," *L'Express*, January 5, 2019, https://www.lexpress.fr/actualite/societe/gilets-jaunes-la-manif-pour-tous-truste-la-consultation_2055939.html.
95 Yves Mény, *Imparfaites démocraties* (Paris: Presses de Sciences, 2019), 238.
96 Danielle Tartakowsky, *Les Droites et la rue: Histoire d'une ambivalence, de 1880 à nos jours* (Paris: La Découverte, 2014), 166.
97 Voir Pippa Norris and Ronald Inglehart, *Cultural Backlash: Trump, Brexit, and Authoritarian Populism* (Cambridge: Cambridge University Press, 2019), 7.
98 Gilles Ivaldi and Joël Gombin, "The Rassemblement National and the New Politics of the Rural in France," in *Rural Protest Groups and Populist Political Parties*, ed. Dirk Strijker, Gerrit Voerman, and Ida J. Terluin (Wageningen: Wageningen Academic Publishers, 2015), 243–64.
99 Nonna Mayer, "From Jean-Marie to Marine Le Pen: Electoral Change on the Far Right," *Parliamentary Affairs* 66.1 (2013): 160–78.
100 Michel Feher, "Solidarité mélancolique: La gauche et les 'gilets jaunes,'" *Analyse Opinion Critique*, January 21, 2019, https://aoc.media/opinion/2019/01/21/solidarite-melancolique-gauche-gilets-jaunes.
101 Bojan Bugaric, "The Two Faces of Populism: Between Authoritarian and Democratic Populism," *German Law Journal* 20.3 (2019): 390–400.
102 *Boulevard Voltaire*.

103   Edmund Burke, *Reflections on the Revolution in France and on the Proceedings in Certain Societies in London Relative to That Event* (London: Dodsley, 1790), 127–28.
104   Walker Connor, "The Politics of Ethnonationalism," *Journal of International Affairs* 27.1 (1973): 4.
105   Guy Debord, *Society of Spectacle*, trans. Fredy Perlman et al. (Detroit: Black & Red, 2010), § 29.
106   Ian Woodward, Zlatko Skrbis, and Clive Bean, "Attitudes Towards Globalization and Cosmopolitanism: Cultural Diversity, Personal Consumption and the National Economy," *British Journal of Sociology* 59.2 (2008): 207–26.
107   Graeme Turner, "The Nation-State and Media Globalisation: Has the Nation-State Returned—or Did It Never Leave?" in *Global Media and National Policies: The Return of the State*, ed. Terry Flew, Petros Iosifidis, and Jeanette Steemers (London: Palgrave Macmillan, 2016), 92–105.
108   Bernard Harcourt, for example, analyzes the links between counterinsurgency practices and methods of policing and surveillance. Bernard Harcourt, *The Counterrevolution: How Our Government Went to War Against Its Own Citizens* (New York: Basic Books, 2018).
109   See my forthcoming book, *Spheres of Injustice: Minorities, Law and Representation*.
110   See William Julius Wilson, *The Truly Disadvantaged: The Inner City, the Underclass, and Public Policy* (Chicago: University of Chicago Press, 1987).
111   Jeannie Suk Gersen, "The Uncomfortable Truth About Affirmative Action and Asian-Americans," *New Yorker*, August 10, 2017, https://www.newyorker.com/news/news-desk/the-uncomfortable-truth-about-affirmative-action-and-asian-americans.
112   See Catherine Koerner and Soma Pillay, "Conceptualising Cultural Identity: The Great Divide," in *Governance and Multiculturalism: The White Elephant of Social Construction and Cultural Identities* (London: Palgrave Macmillan, 2020), 121–80.
113   Bruno Perreau, "Les analogies du genre: Différance, intrasectionnalité et droit," in *Genre, droit et politique*, ed. Charles Bosvieux-Onyekwelu and Véronique Mottier (Paris: LGDJ, 2022), 191–214.. See also Patricia Hill-Collins, *Intersectionality as Critical Social Theory* (Durham: Duke University Press, 2019).
114   Voir Salena Tramel, "Convergence as Political Strategy: Social Justice Movements, Natural Resources and Climate Change," *Third World Quarterly* 39.7 (2018): 1290–1307.
115   Mark Lilla, *The Once and Future Liberal: After Identity Politics* (New York: HarperCollins, 2017), 10.
116   Amy Chua, *Political Tribes: Group Instinct and the Fate of Nations* (New York: Penguin Books, 2018), 197–204.
117   See Rachel Knaebel, "The Gilets Jaunes and the Unions: A Convergence over What?" trans. Joe Hayns, *Inquiry*, December 18, 2018, https://notesfrombelow.org/article/gilets-jaunes-and-unions-convergence-over-what#; see also Matthieu Foucher, "Avec les militants queers qui ont rejoint les

'gilets jaunes,'" *Vice*, December 10, 2018, https://www.vice.com/fr/article/vbap9m/avec-les-militants-queers-qui-ont-rejoint-les-gilets-jaunes.

118 Nina Kirmizi, "Comité Adama, cheminots, étudiants ... et Gilets Jaunes: L'autre cortège de la manifestation parisienne," *Révolution Permanente*, December 1, 2018, https://www.revolutionpermanente.fr/Comite-Adama-cheminots-etudiants-et-Gilets-Jaunes-l-autre-cortege-de-la-manifestation-parisienne.

Gisela Catanzaro

11. Authoritarian Neoliberalism and Neocolonial Subordination: Beyond the National Question (Argentina, 2015–19)

Translated by Ramsey McGlazer

THIS TEXT SEEKS to present some elements for the analysis of new forms of neoliberalism, paying particular attention to the internal complexities of neoliberal ideology in Latin America's "peripheral" countries. I begin from the premise that we need to tear away the aura of impenetrability from the supposed mystery of a form of neoliberalism that is at once deregulating, disciplinarian, and punitive. Such an effort is necessary if we are to move beyond the plane of neoliberal ideology's own self-representations and instead develop a critique of the authoritarian social sensibilities that, in Argentina, the government of Mauricio Macri both expressed and fomented between 2015 and 2019. In order to understand the specificity of this authoritarian form of neoliberalism, however, we have to attend to the dialectic of aggression and submission that unfolded at the level of rhetoric. Unlike both recent nationalist configurations of neoliberalism in countries like Brazil and earlier forms of neoliberalism that prevailed in Argentina, Macrism in the latter country combined xenophobic gestures, a series of dehistoricizing strategies, and a demand that the population meekly assume the subordinate role historically assigned to Argentina in the global order.

From the "Cultural Turn" to the "Authoritarian Turn"

DURING THE 1990S, in his reflections on the idea of a "cultural turn," Fredric Jameson considered the ideology peculiar to an era in which the unprecedented universalization of a single mode of production at the planetary scale was celebrated as a euphoric explosion of cultural diversity in a "globe" imagined as a new and unbounded space of harmonic coexistence for various kinds of difference.[1] Slavoj Žižek likewise interpreted both the idea of a "friction-free capitalism," first formulated by Bill Gates, and capitalism's self-representation as "multicultural" as utopias built on the fantasy of freedom not only from "the reality of material obstacles which sustain any exchange process, but [also] above all [from] the Real of traumatic social antagonisms, power relations and so forth which brand the space of social exchange with a pathological twist."[2] Writing during the same period but from a perspective closer to Michel Foucault's, Wendy Brown defined neoliberalism by pointing both to the market-driven morality that took a heavy toll on the unrestrained subject engaged in a process of constant self-valorization and to the spread of a political rhetoric that proclaimed itself part of the "constructivist" project. In this rhetoric, the marketization of life emerged as a horizon to be reached rather than something already guaranteed or given, like a natural part of existence.[3]

In the two decades that separate us from the historical moment that these descriptions seek to delineate, there have been no important structural transformations in the global economy, and yet many of the traits outlined by Jameson, Žižek, and Brown have become unrecognizable. Far from that moment's optimistic and future-oriented emphases, today the present in capitalist societies would seem to be ever more closed in on itself. At a time when the claims of multiculturalism have clearly been displaced by a worrying rise in xenophobia and explicit militarism, the cult of diversity and of a "borderless" world has given way to the valorization of an "authentic" domesticity capable of protecting the real, vital interests of those "close to home" instead of what are taken to be artificial mediations. Given these contrasts, it is clear that, although in terms of the critique of ideology it does not seem at all possible to give up the term "neoliberalism" in our efforts to disclose the specificities of a certain form of post-Fordist, deregulated, and global capitalism, it is also senseless to ignore the transformations that have taken place under a form of neoliberalism that, after crises in 2001 and 2008, has been reignited but not without transforming some of its most conspicuous features at the level of ideology.

Compared to the more technocratic, consumerist, and multicultural form of neoliberalism that prevailed during the last decades of the twentieth century, the new inflection of neoliberalism that we confront today has effectively been shown to be less concerned with horizons of transcendence, more emotional, and more authoritarian. On the one hand, neoliberal capitalism would seem to have been absolutized, to have lost the internal tension that characterized its drive to realize itself in a global society, one that, according to the cold technocratic utopias of the 1990s, would be by "experts" using the tools of the strictest economic rationality. After the crises of 2001 and 2008, these horizons of futurity and these aspirations for transcendence—these desires to go beyond what already exists—seem to have given way to inexorable claims that the given is absolute. A closure of the present on itself, a new "capitalist realism" that manages to not be perceived as problematic at all,[4] one marked at the level of fiction by the shift from the "United Colors of Benetton" to the endless proliferation of post-apocalyptic films in which infinitely entrepreneurial subjects, having developed all kinds of superhuman capacities for survival, nevertheless find themselves systematically submitting to unsatisfiable demands.

Today, under the conditions of a capitalism without an outside that would allow us to make its limits visible—and one that is itself lacking in internal horizons—it is necessary to argue that the (admittedly ideological) image of a future without borders, defined as a world to be achieved, has given way to the building of walls and enclosures. These walls mark national borders and police enclosures that express the triumph of a disciplinary and punitive form of securitarianism that is ever more entrenched and increasingly regarded as the key to resolving conflicts both outside and within nations. If "openness" was the slogan of what William Davies calls "combative neoliberalism" in its confrontation with socialist regimes, then "punitive neoliberalism"—which emerges when that other form is overcome and at the same time the hinges of capitalism begin to creak after a new global crisis—encourages the social demand for "law and order" or for a "return to order" and interprets these demands as the highest ideals to which collective subjects can aspire.[5] This form of neoliberalism thus neglects the freedoms and rights that then become vulnerable during the course of this process.

But it would be wrong to conclude that this triumph of disciplinary desires and calls to order has happened in a homogeneous way throughout the world. How could the *forms* of order, of discipline, be indifferent to the hierarchies within which "order" as such has historically been consolidated, hierarchies that it also seeks to reproduce? Rather than being expressed in a homogeneous way, calls to order and the administration of proliferating punishments during these times of punitive neoliberalism would seem to imprint new determinations on old geopolitical maps marked by old anxieties. These maps date back to the colonial era, and they established the unequal distribution of roles that became a sine qua non for the reproduction of capitalism, assigning different roles to different countries as well as to the coastal and interior regions of these countries. Refusing to lose sight of this colonial dimension means, among other things, insisting that, far from constituting proof of or evidence for a thesis that critical thought needs only to confirm, the various forms taken by the authoritarian turn in neoliberal capitalism in different geographies imply a challenge for theoretical and analytical efforts that seek to address this transformation.

The emergence of new forms of supremacist nationalism is one of the key manifestations of the punitive and authoritarian call to order in contemporary neoliberalism. This neoliberalism takes shape as an ideology that seeks to shield populations from the experience of their own disposability under current global conditions. But it would be problematic to think of these supremacist impulses as the universal expression of neoliberal capitalism's openly punitive form; this would risk ignoring other forms of authoritarian punitivism that currently prevail in various world regions without necessarily being linked to supremacist aspirations. Conversely, under current conditions of subjugation—whether military, financial, juridical, or cultural—imposed by some nations over others, to generalize the condemnation of invocations of national sovereignty in the name of freedom and justice might entail ignoring one of the dimensions of inequality against which many emancipatory projects are currently struggling. Can the potential politics of "the national question" be thought of "universally" at all—as if we could set aside or abstract from "the colonial question" and the geopolitical asymmetries that continue to make this latter question a current one? Wouldn't such an exercise in abstraction remain colonial in its refusal to recognize the national question *as a question* and a problem, assuming that the meaning of all appeals to the nation can be reduced to their meaning in central, as opposed to peripheral, countries?

Echoing a certain anxiety confronted by contemporary political theory and analysis when they seek to conceptualize the present in capitalist societies, this text undertakes to offer elements for the analysis of new forms of neoliberalism, paying particular attention to neoliberalism's internal complexities and to the particular forms that it assumes in "peripheral" countries like Argentina. I take as my point of departure the claim that the effort to conceptualize these complexities is blocked by the dichotomies that organize classical political thought. This is why I begin by elaborating on the argument, made by authors as different as Wolfgang Streeck and Wendy Brown, that nothing guarantees neoliberalism's compromise with the values of liberal democracy. Nor can we rule out the possibility of a culturally conservative neoliberalism. Building on Brown's recent reading of neoliberal doctrine,[6] I argue that it is necessary to strip away the aura of unfathomability and supposed mystery from a form of neoliberalism that is at once libertarian *and* disciplinarian or authoritarian. This is necessary, that is, if we are to move beyond the plane of neoliberal ideology's own self-representations and instead develop a critique of the authoritarian social sensibilities that, in Argentina, the government of Mauricio Macri both expressed and fomented.

But understanding the specificity of neoliberalism's peculiar, authoritarian form in Argentina means engaging in another effort to complicate the picture, by attending to a dialectic of *aggression and submission* that governmental practices implemented during the period from 2015 to 2019. As Theodor Adorno already noted in the 1940s, considering these two contrasting elements as constitutive components of the authoritarian personality, the desire for order and punishment can be turned against the subject itself, in a logic that exacerbates *both* the tendency to condemn and punish others, on the one hand, *and*, on the other, the ego's drive to sacrifice itself and submit to an external authority.[7] If Macri's government in Argentina could at once be the party of deregulation and the party of order, as has happened in many other neoliberal governments throughout the world, it also showed a peculiar ability to project images in which the disciplinarian community was not defined only as a subject capable of punishing others but also as a community that could reconstitute itself in a salutary form of suffering, undergoing a punishment that it deserved and that allowed it, among other things, to rediscover its natural and subordinate place in the world order. Thus, attending to the ideological traits that distinguish this new form of neoliberalism from emergent nationalist neoliberalisms in the region as well as those that previously prevailed in Argentina, in the last two sections I consider how the promotion of a peculiar form of authoritarianism in Argentina allowed the Macri administration to partly sidestep conflicts between nationalisms and anti-nationalisms as it brought together, apparently without contradictions, the oligarchic tendency to discriminate against ethnic minorities, the devalorization of the idea of national sovereignty that characterized Argentine neoliberalism during the 1990s, a sacrificial logic leading to a neocolonial position, and the displacement of historical conflict with appeals to nature.

Deregulation and Discipline

NEOLIBERALISM HAS OFTEN been characterized as a doctrine driven by processes of privatization that are fundamentally objectionable because of their consequences, which wear away at the social. Thus, according to Streeck, the relaunching of capitalist relations of production in the 1970s had profoundly de-democratizing consequences at the level of ideology in that it led to a dissolution of solidarities in which all political projects that sought to minimize increasing social inequality were shown to be either redundant or badly damaging. This process in turn encouraged, according to Streeck, the generalization of a cynical attitude in the population, which confronted a form of capitalism that no longer pretended to give rise to a just society and sought only to found *"social integration* on *collective resignation* as the last remaining pillar in the capitalist order, or disorder."[8]

Although this emphasis on the process of de-solidarization has the advantage of highlighting the damage that neoliberal capitalism does to the egalitarian promises associated with modern democracies, the diagnosis of anomic individualism characteristic of many sociological analyses that are critical of neoliberal ideology is problematic for two reasons: on the one hand, because this diagnosis tends to underestimate neoliberalism's ability to produce paradoxical social ties and figures of community; and, on the other hand, because it does not question—or it simply reproduces—the opposition between individual autonomy and social justice. This is precisely the opposition that neoliberal ideology, which these accounts seek to criticize, continues to imagine as an either/or. Thus situated within the very ideological coordinates that they work to contest, these theories come up against almost insurmountable obstacles in their effort to conceptualize and problematize specifically neoliberal understandings of justice. But even more importantly for my purposes in this text, these analyses also come up against hard limits in their effort to address how neoliberalism can become authoritarian, damaging individual autonomy by undermining the social—economic, political, and cultural—conditions that allow for it, promoting instead not only openly repressive policies but also anti-intellectual and culturally conservative drives, as happens in many countries in Latin America, including in Brazil, and as happened in a less virulent form in Argentina under Macri's administration.

How can we explain the imperative to submit to the order of existing things and hierarchies, the punitive tendencies, the unlimited criminalization of others who are systematically figured as threats, the subjective dispositions that, all over the world, actually existing neoliberalism continues to exacerbate—how can we explain all of this if we begin from the premise that neoliberalism is essentially associated with the "tolerance" of difference and the defense of individual autonomy? To consider the current emergence of supremacist and xenophobic nationalism, increasing homophobia, and the spirit of crusade, for instance, in current evangelical practices that predominate in Brazil as mere reactions *to* neoliberalism or as deviations *from* its "logic" is uncritically to reproduce a form of neoliberal self-representation that finds its pure form by projecting inverted mirror images (for example, the image of "populism"). Inasmuch as it is *imaginary*, this self-representation is unable to conceptualize the internal complexity of these ideologies, which are not necessarily harmonious or coherent. Thus in order to understand neoliberalism, especially at a time when its authoritarian potentials seem to be so highly developed, it is necessary to *deconstruct* the opposition between individual autonomy and social justice, to interpret this opposition as one of many effects of a cultural disposition already shaped by neoliberalism. Behind the opposition between these terms hides a profoundly conservative dimension of neoliberalism.

In a recently published text, Brown works at once to complicate and to deconstruct familiar understandings of the "liberal" in "neoliberal." Here Brown not only demonstrates that the architects of neoliberal doctrine, including Friedrich Hayek, demonized social justice; she also interrogates the understandings of freedom and justice that subtend this rejection. This allows Brown to investigate the meaning of their efforts to privatize life and to expose the socioculturally conservative character of neoliberalism. For someone like Hayek, Brown writes, all limits to liberty—negatively defined and thus *not* understood as a power to act that requires interventions and limitations in order to unfold at all—in the name of civility, equality, inclusion, public goods, and especially "the dangerous superstition" of social justice are located on a continuum with totalitarianism, while deregulation and privatization emerge as unlimited moral and philosophical principles that extend far beyond the realm of the economy.[9] Elaborating on this last point, Brown shows that the forms of privatization driven by neoliberalism are not limited to the privatization and/or dismantling of public goods and services or to the concomitant, meritocratic hyper-responsibilization of individuals at the level of the reproduction of life. Privatization also constitutes a means by which to introduce family values into public spaces previously organized by democratic norms and laws, and this not only threatens the principles of equality, secularism, pluralism, and inclusion—all principles at the heart of modern democratic society—but also replaces them with traditional moral values belonging to "the personal, protected sphere."

In this familialist form of neoliberal privatization, the promotion of conservative values is also inseparable from securitarian logics, since, according to Brown, "when the twin dimensions of privatization," economic and ethical, "discursively capture the nation itself, it ceases to be figured primarily as a democracy but instead is figured as a competitive business needing to make good deals and attract investors, on the one hand, and as an inadequately secured home, besieged by ill-willed or nonbelonging outsiders, on the other."[10]

There is a traditionalist moralism that is part of neoliberal doctrine and not a mere "deviation" from its logic. This thesis is a key point of departure for global efforts to understand contemporary neoliberal reality and the various de-democratizing tendencies that it both expresses and enables. While the uncritical reproduction of a unitary, imaginary neoliberal self-representation makes the phenomena of xenophobia, racism, and homophobia—phenomena that profoundly shape our present—unthinkable, or thinkable only as matters of radical exteriority, Brown's diagnosis of the double valence of privatization, in its economic and ethical forms, as defended by the architects of neoliberalism, strips away the aura of insolubility from one of the great "mysteries" of our present: how is it possible for the political right to be currently perceived as at once in favor of liberty *and* in favor of law and order?

However, in order to account for these two tendencies—that is, for both the self-promotion and the social perception of these new political forms of neoliberalism, defined as the products of a struggle against the threat of authoritarianism *and* as the promise of an empire of order—it is not enough to study neoliberal doctrine. In the Argentine case, such an effort would require, first of all, locating contemporary neoliberalism within a genealogy of the coups through which neoliberal policies were originally installed in the region during the 1970s and analyzing their long-term effects on subjectivity and society. Second, this effort would require a careful analysis of the rhetoric and policies of Macri's government as well as of the expectations and sensibilities that predominated in Argentine society before the Alianza Cambiemos assumed executive power at the national level in 2015. Although it is impossible within the limits of this essay to undertake these historical and sociological analyses in detail, it is worth signaling their importance as correctives to the constructivist and would-be universalist political tendency that obstructs critical analysis by ignoring, on the one hand, the fact that political forces not only *produce* but also *express* (conflictual) social conditions, and, on the other, the fact that authoritarian neoliberalism already has a long history in Latin American countries, where, in political and cultural terms, its conservative and/or reactionary violence constitutes less a potential that has recently been actualized than a mark of origin that has been reinterpreted and actively resisted during the last decades.

Both at the level of government rhetoric during the period from 2015 to 2019 and at the level of the social sensibilities that gradually came to the fore and constituted an opposition during the second presidential term of Cristina Fernández de Kirchner (2011–15), we can see the combination of deregulatory, disciplinary, and conservative projects that Brown identifies in classical neoliberal doctrine.[11] The prevailing social mood in Argentina before Macri's rise to the presidency was characterized by demands both for more (negative) freedom and for more control, both for less "anarchy" and for less "authoritarianism," both for the opening of "dialogue" denuded of all political conflict and for the reimposition of order, that is, for a return to the hierarchies that "populist"[12] egalitarianism had questioned and the revival of the systems of recompense and punishment that had been neglected, in the opinion of the majority.

This more or less unconscious and widespread ideology found expression in furious denunciations of the "anarchy" that had supposedly been created by social programs that were indifferent to individual effort, and in diatribes against the policies that had sought to establish consumer-friendly standards for the financial market and the market in goods, but that were interpreted as "authoritarian" regulations in keeping with a desire to wield political power over the everyday lives of individuals. In this increasingly prominent sensibility and the narratives of personal responsibility to which it gave rise, the fear of "others"—who were either under- or over-represented but always regarded as a threat—converged with a heightened emphasis on "punitive security" and on family relations, imagined as the only possible means by which peace could be guaranteed.[13]

The most authoritarian features of this constellation of disciplinary discontents and desires for punishment, harmony, and deregulation—all at the same time—were in turn sustained by the policies that Macri's government promoted and the discourse of this government's officials. Among these policies—which include the suppression of a law that sought to limit monopoly power in communications and media, and the decision to lower taxes for the export of grains and minerals—we can single out one that allowed the armed forces to intervene in matters of internal security, through a presidential decree that contravened one of the most stable agreements upheld by various administrations in Argentina since the end of the last civico-military dictatorship (1976–83), an agreement that insisted on the maintenance of a separation between matters of defense and matters of security.[14] Complementing this measure, taken in the name of the struggle against drug trafficking, in the name of freedom of movement and on behalf of a population "fed up" with traffic jams caused by protests and with "insecurity," the Macri government sought to impose a "protocol for conduct" during public demonstrations, effectively allowing the security forces to violently intervene in scenes of social protest; an "anti-occupation" protocol to discourage protests among secondary school students in the City of Buenos Aires; a change in the regulations governing the use of weapons by security forces, granting more firepower to them; a modification to national immigration law that marked a step backward in terms of respect for human rights, in a decree appealing to necessity and national security that was ultimately declared unconstitutional; and the creation of an immigrant detention center.[15]

These policies were compounded by numerous declarations in which government officials expressed their support for the police, the gendarmerie, and the naval prefecture in cases of "trigger-happy" officers. Other declarations offered justifications for vigilante acts by civilians in various cases of "insecurity"; others defended the bearing of arms for the "legitimate defense" against crimes targeting private property and at the same time identified as "terrorist" demonstrations organized in southern Argentina by the Mapuche community.[16] The promotion of racism and xenophobia, which reached its apex in declarations about the Mapuche made by Patricia Bullrich, Macri's minister of security, could also be seen in the stoking of suspicion by other government officials, who suggested that crime rates were higher among immigrants, in complaints about the use of public hospitals by these immigrants, and in the request made to national universities that they declare how many non-Argentines were enrolled in free higher education as well as the courses in which they were enrolled.

To an extent, all of these policies and public acts by government officials—which can only be understood when they are seen as part of the genealogy of coups in the region and which, without openly defending the dictatorships in which these coups resulted, break with certain post-dictatorship social agreements that rendered the doctrines of national security promoted by these regimes of state terror unacceptable—can also be seen as part of a securitarian and punitivist turn among democratically elected neoliberal governments. As Gabriela Seghezzo and Nicolás Dallorso indicate, this turn has shaped subjectivities and social relations since the 1990s, instilling individualizing fears, public distrust of whole sectors of the immigrant population, and doubts about the state's ability, and that of politics more generally, to resolve social problems.[17] Nevertheless, under the administration of Carlos Menem (president of Argentina from 1989 to 1999) this securitarianism was associated with privatizing incentives to consume and with commodified forms of leisure that were clearly compatible with that former president's ironic and hedonistic style and with a cynical attitude that drew attention to the self-interest and particularism of all subjective practices. By contrast, the punitivism promoted by Macri's administration exalted the moral superiority of austerity, discipline, and submission, acquiring sacrificial traits that set it apart both from previous iterations of neoliberalism in Argentina and from other forms of neoliberalism in Latin America. It is these traits that we must attend to in order to understand the particularities of an authoritarian punitivism that is not necessarily fueled by supremacist nationalist aspirations.

The Rhetoric of Sacrifice in Argentina's New Authoritarian Neoliberalism

AFTER THE CRISIS of utopian multiculturalism and the decline of the fantasy of "friction-free capitalism," throughout the world neoliberalism entered a newly punitive phase in which the emphases on everyone's unlimited potential and the hyper-responsibilization of the subject—emphases typical of all entrepreneurial neoliberal discourses—were combined with a new prominence given to figures of punishment. In this new guise, neoliberalism offers, on the one hand, a way of channeling the fears and frustrations generated by capitalism, "liberating" subjects by inviting them to unload their aggression on others. But this new version of neoliberalism can also do something else: namely, encourage the introjection of guilt and thus demand the population's endless self-flagellation. Working within a moralized framework of punitive values, William Davies argues, this form of neoliberalism produces an interiorization of the morality of finance, which produces the sense that we deserve to suffer for the supposed economic irrationality of our past. Understood in this way, the spread of punitivism, which associates suffering with a certain nobility, includes but exceeds the diffusion of preexisting securitarian logics and policies of repression, realizing itself in a new ethos of (self-)sacrifice and punishment (of others). It operates through a projection of guilt (one's own and that of others) that is also characterized by anti-intellectualism or a post-critical orientation: "the moment of judgement has already passed, and questions of value or guilt are no longer open to deliberation."[18]

In the discourse of Macri's administration, the punitivism condensed in the idea of "zero tolerance" for the deviations or infractions of others—and associated both with a hypertrophy of law and with a hardening of restrictions that can nevertheless justify extralegal actions on the part of security forces—is compounded by a form of self-punishment that is equally intolerant. Such self-punishment makes no exceptions when it comes to making the individual responsible for his or her destiny, or when it comes to vilifying our national culture, which by this account has taught us to be lazy and to seek shortcuts, preventing us from recognizing that effort *as such* constitutes a supreme moral value and that "there is nothing more important in someone's life than the dignity of his work."[19]

Viveza criolla, "creole cleverness" or the supposedly special capacity of Argentines to devise tricks that allow them to get ahead even at the cost of deceiving others, the *astucia* or cunning that Menemism celebrated as a sort of cultural gift and that new forms of neoliberalism continue to require, was morally condemned in Macri's discourse.[20] Neoliberal cynicism under Menem showed the exacerbation of private interests, always pointing to the self-interest and particularism of those interests and defending *viveza criolla* unreservedly. Under Macri, by contrast, neoliberal discourse in Argentina moved away even from the logic of interest and self-preservation, proclaiming instead that effort, discipline, and submission were superior moral values, independent of any end.

The Macri administration's discourse called on us to sacrifice *endlessly* and declared openly that we would suffer. We were to suffer—in keeping with a message more or less explicitly delivered by government officials—not so that we could regain a lost supremacy, as in the case of the call to "Make America Great Again" in the United States. Nor were we to suffer for the sake of a struggle against an external enemy, as had been the case with Chile and the United Kingdom in the militarist discourse developed by Argentine military officials during the last dictatorship. Instead we were to suffer because we had regained the awareness of the place that fell to all of us—every country and every individual—in the "normal" world order, an order from which Kirchnerist governments had "isolated" us by pursuing a revanchist and pathological politics that insisted on conflicts with international financial organizations even while it also established political alliances with other countries in the region including Venezuela, Bolivia, and Brazil under Luiz Inâcio Lula da Silva's administration, opposed to the Pacific Alliance and the Free Trade Area of the Americas.[21] Thus what was recovered after the defeat of "populism" was nothing less than the "justice" of inequality crystallized in an order whose restoration promised—when it did not promise even more than this—to resolve "insecurities" related to internal social hierarchies, and also to restore our humble but honorable identity as providers of raw materials and debtors in the international community.

The dual character of contemporary neoliberalism, where self-sacrifice and the punishment of others are inseparable from one another, was visible in the idea, which was already widespread before Macri's rise to power, that economic suffering without social assistance was the sign of an individual's superiority over those who, by contrast, were morally inferior and even condemnable for receiving such assistance.²² This became one of the topics that, after Macri's rise to power, displaced the previously dominant problem of "insecurity": the state of "corruption" and "insincerity" in which, by this account, all Argentines had been immersed until 2015. Although in Macri's discourse "the corrupt" and "liars" referred first of all to officials in the previous government administration, they were also those who "sought to live on our taxes": the beneficiaries of social programs or foreigners who "took advantage" of the supposed generosity of certain public programs in the country, especially its education and health care systems. These figures, and the various political organizations and public demonstrations that insisted on defending such prerogatives as human rights that had been fought for and won, became the main targets of discrimination and punitive rage. But the list did not end there: we had *all* been corrupt and insincere in that we had all more or less directly participated in the sinful arrogance that had led us to imagine that it was possible for much of the population to access goods and services previously reserved exclusively for select minorities, or to live in a country unburdened by debt and sovereign in its ability to develop a political economy that would not be subject to the historical demands made by the International Monetary Fund.²³

In the narratives of a prior state of generalized moral corruption, narratives that Macri's administration promoted, sacrifice appears not simply as an ineluctable but contingent phenomenon; instead it appears as inherent to our nature, as something good and even "liberating" in the sense that acknowledging its necessity lets us detach ourselves from false hopes and redeem ourselves by repenting for the arrogance that sustained these hopes. It teaches us to accept our place in the world order. Above all, it gives us the right to show others— whether those who have fallen prey to the "fable" of social justice or those who have usurped rights that did not belong to them—how to learn to occupy a subordinate position in the world order, even when this implies direct violence. But if this punitive/sacrificial logic is clearly disciplinary, it is disciplinary in a more complex sense than the one implied in easy appeals to the imposition of force through the exercise of repressive apparatuses. Unlike what takes place in this kind of discipline, the Macrist version of discipline is productive, and it depends on the interpellation of paranoid and punishing subjects who are also guilty themselves. While it generalizes a "right to punish," it also generalizes the state of sinfulness and guilt, providing moral codes to allow for self-limitation. Thus the new right in Argentina does not hesitate to rely on the theological vocabulary of guilt, redemption, and sin to justify the politics of austerity implemented during the course of Macri's administration and that it continues to promote, thus justifying the increasing inequality and the resulting devastation of lives.

In this vocabulary, sacrifice and schooling in submission are key figures that appear not only in the context of demands for individual entrepreneurship but also in the functioning of a neocolonial discourse that promotes a sense of vassalage, of subordination to world powers, as if this subordinate attitude were an index of wisdom. The promotion of this attitude is certainly far from new in Argentina: both oligarchic liberal governments in the late nineteenth and early twentieth centuries and previous neoliberal governments sustained these attitudes. But under Macri the element of submission was accentuated or made explicit, whereas it had only been implicit in the idea, formulated by the founding fathers, that Argentina was "the breadbasket of the world," or in the furiously nationalist discourse of the last military dictatorship, or in the supposed egalitarianism of exchange rates and the defense of unrestricted imports that characterized Menem's administration.

Anticipating Macri, Menem espoused a "post-nationalism" during the 1990s, demonstrating a docile will to participate in the world order by assuming the position that this order was ready to assign him. The subordination that his administration encouraged, however, was inseparable from a hedonism associated with images of the pleasure held out as a promise, as in the phrase that then-chancellor Guido Di Tella used to refer to the country's international politics. At a moment when the world promised interconnections, new consumer goods, and a multiculturalism enraptured by the fantasy of a "friction-free" and borderless form of capitalism, Argentina tried, in Di Tella's words, to "maintain carnal relations" with the United States. By contrast, Mauricio Macri's view, expressed on July 9, 2016, during the course of celebrations commemorating the 200th anniversary of Argentina's declaration of independence from Spain—an occasion that happened to coincide with the Spanish prince Juan Carlos's visit to Argentina—was that submission should be interpreted as noble. In a speech in which the illustrious heir to the Spanish crown—which had held Argentina as one of its colonial possessions—played a central role, Argentina's president said, addressing the prince who stood next to him: "I am here trying to think and feel what [those who declared independence] felt at that moment. Clearly they must have been agonized to decide, dear King, to separate from Spain."[24] The punitive and sacrificial neoliberalism that the government sponsored seemed to represent the only form of neoliberal neocolonialism still possible when the "positive" side of this ideology was in crisis. As Horacio González has perceptively noted in an analysis of this scene, which coincided with a request for forgiveness from international capital for the "abuses" of Kirchnerism, a request made by then-finance minister Alfonso Prat Gay, this scene lets us identify a fundamental trait of Macrist ideology: "the profound longing to be forgiven by the most powerful people on earth. Forgiveness, seen as a matter of superficial, seignorial anguish, closed the circle opened by the fathers of national independence in 1816 and became a matter of submission even while remaining in keeping with certain superficial norms of 'autonomy.'"[25]

Neocolonialism and Dehistoricization: Before and Beyond the Problem of the Nation

THE PRIVATIZED, HIERARCHICAL, and culturally conservative ethos that, according to Brown, allows neoliberalism to figure the nation as a home insufficiently protected—an ethos that is particularly conducive to the cultivation of xenophobic, misogynist, and punitivist political formations—came to permeate both dominant sensibilities in contemporary Argentina and the political discourse of the new right in the country. But the rhetoric of Macrism did not exalt the ethos of the nation and in this sense it lacked one of the constitutive elements of supremacist nationalism, instead relying on appeals to submission and sacrifice.[26] Without giving up on selective xenophobia, these appeals nevertheless insisted that "Argentines were at fault," were guilty.[27] As I have been suggesting throughout this chapter, this insistence made the authoritarian trajectory of the Macri administration different both from the trajectories of actually existing nationalisms elsewhere in the world and from the ironic and hedonist forms of neoliberalism previously seen in Argentina during Carlos Menem's administration. In the remainder of this chapter, I would like to further explain the diverse strategies at work in the political promotion of authoritarian neoliberalism.

The Argentine new right brings together multiple and diverse forms of the "familializing privatization" that neoliberal ideology has managed to articulate with economic privatization. If Macri's discourse is privatizing from the ideological point of view—and not only in an economic sense—this is not only because it enables and sustains socially conservative values. Although it exhibited and demanded—especially through the medium of key officials including Patricia Bullrich, Macri's minister of security, and Vice President Gabriela Michetti—ironclad attachments to the classical symbols of identity that the national ruling class historically used to demand submission and ensure discipline in the population, from the conquest of the "desert" to the exaltation of the "countryside" and its simple ways, through to the insistence on unconditional respect for the armed forces, Macri's administration insisted at the same time on making history disappear, in gestures of dehistoricization.

On one hand, traditional symbols of history and authority were restored, and we were asked to reconcile with the institutions tasked with perpetuating the asymmetries and forms of violences that had been consecrated by the nation-state since its foundation. Crudely, neoliberal discourse situated itself "beyond" the efforts to interrogate the nation's dominant history that had been undertaken after persistent social struggle. On the other hand, however, all kinds of historical disengagement were encouraged, leading to the disavowal of history as such, to the wholesale displacement of the historical into the realm of "artifice" and "corruption."

Already in the terms that it chose to name itself as a political movement (PRO, Cambiemos [Let's Change], and later Juntos por el Cambio [Together for Change]), in Macrist interpellations we find that the "future" is turned into a sort of fetish uprooted from all cumulative historical processes. This tendency to dehistoricize the future was programmatically articulated by Macri himself in 2013 in an opinion piece published in the newspaper *La Nación* in which he distinguished between "vindictive positions" and salutary "aspirational perspectives," and it was again confirmed in the course of Macri's electoral campaign for the presidency in 2019.[28] But beyond this fetishization of a "future" that has been tendentiously emptied of all content and that implicitly associates the past with the dead and what's harmful to life,[29] the process of dehistoricization promoted by Macrism between 2015 and 2019 took the form of a discursive tendency that oscillated between the avoidance of references to national history, replaced with a language centered on immediate everyday life, and the explicit demonization of "historicizing discourses" defined as symptoms of a pathological penchant for criticism[30] or as imposed by a partisan minority that disregards the interests of "the people."[31]

The Macri administration's practices are privatizing in this second, dehistoricizing sense, in that from the first they sought to impose an ahistorical political style centered on the "future," "healthy living," and "proximity," presenting themselves as the only truly non-political forces, located "on this side" of all ideologies and struggles over historical symbols, including names, languages, and national emblems. But because of the centrality of the idea of proximity, the erasure of history in the rhetoric of the Macri administration did not function—as such erasure had under the neoliberalism of the 1990s—through a technocratic appeal to a neutral, expert knowledge located above partisan conflict. It relied instead on the constant mobilization of domestic and self-centered passions, re-eroticizing the language of social administration (particularly through an atemporal understanding of happiness as opposed to and stripped of conflict) and, in official rhetoric, locating Macrism below or in a paradisal antechamber of the forms of artifice and the divisions "later" introduced by politics and history.

In other words, Macrist familialization not only makes the patrician history consecrated by dominant tradition appear; it also simultaneously makes history, defined as a matter of conflict and of debates over the conservation or the transformation of current social relations, disappear. Everything in history that is violent—but also everything that is contingent—is displaced by a "nature," a "life," a present, that is always identical to itself, since it is located in the eternity of the whales that took the place of national heroes on Argentine pesos,[32] or in the eternity of parents' love for their children. In President Macri's discourse, this love took the place previously occupied by conflicts over the interpretation of national history. In this context of omnipresent fauna and of kinship relations, struggles for emancipation have certainly been weakened. But even the canonical icons of the national establishment, symbols of the reproduction of the status quo, have tended to disappear. With the endless proliferation of images of a supposedly self-identical, originary, and immediate nature, this ideology does not pursue critical ends related to ecological crisis. Instead it projects the image of an idealized nature[33] and above all seeks to leave history's divisions and its contingency behind, in a leap toward eternity, where only my pet, my neighbor, and I reside.

In this leap, the "national question" loses all disruptive potential. If nationalism is a way of flattening the complications of this question, making the nation into an unproblematic identitarian category, then the latest form of neoliberalism in Argentina has achieved something similar, but by weakening the nation as well as history, by substituting both with a nature that is only ever overcome when another authority intervenes—that is, when the king of Spain, the emissaries of the

Sociedad Rural Argentina,[34] the IMF, or the president of the United States intervenes. In its dealings with these authorities, Macri's government let its insistence on sacrifice and discipline give way to an insistence on a submission consecrated by history. By contrast, when it is a matter of a history that involves the question of the nation, that remains unresolved and requires ongoing prosecutions in cases still pending, the kingdom of nature and the realm of domestic passions replaces history, and the national question evaporates as well.

In effect, neoliberalism tends to make the nation into a political non-issue, into a home that is insufficiently protected. But in the case of Macri's administration, that claim should be understood in a double sense, in terms of a twofold political strategy. On the one hand, I am referring to the strategy that seeks the reconstitution of the historically dominant logic of colonialism, which in peripheral countries leads not to ethnonationalism but to a kind of "ethnos" without "nationalism," that is, to a racialized, feudal logic that governs the interior of these countries. According to this logic, indigenous or mestizo populations form part of the hacienda and are objects, are property. At the same time, however, this logic is itself servile in that it serves the interests of the exterior, renouncing all national aspirations.[35] On the other hand, I am referring to the erasure of everything in the nation's history that continues to index an unresolved past, now recast as the extension of a nature that remains identical to itself. In this sense, we could say that Macrism in Argentina showed us that what punitive, familial authoritarianism required in the periphery was not nationalism—with which it could in fact dispense—but the closure of the national question, given this question's role in efforts to problematize existing hierarchies. Macrism also showed us that an alternative to nationalism can be combined with racial prejudice in different ways. It can be combined with calls for (self-)punishment that give pride of place to the idea of sacrifice and thus reimpose old hierarchies within the nation even while the nation itself assumes a position of neocolonial submission with respect to the "great" world powers. But the alternative can also take the form of a politics of symbolic "subtraction" at the level of history, erasing conflicts over interests and values while, at the social level, sustaining a timeless morality, detached from the socio-historical conditions of its formation, the conditions that also allow for the realization of its precepts.

Clearly, then, the experiences of the new right in the region seem once again to confirm the old intuitions of many popular movements in Latin America: namely, that racial prejudice in these countries is not always used to defend the national cause, and that the national question cannot be equated with nationalism. The reproduction of ready-made national identities, stripped of their complications, excesses, and discontinuities, is certainly not emancipatory. But addressing "the national question" in Latin America does not necessarily mean ignoring or foreclosing conflicts at the level of identity. Rather than a way to consecrate a structure presumed to be beyond dispute, working to address the national question has often been a way to name those conflicts and create space for anxieties and disputes over subaltern participation in society.[36] For precisely these reasons, not all ways of "overcoming" the national question are desirable. How else than as "national questions" can we frame ongoing debates about urgently important issues, indispensable to social justice, that have yet to be addressed: the struggle for the rights of the Mapuche people, for example, or the Qom, within the nation-state; or the last administration's responsibility for increases in malnutrition, unemployment, and indebtedness in Argentina; or its unwillingness to prosecute those responsible for crimes committed within the country by a repressive nation-state during the last civico-military dictatorship? The national question has thus not infrequently turned out to be inseparable from other questions like those addressed here, questions that touch on what Walter Benjamin referred to as the "untimely, sorrowful, and miscarried" dimensions of history.[37] This history is like a "death's head" waiting to be redeemed, and only terms shot through with tensions still have the capacity to name it.

Notes

1 Fredric Jameson, *The Cultural Turn: Selected Writings on the Postmodern, 1983–1998* (London: Verso, 1998).
2 Slavoj Žižek, "Multiculturalism, or the Cultural Logic of Multinational Capitalism," *New Left Review* 225 (1997): 36.
3 Wendy Brown, "Neoliberalism and the End of Liberal Democracy," in *Edgework: Critical Essays on Knowledge and Politics* (Princeton: Princeton University Press, 2005).
4 Mark Fisher, *Capitalist Realism: Is There No Alternative?* (Winchester: Zero Books, 2009).
5 William Davies, "The New Neoliberalism," *New Left Review* 101 (2016): 124, 129.
6 Wendy Brown, "Neoliberalism's Frankenstein: Authoritarian Freedom in Twenty-First Century 'Democracies,'" *Critical Times* 1 (2018): 60–79.

7   Adorno defines "authoritarian submission" as a "submissive, uncritical attitude toward idealized moral authorities of the ingroup" and "authoritarian aggression" as the "tendency to be on the lookout for, and to condemn, reject, and punish people who violate conventional values." See Theodor Adorno et al., *The Authoritarian Personality* (London: Verso, 2019), 228. Both authoritarian submission and authoritarian aggression are variables on the "F scale," formulated to account for the often unconscious authoritarian tendencies in populations.
8   Wolfgang Streeck, *How Will Capitalism End? Essays on a Failing System* (London: Verso, 2016).
9   Brown, "Neoliberalism's Frankenstein," 63.
10 Brown, "Neoliberalism's Frankenstein," 67.
11 For an analysis of the growth of authoritarian sensibilities in Latin America, see Gabriel Kessler and Gabriel Vommaro, "La era de las sensibilidades autoritarias," http://revistaanfibia.com/ensayo/la-era-de-las-sensibilidades-autoritarias/. For a study of the importance of these sensibilities for Macri's electoral base, see, among others, Ezequiel Ipar and Gisela Catanzaro, "Nueva derecha y autoritarismo social," http://www.revistaanfibia.com/ensayo/nueva-derecha-autoritarismo-social/, and a report on public opinion polls identifying similarities between Bolsonaro's electoral base and Macri's: https://www.centrocultural.coop/blogs/ocop/2018/11/bolsonaro-llego-hace-rato-parte-1-por-eugenio-garriga-pablo-villarreal-y-ezequiel. On the imbrication of liberalism and authoritarianism in the region, see Ezequiel Ipar, "Neoliberalismo y neoautoritarismo," *Política y Sociedad* 55.3 (2018): 825–49, https://www.revistas.ucm.es/index.php/POSO/article/view/57514/4564456549083; and Ezequiel Adamovsky, "Bolsonaro-Macri: El neoliberalismo autoritario," https://www.revistaanfibia.com/ensayo/circulo-sin-molestar/.
12 In the South American context, this term is usually pejoratively applied to governments that center on internal markets and that are opposed by the social sectors that benefit from the exporting of raw material and from finance capital. In Argentina, the administrations demonized as "populist" are also associated with the defense of both social and civil rights that are resisted or openly fought against by administrations that instead promote neoliberal policies, including the last civico-military dictatorship (1976–83). "I am less afraid of coronavirus than of populism," former president Mauricio Macri recently said, referring to what he called the "plague" represented by Peronist governments in general and in particular by the political forces associated with the administrations of Néstor Kirchner (2003–7), Cristina Fernández (2007–11, and 2011–15), and the current government of Argentina led by President Alberto Fernández.
13 For an expanded version of this brief analysis of the ideological dispositions that prevailed during the first part of the 2010s, see Gisela Catanzaro, *Espectrología de la derecha: Hacia una crítica de la ideología neoliberal en el capitalismo tardío* (Buenos Aires: Cuarenta Ríos, 2021), chap. 5. As for punitive securitarianism, it is worth noting that it displaces another understanding of security, one tied to social protections regarded as citizens' rights. As

Gabriela Seghezzo and Nicolás Dallorso indicate, in punitive securitarianism "worries about how to ensure social security are diluted, giving way to the imperative to do something about the effects of the cancellation of social protections." See Gabriela Seghezzo and Nicolás Dallorso, "Del punitivismo al cuidado (feminista): El porvenir de la ilusión securitaria," in Nahuel Sosa, Marina Cardelli, and Alejandro San Cristobal, *Emergencias: Repensar el Estado, las subjetividades y la acción política* (Buenos Aires: Ediciones Ciccus, 2018), 174.

14 Decree 683/2018, promulgated by Macri, broke with a sustained political effort to make the armed forces' non-intervention in matters of internal security a matter of state policy. This effort had begun in 1988 with the Ley de Defensa Nacional (Law of National Defense), promulgated during the administration of Raúl Alfonsín; it continued with the security law passed during the administration of Carlos Menem; it continued again with the national intelligence law approved in 2001 during the presidential administration of Fernando de la Rúa; and it was ratified in the defense regulations passed in 2006 under the administration of Néstor Kirchner. Another decree by Macri, in keeping with this one, allowed the intelligence agencies and armed forces in Argentina to regain their self-rule and thus protect themselves from political oversight by democratically elected representatives.

15 According to the section dedicated to immigration in its annual report for 2017, the Centro de Estudios Legales y Sociales (CELS, Center for Legal and Social Studies), referring to the state of human rights in Argentina, the *decreto de necesidad y urgencia*, or national security decree, 70/2017, through which the executive sought to modify previous norms—a decree that was declared unconstitutional by the judiciary in 2018—showed the will to bring about a shift from protection to criminalization in Argentina's immigration policies. "The reform allowed for the deployment of a tool for social control with consequences for the regularization of immigration, especially for those with fewest resources. After the modifications introduced by the decree, the management of immigration is now in the hands of immigration authorities, together with judicial and police authorities in various jurisdictions. The selectiveness that these forms of administration produce is in tension with any program that seeks to recognize the right to immigrate and be regularized. It is a regressive process that undermines even the false classification proposed by the national executive, which differentially regulates immigration according to the conduct of immigrants." For the report as well as other materials related to immigration prepared by CELS, see https://www.cels.org.ar/web/tag/dnu-migrantes/. On the creation of the immigrant detention center, see https://www.pagina12.com.ar/diario/elpais/1-307814-2016-08-26.html.

16 A case that gave rise to what became known locally as the "Chocobar doctrine" is emblematic of government officials' support for police actions even when these took place outside the framework of its own regulations. In late 2017, after a local police officer shot a person who had committed a robbery in the back, the president and minister of security received the officer in the house of government, validating his actions. Something similar had taken place before in relation to the national gendarmerie after the killings of Santiago Maldonado and Rafael Nahuel, which took place while they were

participating in roadside protests organized by the Mapuche in southern Argentina.

17 "Insecurity, defined very generally as related to crime and to the protection of some goods and certain social groups in public space, as a pressing problem that calls for urgent solutions, became increasingly prominent in the 1990s. Despite the blurriness of this definition, the construction of the problem depends, almost without exception, on an ironclad connection between crime and the working class, a linkage that informs ways of seeing, thinking and acting that reify the supposed connection between delinquency and poverty and that produce inequality, fragmentation, and precarity in the most impoverished sectors of the population. Securitization thus functions—and here is its specificity—as a sort of lever of negativity, activated by fear. The thieving kid (*pibe chorro*) is the sinister opposite of the entrepreneur, combining success, creativity, cunning, and risk. A foreigner, but one with familiar values." Nicolás Dallorso and Gabriela Seghezzo, "Itinerary of the Issue of Security Since Neoliberalism Return in Argentina," presented at the international conference "Crises, Economy and Punishment: The Influence of the Great Recession on Crime and Penality," La Coruña, Spain, 2016.

18 Davies, "The New Neoliberalism," 130.

19 This presidential call to sacrifice did not go unnoticed even by newspapers friendly to the administration. These newspapers nevertheless tended, in their ways of editing and presenting Macri's declarations, to justify the necessity of these calls to sacrifice by pointing to Macri's own claims that they were necessary. See, in this context, coverage in the newspapers *La Nación* and *El País* from July 9, 2016: "Hay que alejarse de la viveza criolla," https://www.lanacion.com.ar/1974555-hay-que-alejarse-de-la-viveza-criolla-y-otras-frases-de-mauricio-macri; and "Macri pide sacrificios," https://elpais.com/internacional/2016/07/09/argentina/1468083041_612401.html.

20 "I ask that the truth govern all of us. We have to take distance from the kind of *viveza criolla* that's misunderstood, get rid of the idea that you get ahead by scheming, deceiving, taking advantage. ... We have to show that we can use words and compromise. To recover the culture of work, of effort. We've seen increases in absenteeism and reduced hours. That's not good." Macri made these statements during the course of Independence Day celebrations on July 9, 2016. See "Macri pide sacrificios."

21 The claim that populist governments had "isolated us from the world," placing obstacles in the way of the exporting of commodities and undermining Argentina's "healthy" relationship to the global market for political reasons, was and continues to be central in Macrist discourse. This discourse insists on characterizing our national culture as exceptional, pathological, and revanchist when it seeks justice both in the form of human rights within the country and in the form of economic exchange in the international market. According to it, Argentina's supposed isolationism and its supposed obsession with the past constitute in fact two symptoms of the same national illness, an illness introduced by populism and that must be cured through "healthy" integration into world markets. This was illustrated in 2017 in the comments that a former cabinet chief, Marcos Peña, let slip in a meeting of the Coloquio Idea, a yearly gathering that brings together business, political,

bureaucratic, academic, and media elites: "The obsession that we have [in Argentina] with analyzing the current conjuncture in terms of the past is not normal. In other countries this doesn't happen. And it's good to know that this is a pathology of ours. For me, one of the two nicest small but symbolic things that we did was to put animals on bank notes. ... It's the first time in Argentina's history that there are living things on our national currency, and that we leave the dead behind. Leave death in peace; let it rest in peace, and let us live our lives." Interview with Marcos Peña, https://www.youtube.com/watch?v=yO1UX57nfWY&fbclid=IwAR3oo8pV77PHfRiN7aI4SMV0IaQL7yjNLZ8jNENt9BcdmiGDOuZDiOMu_BA. Regarding the banknotes, the former cabinet chief was alluding to the fact that since 2016 the Central Bank of the Republic of Argentina has replaced the images of the "fathers" of the nation with images of animals native to the country. In a measure that can be seen as symptomatic of a more general politics that seeks to dehistoricize history—a politics to which I will return—Macri's administration introduced the deer, condor, hornero, llama, whale, and jaguar as replacements for Eva Perón, José de San Martín, and Julio Argentino Roca, among others. But what I want to underscore here is that Peña's diagnosis establishes a direct correlation between eccentricity or isolation, on the one hand, and death, on the other. It is our obsession with death that makes us pathologically exceptional, isolating us from the "normal" world of sane and healthy countries. Thus, as I will show, "life" implies leaving the past behind, living in the present and adapting to continual adjustments, forms of indebtedness, and global demands. Or rather, as another former minister under Macri's administration put it more playfully, it implies "learning to live with uncertainty and enjoy it."

22 One of the people interviewed during the course of a study of anti-democratic attitudes in Argentina, which the Grupo de Estudios Críticos sobre Ideología y Democracia (GECID-IIGG-UBA: http://gecidiigg.sociales.uba.ar/) has been conducting since 2011, described himself as "unemployed and proud of not asking for social assistance," giving expression to this disposition, at once sacrificial and punitive.

23 In Latin America and especially in Argentina, the years between 2003 and 2015 saw significant reductions in foreign debt. This feature distinguishes the region from the cases on the basis of which Davies develops his understanding of a punitive neoliberalism that, according to him, follows after a period of economic growth driven by credit and the subsequent creation of a debt whose "irrationality" leads to the necessarily punitive imposition of requirements for painful expiation. As María Stegmayer and I have argued elsewhere, more than a matter of an excess of prior indebtedness, the guilt induced by this form of neoliberalism in Argentina should be thought of, on the one hand, in terms of the demand for unlimited capitalization, in response to which all subjective efforts to turn "opportunities" to profit fall short; and, on the other hand, at the political level, in terms of a break with the inclusive demands and aspirations of previous progressive governments, which sought to strengthen the internal market during the first decade and a half of this century. This was also a break with the "order" that, Stegmayer and I have argued, was perceived by much of the population as

in fact a period of "anarchy" that needed to be brought to an end. See Gisela Catanzaro and María Stegmayer, "The New Neoliberal Turn in Argentina: Omnipotence, the Sacrificial Mandate, and the Craving for Punishment," trans. Pedro J. Rolón Machado, *Critical Times* 2.1 (2019): 133–58.

24 For Macri's statements, see, for instance, https://www.hispantv.com/noticias/argentina/281443/declaraciones-polemica-macri-rey-espana-independencia-juan-carlos; and "'Querido Rey' … Una lamentable frase de Macri tiñó de tristeza los festejos del 9 de julio," Portal de Noticias, July 10, 2016. For the popular reaction to these statements, which were indicative of the resistance that the administration encountered as it preached the need for sacrifice, see "Fiesta popular en las redes: Estallaron los memes por Macri," https://www.eldestapeweb.com/nota/fiesta-popular-en-las-redes-estallaron-los-memes-por-el-bicentenario-2016-7-11-9-1-0.

25 Horacio González, "Modos de historicidad en el macrismo," http://vagosperonistas.blogspot.com/2016/09/modos-de-historicidad-en-el-macrismo.html.

26 Regarding Argentina's supposed inferiority to developed nations—a narrative that is currently being revived, for example, in the social perception that, statistics aside, Argentina has managed the pandemic badly compared to "serious countries"—it is worth emphasizing that even the "nationalist" discourse of the last military dictatorship did not feature the massive and coherent exaltation of the nation, seen as superior to foreign countries, so characteristic of the supremacist discourses of the North. This was expressed in a paradigmatic advertisement from the period between 1976 and 1983 that alerted Argentines to the inferiority of national products compared to those imported from elsewhere; https://www.youtube.com/watch?v=Ys9GlRowehI. The justification for the opening of the national economy to imports that the government then implemented thus depended on a sense of Argentina as inferior even while on the military level Argentina was exalted especially in the context of the war in the Malvinas.

27 In the context of an electoral campaign, the Instagram account of the president of Argentina published a video in which those interviewed declared their guilt and accepted that Argentines were to blame for the economic crisis affecting the country. See https://www.infotechnology.com/online/El-video-de-Instagram-de-Macri-donde-se-afirma-que-la-culpa-la-tienen-los-argentinos-20190307-0001.html.

28 In the first piece, which bore the title "The Answer Is the Future," Macri argued: "We're missing a future. We're missing the will to give form to a new reality. We have too much disenchantment, fear, and frustration. We dedicate more time to describing failure than to leaving it behind. It is urgently necessary that we learn to overcome the *vindictive position* and that we manage to generate *active and vital positions* that enable the solutions that we need. *The vindictive vision considers the past more important than the future, and it makes a reality that no longer exists weigh on all of us.* It abuses references to persons and situations that belong to another age. It seeks revenge, not solutions. *The aspirational vision, by contrast, allows us to focus on what we need to focus on: on the effort and the pleasure of development, on the healthy desire for growth.* My political action, my role as a leader, have always been about gathering together my compatriots in an act of essential rebellion. Rebellion, yes, *a rebellion that*

dares to overcome prejudices, outdated references, fears, sources of shyness, false differences" (my emphases). In 2019, despite the fact that he was running for reelection after having occupied the office of the presidency for four years, Macri returned to these same ideas: "We're not returning to the past, because the Argentina of the future is the one we want [*la que queremos*: also the one we love], because the past has no future." Both of these texts are quoted by Fabio Wasserman in "'No hay futuro en el pasado': Política, temporalidad y orden social en el discurso macrista," http://revistabordes.unpaz.edu.ar/no-hay-futuro-en-el-pasado-politica-temporalidad-y-orden-social-en-el-discurso-macrista.

29 This immediate identification of the past with the dead is illustrated well in the comments of Macri's former cabinet chief cited in note 21 in this chapter.

30 In the words of former presidential advisor Alejandro Rozitchner, there is a sort of "critical madness" that assails national thought and that must be suppressed so that younger generations can be healthy and happy. See the interview with Rozitchner published in *La Nación*, http://www.lanacion.com.ar/1968830-alejandro-rozitchner-el-pensamiento-critico-es-un-valor-negativo.

31 "I think that the twenty-first century realigned ideologies on the basis of an outcome. People want better lives; people want to lead healthy lives; they want to be in constant communication with one another and to envision a future for their children. So they ask who it is who can guarantee that. Then there is a minority that wants to relate that to histories and reasons and philosophers. … But the truth is that, at the end of the day, what matters is my child. Will he have a future better than mine? Or rather, that narcissistic love that one channels into one's children. One wants guarantees, and this is what people are looking for." See the interview with Mauricio Macri in *Perfil*, March 20, 2016, http://www.perfil.com/politica/he-tenido-dias-de-abrumarme-0319-0100.phtml.

32 See note 21 in this chapter.

33 This image is compatible both with the model of agricultural exports that predominates in Argentina and with the demands of real estate developers who promote their businesses in the City of Buenos Aires, whose coast was recently reprivatized.

34 The Sociedad Rural Argentina brings together the representatives of the most traditional and concentrated sectors in Argentine agriculture, those dedicated to export, who own the most fertile lands in the country. Macri promised not to increase taxes on them even when an extraordinary devaluation of the peso, which led to an equally extraordinary increase in revenue for these sectors in the international market for its products, took place during his administration.

35 As Álvaro García Linera indicates, considering neoliberalism in Bolivia, despite their techniques, which are modernizing, many of the dominant sectors that form the social basis of neoliberalism in Latin America "never stopped imagining power and territory in patrimonial ways, thinking of power as a privilege that follows from ancestry, and of territory as an extension of the feudal logic of the hacienda system. … In this sense, their vision of the spatial role of the state is pre-modern, feudal, similar to that of the

Andean elites of the nineteenth century to whom, as [René] Zavaleta says, the wellbeing of the statue of the Virgin in Copacabana [in Bolivia] mattered more than the mutilation of the coast [which Bolivia lost in 1879]." Álvaro García Linera, *La potencia plebeya* (Buenos Aires: Prometeo, 2008), 365. It is worth emphasizing the similarities between this "carelessness" on the part of the Bolivian elite, their disregard for the national territory, and the Macri administration's attitude toward the Malvinas, which were all but surrendered to the United Kingdom during Macri's presidency.

36 For a discussion of this question that interweaves the philosophy of history with various invocations of the nation in twentieth-century essay writing in Argentina, see Gisela Catanzaro, *La nación entre la naturaleza y la historia: Sobre los modos de la crítica* (Buenos Aires: FCE, 2011).

37 "History, in everything untimely, sorrowful, and miscarried that belongs to it from the beginning, is inscribed in a face—no, in a death's head. And though it is true that to such a thing all 'symbolic' freedom of expression, all classic harmony of form, and everything human is lacking, nevertheless in this figure, the most fallen in nature, is expressed meaningfully as enigma not only the nature of human existence in general, but also the biographical historicity of an individual." Walter Benjamin, *Origin of the German* Trauerspiel, trans. Howard Eiland (Cambridge, MA: Harvard University Press, 2019), 174.

Ramsey McGlazer

12. Gramsci's Grave

IN BRAZIL, ANTONIO Gramsci's detractors on the political right still see him as an undead red menace. This chapter seeks to account for the persistence of this image and asks how and why right-wing discourses in Brazil privilege Gramsci's views on the school in particular. Whereas in Gramsci's educational theory, the school is figured as a democratic training camp, in the discourse of the Brazilian far right it becomes a veritable battlefield. At stake in this ongoing culture war, centered in schools, is not only the defeat of a supposedly still-widespread "Cultural Marxism" but also the suppression of an "ideology of gender" said to have infiltrated, or rather to have already conquered, Brazilian public education. It is counterintuitive to make Gramsci represent this latter "ideology," given that, as commentators in Brazil have noted, questions of gender and sexuality are not central to his work. And yet that is what the highly visible and increasingly influential movement Programa Escola Sem Partido (Program for a School without Party, or a Nonpartisan School) has done repeatedly and consequentially as it has gathered support first for its own legislative agendas and then for the administration of Jair Bolsonaro.[1] In this way, the movement's members have, like the Brazilian right more broadly, brought together Marxist, feminist, queer, and trans arguments and have inadvertently revived Gramsci even while they have ostensibly worked to destroy his legacy, to banish every last trace of his thought from schools, to bury his writings permanently. Reading the movement's engagements with Gramsci symptomatically, I consider this effort's implications for the left in and beyond Brazil. I argue—writing against persistent calls to move both beyond Gramsci and "beyond education"—that the ESP's efforts challenge us to reimagine the scene of teaching even while they remind us that this scene remains one to which we should return.

I

IN THE IMAGE and caption shown below (Fig. 14), posted to Facebook in August 2015, Miguel Nagib, founder of the Programa Escola Sem Partido (ESP), proclaimed that Antonio Gramsci's death was imminent. Going further, he figured the theorist as dying but still undead. A specter was haunting Brazil, according to Nagib, who identified this ghost as "Count Gramsci, the vampire who's vampirizing Brazilian education with the help of Paulo Nosferatu Freire—his days may be numbered."[2] The caption ends by referring to a possibility rather than to an absolute certainty, as if to say, *if we're lucky*, or rather *if we work together to bring about this vampire's demise*, it will happen, and his remaining blood-sucking days will be few. But the image more than makes up for any confidence that this caption, with its final, modal construction, might appear to lack. In his coffin, Count Gramsci lets out a scream so vivid that it's all but audible as a stake bearing Escola Sem Partido's logo is driven through his heart. That no one other than the vampire himself is shown committing this act of aggression suggests not so much that this Dracula will die of self-inflicted wounds as that the viewer herself should wield the stake, deliver the blow, silence Gramsci for good by joining the movement.

Readers may already feel that it's perverse to lavish such attention on a post that's clearly wrong on several levels: Wrong-headed politically, the image is as crude in its anti-intellectualism as it is (perhaps willfully) confused about what Gramsci stood and still stands for. Here the Sardinian Marxist, theorist of the "Southern Question" and of subalternity, is associated with a foreign, though fading, aristocracy, with a cosmopolitan elite or oligarchy. Indeed, Gramsci is implicitly recast in this image as the sort of Southern intellectual that he criticized, disconnected from his region, his interests aligned with institutions that are supranational and anti-popular.[3]

Figure 14. Count Gramsci.

The post is distasteful and in many ways dumb, and yet it discloses key dynamics on the Brazilian far right. These dynamics offer important lessons for the left—not only in the banal sense that it's good to know your enemy or to see clearly what you're up against, but also for reasons related to timing: The Brazilian right takes Gramsci to be diabolical—spinning out paranoid scenarios about his reach and current influence even while it insists that his days are "numbered"—at a moment when his work appears to thinkers on the left either to be obsolete or "dead,"[4] or to have been co-opted by the right, to whom Gramsci's *Prison Notebooks* are seen to "offer many lessons in strategy of great importance."[5] How should we understand these divergent readings, or these various misreadings, of Gramsci, and what does it mean to make the school into a stake to be driven through a vampire's heart?

II

IT IS INDEED a misreading to figure Freire as Gramsci's helpmeet, as though there were no real difference between the two, or as though Freire did nothing more than build on Gramsci's theories, transpose them to South America, or sound variations on Gramscian themes. In fact, as I have argued elsewhere, Gramsci offered a qualified defense of the "instruction" or traditional, even old-school education that Freire famously denounced.[6] But this is far from the most egregious misreading of Gramsci on the Brazilian far right, where, as Nagib's post already suggests, denunciations of Gramsci and his influence continue to abound, strikingly. What accounts for this influence, and what should we make of the fact that these denunciations in Brazil continue, registering as they do a sense of Gramsci's persistence at a time when, for at least some on the left, his texts seem to have lost their prestige if not always their explanatory power?[7]

This loss of prestige is related to the emergence and reemergence of far-right, authoritarian, and neofascist regimes from the United States to Brazil and beyond, regimes that have seemed to render Gramsci's theories of hegemony obsolete. As William Davies notes and Gisela Catanzaro emphasizes in her chapter in this volume, these regimes point to the consolidation of a new, "punitive" form of neoliberalism that rules by way of dominance without hegemony. In the current, "post-hegemonic phase" of neoliberalism, according to Davies, we see a "relentless" impulse to punish "that acts in place of reasoned discourse, replacing the need for hegemonic consensus formation."[8] "Neoliberalism has become incredible," shocking in its brutality, its venality, and its naked coerciveness,

> but that is partly because it is a system that no longer seeks credibility in the way that hegemonies used to do, through a degree of cultural or normative consensus. Sovereign power has always had a circular logic, exercised to demonstrate that it can be exercised. Yet today, that sovereignty is found in technical and technocratic spheres: policies, punishments, cuts, calculations are simply being repeated, as that is the sole condition of their reality. The coercions of post-2008 policy-making are those of a system in retreat from both the ideology and the reality of rational public dialogue, and the epistemological constraints which that involves.[9]

If this is true—if neoliberalism today does not function hegemonically or even pretend to seek the "cultural or normative consensus" that its precursors sought in the past—then it stands to reason that theories of hegemony cannot show us ways out of the current political impasse. We need another set of analytical tools, other resources for responding to and confronting sovereign power in its current forms.

And yet, to return to the distinction between prestige and explanatory power that I made a moment ago, in their effort to account for the contemporary right's resurgence, some critics emphasize the cultural (which is not to say the "merely cultural") dimension precisely.[10] Even when they do not rely on Gramsci directly, these critics' accounts attest to the continued relevance of his questions and categories, including the category of hegemony. Alberto Toscano, for instance, writing in another context, underscores the centrality of culture in "racial fascism": "Enlisting bodies and psyches into endless culture wars," today this fascism or neofascism also marks a place "where the superstructure sometimes seems to overwhelm the base, as though forces and fantasies once functional to the reproduction of a dominant class and racial order have now attained a kind of autonomy."[11] Toscano is not thinking here of Gramsci specifically, but his formulations do suggest that Gramsci's thought—famous for its heterodox recognition of the relative autonomy of the superstructure—might remain salient or become salient again. Catanzaro, meanwhile, goes so far as to posit a shift "from the 'cultural turn' to the 'authoritarian turn,'" as if new authoritarianisms that she considers represented a superseding or suppression of culture. Elsewhere in her essay, however, Catanzaro highlights a range of cultural initiatives coordinated and sustained by the government of Argentine president Mauricio Macri. These demonstrate that the turn away from multiculturalism in punitive neoliberalism is not at all a turn away from culture as such. By way of conclusion, moreover, Catanzaro returns pointedly to the question of "subaltern participation in society." Inasmuch as this question "remains unresolved," Catanzaro suggests indirectly, Gramsci's work is still worth rereading.

To reread this work is to recall that Gramsci's account of subalternity is inseparable from his account of hegemony.[12] And the latter account, like Gramsci's writing overall, frequently calls attention to the school, defined as "the instrument through which intellectuals of various levels are elaborated."[13] Asking us to hear the "labor" in this process of elaboration, Gramsci teaches us to see the school as a place for both the consolidation and the potential contestation of hegemony. Just as Louis Althusser would later insist that the school is both the "site" and the "stake" of class struggle,[14] Gramsci argues that even formal education is not merely practice for, but is itself integral to, the functioning of real democracy. Schooling is a means by which to begin to create the kind of society and state in which, Gramsci writes, any and "every citizen can govern [*diventare 'governante'*]."[15]

Thus, although they are clearly and thoroughly confused about many things, Gramsci's enemies on the contemporary Brazilian far right are not wrong to identify the school as central to the Gramscian project or the project of communism more generally. This is an instructive reminder, a lesson that the left might need to learn again, at least in the United States: If advocacy for public education, the assertion of the school's (though not teachers' unions') importance today, often takes the form of mouthing liberal pieties or finds its way into breathless right-wing responses to what's called "intersectional" or "woke" overreach and the supposed incursions of "critical race theory," there is a serious risk involved in efforts to move "beyond education" altogether, in the continued pursuit of "deschooling" as an end.[16] This pursuit risks colluding with ongoing neoliberal assaults on social goods and even arguably with neoliberal forms of privatization. This is not to suggest that any alternative school can only ever be or become a charter school. But if, as Wendy Brown writes, neoliberal "logics and energies organize aspects of left response to contemporary predicaments," the left critique of education as such may be one such site of convergence.[17] We may forget or write off the public school at our peril, then, and now may instead be a time to return to and repurpose it. But in order to begin this work, we may need to take far-right denunciations of the school more seriously than we are used to doing.

III

IT HAS BECOME something of a commonplace to claim that the contemporary right, especially the alt-right, understands Gramsci and applies his lessons better than the left does. This claim can take facile forms, as in the work of Angela Nagle,[18] for instance, but there are reasons to consider other versions of the argument more carefully. These do not typically center on the school; rather they refer to the alt-right's or the far right's broader understanding of cultural politics, its willingness to play a long game in pursuit of ends that it considers counterhegemonic. "Counter-" because by this account the left is currently culturally in control, and the right's aim should therefore be to organize counteroffensives in an effort to reclaim this lost cultural ground.

Indeed, Bernard Harcourt goes so far as to assert that "Gramsci is at the heart of Alt-Right praxis."[19] Here Harcourt is thinking in particular of Gramsci's role in the Swedish businessman and far-right figurehead Daniel Friberg's account of "metapolitics" in his book *The Real Right Returns*. "Conquering power," Friberg writes there, concluding what he presents as a paraphrase of Gramsci, "is only the last step in a long process, a process that begins with metapolitics." For Friberg, that last term refers to an undertaking that, "simply put, is about affecting and shaping people's thoughts, worldviews, and the very concepts which they use to make sense of and define the world around them. ... Metapolitics can thus be seen as a war of social transformation, fought on the level of worldview, thought, and culture."[20] Because he thinks the right has been losing this war for decades, Friberg looks to Gramsci for "lessons in strategy" and works to wrest Gramsci's legacy from the left, to recast the *Prison Notebooks* as a primer for a renewed far-right effort to win (back) hearts and minds.

Perversely, this way of reading recasts Gramsci's own determination to learn from the Italian left's historical losses, to take stock of workers' and radicals' defeats from the Risorgimento through to the rise of Fascism. But Friberg, who is nothing if not an idealist, empties Gramsci's *Notebooks* of their historical as well as their political specificity. A media magnate and not an imprisoned organizer, Friberg writes from a position of defensiveness rather than one of veritable, material, or military defeat or ongoing exploitation. He thinks that the right has long since lost a culture war, that its members have been made ashamed if not rendered invisible by those elsewhere called "Cultural Marxists" and by the purveyors of political correctness in its many forms. He addresses readers whose humiliation he anticipates and works to counter and thus overcome. But from the first he makes this humiliation synonymous with subalternity. It is as if a culture war, in other words, and not a calamity, were what Gramsci's subaltern had been up against all along.[21]

These are of course familiar rhetorical moves on the contemporary far right (and by some accounts not only there): the exaggeration of harm; the claim that one's views have been silenced, censored, and suppressed; the performance of "wounded attachment" to an identity said to be under siege.[22] Although Friberg's recourse to this set of tropes is entirely unsurprising, it is worth recalling in this context, not least because it lets us relate his appropriation of Gramsci to engagements with Gramscian thought in Brazil. At first these latter engagements seem to rely on an image of Gramsci that is altogether different from the affirming if misleading one that we find in Friberg's prose. Far from being figured as a leftist whose thought the right can now use, a communist whose ideas can be co-opted, Gramsci is imagined in Brazil as a villain and vampire, as we have already seen.[23] And yet this image allows for a series of slippages whose logic or paralogic discloses a family resemblance between these Latin American conservatives and Friberg's European, proudly Eurocentric new right. (To say this is not, however, to suggest that the resemblance is one Friberg and his followers would themselves avow.[24])The slippages are as follows:

   a. If the Marxist is not well and truly dead but rather undead, Dracula-like, then he remains menacing.
   b. Since he—or she, as we'll see—stands synecdochically for the whole apparatus of "Cultural Marxism," this latter force still presents a clear and present danger.
   c. Those endangered by the hordes of hegemonic "Cultural Marxists," who are Gramscians, who are undead, face a threat that is not abstract but rather concrete and existential.
   d. In fact, this threat is not only, and perhaps not even primarily, a matter of potential future harm, for it has already resulted in grave and widespread injuries to Brazilian people and to hallowed institutions ranging from the family to the Church to the school to the state itself.
   e. This, then, makes the supposed victims' most vitriolic interventions in public life, including their interventions in public education, wholly justified, even a matter of righteous obligation.

These last two claims in particular can be seen in the Programa Escola Sem Partido's recasting of the scene of teaching as the scene of a crime that has happened and keeps happening, taking lurid forms as it repeats itself compulsively. This is classic projection, of course: it's the *fantasy* of the scene's repetition that's compulsive, not the teaching practices that these members of the Brazilian right purport to describe. Theirs is, in other words, a compulsion to fantasize about the child who's being beaten, and it's this compulsion that drives their effort to expose the bad teacher's death drive, as in Figure 15, first posted in a comment on Escola Sem Partido's Facebook page.

Figure 15. Garbage In.

IV

THE IMAGE IS crude but richly instructive. Indeed, it is arguably even richer and more instructive than the image with which I began this chapter, because it stages the fantasies of the Brazilian far right more vividly. The text at the top right means: "Religion is for stupid people … all you need is sex, sex, sex, sex, sex."[25] This is presumably the content of the "garbage" (*lixo*) that is being vomited into the "young innocent" student's head by the busty teacher bearing the insignia of the left and wearing a shirt that identifies her as an allegorical figure for the "public school." The boy is dismayed, stunned, even moved to frightened tears. But it's also possible to read something else in his expression, his wide-open eyes: an awakening. He's not just terrified but excited, in other words, as in aroused, by the teacher's not-so-enigmatic signifiers, her repetition of the word for and insistence on the idea of sex.

The teacher's prominent breasts, her features, and her hair might all prompt us to think of the Black *babá*, the wet nurse or nanny whose role in Brazilian history and whose foreclosed centrality in the "national psyche" Rita Segato has analyzed.[26] This would make the public school pupil shown in Figure 15 into an Oedipus, and this image into a scene of interracial seduction.[27] Though at a far remove in every sense from the image that occasions Segato's analysis—a painting of the emperor Dom Pedro II with his nurse, hanging in the Imperial Palace in Petrópolis—this image shares at least one key feature with that earlier one. This innocent is not an infant, like the baby Dom Pedro II. But here, as there, the artist lays stress on a young white boy's being *held* and *handled*. Note the placement of the teacher's hand on the boy's cheek: even while he's being used as a garbage bin or toilet bowl, the boy isn't being held with the violence or desperation that we typically associate with vomiting. Rather he is held in place with a care that may even verge on tenderness.

No wonder the "young innocent" who's shown being slaughtered here shudders, his hair standing on end as his mind is laid to waste. He's not being caressed, but he's not being beaten either—and even if he were, of course, this schoolroom scene might still be sexualized. In a strictly Freudian fashion, the student in this scene would still be *feminized* like the one shown here, recast as a receptacle open to the unclean liquid stream by which he is being brainwashed.[28] But this still leaves one key claim in the image, attributed to the teacher, unaddressed: "all you need is sex."

As in the case of the Brazilian right's conflation of Gramsci's theory and Freire's, it would be easy to dismiss this as a matter of confusion or mere ignorance. It is both, undoubtedly; there really is no daylight, in the cartoonist's view, between Marxism, feminism, and queer theory. (All of these are seen as so many forms of what the contemporary right in the United States would call "grooming.") But I want to suggest that the conflation here is symptomatic of something else as well: an unconscious awareness and envy of the left's capacity to alter and inspire, indeed to *tempt* and *seduce*.[29] I borrow these last two words from the Argentine sociologist Emilio de Ípola, and specifically from an essay about his time spent as a political prisoner during Argentina's last civico-military dictatorship (1976–83). Here, de Ípola notes, prisoners and guards were compelled to observe a "strict rule of reciprocal silence." His speculations as to why are interesting. The authorities, de Ípola writes,

> were less afraid of the revolts and riots that the political prisoners might organize—in this realm the prison authorities knew how to respond—than they were afraid of *the temptations and seduction* that, especially among lower-ranking personnel [*personal subalterno*], the prisoners' discourse might provoke. This was an insidious and cunning discourse that was all the more

dangerous because it was underpinned by an uncontrollable and unalienable knowledge. There could thus be no occasion for the exercise of the power of that discourse. The resulting hierarchies and forms of discipline were based on and made efficacious by the strict rule of reciprocal silence.[30]

At this point in his essay, de Ípola is describing the threat that he and his comrades were thought to pose, the reason for their silencing: "For some time, the prison authorities have understood that the stereotype of the fanatical, semi-demented guerrilla fighter (the image of the political 'delinquent' publicized in the mass media) is easily contradicted by experience." But this makes it all the more necessary for the right and for prison authorities in particular to double down on their insistence—or what de Ípola pointedly calls their "indoctrination," which teaches—that the political prisoners are "diabolical," and so is the left as a whole.[31]

This last claim is literalized in an earlier cartoon (Fig. 16), this one published in January 1964, two months before the U.S.-backed military coup that overthrew Brazil's president, João Goulart.[32] Here gender difference recedes, since both the diabolical teacher and his student are male, but class difference is accentuated: the teacher is a buttoned-up, bespectacled bourgeois, or at least a Communist in bourgeois clothing, whereas the slouching student is a member of and stand-in for the huddled masses, awaiting a secular "S-A-L-V-A-T-I-O-N" that the caption invites us to spell and to sound out, letter by letter. Training in literacy is in this way shown to be a front for Communist indoctrination,[33] where the stress falls on doctrine or indeed "dogma."[34] Smuggling liturgy into literacy, or making the two indistinguishable, the reformist campaign also makes a salvific promise that leads would-be Catholics astray, just as the teacher shown in Figure 15 will disparage religion. Long before "sex" enters the picture explicitly, then, as in the more recent cartoon (Fig. 16), *coercion* indelibly marks the scene of mass education as it is figured by the Brazilian right. Far from teaching students to think for themselves, educators in this context put words and ideas directly into students' heads. In this way, in Armindo Moreira's words, they undertake to "prepare the people's mind for the acceptance of [left] fascism [*mentalizar o povo para que aceite o fascismo*]," where the verb *mentalizar* is more forceful and vivid and less euphemistic than any English equivalent.[35] This is education, in other words, recast as mind control.

Figure 16. "The Literacy Campaign," from *O Globo*, January 25, 1964.

But de Ípola teaches us to recognize the right's insistence on this coercion as a cover, or an effort to compensate, for its perception of the "temptations and seduction" of the left, or rather the temptations of what de Ípola takes pains to specify is the left's "discourse."[36] Crucially, this is not a matter of "temptations and seduction" that are embodied in or "exercised" by any individual teacher, let alone any political leader or ruler; de Ípola is instead referring to the allure of "knowledge," of speech, of words, even of letters. It is this allure that is, I think, tacitly acknowledged in both cartoons, where irresistible siren songs are parsed into individual signifiers. To tarry with these is to come into contact with a truth, de Ípola writes, that is "uncontrollable and unalienable."[37]

Without granting it the status of truth—on the contrary, while insisting on its status as lie—the cartoons nevertheless recognize this too: the power of what's transmitted in and through such tarrying, such teaching, the danger to "authorities" that is really represented by such lessons. Despite themselves, the images attest to the power of the word for "sex" and of the idea of "salvation" through liberation. Though grotesque, the teachers in both images are in this sense conduits for these words and ideas, and it is this—their status as such conduits, opening onto whole discursive worlds, whole linguistic realms, and whole ways of knowing—rather than their individual, charismatic features or perverse proclivities, that ultimately makes them such a threat to youth and white innocence.

V

"IT IS THE left alone that is responsible for instrumentalizing teaching for political and ideological ends; and being opposed to this practice, we are seen as [their] ideological adversaries." So the Movimento Escola Sem Partido claims in its response to the frequently asked question: "Is the ESP right-wing?"[38] The patently right-wing movement insists on its own political neutrality. ESP's spokespersons concede in their response to another question ("Isn't there right-wing indoctrination?") that there may be individual teachers on the right who, for their own reasons, bring their views into the classroom. But they argue that the left alone pursues the aim of indoctrination "in a systematic and organized way, with support that is theoretical (Gramsci, Althusser, Freire, Saviani, etc.), political (left governments and parties, with the PT [Workers' Party] in the lead), bureaucratic (the Ministry of Education and secretaries of education), editorial (the textbook publishing industry), and union-based."[39] Note that theory is given pride of place here and that Gramsci in particular is given pride of place in the list of dangerous theorists.

As a presidential candidate, Jair Bolsonaro himself would follow the ESP's lead, as would his first minister of education, Ricardo Vélez Rodríguez.[40] Bolsonaro's 2018 campaign materials, for instance, included this potted history: "In the last thirty years, 'Cultural Marxism' and its offshoots including 'Gramscianism' have joined forces with corrupt oligarchies to undermine the values of the Nation and the Brazilian family."[41] Key here is the notion that the Gramscians' goal *already* stands nearly if not completely achieved. The "Cultural Marxist" reinvention of Brazilian education is not merely a work in progress, then, not simply an imminent threat; it has already successfully undermined, or at least long since begun to undermine, the values that Bolsonaro seeks to restore or indeed to "rescue" (*resgatar*).[42] What allows Bolsonaro to make such a claim?

Others have offered historical answers to this question, by tracing Bolsonaro's debts to the infamous right-wing intellectual Olavo de Carvalho, or examining Carvalho's readings of Gramsci in detail.[43] "Carvalho does not hesitate to say that Gramsci and the Gramscians have already won in Brazil," Carlos Nelson Coutinho wrote already in 1999, "as they control not only the government and the state bureaucracy, but also the press and the whole education system. ... [O]nly the armed forces have resisted 'Gramscianism': the call for a military coup is therefore clear."[44] This call has only grown louder and clearer during the years since 1999. Bolsonaro's rise is thus not the call's second coming but its continuation in an amplified form. And there is a sense in which the exaggeration of the "Gramscian" threat simply serves his political interests; "Gramscianism" names just one of many internal political enemies, as does "communism" more generally.[45] To this list of enemies, we can add queers, trans people, Black and indigenous communities, and of course "delinquents." And since the ESP has led efforts to criminalize various kinds of teaching, as well as other efforts to allow for "extrajudicial notification" processes involving the naming and shaming of public school teachers,[46] *all* such teachers are, at least potentially, delinquents awaiting exposure and useful foils or lightning rods in Bolsonaro's politics of resentment. Like "Count Gramsci" in the image with which I began, they're not going anywhere even if their days may be said to be numbered.

All of the above is undeniable. Yet I have been working to develop another account, less historical than theoretical, of why Gramsci so often looms so large, of why, perhaps improbably, his name not only recurs but also figures so prominently in so many of the screeds of Bolsonaro's forerunners and followers and those loyal to the cause of the ESP.[47] As I have indicated, he is singled out in these screeds with striking consistency, and the central place that he's assigned in them indexes a right-wing "reading" of Gramsci, despite the distortions, mischaracterizations, and outright lies about him that proliferate. "Prophet of imbecility, guide to hordes of imbeciles,"[48] he is not only a bad teacher among bad teachers in Brazil, not only a dangerous, dissolute, and even demonic influence, and not only an emblematic educator of overreaching, sex-obsessed educators, but the "indoctrinator" par excellence. Robbing schoolteachers of the capacity to think for themselves, "with their own heads," he exercises a form of mind control that is also a way of remaking teachers "in his image and likeness," or rather in "the image and likeness of his own inner obscurity."[49] For he is a prince of darkness, and his is "a malice that obscures, not an intelligence that clarifies."⁵⁰ So too does teaching in actually existing Brazilian schools take the form, for Carvalho and the ESP, of an "indoctrination" that clouds students' perception of their faith, family, and rightful social place and otherwise blackens Brazil.

It is worth emphasizing that in this context "indoctrination" is also explicitly figured as *estupro intelectual*, or "intellectual rape." According to Carvalho, who wrote a statement called "The Intellectual Rape of Childhood," introducing and helping to publicize Nagib's cause, that is, the cause that became Escola Sem Partido: "The pedagogical method implanted in this country is a form of intellectual rape devised by Antonio Gramci [sic] to reach its victims at an age when their brains are not ready to critically react to tireless and brutal ... assaults."⁵¹ It gets worse: "the manipulators aren't satisfied with indoctrination by propaganda." They proceed, Carvalho writes, "to active regimentation, using their students as a reserve army" for left parties, enforcing "docility" and "communist or fascist" discipline.⁵² Gramsci, according to this influential statement—which became something of a founding document for the ESP—masterminded a left strategy that is simultaneously pedagogical and pedophilic.⁵³ More than a strategy, he set in motion a practice or *policy* in actually existing schools that's at once indoctrination, regimentation, and rape. Indeed, Carvalho writes in all seriousness, "although he was never here"—although, that is, he never visited Brazil, and although "the majority of Brazilians have never heard of him, and moreover he's been dead for over half a century"—from his place in the underworld, "from the kingdom of shadows, he secretly directs [*dirige*, so also 'leads,' a Gramscian word] events in this part of the world."⁵⁴ Among many other questions, this deranged but not for all that inconsequential account confronts us with the following: Why Gramsci, and what form if any might a Gramscian response to these charges take? These questions have guided my argument throughout in the preceding pages. In the next section, this essay's last, I offer some provisional answers while also venturing briefly beyond Brazil.

VI

DONALD TRUMP WAS taking a page out of Bolsonaro's playbook—also Escola Sem Partido's—when, in his 2020 State of the Union address, he denounced not public schools but "government schools."⁵⁵ "Public" was apparently still too positive, whereas "government" in the phrase "government schools"—a phrase borrowed from Milton Friedman—carried the Reaganite sense of encroachment (as in "I'm from the government, and I'm here to help").[56] Painting with a broad, Brazilian brush, Trump thus indicated that the problem wasn't this or that school, but the (public, non-charter) school as such, an institution that was partisan by definition. This was a prelude to his more recent and more widely publicized denunciation of *The 1619 Project* and what he called critical race theory, "a form of child abuse" that Trump claimed had infiltrated schools, which were now "indoctrinating" students throughout the United States.[57] Complaints about "indoctrination" in schools have proliferated on the far right since Trump's departure from office. But objections to "the church of intersectionality" and its educational offshoots have also appeared in columns in the *New York Times*.[58] Appealing as ever to liberal common sense—to "balance" even in the paper in which *The 1619 Project* first appeared—these columns suggest that a close association between literacy and liturgy still obtains not only in Brazil but in the United States as well. In both contexts, bad education still takes the form of brainwashing, and would-be secular leftists are branded sectarians, said to be promoting uncritical adherence to "ideology" rather than the critical thinking in which they purport to believe. This is not to discount the liberal provenance of some antiracist curricula or to repeat the specious claim that all such projects are Marxist.[59] My point is that projects that *are* Marxist are implicated, swept up in such breezy and broad dismissals of the "doctrinaire" left.

It would be absurd to argue that the left should embrace these kinds of caricatures. I am not suggesting that we should grant or give anyone to understand that we are indeed "indoctrinating" or even counterindoctrinating, since, as de Ípola reminds us, if we need reminding, the right consistently depends on the "indoctrination" of which it accuses the left.[60] What I have tried to suggest, instead, following Gramsci, is that there is an *instruction* that is irreducible in education: an "imposing" and an impersonal, a discursive and indeed, for Gramsci, a "coercive" dimension in education, even in education for equality, where "mechanical coercion" in his limited and specific sense is a matter of performing drills, repeating exercises, sitting through lectures, or just getting through readings or rounds of study.[61] It is a shared, provisional, and enabling if occasionally mind-numbing experience. It is preparation, again, for the practice of "governing," or literally "becoming 'governing' [*diventare 'governante'*]" in a truly democratic state, where this practice—a practice that, Gramsci's scare quotes suggest, is itself provisional, alternating rather than permanent—would not be the province of a privileged few but a real possibility for anyone and everyone.[62] Such instruction through "coercion" is not, in other words, a matter of invasive disempowerment, of lasting damage done to the body or mind (or both, as in Figure 15), but rather one of democratizing discipline—"discipline," then, not in the "communist or fascist" sense that the anti-Gramscian Carvalho denounces, as leading to or simply enforcing a surrender of students' critical capacities.[63] On the contrary, it strengthens these capacities, albeit slowly and at times through rote learning and other forms of repetition, recall, and ritual. "Coercion" in Gramsci's sense can open onto conviction, but it does not prescribe belief ("all you need is x"), promise secular "salvation,"[64] or preclude questioning. In fact, as I have argued elsewhere, instruction's very reliance on imposed tasks *that know themselves to be imposed*—rather than on work disguised as "play," like the exercises in child-friendlier and student-centered classrooms—can be conducive to such questioning. I mean this not only in the sense that scholastic chores can, at their best, themselves model the formation of questions but also in the sense that being *de*centered, being spoken to but not directly addressed, being made to go through motions—all of this can allow the student to pose questions behind the teacher's back, whether to peers (as in the passing of notes) or inwardly (as when one spaces out or daydreams in class).[65]

To be clear, I have been using the word "instruction" in Gramsci's sense rather than in the sense it currently has on the Brazilian right, where, as Bernardo Bianchi writes, paraphrasing Armindo Moreira, the distinction between education and instruction is understood as follows: "While education is the purview of the family, [instruction] is the responsibility of the school"; it is a matter of "'providing knowledge and skills' that allow people to easily earn a living and livelihood. ... For Nagib," the founder of the ESP, schools thus "usurp a right that is the exclusive purview of parents and the family. The teacher should limit him- or herself to imparting neutral knowledge, avoiding the promotion of any type of value or perspective on the student's reality and instead concentrat[ing] on preparing him or her for [his or her] professional future."[66] By contrast, for Gramsci, education and instruction are not aligned with the family and the school, respectively; instead, as in the discourse of earlier Italian educational theory, they refer to two of the school's modes or functions. Far from being vocational, "instruction" impedes or at least delays the acquisition of vocational skills. It is, in the eyes of its detractors, useless and outmoded. For Gramsci, who defends instruction on these grounds, it is disinterested and politically promising for this very reason: because it lets students take distance from their immediate world. In all of these ways, Gramscian instruction reminds us of what de Ípola, referring to Marxism, calls "the power of that discourse": the power of some words, of some modes of transmission, of some uses of culture to open perspectives, point to horizons, and contest "authorities," even in prisons.[67]

It is Gramsci—more than Freire, I have argued, despite Freire's abiding claim to greater relevance—who puts us in touch with this kind of instruction's irreducibility and critical importance.[68] That he also puts the Brazilian far right in touch with its potential, though of course incoherently and unconsciously—this is what accounts for the theorist's persistence and outsized presence in contemporary debates in Brazil, for his depiction as a monstrous degenerate and destroyer of nations, poisoner of minds, wrecker of homes, and corrupter of "young innocent" children. If he poses such an immense threat in far-right fantasy, then perhaps, I have wagered, there is something to what Gramsci argues, theoretically outmoded and politically "dead" though he has recently seemed.[69] Perhaps Gramsci's deadness or undeadness should be rethought in light of what he teaches us about the paradoxically enlivening—the collectively and not merely individually animating—power of instruction in dead languages and other "dead things."[70] Perhaps rather than abandoning or attempting to move beyond the scene of instruction, then, we should revisit this scene in an effort to remain in touch with its potentials even while we refuse the imperative to repeat the same.

Finally, I have worked to argue that we should learn to see ourselves in the right's broken mirror—not as "indoctrinators" but as educators and thus necessarily instructors in Gramsci's sense. Unwittingly, against all odds, and in a kind of negative image, the caricatures of "Cultural Marxist" teachers peddling Gramsci's *Notebooks* show us an inverted world in which the prisoner's dream is not yet dead or defeated. In this other world, a collective is under construction, and divergent forces are colluding to emasculate the *pátria* and do away with the patriarchal family.[71] These forces are gathered in public schools. They haven't left forever but have only gone underground.[72]

Notes

1. For studies of the ESP, see Gaudêncio Frigotto, ed., *Escola "Sem" Partido: Esfinge que ameaça a educação e a sociedade brasileira* (Rio de Janeiro: Laboratório de Políticas Públicas, 2017); Guilherme Costa Garcia Tomaselli, *Escola sem Partido: Síndrome de uma educação autoritária* (Curitiba: Appris, 2019); Fernando Penna, "Understanding 'Hate Against Teachers' in Brazil," in *Disrupting Hate in Education: Teacher Activists, Democracy, and Global Pedagogies of Interruption*, ed. Rita Verma and Michael Apple (New York: Routledge, 2021), 153–73; and Luciano M. Roza, "Against Indoctrination: The Movement *Escola Sem Partido* in Educational Media of Present-Day Brazil," in *The Politics of Authenticity and Populist Discourses: Media and Education in Brazil, India, and Ukraine*, ed. Christoph Kohl et al. (London: Palgrave, 2021), 175–96.
2. https://www.facebook.com/photo.php?fbid=425336157671680&set=a.222885187916779.1073741827.100005858980838&type=1&theater.
3. The image might also draw, ironically and no doubt unconsciously, on Marx's account of capital's blood-sucking tendencies: "Capital is dead labour which, vampire-like, only lives by sucking living labour, and lives the more, the more labour it sucks." Karl Marx, *Capital: A Critique of Political Economy*, vol. 1, trans. Ben Fowkes (New York: Penguin, 1976), 342. The anti-capitalist, condemned for his anti-capitalism, thus acquires capital's traits.
4. Richard J. F. Day, *Gramsci Is Dead: Anarchist Currents in the Newest Social Movements* (London: Pluto Press, 2005).
5. Daniel Friberg, *The Real Right Returns: A Handbook for the New Opposition* (London: Arktos Media, 2015), 21–22.
6. I consider this contrast in my book *Old Schools: Modernism, Education, and the Critique of Progress* (New York: Fordham University Press, 2020). This chapter picks up where that book's argument leaves off, in the Brazilian context and with an effort to think through the right's co-optation of a discourse of resistance to oppression. See, for instance, Armindo Moreira, *Professor não é educador* (São José dos Pinhais: Autores Paranaenses, 2012).
7. See, for example, Rei Terada, "Impasse as a Figure of Political Space," *Comparative Literature* 72.2 (2020): 144–58; and for an earlier, influential instance, Frank Wilderson III, "Gramsci's Black Marx: Whither the Slave in Civil Society?" *Social Identities* 9.2 (2003): 225–40. For Terada, whose reading of the *Notebooks* is both close and sympathetic, Gramsci's account of political conflict ultimately forecloses other, non-political possibilities. Wilderson argues that "black subjectivity ... disarticulates the Gramscian dream as a ubiquitous emancipatory strategy, because Gramsci (like most US social movements) has no theory of, or solidarity with, the slave" (238). By this account, Gramsci's writings are centered on the worker, who enjoys an access to and a mobility within civil society that are structurally unavailable to Black people, because civil society is constitutively anti-Black (239). There is much more at stake here than a reading of Gramsci, and I am not interested in pretending to adjudicate the accuracy of Wilderson's claims. Still, I note that other readings of Gramsci that do not center on the worker and the wage remain possible. For one rejoinder to Wilderson, see Nikhil Pal Singh, "On Race, Violence, and So-Called Primitive Accumulation," *Social*

Text 34.3 (2016): 27–50. For another that develops an alternative reading of Gramsci on race, see Marcus E. Green, "Race, Class, and Religion: Gramsci's Conception of Subalternity," in *The Political Philosophies of Antonio Gramsci and B. R. Ambedkar: Itineraries of Dalits and Subalterns*, ed. Cosimo Zene (New York: Routledge, 2013), 116–28.

8   William Davies, "The New Neoliberalism," *New Left Review* 101 (2016): 123–24.
9   Ibid., 134.
10 See Judith Butler, "Merely Cultural," *Social Text*, no. 52–53 (1997): 265–77. For an overview of how the "culturalist Gramsci" came to be constructed posthumously by the PCI (Italian Communist Party) and on some of "the global (mis-)fortunes of this culturalist Gramsci," see Roberto Dainotto's introduction to *Gramsci in the World*, ed. Roberto Dainotto and Fredric Jameson (Durham: Duke University Press, 2020), 20–23.
11 Alberto Toscano, "The Long Shadow of Racial Fascism," *Boston Review*, October 28, 2020, http://bostonreview.net/race-politics/alberto-toscano-long-shadow-racial-fascism. For another analysis of some of the "forces and fantasies" to which Toscano refers here, see Eva von Redecker, "Ownership's Shadow: Neoauthoritarianism as Defense of Phantom Possession," *Critical Times: Interventions in Global Critical Theory* 3.1 (2020): 33–67.
12 Green, "Race, Class, and Religion," 116.
13 Antonio Gramsci, *Quaderni del carcere*, ed. Valentino Gerratana (Turin: Einaudi, 2007), 3:1517; *Selections from Prison Notebooks*, ed. and trans. Quinton Hoare and Geoffrey Nowell Smith (New York: International, 1971), 37. Further citations use the abbreviations *QC* for the Italian and *PN* for the English.
14 Louis Althusser, "Ideology and Ideological State Apparatuses (Notes Towards an Investigation)," in *Lenin and Philosophy and Other Essays*, trans. Ben Brewster (New York: Monthly Review Press, 1971), 147. See also Ben Conisbee Baer, *Indigenous Vanguards: Education, National Liberation, and the Limits of Modernism* (New York: Columbia University Press, 2019), 30.
15 Gramsci, *QC* 3:1547; *PN* 40.
16 Eli Meyerhoff, *Beyond Education: Radical Studying for Another World* (Minneapolis: University of Minnesota Press, 2019). I should note that Meyerhoff focuses on higher education, and that this emphasis perhaps necessarily leads to conclusions that differ from mine here. On deschooling, see Ivan Illich, *Deschooling Society* (New York: Harper & Row, 1971). In some ways, Lee Edelman's recent work might also be seen as part of the tendency that I am describing, although importantly Edelman does not envision a "beyond." For him, "bad education, while insisting on [the] nothing, offers nothing by way of repair," let alone revolution. See *Bad Education: Why Queer Theory Teaches Us Nothing* (Durham: Duke University Press, 2022), 43.
17 Wendy Brown, "Neoliberalism's Frankenstein: Authoritarian Freedom in Twenty-First Century 'Democracies,'" *Critical Times: Interventions in Global Critical Theory* 1.1 (2018): 75.
18 Angela Nagle, *Kill All Normies: Online Culture Wars from 4Chan and Tumblr to Trump and the Alt-Right* (Winchester: Zero Books, 2017), 53.

19 Bernard Harcourt, "Introduction to 'Critique and the Alt-Right,'" *Critique & Praxis* 13/13, http://blogs.law.columbia.edu/praxis1313/bernard-e-harcourt-introduction-to-critique-the-alt-right/.
20 Friberg, *The Real Right Returns*, 24.
21 On calamity, see Anahid Nersessian, *The Calamity Form: On Poetry and Social Life* (Chicago: University of Chicago Press, 2020).
22 On the exaggeration of harm, see Sarah Schulman, *Conflict Is Not Abuse: Overstating Harm, Community Responsibility, and the Duty of Repair* (Vancouver: Arsenal Pulp Press, 2016); on the claim to have been silenced and the rhetoric of victimization, see Barbara Johnson, "Muteness Envy," in *The Feminist Difference: Literature, Psychoanalysis, Race, and Gender* (Cambridge, MA: Harvard University Press, 1998), 129–53; on "wounded attachments," see Wendy Brown, "Wounded Attachments," in *States of Injury* (Princeton: Princeton University Press, 1996), 52–76.
23 But see Mitchell Abidor, "The Gramsci of the Brazilian Right," *Dissent* (Summer 2020), https://www.dissentmagazine.org/article/the-gramsci-of-the-brazilian-right, on Olavo de Carvalho, to whom I will return.
24 I am thinking of the scene in Kleber Mendonça Filho and Juliano Dornelles's film *Bacurau* (2019) in which the assembled European tourists laugh at a Brazilian couple's claim that they, too, are white.
25 For a reproduction of this image, see https://liberdadeparaensinar.wordpress.com/2015/09/18/o-odio-aos-professores/.
26 Rita Segato, "O Édipo brasileiro: A dupla negação de gênero e raça," *Série antropología* 400 (2006), http://www.dan.unb.br/images/doc/Serie400empdf.pdf; in Spanish, "El Édipo negro: Colonialidad y forclusión de género y raza," in *La crítica de la colonialidad en ocho ensayos y una antropología por demanda* (Buenos Aires: Prometeo, 2013); in English, "Black Oedipus: Coloniality and the Foreclosure of Gender and Race," in *The Critique of Coloniality: Eight Essays*, trans. Ramsey McGlazer (New York: Routledge, 2022), 133–58; for the phrase "national psyche," see 137.
27 See also Jean Laplanche's "general theory of seduction" in *New Foundations for Psychoanalysis*, trans. David Macey (Oxford: Basil Blackwell, 1989).
28 I thank Ellen Nerenberg for encouraging me to think through the workings of feminization in instruction. See Sigmund Freud, "A Child Is Being Beaten: A Contribution to the Study of the Origin of Sexual Perversions," in *The Standard Edition of the Complete Psychological Works of Sigmund Freud*, vol. 17 *(1917–1919)*, trans. and ed. James Strachey, with Anna Freud, Alix Strachey (London: Hogarth, 1955), 197–98.
29 Thanks to Joshua Branciforte for helping me to see the envy in particular; on sadistic destructiveness as compensation and alternative lure, offered in the absence of any other seductive vision or promise, see Branciforte's essay in this volume, "Fascism Without Men."
30 Emilio de Ípola, "La bemba," in *La bemba: Acerca del rumor carcelario y otros ensayos* (Buenos Aires: Siglo XXI, 2005), 27–28.
31 Ibid., 27.
32 https://twitter.com/Vinncent/status/1102557987351265280. See also Vincent Bevins, *The Jakarta Method: Washington's Anticommunist Crusade and the Mass Murder Program That Shaped Our World* (New York: Public Affairs, 2020), 105.

33 In Brazil, the illiterate would not be given the right to vote until 1985. For more on the relationship between literacy and citizenship in Brazil, see Bernardo Bianchi, "Paulo Freire's Legacy and the Ideological Battle in Brazil," in *Democracy and Brazil: Collapse and Regression*, ed. Bianchi et al. (New York: Routledge, 2020), 140.
34 Olavo de Carvalho, *A nova era e a revolução cultural: Fritjof Capra e Antonio Gramsci*, 4th ed. (Campinas: VIDE Editorial, 2014), 127.
35 Moreira, *Professor não é educador*, 7.
36 De Ípola, "La bemba," 27–28.
37 Ibid.
38 http://escolasempartido.org/perguntas-e-respostas/; quoted in Bianchi, "Paulo Freire's Legacy," 135; translation modified.
39 http://escolasempartido.org/perguntas-e-respostas/.
40 "Vélez exalta igreja e família e diz que MEC vai combater marxismo cultural," *Folha de São Paulo*, January 2, 2019, https://www1.folha.uol.com.br/educacao/2019/01/velez-exalta-igreja-e-familia-e-diz-que-mec-vai-combater-marxismo-cultural.shtml.
41 Bolsonaro 2018, "O camino da prosperidade: Proposta de plano de governo," https://divulgacandcontas.tse.jus.br/candidaturas/oficial/2018/BR/BR/2022802018/280000614517/proposta_1534284632231.pdf, 8.
42 Ibid., e.g., 80.
43 On Carvalho's influence on the ESP, and for a study that considers Brazilian anticommunism, the right-wing reception of Gramsci, and the war on "gender ideology," see Garcia Tomaselli, *Escola sem Partido*.
44 Carlos Nelson Coutinho, "Gramsci and Brazil," in *Gramsci's Political Thought*, trans. Pedro Sette-Câmara (Leiden: Brill, 2012), 174.
45 Rodrigo Nunes explains: "The seeds of the staggering resurgence of anticommunism in Brazil started being sown during PT's first term in power. At a time when the economy was booming and most people's material standards were improving, red scares manufactured with the aid of the media were among the few weapons in the opposition's armour. The contrast between these and the embracing of Lula by the international establishment produced a cognitive dissonance that conspiracy theories about a global leftist conspiracy would subsequently help solve. It was the social media–fuelled spread of the latter that operated the shift from Cold War discourse as a tool in parliamentary struggle to anticommunism as an overarching geopolitical narrative pitting Trump and Bolsonaro as the Asterix and Obelix of the struggle against 'cultural Marxism-driven economic globalisation.' The very fact that no concrete threat existed only made this discourse more efficient, as its 'abstractness' meant that 'anything that … [did] not fit [could be] subsumed under [an] all-purpose term' like 'communism' or 'globalism.'" Rodrigo Nunes, "Of What Is Bolsonaro the Name?" *Radical Philosophy* 2.9 (2020), https://www.radicalphilosophy.com/article/of-what-is-bolsonaro-the-name#fnref41.
46 https://escolasempartido.org/blog/notificacao-extrajudicial-arma-das-familias-contra-a-doutrinacao-nas-escolas/.

47 A search for "Gramsci" on the ESP's site suffices to demonstrate this, yielding copious results, including blog posts purporting to locate various Gramscian dimensions in contemporary Brazilian education at all levels.
48 Carvalho, *A nova era*, 53.
49 Ibid., 54.
50 Ibid., 53.
51 Olavo de Carvalho, "O estupro intelectual da infância," September 19, 2003, http://old.olavodecarvalho.org/convidados/mnagib.htm.
52 Ibid.
53 On the statement's status, see Penna, "Understanding 'Hate,'" 162.
54 Carvalho, *A nova era*, 45.
55 "For too long, countless American children have been trapped in failing government schools. ... [N]o parent should be forced to send their child to a failing government school." "Full Transcript: Trump's 2020 State of the Union Address," *New York Times*, February 5, 2020, https://www.nytimes.com/2020/02/05/us/politics/state-of-union-transcript.html. Note that school here is not only the site of failure but also a space of coercion: a trap into which parents and children alike are "forced." Compare, again, Moreira, *Professor não é educador*, 9. On the not strictly national implications of Bolsonarismo, Nunes is eloquent. To quote at length again from "Of What Is Bolsonaro the Name?": "Bolsonarismo is not reducible to either a national atavism or a simple repetition of historical fascism. It is a very contemporary tragedy, the conditions for which are given far and wide today, and tend to worsen as political and economic inequality grows and the effects of climate change intensify. Some form of overseer capitalism may well be part and parcel of that 'Brazilianisation' with which the developed world is menaced from time to time." For a sense of the current reach of the "Brazilianization" thesis, see Alex Hochuli, "The Brazilianization of the World," *American Affairs* 2 (2021), https://americanaffairsjournal.org/2021/05/the-brazilianization-of-the-world/.
56 Milton Friedman, "The Role of Government in Education," in *Capitalism and Freedom* (1962; Chicago: University of Chicago Press, 2002), 99.
57 "Trump 'Patriotic Education Plan' to Counter 'Left-Wing Indoctrination' in Schools," *Democracy Now*, September 18, 2020, https://www.democracynow.org/2020/9/18/headlines/trump_patriotic_education_plan_to_counter_left_wing_indoctrination_in_schools.
58 Ross Douthat, "How Michel Foucault Lost the Left and Won the Right," *New York Times*, May 25, 2021, https://www.nytimes.com/2021/05/25/opinion/michel-foucault.html. See also Douthat's subsequent columns including "The Excesses of Antiracist Education," *New York Times*, June 3, 2021, https://www.nytimes.com/2021/07/03/opinion/antiracist-education-history.html.
59 For one critique of the distance taken in *The 1619 Project* from "materialist ... anti-racist historiography," see Harvey Neptune, "#1619Project and the Anti-Racist Road Not Taken," *Small Axe*, January 7, 2020, http://smallaxe.net/sxlive/1619project-and-anti-racist-road-not-taken-essay-harvey-neptune.
60 To be clear, I am also not suggesting that we should court political danger by recasting teaching as outright "seduction."

61 On "mechanical coercion," see Gramsci, *QC* 3:1544; *PN* 37; and McGlazer, *Old Schools*, 4–5.
62 Gramsci, *QC* 3:1547; *PN* 40.
63 Carvalho, "O estupro intelectual."
64 Not for nothing is Carvalho's chapter on Gramsci in *A nova era e a revolução cultural* called "St. Antonio Gramsci and the Salvation of Brazil."
65 I develop this argument in more detail, contrasting "instruction" with progressive educational ideals up to and including Freire's, in *Old Schools*.
66 Bianchi, "Paulo Freire's Legacy," 136. See also Moreira, *Professor não é educador*, e.g., 7–8.
67 de Ípola, "La bemba," 27–28. Here I am not downplaying the severity of carceral constraints but rather remembering what Ruth Wilson Gilmore writes: "If people living under the most severe constraints, such as prisoners, can form study groups ... then free-world activists have no excuse for ignorance, nor should they rely on funder-designed workshops and training sessions to do what revolutionaries in all times have done on their own." Ruth Wilson Gilmore, "In the Shadow of the Shadow State," in *The Revolution Will Not Be Funded: Beyond the Non-Profit Industrial Complex*, ed. INCITE! (Durham: Duke University Press, 2007), 48.
68 For another critique of Freire, one that I regrettably learned about too late to address it in *Old Schools*, see Eve Tuck and K. Wayne Yang, "Decolonization Is Not a Metaphor," *Decolonization: Indigeneity, Education, & Society* 1.1 (2012): 1–40; see especially 19–20. Here the authors are contrasting Freire and Fanon, rather than Freire and Gramsci, but their argument is relevant to the one I am making here.
69 See especially, again, Day, *Gramsci Is Dead*.
70 Gramsci, *QC* 1544; *PN* 38.
71 On Bolsonarismo and masculinity, see Rosana Pinheiro-Machado and Lucia Mury Scalco, "From Hope to Hate: The Rise of Conservative Subjectivity in Brazil," *HAU: Journal of Ethnographic Theory* 10.1 (2020): 21–31.
72 For an ominous instance of going underground—where it's the colonizer who does this rather than the forces of anticolonial resistance—see the end of *Bacurau*. For a more affirmative understanding of what hasn't disappeared but has only "gone away," see Paula Berbert and Roberto Romero, "Drawing, Healing, and Transformation Among the *Yãmĩyxop*," trans. Ramsey McGlazer, *Critical Times: Interventions in Global Critical Theory* 4.3 (2021): 599–603. In the Atlantic Forest, though under conditions of deforestation and species extinction, the indigenous "Tikmũ'ũn often refuse to say that animals 'have disappeared.' They prefer to say that they 'went away' after the whites destroyed their homes, that is, their forests. But just as they went away, they can return."

About the Contributors

TY BLAKENEY is Assistant Professor of French at Northwestern University. He is the author of several articles on literature, sexuality, and politics. His first book project examines a novel archive of literary and historical texts about gay sex in prison from 1830 to the present in order to rethink the relationship between state power and sexuality more broadly.

CHIARA BOTTICI is a philosopher and critical theorist. She is Director of Gender Studies and Associate Professor of Philosophy at The New School, and she is the author of *Imaginal Politics: Images beyond Imagination and the Imaginary* (Columbia University Press 2014), *A Philosophy of Political Myth* (Cambridge University Press 2007), *Anarchafeminism* (Bloomsbury 2021), and *A Feminist Mythology* (Bloomsbury 2021).With sociologist Benoit Challand, she also co-authored *Imagining Europe: Myth, Memory, Identity* (Cambridge University Press, 2013) and *The Myth of the Clash of Civilizations* (Routledge, 2010). She also co-edited the collections of essays *The Politics of Imagination* (Routledge, 2011), *The Anarchist Turn* (Pluto 2013), and *Feminism, Capitalism and Critique* (Palgrave 2017). Her work has been translated into ten foreign languages and impacted the fields of philosophy, sociology, political science, and aesthetics.

JOSHUA BRANCIFORTE is an independent scholar. He co-edited the "Queer Bonds" special issue of *GLQ* (17:2-3), and his work has also appeared in *Modern Language Quarterly*. A companion piece to his chapter in this volume appears in the Winter 2022 issue of *GLQ*.

GISELA CATANZARO is a sociologist. She is a Professor in the Departments of Political Science and Sociology at the Universidad de Buenos Aires and an independent researcher affiliated with the Consejo Nacional de Investigaciones Científicas y Técnicas and the Instituto de Investigaciones Gino Germani. She currently directs the research project "Transformations in Contemporary Neoliberal Ideology: Ethico-Political and Critical Shifts in the Present, the Frankfurt School, and Poststructuralism" at the Secretaría de Ciencia y Técnica at the Universidad de Buenos Aires.

MELINDA COOPER is Professor in the Research School of Social Sciences at the Australian National University. She is the author of *Family Values: Between Neoliberalism and the New Social Conservatism* (Zone Books, 2017) and is currently completing a manuscript *On Capital Gains: The Counterrevolution in Public Finance*.

JULIAN GÖPFFARTH completed his Ph.D. at the European Institute at the London School of Economics in 2020. Currently he is an independent researcher and a fellow at the Centre for the Analysis of the Radical Right. Julian's work focuses on the intellectual roots of the populist far right in East Germany; the ideological transformations of this right; and the role that intellectuals play within it.

RAMSEY McGLAZER is Assistant Professor of Comparative Literature at the University of California, Berkeley, where he is also affiliated with the Program in Critical Theory, the Department of Italian Studies, and the Center for Latin American Studies. He is the author of *Old Schools: Modernism, Education, and the Critique of Progress* (2020), published by Fordham University Press in the Lit Z Series.

BENJAMIN NOYS is Professor of Critical Theory at the University of Chichester. His latest book is *The Matter of Language* (Seagull Press, 2022).

BRUNO PERREAU is the Cynthia L. Reed Professor of French Studies at the Massachusetts Institute of Technology. He is the author of ten books on political institutions and ideas, bioethics, gender in translation, and queer theory. He has recently published *The Politics of Adoption* (MIT Press, 2014), *Queer Theory: The French Response* (Stanford University Press, 2016), *Les Défis de la République* (co-edited with Joan W. Scott, Presses de Sciences Po, 2017), and *Qui a peur de la théorie queer ?* (Presses de Sciences Po, 2018). He is currently working on a new book on minority politics in France and the US, titled *Spheres of Injustice*.

RAHUL RAO is Lecturer in International Political Thought at the University of St Andrews. He is the author of *Out of Time: The Queer Politics of Postcoloniality* (2020) and *Third World Protest: Between Home and the World* (2010), both published by Oxford University Press. He is a member of the Radical Philosophy collective.

SHAUL SETTER is a critical theorist. He is the head of the Master's Program in Policy and Theory of the Arts at the Bezalel Academy of Arts and Design, Jerusalem, and the editor of the journal *Theory and Criticism* at the Van Leer Jerusalem Institute. He is the author of *Collectivity in Struggle: Godard, Genet, and the Palestinian Revolt of the 1970s* (Lexington, 2021).

M. TY is an Assistant Professor of English at the University of Wisconsin, Madison.

Index

Abbott, Greg, 275
accelerationism, 15, 243, 246, 248–250, 253–258; right and left versions of, 254–257
Adorno, Theodor, 6, 24, 59, 63–65, 67–68, 73–80, 157, 300
Agamben, Giorgio, 120, 152
al-Assad, Hafez, 194
Alternative für Deutschland (AfD), 207–212, 217–228
Althusser, Louis, 328, 336
Ambedkar, B. R., 192
American Activist Collective, 33–34
Anderson, Benedict, 3
anti-Semitism, 155, 213, 242, 247, 272
Arendt, Hannah, 24
Aristotle, 123
Art, David, 214
Aster, Ari, 40
Aydemir, Fatma, 214, 229

Bachofen, Johann Jakob, 29, 36
Badiou, Alain, 245, 256
Balibar, Étienne, 214
Bannon, Steve, 36
Barrett, Amy Coney, 277
Barthes, Roland, 89
Bataille, George, 24–25, 255
Bechhaus-Gerst, Marianne, 211
Benjamin, Walter, 24, 128, 316
Benoist, Alain de, 180, 216–217

Berardi, Franco "Bifo," 162
Berlusconi, Silvio, 75
Bernasconi, Robert, 218
Bernstein, Jay, 64, 68
Bersani, Leo, 25, 27, 48, 98
Bianchi, Bernardo, 340
Biden, Joe, 91
Billig, Michael, 209
Blanquer, Jean-Michel, 273
Böckelmann, Frank, 219
Bolsonaro, Jair, 1, 3, 324, 336–338
Bolton, Kerry, 180
Bosch, Hieronymus, 249–250
Bouie, Jamelle, 31
Bourdieu, Pierre, 99–100
Boutin, Christine, 269
Boyarin, Daniel, 157
Boyarin, Jonathan, 157
Boycott, Divestment and Sanctions (BDS) Movement, 155
Breitbart, Andrew, 2
Brody, Richard, 40, 43, 49
Brown, Wendy, 127, 150, 298, 300, 303–305, 312, 329
Buchanan, Patrick J., 10, 173–174, 179–184
Buckley, William F., 172, 174
Bullrich, Patricia, 307, 313
Burke, Edmund, 268, 285–286
Butler, Judith, 24, 66–68, 157, 269, 271–272

Calhoun, John C., 168, 170–171, 176, 181
Camus, Renaud, 7, 88–113, 282
Canetti, Elias, 62–63
Carvalho, Olavo de, 337–338, 340
Carlson, Tucker, 91
Catanzaro, Gisela, 327–328
Cathy, Daniel Truett, 275
Céline, Louis-Ferdinand, 35
Chin, Rita, 209
Chinese Exclusion Act (1882), 122
Citizenship (Amendment) Act, 11, 190–196
Clover, Carol, 47–48
Clover, Joshua, 4, 252
communism, 9, 227, 253, 329, 334, 337
Confino, Alon, 211
Connor, Walker, 267, 286
constitutionalism: in India, 190–192, 197–201
Conway, Kellyanne, 2
Copjec, Joan, 33
Coughlin, Charles, 180, 183
Coulter, Ann, 36
Crenshaw, Kimberlé, 272
Creton, Pierre, 288
critical race theory, 6, 329, 339
Cultural Marxism, 15, 17, 324, 330–331, 336, 341

Dallorso, Nicolás, 307
Davies, Peter, 36
Davies, William, 299, 308, 327
Dayan, Hilla, 155
De, Rohit, 197
De Beauvoir, Simone, 67
de Ípola, Emilio, 333–335, 339, 341
Debord, Guy, 77, 286
Decker, Oliver, 209
Die Linke, 209
Doan, Laura, 98
Douglas, C. H., 180
Dugin, Alexander, 5, 12, 30
Duterte, Rodrigo, 1, 3
Dyer, Richard, 32

Eichberg, Henning, 215
El-Tayeb, Fatima, 209, 227, 229–230

Enoch (Peinovich), Mike, 166, 180
Erdoğan, Recep Tayyip, 3–4
Esposito, Roberto, 120
ethnonationalism, 158, 160, 264–272, 278, 283, 286; as keyword, 5; in France, 267–268; in peripheral countries, 315; and populism, 284; and technology, 242, 253, 257; as transcendental thought, 264. *See also* new conservative humanism
ethnopluralism, 208–211, 214–215, 219, 222, 228
eugenics, 12–13, 28–30
Evola, Julius, 5, 29–30, 35

Fanon, Frantz, 79
fascism, 4, 9, 12–13, 179; as heuristic tool, 58–59; older versus contemporary, 30–31, 40; racial, 328
Faust, Sigmar, 212
Faye, Guillaume, 242
Federal Reserve Act, 167
Feder, Gottfried, 180, 183
Fernández de Kirchner, Cristina, 305
Finkielkraut, Alain, 104, 106, 112
Fisher, Gaëlle, 212
Fleming, Thomas, 176
Ford, Henry, 182
Foucault, Michel, 29, 125, 298
Four, Jean-Marc, 264
Francis, Samuel T., 176, 180–181
Frankfurt School, 23
Fraser, Nancy, 78, 159
Freire, Paulo, 325, 327, 333, 336, 341
French Revolution (1789), 268
Freud, Sigmund, 5–8, 30, 41, 51; and group psychology, 59–63, 71, 73, 78–80; and primary susceptibility, 17, 119, 123–124, 129–137; and psychopathological structures, 25–27, 43; and sublimation, 149–150; and education, 333
Friberg, Daniel, 330
Friedman, Milton, 170, 339
Friedrich, Caspar David, 217
Fuchs, Christian, 73, 77
Funès, Julia de, 103–104

Gallagher, John, 92–98, 110
Gandhi, Mahatma, 192, 203
Garbagnoli, Sara, 281
Gates, Bill, 298
Gauland, Alexander, 221
Gellar, Pam, 95
gender: collapse of, 47–48, 53; as cornerstone of civilization, 269–270; and discrimination, 269; and nature, 273–274; as ideology, 6–7, 65–66, 324; mobilizations against, 269–274; and race, 66; and subject formation, 25–26; Vatican struggle against, 269, 273. *See also* LGBT groups
Gibson, William, 252–253, 257
Gingrich, Newt, 263
Gogoi, Ranjan, 198
González, Horacio, 312
Gottfried, Paul, 166
Goulart, João, 334
Gramsci, Antonio, 16–17, 324–341
Griffin, Roger, 28
Grossman, David, 148
Guadagnino, Luca, 5, 37–53
Guénon, René, 30
Gurion, Ben, 152
Guru, Afzal, 198

Habeck, Robert, 208
Halberstam, Jack, 25, 27, 98
Hamilton, Alexander, 181
Harcourt, Bernard, 330
Harris, Kamala, 15
Hayek, Friedrich, 304
Hazony, Yoram, 263
Hegel, Georg Wilhelm Friedrich, 218
Heidegger, Martin: and nativism, 13, 217–219; and technology, 15, 241–248, 250–251, 253–254, 256–258
Heimat (Homeland), 207–230
Heimbach, Matthew, 180, 184
Herf, Jeffrey, 242
Herrnstein, Richard, 173
Herzl, Theodor, 147
Herzog, Dagmar, 25, 28–30
Hesse, Barnor, 229

Hewitt, Andrew, 25, 35
Hitler, Adolf, 60, 65, 67–68, 74, 90, 250
Hobbes, Thomas, 32, 71
Hobsbawm, Eric, 72, 267
Höcke, Björn, 217, 221, 225
Hölderlin, Friedrich, 244–246
Hollande, François, 283
Holocaust, 49–51, 65, 90, 211, 251, 275
homosexuality: and bestiality, 271; and fascism, 24–25; legal cases involving, 269–272; and outlaw thesis, 88–112. *See also* LGBT groups
Hoppe, Hans-Hermann, 179
Hood, Gregory, 166, 184
Hoof, Thomas, 221
Horkheimer, Max, 64, 67
Huckabee, Mike, 275
Hughey, Matthew, 210–211
Huntington, Samuel, 227
Huyssen, Andreas, 252

intersectionality, 272, 339
Islam: in France, 226–228, 278, 280

Jackson, Andrew, 182
James, Jason, 212, 220
Jameson, Fredric, 298
Jefferson, Thomas, 171
Johnson, Boris, 264
Johnson, Greg, 180
Jones, Donna, 216
Judaken, Jonathan, 218
Jung, Carl, 41, 52
Jünger, Ernst, 15, 242–246, 248–256
Jünger, Friedrich-Georg, 249

Kant, Immanuel, 129
Karim, Imrad, 225
Karnad, Raghu, 202
Karta, Neturei, 157
Keskinkılıç, Ozan Zakariya, 211
Khan, Masud R., 27
King, Martin Luther, 280
Komporozos-Athanasiou, Aris, 78
Kristeva, Julia, 31, 35
Kubitschek, Götz, 219–220, 224

Kumar, Kanhaiya, 193
Kushner, Jared, 184

Lacan, Jacques, 25–26, 33, 41–42, 52
Land, Nick, 15, 243, 252, 255
Le Bon, Gustave, 60, 63
Le Bras, Hervé, 104–105, 107
Le Gallou, Jean-Yves, 274
Le Pen, Jean-Marie, 1, 36, 264, 280, 282, 284
Le Pen, Marine, 1, 36, 91, 280, 282, 284
Lemaître, Éric, 279
Lemke, Thomas, 136
Lengsfeld, Vera, 212, 225
Leona, Amulya, 202
Leopold, Aldo, 125
Letac, Anne-Sophie, 103
LGBT groups: demonstrations against, 268–281; legal cases involving, 274–278; and religious freedom, 278, 281; Vatican view of, 273. *See also* gender; homosexuality; transphobia.
Lloyd, David, 11, 195
Locke, John, 123, 168
Love, Heather, 98

Macri, Mauricio, 16, 297, 300–316, 328; and sacrifice, 309–312, 315
Macron, Emmanuel, 280, 283
Marcuse, Herbert, 149–150
Maréchal-Le Pen, Marion, 263–264, 267, 273, 282, 284–286
Maron, Monika, 212
Marx, Karl, 4
May, Karl, 211
Maza, Carlos, 95–96
Meloni, Giorgia, 3, 263
Menem, Carlos, 307, 309, 311–312
Menger, Carl, 167
Merkel, Angela, 121, 208, 225
Meuthen, Jörg, 224–227
Michetti, Gabriela, 313
Mishra, Kapil, 191
Modi, Narendra, 1, 3, 198, 203
Morawiecki, Mateusz, 126
Moreira, Armindo, 334, 340
Mosse, George, 23, 28–29

Murray, Charles, 173
Musk, Elon, 253
Mussolini, Benito, 60

Nabokov, Vladimir, 27
Nagib, Miguel, 325–327, 338, 340
Nagle, Angela, 329
nationalism, 209–210, 266; in Germany, 207–212; in India, 195–197
Nationality Law (2018), 151
nativism, 4
Nazism, 4, 47, 60, 65, 68; and Heimat, 211–220; as perversion, 23–30; and technology, 247, 258
Negro Act (1740), 122
Nelson Coutinho, Carlos, 337
neoliberalism, 15, 73, 146; and the alt-right, 167, 182; in Argentina, 307–316; punitive inflections of, 297–316, 327
Netanyahu, Benjamin, 3, 154
Neumann, Erich, 38, 51
New Left, 169–170, 172, 213, 215
new conservative humanism, 264–288; and sexual minorities, 268–280
Ngai, Mae, 124
Nietzsche, Friedrich, 248
Nixon, Rob, 128
Nuremberg Laws, 122

Obama, Barack, 15
Ohana, David, 149
Orbán, Viktor, 1, 3, 263–264
Ortega y Gasset, José, 24
Otoo, Sharon Dodua, 229
Otte, Max, 224, 226
Owaisi, Asaduddin, 202

paleoconservatism, 173–178, 184; as distinct from libertarianism, 180–181; as distinct from neoconservatism, 174–175
paleolibertarianism, 173–179, 184; and the alt-right, 179–180; as distinct from paleoconservatism, 180–181; and anti-capitalism, 182–183

patriarchy, 67
Paul, Ron, 166, 174–175, 179
Pedaya, Haviva, 152
Peele, Jordan, 40
PewDiePie, 90
Philippot, Florian, 280
Phule, Savitribai, 192
Plant, Sadie, 255
Pope, John Paul II, 263, 273
Pope, Benedict XVI, 66, 273
populism, 4, 8, 67, 120, 137, 303; in Argentina, 309; far-right, 177–178; as distinct from popular, 283–284
Porter, Charles A., 89–90
Prearo, Massimo, 281
Programa Escola Sem Partido (Program for a School without Party), 16, 324–326, 331, 336–338
Puar, Jasbir, 94, 98
Putin, Vladimir, 3
Pynchon, Thomas, 250

race, 6, 29, 122, 217–218, 228, 271; and the alt-right, 171, 175, 177, 183, 215, 282, 332, 336; empty character of, 64–65; and gender, 66; new conceptions of, 12–14. *See also* eugenics
Rancière, Jacques, 94–96
Rand, Ayn, 166, 174
Raz-Krakotzkin, Amnon, 156
Reagan, Ronald, 2, 174, 182, 263
refugees, 118–138, 221, 223
Reich, Wilhelm, 24
Reichardt, Sven, 213
Rey, Olivier, 105
Rilke, Rainer Maria, 246
Roberts, John, 276
Rockwell Jr., Llewellyn H., 172–173, 175, 176–178
Roosevelt, Theodore, 182
Röpke, Wilhelm, 183
Roquette, Guillaume, 102
Ross, Alexander Reid 24
Rothbard, Murray, 10–11, 166–180, 183
Roy, Arundhati, 201
Roy, Srirupa, 194

Safatle, Vladimir, 75
Salvini, Matteo, 118, 121
Sanyal, Debarati, 128
Sapiro, Gisèle, 99–101
Sarrazin, Thilo, 225–226
Sayre, Nathan, 124
Seidman, Steven, 105
Schacht, Hjalmar, 183
Schehr, Lawrence, 89–90, 100–101, 112
Schlafly, Phyllis, 36
Schmitt, Carl, 216
Scholem, Gershom, 151, 156
Sedgwick, Eve Kosofsky, 25
Seehofer, Horst, 128, 134
Segato, Rita, 332
Seghezzo, Gabriela, 307
Serwer, Adam, 31
Shah, Alpa, 200
Sheik, Fatima, 192
Shooman, Yasemin, 215
Sieferle, Rolf Peter, 221
Silverman, Kaja, 48
Singh, Bhagat, 192
Smith, Anthony, 211
social media, 76–78
socialism, 69, 212
Sotomayor, Sonia, 275
Southern Agrarians, 175, 181
Southern, Lauren, 108
Southern Partisan, 176, 179
Spackman, Barbara, 23
Spencer, Richard, 166, 180, 184
Spengler, Oswald, 216
Stanley, Jason, 30
state: libertarian critique of, 10–11, 167–179, 183; populist critique of, 153–154; as distinct from nation, 8, 29, 68–70, 72, 105–106, 112–113, 151, 155, 183; nationalist critique of, 195–198, 202; receptive capacity of, 118–138
Steinmeier, Frank-Walter, 208
Sternhell, Zeev, 28
Streeck, Wolfgang, 301–302
Suspiria (Guadagnino), 37–53

Tagore, Rabindranath, 196–197

Taguieff, Pierre-André, 215, 223
Tarrant, Brenton, 91–92, 109
Taubira, Christiane, 271–274
Taylor, Jared, 216–217, 228
technology, 241–258
Théry, Irène, 268
Theweleit, Klaus, 23–24, 30
Thiel, Peter, 9
Toscano, Alberto, 328
transphobia, 17, 63, 106
Trump, Donald J., 1, 3, 6, 10–11, 15, 123, 128, 135, 154, 264, 277; and education, 338; iconography of, 31–36; ideology of, 59; and paleolibertarianism, 179–180, 184; public performance of, 64–66, 68–78

Urban, Jörg, 223

Vadolas, Antonios, 25, 28
Valentin, Caroline, 99, 102–103, 108–109, 112–113
Vallaud-Belkacem, Najat, 272
Vélez Rodríguez, Ricardo, 336
Vemula, Radhika, 190, 193
Vemula, Rohith, 190, 193
Verhaeghe, Paul, 26
Virilio, Paul, 241
von Mises, Ludwig, 166–167

Walia, Harsha, 122
Wallerstein, Immanuel, 214
Webster, Jamieson, 64
Wedeen, Lisa, 194
Wei Wei, Ai, 121
Weinstein, Harvey, 27
Weißmann, Karlheinz, 219–223, 226
white identity, 282; in Germany, 209–216, 223–224, 226–230
Wiegman, Robyn, 98
Wilde, Oscar, 101
Wilders, Geert, 95
Wilson, Clyde N., 176
Wilson, Elizabeth, 98
Wilson, Woodrow, 167
Wirth, Herman, 37
Woods, Thomas, 179

xenophobia, 137–138, 298

Yaghoobifarah, Hengameh, 214
Yellow Vests, 283–284, 288
Yiannopoulos, Milo, 95–99, 110
Young, Damon R., 90

Zemmour, Éric, 282
Zionism: in opposition to Neo-Zionism, 10, 145–163
Žižek, Slavoj, 25, 35, 195, 298
Zreik, Raef, 151

www.ingramcontent.com/pod-product-compliance
Lightning Source LLC
Chambersburg PA
CBHW020240030426
42336CB00010B/551